The *Third Text* Reader on Art, Culture and Theory

The *Third Text* Reader

on **Art, Culture** and **Theory**

Edited by

RASHEED ARAEEN
SEAN CUBITT
ZIAUDDIN SARDAR

continuum
LONDON • NEW YORK

Continuum

The Tower Building, 11 York Road, London, SE1 7NX
370 Lexington Avenue, New York, NY 10017–6503

This selection first published 2002

© *Third Text* 2002 and original contributors

British Library Cataloguing-in-Publication Data
A catalogue record for this book is available from the British Library.

ISBN 0–8264–5850–5 (hardback)
     0–8264–5851–3 (paperback)

Library of Congress Cataloging-in-Publication Data
A catalog record for this book is available from the Library of Congress

Typeset by RefineCatch Limited, Bungay, Suffolk
Printed and bound in Great Britain by
Biddles Ltd, Guildford and King's Lynn

Contents

Prologue

In the Beginning: *Third Text* and the Politics of Art

SEAN CUBITT

In the years since 1987, when the first issue of *Third Text* appeared, the terrain of global art practice has changed. To that extent, the project of the journal has also developed. It is not just that art-making has evolved, as is its nature, but that the institutional landscape has undergone a profound if belated revolution. Where once the task was to champion the silenced voices and invisible canvases of artists outside the pale of the power-broking metropolitan galleries, now it is to understand in what ways global art practice has become a spice to flavour the pot of the new multiculturalism.

WORLD ART

Over the seven thousand years of recorded history, there has been incessant trade across the vast expanses of the known world, from the Yangtse to the portals of the Mediterranean, along the rivers and the navigable seas. Pilgrims, crusaders, nomads and merchants have criss-crossed Africa, Asia and the European peninsula for millennia. Polynesian navigators have been traversing the Pacific for as long as memory records. All the evidence we have suggests that the social animal has always been ready to move and to mingle. Why should our epoch be any different? Why should communication between cultures be harder now than then?

One answer is provided by the great Uruguayan literary critic, Angel Rama. He notes that 'while European writers could address their audiences without worrying about the marginal readers outside Europe', writers from other regions of the world continue 'to yearn for European readers and regard their reading as the true and authorizing one'. Rama gives the example of the Cuban novelist Alejo Carpentier, who 'certifies the continued sense, on the part of some twentieth-century Latin American *letrados*, that they remain exiled in the fringes of a civilization whose animating centre lies in the metropolitan powers of Europe'.[1] Two factors arise here. One is the lure of the colonial mindset so astutely and politically understood by Fanon: the readiness of the colonized not only to submit passively but to participate actively in their own subordination.[2] The second is the root of this colonized mentality in the communicative structures that ensure the imbalance of cultures. Dialogue can occur only between equals. In a command structure, communication is limited to the confirmation that an order has been understood and carried out, or at best to seeking approval for initiatives designed to please the colonial power. The *letrados*, originally the clerks of imperial bureaucracy in the Baroque period, but increasingly the displaced literati, caught between the claims of indigeneity and loyalty to the culturally authenticating power of Spain, between mestizo hybridity and the demands of literary language dependent on an otherwise alien Europe, act out a dialectic of anger, exile and longing which both powers the rich literature of Latin America in the last century and limits its ambitions. The circumscribing factor is the imbalance in cultural power, the anthropological limit on true dialogue.

Perhaps there is an explanation in the millennial isolation of Europe. The storm-tossed waters of the North Atlantic were poor sailing, and the scraggy isthmus, in Joyce's phrase, had little to offer the thriving, complex trades based on fine horses, silks, spices and precious metals. The Phoenicians would risk the waters for Cornish tin and gold: there was little else to tempt the great empires and the travelling merchants. Feudalism merely chained the European peasantry to the land. Perhaps this is why the European age begins with such a virulent, necessarily global ambition in the invention of capitalism. Unused to the commerce that civilized the rest of the world in mutual (if often armed) dialogue, capitalism emerged without ethics and without the system of mutual obligations and trust that fuelled ancient trade. Not that all that it brought was bad. But while the philosophical doctrines of freedom offered a utopian lure, the institutional apparatus of modernity – in particular, the nation-state and the commodity form – would be profoundly mixed blessings for the world it colonized.

To take only one example, the concept of nationality has a direct impact on art. As Laura Marks points out in relation to media arts, 'national funding policies that give priority to exclusively national artists constrain production, distribution, exhibition and criticism of intercultural cinema, realigning this work with the very nationalist discourses that it critiques'.[3] In similar ways, the necessity for national galleries to promote the art of national citizens, and of funding bodies to aid journals that record the national life of art, work to help form the artistic culture in an image of the nation as it is conceived in any specific moment in political history, even if that means burning the art of 'Jews'. Nationhood is an export of European modernity. In Europe itself, it is undergoing immense changes. The possibility of a regional union has provoked an outcry among national media, who see their franchises at risk. Nationhood under threat becomes nationalism of the most profoundly dangerous kind, as witness the rise of ethnocide in the Balkans, of neo-Nazism in Germany. At the same time, the very notion of Europe is itself dissolving under the impact of the rich and diverse populations that move through it. The old colonial powers, as Robert Reich argues, retain their strategic position through what we can isolate as a monopoly on communication: wealth accumulates neither in the home country of a transnational corporation, nor at the sites of manufacture, which may be scattered across the globe, but at the centres where technologists and managers govern research and development.[4] This explains too the problem identified by Saskia Sassen: why do cities play such a vital role in contemporary capitalism, when the global economy is so powerfully based in communications networks?[5] Economic power operates by blocking communication flows: by creating nodes through which the flows of human intercourse are forced to pass, and in which they can be mined for profit. Money is not a very complex mode of communication, but it does communicate. The city of managers and experts is the most characteristic of these nodes.

The same cities that govern the stock exchanges govern art exchanges: New York, Paris, Milan, London, Frankfurt, Tokyo . . . Each controls the global flow of communications, and each attempts to cling to a fading uniqueness in the guise of national art, even while, by the nature of the information economy, each becomes more like the others. Curiously, the effect of this is not to produce distinctive forms of art, but to encourage even further the development of a transnational class, equally at home in any world city, and recognizing one another by their shared taste in an increasingly homogeneous world art.

These are the conditions under which *Third Text* entered its second decade. If the first was pre-eminently devoted to revealing the institutional closures of the art world and the artists they excluded, the second began the enquiry into the emergent phenomenon first signalled by the notorious show 'Magiciens de la terre' of the assimilation of the exotic Other into the new world art. In this Paris exhibition, contemporary European artists were mixed indiscriminately with shamans and artists from ex-colonial cultures in a show with a major cultural impact, but one in which the distinctive dominance of the Eurocentric institution remained. On the one hand, there were works of autonomous, enlightenment art whose concept would have been perfectly recognizable to Immanuel Kant. On the other were the rest: spectacle rather than concept, materials and methods rather than art, crafts and beliefs rather than the specificity of art engaged almost exclusively with defining itself. They came to bring images for the real artists: the Europeans. *Third Text* devoted the whole of its sixth issue to the criticism of the exhibition.[6] The journal continues its task to expose and attack such racist parochialism wherever it persists. But the nature of the art institutions has changed over these years, and the critique must evolve with it.

METROPOLITAN COSMOPOLITAN

Among the most persuasive accounts of contemporary racism, Etienne Balibar notes a discursive shift from the older language of a supposedly biological ground of races to a new language of culture. Behind this apparent political correctness, a new formation of the old racism is in hand:

> It is a racism whose dominant theme is not biological heredity but the insur-
> mountability of cultural differences, a racism which, at first sight, does not
> postulate the superiority of certain groups or peoples in relation to others but

'only' the harmfulness of abolishing frontiers, the incompatibility of life-styles
and traditions.[7]

Commenting on this 'differential racism', Hardt and Negri observe that the new
racism operates not so much by binary oppositions between colonizer and
colonized, the strategy of the older, biological racism, but by inclusion. This
'hatred born in proximity' proper to a world of massive migration ensures that
'racial exclusion arises generally as a result of differential inclusion'. The new
global social order which they refer to as Empire poses racial differences 'never
as a difference of nature but always as a difference of degree'.[8] The old racism
saw exclusion as necessary and absolute, the product of the innate, genetic
heritage of non-Europeans. The new abandons this universalism in favour of
inclusions, but inclusions that are highly differentiated. In the new Europe, for
instance, 'we' are all Europeans, but the old Europeans continue to occupy the
centre stage exclusively.

In this new domain, every success from among the despised 'others' is used
to 'prove' that there is no racism: Colin Powell in G.W. Bush's cabinet shows
that the Republicans have no colour bar, despite the virtual apartheid governing almost every major city in the USA. The same principle now governs
the metropolitan art world. World art demonstrates the inclusiveness of the
new world order, while at the same time serving to reinforce the fundamental message of differential inclusion. Art that demonstrates unredeemable
cultural difference is of the highest value, since it undergirds the fundamental
argument of neo-racism: that there exist cultural differences that cannot be
overturned, differences that provide ideological and discursive explanations for
the continuation of white dominance.

The globalization processes of contemporary culture cannot afford to ignore
the reality of intercultural, transcultural geographic and communicative flows.
The immense increase in tourism indicates something of this: in 1994 alone, the
world saw 455 million tourists; and the numbers continued to escalate until the
events of 11 September 2001. The popularity of long-haul destinations speaks
of an increasing desire for the exotic as counterbalance to the increasing homogeneity of the metropolitan centres. Postmodern theory understands long-haul
tourism, in some respects the vanguard of expanding capitalism, as the result of
the lure of an authenticity which is no longer available in the postindustrialized,
overdeveloped areas of the world, sunk as they are into societies of spectacle
and simulation. As Ziauddin Sardar has argued, the consumption of the Other,
in material, intellectual and spiritual forms, has become a hallmark of postmodern times.[9] World art, like world music, heralds a sentimentality among
the powerful, an enjoyment without responsibility, and a false nostalgia for a
mythologized state of cultural innocence which never prevailed in the West and
does not in the poor regions of the present day. The sentimentalist cult of
authenticity, that bogus respect for the cultures of others, permits, indeed
demands, the policing of traditions and the preservation of ways of life to
supply a stream of novelty entertainments for the élite.

This new formation of art-institutional racism requires ever-new modes of creativity from artists who are not content to see their work assimilated into the system. In addition to the challenge faced by all artists, to create work which does not finally take the shape of a commodity, Third World artists must confront the immensely difficult task of remaining true to themselves while refusing the imposed signification of tradition, typicality and authenticity; of making work that can communicate, or in some way be habitable across the world, without thereby becoming proof of the inclusiveness of neo-liberal globalization programmes. For some artists, the struggle has led to a retreat from international arenas and a return to the local. While there may be many motivations for such an action, it is not a possible strategy for countering the globalizing assimilation of Otherness, since it merely proves, once again, the unassimilability and, therefore, 'racial' difference on which the system thrives.

The purpose of this introduction is not to resolve this dynamic into a single strategy for global arts. It is not just the arrogance of the idea of a single strategy, so typical of the neo-conceptualism so fashionable at present. Nor is it merely the impossibility of a single resolution suitable for all situations. Many makers have abandoned the concept of art altogether, and begun to practise in emergent media or alternative modes of cultural practice, but this, while vitally important, does not remove the responsibility to fight for and within the institutional structures of the art world as well, not least since their popularity has grown exponentially over the last decades. To a great extent, there is no resolution to be had. This is the condition under which the policing of the metropolitan galleries and museums, journals and biennials is undertaken and maintained. The condition of working in them is that they must also be resisted.

It is clear from the history of art in the twentieth century that art does not necessarily represent. It is increasingly clear in the first years of the twenty-first that it cannot claim simply to be: the Kantian autonomy of artworks is given the lie with every gallery purchase. What art does is mediate. Standing in the zone between people, that space so often dominated by money and power, art offers another way, a praxis-based method of relating. This is what makes the challenge to the art institution so critical. Art's promise of a different mode of relationship between people is constantly broken by the intervention of an institutional organization that presumes to know, in advance, what is being communicated, by whom and to whom. By restructuring mediation as a transmission of meaning, authenticity or exoticism from A to B, the art institution diminishes the utopian potential of art. Gatekeeping ensures that the permission to mediate is restricted, and that it is always open to the structuration of the institution. Most of all it ensures that, just as metropolitan R&D keeps the accumulation of wealth in the control centres of the West, so the circulation of art's mediations always foregathers at the central nodes of the gallery circuit so that control over its circulation remains in the same hands. It is that control which restrains and diminishes the function of art in the twenty-first century, and it is that diminution against which *Third Text* stands.

But this in itself raises further problems. To what extent is the project of *Third*

Text itself an unwitting participant in the processes of assimilation? If it is true that there exists a new transnational class, their culture is appropriately not metropolitan but cosmopolitan. Though the politics of the World Trade Organization is based in the free flow of goods and controlled flow of people, the barriers to migration and travel are lifted for the transnational executive. A citizen of the world, basking in the glow that comes from knowing that he or she embodies the cosmopolitanism that Kant saw as the sole basis for universal peace, not only moves happily in space but embraces, warmly embraces, every cuisine and every culture. Every difference is an opportunity for trade, but trade in the conditions that obtain under globalization is never the communicative trade of the ancient bazaar. It is instead an opportunity to extract profit, most typically not by either buying or selling but by lending: supplying and controlling the medium in which the trade occurs. As finance capital overtakes production, so the contemporary art institution, as it were, dematerializes art. The accommodation of conceptualism into the institution is remarkable.

Slavoj Žižek argues that the response to universalist cosmopolitanism cannot be the cultural relativism of so much western Marxist cultural theory. Nor, *Third Text*'s consistent criticism of western instrumental rationalism suggests, can it be a Habermasian universal rationality.[10] We already have universal citizenship governed by the cultural relativism of inclusive differentiation and the results are punitive. Žižek argues that universalism can only be countered by a further universalism.[11] In our context, the assimilation of world art to the global hegemony of universalist art institutions can only be radically overturned by another universal, the necessity of emancipation. But since emancipation can only be spoken from the position of its realization, that is, from its position as a universal that does not yet exist, the purpose of artistic struggle is to voice a yearning for a freedom that we do not possess, to speak to us from the future that, through art's mediations, we can feel as immanent but unrealized. Whether that future takes the form of a new mode of universal, or whether, as Arif Dirlik[12] suggests, it emerges as a non-totalizing politics, it remains a future. *Third Text*'s object is then not to reveal what already exists but is ignored, nor to produce real differences that somehow might be more resistant to assimilation, but to propose a counter-hegemony. What the essays that follow share, in spite of their dissimilarities, their diversity, their conflicting and contradictory methods and models, is an alternative cosmopolitanism to that generated in the metropolis: a global culture of radical democracy. That this democracy exists only in an attainable future, far from negating it, provides it with the ethical structure underpinning its aesthetic.

READING THE *THIRD TEXT* READER

Making the selections for this volume has been a difficult task. Relying on volunteer labour and small grants from the Arts Council of England throughout its existence, the journal has remained self-published, surviving from crisis to crisis. Nonetheless, it has achieved an international reputation for insight and aggression. The price of independence has been high, and valued collaborators have been lost along the way, run ragged by the strain. Yet contributors of the highest calibre have written at their best for these pages. We decided early on to avoid articles written by or dealing with single artists, although these are among the most significant pieces in the journal, and in many respects the clearest indication of why it exists. We felt, however, that articles addressing wider issues and major themes would give a stronger sense of the journal's commitment, and allow readers new to the idea of a postcolonial art practice a broader sense of the issues at stake.

The selection also respects a key aspect of *Third Text*'s project, its embrace of popular and vernacular arts as well as the gallery and museum version. In this sense, since its beginning, *Third Text* has been at the forefront of the movement from art history towards visual culture. At the same time, the journal has rarely acted as an apologist for the popular. The alibis offered by much contemporary cultural studies – that what the people like cannot be wholly bad – have rarely convinced its authors, who fear too much the act of representation, by which is understood not just depiction but the political system of speaking on behalf of another. The struggle to speak for ourselves is too precious to be lost in enjoying being spoken fluently by the professional élites. Thus the section on Film not only critiques the entertainment cinema's presumptions but celebrates and articulates, as the journal has throughout its life, the struggle to realize Third cinema. More recently that interest has spread to radical global use of the digital media,[13] a field which is likely to be significant in the journal's future growth.

The eschatological orientation towards the future does not stop *Third Text* engaging with the past. In almost every selection here, and especially in the section devoted to History, Santayana's warning that whoever fails to understand history is condemned to repeat it returns again and again. Globalization and the problems of the formation and construction of identities cannot be understood without a sense of history, and their futures too demand a crafted understanding of the past. If it is true that the cultures of the 'post' – postmodernity, postcoloniality – are spatialized, then part of our task today is to undertake a re-temporalization against the stasis invoked by the idea that history is over, and we lost.

The mere existence of *Third Text* is a tribute to the belief that the immensely difficult task of communication across cultures is thinkable. For all the reasons outlined above, it is not necessarily immediately doable. Instead, it is a project, a task and a practice that we undertake. The journal has provided its own utopian space, a place where argument and debate, celebration and critique have been enabled across every continent and, when funds have permitted, in other languages than English. The journal began as the personal vision of its founding editor, Rasheed Araeen, and specifically as a continuation in another medium of the experiments he had already been engaged with, addressing the possibilities of participation in highly conceptualized but nonetheless open-ended artworks. When Araeen speaks of the journal as the continuation of a personal artistic project of collaboration and conceptualization, he points towards a key quality. *Third Text* is less an accumulation of readings, nor even the documentation of interventions. It is a practice and a resource for further practice. It exemplifies as much as it describes the emergence of alternative planetary networks of cultural, political, ethical and aesthetic action. All those who have worked on the magazine, every contributor, but especially every reader who has picked up an idea, an image or a flash of insight or anger, continue this challenging, exhausting but wholly necessary project. We hope we have captured this spirit in the *Third Text Reader*.

A NOTE ON THE TEXT

Some cuts to the original articles have been necessary in order to accommodate as diverse a selection as possible. No indication is given where material is omitted at the start or end of articles, but major excisions are indicated by three asterisks. Deletion of words, phrases or sentences is not marked. Editorial changes have been made in order to standardize articles, improve clarity, and correct occasional errors. Readers who wish to trace a complete original article should consult the *Third Text* online index, which gives the original publication details and is located at www.waikato.ac.nz/film/research/thirdtext/thirdtext.html

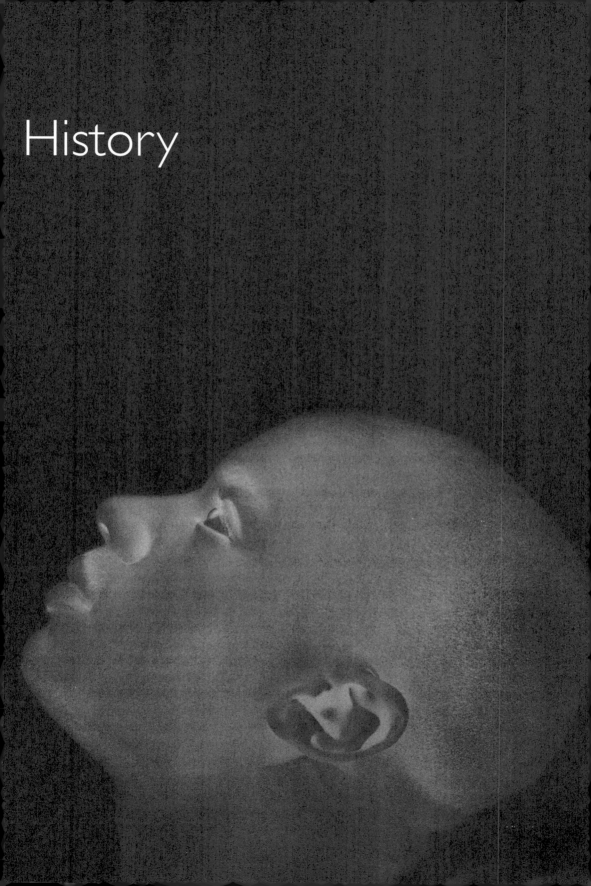

History

Introduction

ZIAUDDIN SARDAR

We make history; but we are also made by our history. Individuals and societies constantly move in history and use it as a reservoir of experience, allegiance and ideals that craft identities and outlooks. The patina of history ages the present. But more important: when today is steeped in a vision of the past it becomes a means to envision and shapes a trajectory into the future. History is never a dead letter, even if we fail to learn its lessons, or refuse anything except reliving its mistakes.

Conventionally, history as taught and studied has been hopelessly selective: it ignored most of the human experience and concentrated almost exclusively on the story of the victors, and wholly on gathering 'facts' and showing the interplay of power politics. This approach to history, akin to stamp collecting, led Karl Popper to talk of the poverty of historicism and argue that 'history has no meaning'.[1] But this view of history had a specific and particular meaning for the western civilization. Often referred to as the 'positivist' approach to history, it is based on the assumption that the 'truth' of history can only be derived, like the 'truth' of natural sciences, by the use of 'scientific method'. It is designed to generate an illusion of clinical objectivity and hide the value judgements that are implicitly placed on historical interpretation. It enabled western civilization to project itself as the only maker of global history,[2] while the histories of all other civilizations, cultures and societies became so many small tributaries, all flowing into the Grand Universal History of western, secular civilization.

The closing decades of the twentieth century witnessed a series of powerful discourses that attempted to transform the dominant conception of history. Jean-François Lyotard introduced a radical departure with his now-ubiquitous concept of the end of the *grand recits*.[3] But the loss of the large-scale narratives of emancipation, progress and reason identified by Lyotard was not the beginning of a season of anomie, but rather the fertile soil on which other stories could be told. Stories of the sciences of other civilizations; stories of peasants and ordinary people, the subalterns; stories of the European working classes; stories of women's work and worlds, 'hidden from history' in British historian Sheila Rowbotham's phrase;[4] and the complex, angry narratives of the origins of globalization in empire, exile and slavery. Far from losing a sense of interconnectedness, new political formations introduced a darker sense of history. Once, Adorno had been able to claim that, after Auschwitz, there could be no more lyric poetry. The realization that the only unique quality of the Holocaust was that it was conducted against Europeans demanded a new understanding of global histories as we contemplated the genocides conducted against Africans in the Atlantic slave trade and against the indigenous populations of North America, the Caribbean and Australia. Where Lyotard had expected the collapse of grand narratives, suddenly there was a proliferation.

One of the main features of the dominant notion of history is its subdivision into 'ancient', 'medieval' and 'modern' that was first introduced in the nineteenth century. Initially, in this linear framework, the terms 'civilization' and 'culture' were used in the singular; but later they coalesced into 'Western Civilization', which became the yardstick by which all other civilizations and cultures were measured.[5] Thus, by definition, western civilization, the final stage of human evolution, became 'modern': it not only defined modernity, but modernity itself could only be acquired through western culture. The present of all other cultures thus became the past of western culture; and the present of western culture became the future of all other cultures. Western modernity became a natural, binary opposite of non-western tradition, which came to be defined as 'old', 'medieval', unworthy and inferior.

In reclaiming their histories, 'Third World' societies not only contested the terms but, as Geeta Kapur demonstrates, often turned the dialectical relationship between tradition and modernity into a profoundly productive one. Tradition 'emerged in the decolonizing process', she writes, 'as an oppositional category': it thus had the power of resistance so eloquently and effectively used by Gandhi. Modernity, on the other hand, had a rather undefined relationship with its two companion terms: modernization and modernism. 'Modernization', Kapur tells us, is 'a social and economic process' applicable to developing countries; it is a term full of 'ideological import' and Eurocentric assumptions. Modernism is a cultural term 'squarely situated at a particular point of western history – the nineteenth century'. While it can 'take on an imperialist character', Kapur contends that it also has 'the potential to evolve into a revolutionary culture'.

The tendency to structure history in linear terms has not altogether evaporated with the emergence of new political discourses. Allowing for differences of vocabularies in various disciplines, the chronologies of intercultural relations tend to run from imperialism (the military and political domination of territories), through colonialism (the pre-eminence of political domination), via neo-colonialism (political independence structured in dominance by ex-colonial economic relations) to the triumph of globalization (the economic domination of the metropolitan and peripheral by transnational corporations beyond the reach of democratic movements). A simpler version of the scheme could be premodern–modern–postmodern. Here, as in its nineteenth-century counterpart, the most evolved category – postmodernism – becomes the defining element. Thus, as David Craven points out, by definition 'modernism is bad; postmodernism is good'. Craven argues that modernist art from the late nineteenth century to the late 1940s is a product of a plurality of related but also notably divergent and even fractious tendencies, some of which are grounded in a broad-ranging multiculturalism and were part of an uneven, non-linear development that contravenes the linear concept of historical progress intrinsic to western modernization. These later tendencies within modernism became known as 'alternative modernism'. Craven shows how this movement was conceived and developed in Latin America, where the very term 'modernism' (*modernismo*) was invented in the late 1880s.

The dominant notion of history not only insists on reducing complex, multiple histories to one single linear hierarchy but also prioritizes ancient over living culture. Thus western civilization not only 'discovers' the pasts of other cultures and civilizations it also becomes the guardian of the 'authenticity' of the colonized cultures. As Johan Lagae shows in his insightful deconstruction of the Universal Exhibition of 1867 (only ten years after the 'Indian Mutiny'), the display of the colonies at such exhibitions emphasized their 'authenticity'. The intent was to invent a tradition – in this case Congolese architecture – and then to become the guardians of its authenticity.

Artists from the 'Third World' had to resist and fight such notions of authenticity that froze them in history and enframed them in a dead and distant past. As Olu Oguibe shows, colonial education policies in Africa were specifically designed to deny modern education to the locals, as cultural and creative education was considered irrelevant for the Africans. The first artist to defy this convention was Aina Onabolu, who began 'a modern art practice by teaching himself'. Onabolu was followed by two South Africans: landscape painter, John Mohl, and naturalist painter, Gerard Bhengu. Mohl was once approached by a white admirer, relates Oguibe, and advised not to concentrate on landscape painting, but to paint figures of his people in poverty and misery. Landscape, he was advised, had become a field where Europeans excelled. 'But I am an African,' Mohl replied, 'and when God made Africa, He also created beautiful landscapes for Africans to admire and paint.' Mohl's elegant reply defies the hierarchical categories within which the Europeans sought to place and thus control the colonial subject. But Mohl's stand against European hegemony was still based on the notion that African modernism (or should it be alternative African modernism?) had to follow the trajectory of the West. A redefinition of African modernism was offered by South African artist, Ernest Mancoba. Mancoba, writes Oguibe, 'displaced the iconography of the European Enlightenment and chose African sculpture and forms as the source of inspiration, the point of departure and yet, the frame of reference'. The whole purpose of the exercise was to produce a 'new aesthetic' that synthesized European and African modernisms 'by writing African art as the common frame, the subtext of all modernisms'.

Zeynep Çelik uses the concept of *lieu de mémoire*, attributed to historian Pierre Nora, to show how similar redefinitions occurred in the Algerian context. *Lieu de mémoire* is defined as 'any significant entity, whether material or non-material in nature, which, by dint of human will or the work of time, has become a symbolic element of the memorial heritage of any community'. 'Memory is life', writes Çelik, 'subject to remembering and forgetting', 'appropriation and manipulation', and can be dormant for long periods before it returns with full force; whereas 'history is the reconstruction of what is no longer'. The *lieux de mémoire*, 'the material, symbolic and functional sites, are the products of the interaction between memory and history. They embody a will to remember (memory) and record (history).' Çelik uses the urban spaces of Algiers – the rooted *lieu de mémoire* – and Eugène Delacroix's famous painting, *Les Femmes d'Alger* – the portable *lieu de mémoire* – to show how contemporary Algeria maintains the colonial *lieu de mémoire*, but transforms it to serve as a critique of modern realities.

'Ethnic minorities' and people of non-European lineage are now involved in similar struggles in the West in relation to the heritage industry. As Stuart Hall reminds us, heritage works as 'selective tradition': 'social memory is also highly selective, it highlights and foregrounds, imposes beginnings, middles and ends on the random and contingent. Equally, it foreshortens, silences, disavows, forgets and elides many episodes which – from another perspective – could be the start of a different narrative.' So, how do *we* ensure that our own narratives survive in the heritage of Britain/Europe/United States? First, Hall suggests we ought to have a good idea of who *we* are. Second, we need to ensure the survival of the 'unprecedented, creative explosion by contemporary practitioners' from 'minority communities' in all the branches of art. Third, we need to preserve 'the record of the migrant experience itself'. Fourth, we must make sure that the younger generation has access to the cultural repertoire of their traditions of origins and 'can understand and practise them' from 'the inside'. Only then will we have the requisite 'cultural capital' and resources for our own heritage and be able to engage with other traditions.

Tradition, heritage, modernism – all contested terms. But no less contested are the very words 'art' and 'history', the one leading away from, the other towards, a time-based judgement of the ethical outcomes of creative practice. But it is precisely when the terms are held in dialectical conflict that they function together to produce illuminations not just of the past, not just of the present, but of the processes of change in which we – all humanity now alive – must take our places.

Contemporary Cultural Practice
Some Polemical Categories[1]

GEETA KAPUR

THE ARGUMENT

The persistence of the terms 'tradition' and 'contemporaneity' as they figure in Third World debates are best appreciated if we see them as notations within the cultural polemic of decolonization. They may be used in all earnestness as essential categories and real options but in fact they are largely pragmatic features of nation-building. Indeed, the terms function in a hyphenated form and mark the double (or multiple) register of a persuasive nationalist discourse. Sufficiently historicized, either tradition or contemporaneity can notate a 'radical' purpose in the cultural politics of the Third World.

TRANSACTING TRADITION

Certainly the term 'tradition' as we use it in the present equation is not what is given or received as a disinterested civilizational legacy, if ever there should be such a thing. This tradition is what is invented by a society's cultural vanguard in the course of a struggle. It marks off territories/identities of a named people, as, for example, Indians. In that sense it is a loaded signifier drawing energy from an imaginary resource (the ideal tradition), but always remaining by virtue of its strongly ideological import an ambivalent, often culpable, sign in need of constant historical interpretation so that we know which way it is pointing.

What in India we call tradition today was put in the fray by nineteenth-century nationalists. The manifestos of *Swadeshi* (political and cultural self-reliance) in the first decades of the twentieth century produced, in conjunction with the ideal tradition, a kind of aesthetic at once didactic and contemplative. This is best exemplified by the great scholar A.K. Coomaraswamy and followed in Bengal by artists with arguable success.

Since tradition even in its conservative allegiances emerged in the decolonizing process as an oppositional category, it has the power of resistance, as we know very well from Gandhi; the power to transform routinely transmitted materials from the past into discursive forms that merit in consequence to be called contemporary even radical. If the savants of the twentieth century, among them Coomaraswamy, have excavated the past to provide the present (in their opinion an errant and impoverished century) with perennial life-symbols, the exercise has a rather special significance when this is contextualized within an anti-imperialist struggle. Coomaraswamy (in the context provided by Gandhi), even when he addresses national cultural issues from a conservative position, produces an interventionist discourse opening up new and numerous other issues besides 'Indianness' – issues about the function of art in society and about the advanced role of artists in the formation of a more universal world culture. These are the issues Rabindranath Tagore takes up in virtual opposition to the more severe injunctions of *Swadeshi*.

Let us look at this a little further. With Coomaraswamy, tradition, besides its metaphysical status, is the code derived from and applied to actual/ideal iconographic forms. Being also a set of working canons, it can include, in an intricately worked hierarchy, high art with everyday objects. For canonical rigour, despite the transcendent meanings to which it refers, is based on the form and function of idols and objects. But it is precisely Coomaraswamy's contemporary, Rabindranath Tagore, who handles tradition in a way that dismantles the code. Tradition with him is a notional category allowing an infinite extension of its own nurturing body through poetic allusion and metaphor. The Tagorean way is as we know the romantic way and it deals with immanent energies that are inexhaustable in the mythical fashion and encourage continual transfiguration of material resources within and beyond a given culture. This includes the anthropological evidence and spiritual experience of extant forms. It includes the emotional resonance of the *rasa* theory, for example; or an encounter with the numen which irradiates from the heart of iconic forms. It includes the linguistic particularities of folk objects that are seen to provide the infrastructure of the civilizational process.

Rather than the canonical, it is the romantic designation of culture that gains ground in India. It is in a sense the more projective, utopian dimension. It is in line with the modern – the romantic tradition is a direct antecedent of the modern in Europe. And it allows non-systematic or intuitive interpretation of traditions with two quite opposite options: the option of finding elective affinities at the level of feeling; but also of triggering more anarchic disjunctions, of loosening and then upturning the forms of tradition. The two filmmakers, Satyajit Ray and Ritwik Ghatak, both heirs of Tagore, reflect the one and the other option within the broadly romantic view of tradition.

But even the very act of handling the tradition is in a sense political: it involves personification/mediation/representation of material that is seen to have been hitherto buried. Received like a patrimony, tradition has a heroic and authoritarian aspect. Is the Code for Coomaraswamy like the Name of the Father (or like the Canon of the Master-Craftsman)? On the other hand, are the affiliations to tradition understood as a nurturing body or as the matrix embedded in the unconscious, more difficult to wean off, leading to softer options in aesthetics and art practice? These personifications themselves are tricky and it becomes necessary to demystify the sustaining figures of Father (law) and Mother (womb) through less tenacious symbols that stress the engendering *function* at once masculine and feminine. We can, for example, take tradition as an androgynous figure and empower it all the more; but also, by this hypothetical entity, subvert the very knowledge of it. Part of the politics in the handling of tradition is to play both with its fantastic figures and its actual functions. There is a kind of plunder involved, and continual replenishment of the desacrilized resources.

When I use the word function I mean the study of genres, conventions, rhetorical devices, symbologies and other linguistic features. If tradition is functional it will also contribute to cultural praxis.

This has further implications: that we work less with seamless systems like myths and more with constructed forms like epic and allegory. Remember Brecht. Or we subject myths to allegorical readings, turning them inside out and placing them as open secrets within larger epic structures that give the myths transcendent purpose and an existential exit into new meanings. Ritwik Ghatak achieves precisely this in his six films. It also means that we work less with spiritual consensus on life-symbols and more with morphologies of art objects; more with formal analyses of given imageries where the signs float up, so to speak, each with its memory cell intact but impelled nevertheless to manoeuvre itself into new formal configurations. Into elaborate montage. I am thinking of the films of Mani Kaul. Is such functionality a reductive process, giving us only the mechanics of traditional forms? There is a function beyond functionalism that can point to the sensuous efficacy of images acted out in iconographic elaboration, that can push towards more reflexive structures, towards further narratives. I am referring to the cinema of Kumar Shahani. But this functionality is nothing without wit or what I called play, which displaces the relationship between canon and craft, between metaphor and structure. A wit that uses dissembling devices that are both naive and irreverent. The work of two artists, K.G. Subramanyan and Bhupen Khakhar, shows this to marvellous effect.

There are other, broadly sociological, ways of looking at the Indian tradition as it has come to us since the nineteenth century. The social matrix yields at least two distinct aspects, the aristocratic and the middle class, each with its own way of interpreting cultural nationalism. The princely attribute of 'Raja' Ravi Varma of the House of Travancore makes up one part of the lineage, a quasi-classical art aspiring to restore a civilizational poise to its people. On the other hand, the ambience of the landed gentry of nineteenth-century Bengal inclines them, as, for example, the Tagore family, towards a pastoral nostalgia for a people of the land. Against the courtly (and sometimes kitsch) pictures of Ravi Varma, the Tagore legacy includes poetic references to the Upanishadic hymns as well as to peasant songs. We know that the courtly tradition may on the whole be conservative. But we must also acknowledge that even the quasi- (or neo-) classical mode can attempt an allegorical/heroic model that provides valour and rationality to a contemporary society and plays, in that sense, a progressive role. As for the romantic view, the Tagore family, for instance, combines noble learning with dilettante experimentalism within the framework of the new national enlightenment called the Indian renaissance, and brings into this frame of reference the *art of the folk*. There is a strongly pedagogical aspect to this project, particularly as it is carried out in Tagore's university at

Santiniketan. It also points to a larger sociological context, the aristocrats' alliance with the folk in matters of culture, a principle on which romanticism in Europe and realism in Russia developed. In this lineage as well, there is then a definite democratic urge.

Indeed, it is this aspect which combines in the first half of the twentieth century with the artisanal basis of Gandhian ideology and the craftsman's canonical aesthetic of Coomaraswamy to give us the threefold composition of nationalist culture in the area of arts and crafts. In the actual practice of artists such as K.G. Subramanyan and his pupils, heirs of this nationalist culture, the aristocratic mentality vanishes completely to arrive, after a series of modernist mediations, at a strategic notion of the *contemporary*.

The other aspect of this invented tradition is less indigenist (less connected with ancient India or the Indian soil), more bourgeois/metropolitan. It is most clearly attributable to the Indo-Hungarian artist, Amrita Sher-Gil, who trained in Paris in the 1930s, and it develops in the late 1940s in Bombay, as well as in Calcutta and Madras during the 1940s and 1950s. One need hardly reiterate the progressive elements in the bourgeois consciousness as such or its initial engendering and later appropriation of a further, more revolutionary, consciousness.

In India the progressive element in the programme of the metropolitan (or simply urban) artists is once again mediated via nationalist aspirations, or the promise in existential and political terms for self-determination. Taken in the direction of modernization, this leads the cultural aspirations of what now comes to be called, in liberationist terminology, a Third World polity towards a more comprehensive, more radical, more sympathetic *international* formation. Calling themselves Progressives, several generations of Indian artists, including writers, seek to represent the people's voice – even if this be a rhetorical (or perhaps more correctly, emblematic) stand. At any rate, the progressives among the painters as, for example, F.N. Souza, M.F. Husain, S.H. Raza and Ara, in Bombay, and Ram Kumar and Satish Gujral in Delhi, can be seen as fellow-travellers in what is still believed through the 1950s to be a transitive society – a newly independent people transiting towards socialism.

The paradigm I have proposed for this invented Indian tradition is of course extremely schematic. It sees the folk as appropriated by the aristocratic élite, and progressive (socialist) ideologies as appropriated by the metropolitan intelligentsia. Even if such a schema works, its truth is of the most general kind. But there are several cross-references involved. First, the appropriation of the folk by the élite could be a way, for example, of correcting a too easy coincidence between the norms of progressivism with those of imperialism; it is a way of deferring the question of modernism until it can be handled by a more independent intelligentsia with a more questioning mentality. Second, it is precisely folk traditions (rather than the indeterminate proletarian culture) that are taken up by the Indian communists. The Indian Peoples' Theatre Association (IPTA) experiment in the 1940s and 1950s mediates folk traditions, especially in the area of performance, to progressive, clearly socialist, ends.

Third, there is another kind of mediation towards an indigenous variant of socialism – the Gandhian framework – where peasant communities are seen as the self-complete prototypes for a new and utopian social structure.

The artists and intelligentsia assigned to the bourgeois/metropolitan category in this simple paradigm also show strong nationalistic sentiments, and their modernism can be seen as not only mediated but in fact fashioned to serve the cultural self-image of a nation declaring its resistance towards imperialist nations of the First World. In India, one might say, the inhibiting, the camou-flaging, as well as the liberating, aspects of modernism are held at bay by a fairly independent bourgeoisie, and a fairly self-conscious intelligentsia, who are able to pose the issues of their own identity even when they cannot so easily resolve the cultural problematic that fetters the process of their own liberation.

CONTEMPORANEITY AND ITS DOUBLE MANTLE

Though obviously a temporal category, the term contemporary assumes a kind of neutrality and stands in an asymmetrical relationship to the value-loaded term tradition. We can, if we want, 'correct' the situation by giving con-temporaneity the ideological mantle of the term modernity. Immediately, of course, complications arise, but that is perhaps the point: to induce the turmoil and give a definitional ambiguity to the present so that the future is predicated at a higher level of consciousness.

But modernity, a word commonly used in India, stands in a relatively undefined relationship to its two other companion terms, modernization and modernism. Modernization is a social and economic process now applicable mostly to the underdeveloped/developing societies (of the Third World). It is a term full of ideological import, even over-determined one might say by socio-logical theory and usage. Modernism, on the other hand, is a cultural term now seen to be squarely situated at a particular point of western history – the nineteenth century. It can take on an imperialist character, but it has also the potential to evolve into a revolutionary culture. In envisaging socialist internationalism, modernism plays a mediating role.

Non-western nations, though struggling with the processes of modernization, are excluded from claiming modernism. Or they are seen as incidental to it. They stay, therefore, quavering a little, with a neutral term like contempora-neity. Yet so far as they undertake to modernize, the thorny face of the modern must be examined even as the aura that surrounds it must be seen to be what it is, a signalling device for the future. On the one hand, then, there is the specific-ally bourgeois ideology of modernism that makes it assume for itself a noble universality while obviously imposing a Eurocentric (imperialist) set of cultural criteria on the rest of the world. On the other hand, a unitary logic of advancement, as this was conceived of in nineteenth-century Europe, continues to be imposed so that some one or the other among the peoples of the world are always seen to be out of step. Further, the same linear model assumes, in the metropolitan concentration of culture, other geometrical figures like the centre and the periphery. This camouflages the crude progressivism of the linear model. Backwardness is not spelled out as such but questions of marginality (minor groups/minorities) emerge in its stead.

In view of the critique mounted from all parts of the world on the euphemistic projection of bourgeois culture as the 'universal modern', there is an attempt by western ideologists to change tactics. A good deal is now said about the abandonment of the linear model and of the model of the centre and the periphery as well. The new system for perceiving *difference*, the key word, is to project cultural phenomena into an infinite series. A problematic universe is mapped out into a differential system that is, as system, considered neutral. There is, in consequence, the reduction of the world into sameness. The Third World can hardly gain from one or the other model.

THE THIRD WORLD

The problematic term Third World comes in handy for primarily ideological reasons. In a sense, it supersedes or even denies historical specificity in order to be polemically effective. The Third World is a new world emerging to chastise the First and the Second Worlds. By definition volatile, it is possible that the Third World wedges itself in the global bind established between the First and the Second Worlds. But issues are confounded when the term is used not as a simple lever but substantively, as a concept: when it attempts to condense past struggles and present crises of a medley of postcolonial societies. Telescoped in history, the Third World becomes the symbolic option, and the polemic enters the realm of possibilities.

The political truth of colonial experience and of the anti-imperialist struggle is self-evident but its logic excludes several other political truths. Even fundamental categories like production systems and class relations are bracketed. Nor do Third World countries yield comparative cultural formations. Historically invented in the process of decolonization, tradition, governed in each case by a national ideology which emphasizes difference, becomes a sufficiently variegated sign to merit close and special attention.

Matters are altogether far from simple in societies designated as postcolonial. Here, if anywhere, capitalism and socialism are contested. Here is the world arena for ideological battle. This generates deeply vexed identities in terms of class and language, race and gender. Individual destinies are at stake as much as new collectivities. Indeed, the profoundly paradoxical nature of existence in the societies newly inducted into world history offers less rather than more possibilities of generalization. If we must, in any case, undertake to bring the anarchy of differential practices (including custom, knowledge, art) into some kind of recognizable order, one frame for which is the Third World, it also means that the theorizing must need be so much more complex. Once independence has been gained, nationalism itself poses ontological questions –

what is at stake in being Indian? And though the question may easily devolve into rhetoric, there is a burden of it that rests on a particularly fraught class of individuals: namely, the urban middle-class intelligentsia, including artists.

This cultural elite rests uneasily on its privileges even after a century of self-identification within the nationalist paradigm. The left-wing intelligentsia finds that the status of fellow-traveller is ambiguous since the goal of socialism remains unfinished. Moreover, when nationalism and unrealized socialism no longer suffice, the middle-class intelligentsia must cope with further states of social entropy – in a way that other sections of society do not – predicated, as it is, on a consciousness of self and identity within the nation state. This is the sort of burden, perhaps unreal and pretentious, that Rabindranath Tagore envisaged for the individual intellectual and artist in India. The responsibility to evolve his or her own subjectivity into an exemplary selfhood that indirectly but surely fulfils the demands of an exemplary nationhood. This burden assumes by proxy the ideal of a collective identity that may, moreover, come to resemble a form of socialism, as Nehru hoped. Certainly the left constituency of the intelligentsia can envisage totalities of another, more egalitarian, order. The imagination turns these expectations to allegorical account: all Third World narratives are national allegories, says Fredric Jameson.[2]

What is to be remembered in the Indian and presumably the Third World context is that contradictions are rife and you have to put up all the fights at once. If the primary fight is against the imperialism of the First World, you have equally to fight the anti-democratic forces of local dynasties and dictators. The fight is also against reactionary forces, especially aggressive in traditional societies like ours; indeed, against the anti-modern forces that use tradition, which served a useful function in the national struggle, as a ruse to regress into communal and religious fundamentalisms.

In view of this, definitions of tradition and modernity are constantly being repositioned in the discourses of the Third World. What is more, the relationship between the two at a substantive level has to be thought through at every point so as to avoid replicating the exploitative relationship the West has established towards traditional societies in the non-western world. From the over-determined nationalist bind in which tradition and modernity have hitherto coexisted, we have to bring them into a larger, more universal, discourse.

The point is to tackle the very problems western cultural hegemony suppresses or neglects. This requires above all that the two concepts, tradition and modernity, be disengaged from the abstracting ideology of capitalism – restoring to the one a self-reflexive mechanism, and to the other the utopian dimension. We have to bring to the term tradition, for example, the concreteness of extant practice, and to make the genuine extension of small particularities into new and contemporary configurations. Also, at the same time, we have to bring to the term modern a less monolithic, a less formalistic, indeed a less institutional, status so as at least to make it what it was once, a vanguard notion leading to a variety of experimental moves. Only with such initiatives can Third World cultures begin to justify their worth as alternative cultures.

Nor is this an entirely hypothetical proposition. Already in the nationalist phase the colonial intelligentsia contextualizes the terms tradition and modernity via patriotic norms. Tradition is not simply an anthropological phenomenon as it was conceived of by western modernists when they discovered primitive cultures. Even though nationalism as ideology introduces its own measure of abstraction into the concept of tradition, it also, in the very moment of inventing it, poses the problematic in contemporary terms and thereby sees it as *process*. A tradition-in-use, shall we say. Rather than producing, as in the case of the West, a discourse *about* the Oriental (including primitive) cultures, rather than distancing alternative civilizations into objects to be processed by western subjectivity, the nationalists at least make some genuinely anxious, and possibly responsible, appropriations within their own societies. If all Third World texts are national allegories, all national allegories are attempts to restore conceptual wholeness to lost communities.

Appropriated tradition in the nationalist phase may in fact resemble that endemic form of eclecticism the modern imagination encourages, but without the extremity of otherness which produces forms alienated from function and meaning. At the same time, this eclecticism can yield, as with the moderns, *acts of transgression* which lead to cultural radicalism. Thus, positing a tradition-in-use in Third World societies encourages an effective method of politicizing culture. It must, in addition, find a way to resist the business of *reification* to which the artefacts of 'other' civilizations succumb in the wake of western modernism. It is true, of course, that capitalism anywhere produces reifications, and that correctives are not easily at hand. In societies like India, modernization after the capitalist mode has produced a commodification of traditions as such, and of traditional forms and artefacts, to serve both the State and the market.

One might also add that today the political mode of aesthetic transgression followed by the moderns is considered ineffectual in the context of multinational capitalism and its appropriating (devouring) techniques. The postmodern vanguard proposes other means of politicizing cultural practice – by a more strategic form of 'minority' (class/race/gender) *resistance*. And the question arises whether postmodernist strategies are especially useful to us as well?[3]

Postmodernism, while it seems to accommodate otherness as never before in the history of capitalist culture, does so, as I said before, through a process of such infinite differentiation that all questions of identity are shredded, along with the normative function of culture and even the necessity of choice. This makes us more captive within the capitalist art market. We, who still must speak in favour of subjective identity at the individual level and living collectivities at the social level, have to learn to question the tendency towards formalism within the modern. But we must equally question the careless and aggressive laissez-faire of the postmodern which throws entire cultures to the gambler's wheel, treating cultural artefacts like so many fetishist pawns in the game.

Although the Indian intelligentsia must engage in transnational discourse on the question of Third World and alternative identities, Indian artists must derive the norms of their actual practice from the very specific aesthetic and ideological issues that they find pressing in their own (geographic/national) environment. That is to say, we have to beware a little of a Third Worldist mentality. There is now a Third World rhetoric surpassing Third World solidarity and over-determining the representations of radical issues for us. The First World (if not the Second) continues to use the principle of primacy quite literally to subsume the polemic into a larger appropriative project – sometimes through theory, sometimes through cultural consumerism. And sometimes through radicalism by proxy that pre-empts and forecloses praxis on site, where it may matter most.

It may also help to resist letting the postmodern categories of discourse coincide entirely with the political entities that arise in consequence of decolonization. Third World people must not simply lend body to the stripped phantoms of the deconstructionists' art. By not allowing too neat a fit between the dilemmas of decolonized cultures and postmodern theorizing, one may safeguard the material and political struggle, save it from appearing subordinate to categories within western academic discourse. It is, however, in our interest to recognize one thing. The sea-change created by the emergence of other cultures, that is our cultures, in the role of historical protagonists, has required western intellectuals to fashion different perceptual modes (and theoretical models). The postmodern phenomenon may be the consequence, not a description, of a universe realigned by social praxis within hitherto displaced societies, necessitating in its turn a theory of displacement.

Even in relation to the discourse set up by the ex-patriots, this tends for our purposes to become too much the privileged voice of the diaspora, whose members are themselves positioned in the western academic world. They are inclined to establish canons for radical discourse for the rest of the world. It is true that there is a certain urgency in their task, but there is also this tendency to establish a hierarchical superiority for a culture-in-exile which declares itself more militant. It should be recognized for what it is, a mode of operation suitable precisely to the mentality of the diaspora in the heart of the white world. Theirs is not the only call for militancy, though we should listen to it all the same.

We have, in other words, to look at the peculiarly structured inter-referentiality of Indian national culture as a continuous formation; to look at ourselves aspiring to enrich the neutral ground of our contemporaneity with a transplanted tradition; as also with the universal marker of the age: modernity. And then to look at ourselves, again, in the form of a postcolonial nation-state coalesced into the Third World to gain political solidarity. And, finally, rather than allowing ourselves to be theorized into political homogeneity, we must engage in a dialectic that takes into account the material factors within our own traditions but in terms of our projected history that can no longer be less than a universal project.

Meanwhile, the artists are in any case engaged in the less ideological, more concrete, task of making a tradition-in-use that nurtures contemporary existence. If the Third World is a political entity, an oppositional discourse and a compendium of cultural practices, then it is the last that will engage the artists' sustained attention.

If the Third World intelligentsia, among them artists, perform a task, it is to bring existential urgency to questions of contemporaneity. And, as with all existential expressions, it is split into two aspects. Tradition is turned into a critique and culture into a matter of practice, and both together into a civiliza- tional discourse that goes beyond nation-state and Third Worldist dogmas, beyond also the dividing bigotries of the present world. In this respect, the artist and intellectual of India and the Third World are no different from their coun- terparts in the First and Second Worlds. It is important to remember this, too, so that we are not simply overtaken by ideologies and left with polemical rather than life-sustaining forms of cultural practice.

The Latin American Origins of 'Alternative Modernism'

DAVID CRAVEN

RUBÉN DARÍO AND THE INVENTION OF EARLY MODERNISM

It comes as a surprise for many of us to discover that, far from being coined in the metropolitan West, the term 'modernism' (or *modernismo*) was in fact invented in the 1880s on the periphery of the world economic order by Rubén Darío of Nicaragua, Latin America's first internationally acclaimed modern author and still one of her most influential poets. Darío, who lived from 1867 to 1916, inaugurated Latin America's earliest genuine avant-garde movement under the banner of *modernism*. He evidently first used this term around 1888/9 to refer to novel attributes in the writings of Mexican author Ricardo Contreras.[1]

In formal terms, Darío's own *modernismo* in such poems as *Azul* (1888) consti- tuted a hybrid fusion of various artistic modes featuring heterogeneous cultural citations that were both European and non-European, along with being at once precolonial, colonial and postcolonial in origin. All of these divergent elements were in turn densely interwoven with references to experiences gleaned from the five senses.[2] Among the contemporary visual artists about whom Darío wrote were the French sculptor Rodin and the late Symbolist Latin American painter Angel Zárraga.[3]

Revealingly, when in 1912 he wrote an essay for *Mundial Magazine* about the paintings of Zárraga, Darío selected Rivera's portrait of Zárraga to accompany his essay. Furthermore, in this same issue of *Mundial* there was a brief discussion of Diego Rivera's modernist paintings by another Latin American author.[4] To a considerable extent, Darío was to *modernismo* what Apollinaire was to Cubism, Marinetti was to Futurism and André Breton was to Surrealism. In all four of these cases, a literary figure, specifically a poet, played a key role in articulating the project of an avant-garde movement many of whose most well-known practitioners turned out to be painters. (And here I am using the term 'avant-garde movements' so as to draw on the key concepts associated with them in the now classic studies by Renato Poggioli and Peter Bürger.[5])

The general dynamic of his poetry was driven, on the one hand, by a reaction against the outdated and ossified literary conventions of official Spanish letters, and it was motivated, on the other hand, by an assimilation of certain new developments in nineteenth-century French literature that were then combined with pre-Columbian cultural traditions of the remote past. The view motivating this unlikely synthesis was articulated by Darío as follows in *Prosas profanas* (1896): 'If there is poetry in our America, it is to be found in the old things.'[6]

Indeed, this notable reference to the artistic representation of '*nuestra América*' by the founding figure of modernism also reminds us of the earlier and still celebrated essay of 1891 that had first popularized throughout Latin America the explicitly non-Eurocentric phrase of 'our America'. This essay, entitled simply 'Nuestra América', was written by José Martí (1852–95), the only Latin American writer of the second half of the nineteenth century who rivalled Darío in prestige and importance.[7] (Incidently, Martí was also an art critic of note who praised French Impressionism and wrote reviews of Mexican artists, such as Diego Rivera's teachers Santiago Rebull and José María Velasco.[8]) Revealingly, Martí's celebrated essay called for the construction of a postcolonial, multiracial and transcultural society. In fact, Martí, who was a leader of the movement for national liberation in Cuba, was killed in 1895 while he was engaged in the armed struggle against western, specifically Spanish, colonialism.[9]

Such a new multi-ethnic society would presuppose a fundamental rethinking of history, so that, according to Martí, 'The history of America, from the Incas to the present, must be taught in clear detail and to the letter, even if the archons of Greece are overlooked. Our Greece must take priority over the Greece that is not ours.'[10] Aside from colonial peonage, there were the grave impediments of racism and imperialism that blocked the path of reconstituting the Americas along more socially just lines. Accordingly, Martí closed his 1891 essay with two warnings: first, 'Whoever foments and spreads antagonism and hate between the races, sins against humanity'; and second, 'The scorn of our formidable neighbor [the United States] who does not know us is Our America's greatest danger.'[11]

These themes of anti-imperialism and of racial harmony in concert with multiculturalism were abiding artistic concerns of Darío's mosaic-like concept of modernism. In Canto VII of his book *Cantos de vida y esperanza* (1905), which is entitled 'To Roosevelt', Darío penned a critique of imperial intervention and soulless utilitarianism that, because of its soaring poetry and pungent politics, has remained a favourite of Central American audiences ever since (particularly in the mid-1980s during the high point of the Sandinista-led Revolution in Nicaragua).[12] In the opening section, Darío declared as follows:

Es con voz de la Biblia, o verso de Walt Whitman
que habría que llegar hasta ti, Cazador!
¡Primitivo y moderno, sencillo y complicado,
con un algo de Washington y cuartro de Nemrod!
Eres los Estados Unidos,
eres el futuro invasor
de la América ingenua que tiene sangre indígena,

(It was with a biblical voice or the verse of Walt Whitman
that you arrived amongst us, O hunter!
Primitive and modern, simple and complex,
With something of George Washington and a quarter Nemrod!
You are the United States
You are the future invader
of the ingenuous America that has indigenous blood.)[13]

Further on in the same canto, Darío critically contrasts, on the one hand, the threatening colossus of the North, which had cynically combined the cult of Hercules and the worship of money, with, on the other hand, *'la América nuestra, que tenía poetas/desde los viejos tiempos de Netzahualcoyotl . . . la América del grande Moctezuma, del Inca'*.[14] (This criticism of the materialism and positivism of North American modernization was also a prominent theme during this same period in the work of the other Latin American *modernistas*, such as José Enrique Rodó of Uruguay.) Furthermore, the nature of his own critique of the West helps us to understand Darío's recorded sympathy for the 1905 Revolution in Russia – a fact that had gone largely ignored until Sandinista commandante Carlos Fonseca did research on it during the mid-1960s.[15]

Darío's critique was coupled with stark depictions of a view that had first emerged with European Romanticism, namely, that of the artist's alienation from bourgeois society. (Darío's relationship to this theme has been discussed brilliantly by Jean Franco.) In his story *El rey burgués*, Darío described the contemporary fate of the artist as one of being condemned to play a barrel-organ in the snow because he had defied the values of middle-class society.[16] Similarly, in his prose poem 'La canción del oro', Darío wrote of a poet/beggar who sings ironic odes to the Golden Calf, or cash nexus, that is widely worshipped in a society undergoing transformation by economic modernization.[17]

In sum, the original modernism of Darío – with its collage-like formal language of *mestizaje* and multiculturalism – embodied precisely that multilateral trajectory that Dore Ashton perceptively identified when she spoke of how modernist art at its most profound 'moved backward and forward at the same time'.[18] As such, Darío's modernism was inflected by an alienation from capitalist social values, pervaded by an opposition to western colonialism, imbued with a desire to revivify, or at least reuse, the non-western and precolonial artistic traditions of Latin America without, however, repudiating that which was still of great value in western art – and, finally, it was marked by an ambivalent embrace of what Charles Baudelaire had earlier called *modernité* (or modernity) in a well-known essay of 1863.[19]

Here, I think, it would be worthwhile to correct a very common misconception in art historical literature of the West. For Baudelaire's essay, 'Le Peintre de la vie moderne' (The Painter of Modern Life), was neither a definition nor a theorization of modernism, however much it did contribute to Darío's more theoretically self-conscious formulation of modernism later on.[20] When Baudelaire wrote: 'By "*modernity*" I mean the ephemeral, the fugitive, the contingent, the half of art whose other half is the eternal, the immutable'[21] he was simply defining modernity as the social experience of economic modernization, to which the cultural practices and artistic responses of modernism would subsequently come to constitute a more self-conscious, often dissident, and increasingly self-critical rejoinder.

This latter point was unintentionally made clear by Baudelaire's choice of the minor late Romantic artist Constantin Guys, rather than his proto-modernist friend Edouard Manet, as the 'painter of modern life'.[22] In fact, Darío's closest counterpart in French literature was Stéphane Mallarmé who, according to Roland Barthes and Marcel Duchamp, was the first French modernist, even though he himself generally employed the more restrictive but also early modernist term of *Symbolist*. This Symbolist movement of the late 1880s and 1890s is justifiably seen as marking the advent of both modernism and the avant-garde in France.[23] The modern visual artists for whom Darío showed a preference were themselves late Symbolists.

Here, of course, I am following Perry Anderson and Marshall Berman in defining these terms, so that *modernism* designates the minority artistic tendencies in opposition to, yet also tied to, the official high culture in the West. Similarly, just as the various tendencies of modernism were ambivalent and varied responses to the social experience of *modernity*, so the latter was a complexly mediated manifestation of the economic project of capitalist modernization and its allied programme of western imperialism.[24] Despite the fact that modernism, modernity and modernization are routinely used as synonyms in much art historical literature, it must be emphasized that they *have always existed only in asymmetrical and unsettled relation to each other.*

Consequently, we need also to note that the orthodox Marxist framework of base/superstructure is simply inadequate to grapple empirically with this asymmetry and the attendant relative autonomy of each of these various domains within society, as Raymond Williams and E.P. Thompson, among others, have noted.[25] The first step towards clarifying the plurality of practices known as 'modernism', then, involves an understanding of how these three terms (modernism, modernity and modernization) have assumed quite different historical relationships and tensions, depending on *which tendency within modernism one has in mind and also on the moment in history that is being addressed.*

EARLY ALTERNATIVE MODERNISM IN THE VISUAL ARTS

It was only after the Latin American term 'modernism' crossed the Atlantic to discover Europe in the 1880s – and its first port of call was Barcelona, not Paris – that it began to designate certain formal strategies and thematic concerns in the visual arts that were analogous to those that were found in Rubén Darío's modernist poetry and which are now associated with the European avant-garde and various tendencies of modernism in the more widely acknowledged sense. Just as Darío, while living in Spain, would have a significant influence on 1890s Spanish literature, so three of the major alternative modernists of the early twentieth century, namely, Antoni Gaudí, Diego Rivera and Pablo Picasso, spent formative years in Barcelona. Like Darío, the latter two figures frequented the anarchist and bohemian enclave of the Els Quatre Gats café. Indeed, Picasso even designed its menu and Rubén Darío left us a vivid description of its décor.[26]

The label of *modernismo* (or *arte modernista*) was evidently first used in the visual arts, while Darío was in Spain, to refer to such work as Antoni Gaudí's architectural projects in Barcelona, the *fin-de-siècle* city where Pablo Picasso lived and worked from 1895 to 1904. It was, then, the distinctly anti-colonial modernism of Barcelona, with a Latin American accent, that first gave us Gaudí and then helped to spawn Picasso's *Demoiselles d'Avignon* plus the 'Anáhuac Cubism' of Diego Rivera, as Justino Fernández has aptly labelled it.[27] (And while the term *modernismo* generally denoted the Catalán version of art nouveau, in the case of both Gaudí and Picasso this early designation of *modernist* obviously signified much else as well, thus expanding the concept of modernism to accommodate the even more divergent network of artistic directions that would soon emerge elsewhere.) In this sense, Catalán *modernismo* was both a distinct tendency *within* modernism proper and a point of departure for developing other tendencies of modernism later on.[28]

As is now widely noted, Catalán modernism in the work of Gaudí evinced a strikingly ambidextrous ability to go both forward and backward in history simultaneously. At once a person of the past and a partisan of the future, Gaudí used ultra-modern materials (he was the first architect in Spain to use reinforced concrete, which he employed for example in the Parque Güell) in conjunction with the time-hallowed artisanal approach to traditional materials such as ashlar, plus archaic building motifs that were both western and non-western in nature.[29] The singular-looking towers of Sagrada Familia came from the Berber building traditions of North Africa; the use of *azulejos* (or blue ceramic tiles) on the façades of edifices was *mudéjar*, or Moorish, in origin; the inclusion of Gothic arches was Catalán in derivation; and the recourse to modern engineering techniques along with new materials such as steel arose from the influence of northern European modernization, even as Gaudí was also apparently inspired by the utopian socialism of William Morris and the Arts and Crafts movement (as Kenneth Frampton has noted[30]).

Perhaps Gaudí's best-known aphorism is that 'originality is achieved by returning to origins',[31] and it should be connected not only to his reaffirmation of the local artisanal traditions of Cataluña (his father was a coppersmith and his grandfather was a ceramicist), but also to Gaudí's ardent commitment to the Catalán national autonomy movement against the imperial hegemony of Castile. It was, for example, this preoccupation with contesting the hegemonic dominion of the Spanish national state that led Gaudí to design a serrated roofline for the Casa Milá, which symbolically echoed the shape of Montserrat, the mountain that had long been a signifier of Catalán independence and which also served as an important subject for Diego Rivera's own landscape paintings while he was in Barcelona in 1911.[32]

Easily the best metaphor for Gaudí's distinctive concept of modernism is an invention resulting from it, namely, the modernist 'collage' that he used at Parque Güell only shortly before Picasso introduced collage into painting in 1912. On the upper deck of Parque Güell, above the market area that is sheltered by reinforced concrete beams and supported by a whimsical red sandstone Doric portico, there are outdoor benches that feature what was probably the first and what still remains one of the most striking architectonic 'collages' or modernist mosaics ever produced in the visual arts. This mosaic collage was fashioned from the broken shards and left-over fragments of rejects from a local Catalán ceramic workshop, as well as from the rubble of fractured glass and tableware.[33] A cobbled-together *mélange* of ruins that signify the unevenness of historical development to which Gaudí's entire *oeuvre* so eloquently attests, this modernist mosaic/collage was also a metaphor for the multifacetedness of Catalán national identity that wedded a utopian gesture of shared public concerns in the future to a sombre sense of the past along with a view of the present as a field of ruins. Here it is important to recall that Sagrada Familia, to which Gaudí devoted the last decade of his life, originated as a lay church for the expiation of the sins of the modern materialistic age, that is, of modernization.[34]

The 'collage' at Parque Güell, then, literally embodies the multiculturalism and dynamic open-endedness that have generally been a hallmark of the best alternative modernism. In addition, it encapsulated a telling historical ambivalence at once hopeful in its vision of the future and yet harsh in its view of what would precede it. A parallel for Gaudí's modernist belief in redemption among

the ruins of history can be found in the late writings of Walter Benjamin, who
remains one of the major theorists of modernism even as he is now routinely
cited by postmodernists. (And quite rightly so, since he introduced such themes
as the 'death of the author', and the historical construction of the subject in his
famous essays from the mid-1930s.[35]) Shortly before his death in 1940, Benjamin
wrote eighteen Theses on History, in which he famously observed that 'There is
no document of civilization that is not also at the same time a document of
barbarism.'[36] The apocalyptic yet also redemptive concept of history put forth
in Thesis IX bears repeating in view of how deeply it relates to the alternative
modernist work of Darío, Gaudí, Picasso and Rivera. It goes as follows:

> A [Paul] Klee painting named *Angelus Novus* [which was in Walter Benjamin's
> personal collection at the time] shows an angel looking as though he were
> about to move away from something he is fixedly contemplating. His eyes are
> staring, his mouth is open, his wings are spread. This is the angel of history.
> His face is turned toward the past. Where we perceive a chain of events, he
> sees one single catastrophe that keeps piling ruin upon ruin and hurls them in
> front of his feet. The angel would like to stay, awaken the dead, and make
> whole what has been smashed. But a storm is blowing from Paradise; the
> wind has caught his wings with such force that he can no longer close them.
> This storm irresistibly propels him into the future to which his back is turned,
> while the pile of ruins before him grows ever skyward. This storm is what we
> call progress.[37]

Indeed, as Karl Werckmeister has shown, unbeknown to Benjamin, Klee himself discussed his artworks in similar terms in 1915: 'Today is the great transition
from past to present. In the huge pit of forms there lies rubble to which one still
clings in part. It furnishes the stuff for abstraction . . . In order to work myself
out of my rubble, I had to fly.'[38]

Similarly, one of Pablo Picasso's most famous aphorisms, or anti-definitions,
was that 'A painting used to be considered a sum of additions. In my case a
painting is a sum of destructions.'[39] This alternative modernist concept of art,
which seems so manifestly linked to collage, is no doubt related both to Picasso's
tenure in Barcelona *modernista* and to his commendable commitment to the cause
of anti-colonialism, in addition to his important affiliations with anarchist thought
(at this time, Barcelona was one of the main centres in Europe for anarchism).
In an excellent article and an equally commanding book, Patricia Leighten
has compellingly documented not only Picasso's anti-colonialist views and concomitant anarchist vantage point but also how they figure so significantly in
his artworks of the early twentieth century.[40]

The celebrated *Demoiselles d'Avignon* of 1907, for example, which is named
after a street in Barcelona's red-light district, is not only about the uneasy
confrontation of the two sexes, as Leo Steinberg has argued, and about a
competition with Matisse's work, as Richard Wollheim showed in a recent
lecture.[41] It is also about the conflict of two cultures – those of western Europe

and west Africa – whose formally conflicted convergence gains in pictorial resonance precisely because of the tensely jarring transcultural quality of the work.

And this is a quality that has now become amplified even more so because of what we have recently learned about the depth of Picasso's opposition to French colonialism in Africa at precisely the moment in history, 1906/7, when this painting was being executed. Similarly, it has also been shown that some of Picasso's collages, such as the *Bottle of Suze* of 1912, feature newspaper articles about the horrifying loss of life in Turkey during the First Balkan War of 1912 and about anti-war speeches made by anarchists before huge crowds that were protesting the 'menace of a general European war' (to quote from one of the articles contained in the collage that was taken from *Le Journal* in November 1912).[42]

As for the use of the idea of the *fragment* to explain the historical import of Cubism, we need only recall how Diego Rivera incisively defined Cubism along these lines:

> It was a revolutionary movement, questioning everything that had previously been said and done in art. It held nothing sacred. As the old world would soon blow itself apart, never to be the same again, so Cubism broke down forms as they had been seen for centuries, and was creating out of the *fragments* new forms, new objects, new patterns and – ultimately – new worlds.[43]

It was the deftly understated, even camouflaged, quality of Cubist fragments that Thomas Crow had in mind when he observed the following of the internal dialogue between high art and mass culture, as well as between western and non-western art, in many Cubist collages:

> The mixing of class signifiers was central to the formation of the avant-garde sensibility . . . to accept modernism's oppositional claims, we need not assume that it somehow anscends the culture of the commodity; we can see it rather as exploiting to critical purpose contradictions within and between distinct sectors of that culture . . . This ceaseless switching of codes is readable as an articulate protest against the double marginalization of art . . . [so that] Cubism is . . . a message [with critical intent] from the margins of society.[44]

Similarly, the origins of the visual language associated with Cubism in general and with collage in particular both presupposed and concretely enacted a profound critique (or deconstruction) of the nature of painting in the West. At issue was something more than the reductive exercise of working with the essence of the medium, as proponents of formalism maintain. (In fact, in a recent series of lectures, Wollheim largely disallowed this Greenbergian reading of modernism by defining the medium as contingent on 'the way the artist shapes the materials', and *not* as an *a priori* given with which an artist must be resigned to work.) As such, the inception of Cubism entailed both an expansion of the communicative resources of the medium *and* a necessary contraction of the pictorial claims of European Renaissance art – that is, its illusions and illusionism.

Simultaneously, a Cubist painting both evokes and then undermines the high-art conventions in the West for constructing perspectival space: as in the abbreviated use of chiaroscuro, in the coy and inconsistent deployment of overlapping, and in the original suggestion but subsequent dissolution of figurative references. In addition, there is an artful decentring of the images, so as to disallow through an almost 'anarchistic' annulment the hierarchical structure along with the sense of formal resolution that were almost always salient traits of the classical tradition. As such, a Cubist painting, with its all-over tension between the actual two dimensions of the picture plane and the fictive three dimensions of Renaissance vintage, is not just about an interrogation of the medium (as Greenberg contended).[45] More importantly, modernist space in Cubist work resulted, whether intentionally or not, in a critique of the official pictorial language in mainstream western art, of which the medium itself was one, but only one, component. Indeed, it is precisely because modernist art at its most profound was a de-hierarchizing and demotic critique of the overarching *conventions* of official western art that the collage aesthetic could become so effective at accommodating a multicultural interplay of western and non-western elements on equal terms.

In one of the most incisive post-formalist discussions of modernism (and I would like to insist here along with Mikhail Bakhtin that we not confuse the necessity of formal analysis with the fetish of formalism[46]), Rosalind Krauss has deftly illuminated further how a Cubist collage, with its distinctive use of modernist space, addresses the mechanics of pictorial logic *per se* in the West.[47] As Krauss has rightly observed, two of the formal strategies that develop out of collage space are those of figure/ground reversal and of the continual transposition between negative space and positive form, so that there is no visual sign without the attendant eclipse or negation of its material referent.

Thus, Cubist collage and modernist space end up critically exploring the cultural preconditions of western representation itself, that is, how images have been produced in pictorial terms and how these images have traditionally come to assume the status of signs. Such a self-critical investigation of *how* and *why* western painting has traditionally worked, specifically of how its system of representation has been culturally mediated, strongly disallows the assertation by Thomas McEvilley that modernism in all its forms hegemonically privileges – *that is, naturalizes* – western art at the expense of non-western art. (This latter point about avant-garde modernism as a critical engagement with western hegemony, instead of being an uncritical presentation of it, was made by Meyer Shapiro in a series of classic essays from the 1930s up to and through the 1970s.[48])

In fact, the Cubist contestation of western cultural hegemony is precisely what allowed Diego Rivera (one of the greatest of the Cubist painters) to recruit Cubist collage and modernist space on behalf of the Mexican Revolution of

1910, with its unequivocal commitment to constructing a non-Eurocentric national identity. There are two key works in this regard by Rivera that fuse the shifting planes of Cubism with the forces of revolutionary upheaval. These are his *Portrait of Martín Luís Guzmán* (1915) and his *Zapatista Landscape: The Guerrilla*, which was painted in 1915 after Emiliano Zapata and Pancho Villa had taken and briefly occupied the capital of Mexico City.[49] (In fact, Guzmán, a Mexican novelist, did serve at one point with Villa.)

A rival and generally unrelated movement that used modernist collage to quite different ends, but for very critical reasons nonetheless, was Surrealism, which numbered among its ranks at various points such major Latin American artists as Wifredo Lam, Frida Kahlo and Roberto Matta.[50] And, of course, no other avant-garde movement contributed more to the emergence of anti-colonialist discourse or to the course of multi-ethnic identity in the arts than did the Surrealists.[51] In 1943, André Breton called Aimé Césaire's damning indictment of European colonialism and western racism, in *Cahier d'un retour pays natal* (*Return to My Native Land*), as 'nothing less than the greatest lyrical monument of our times'.[52] Picasso, who was also deeply moved by this Martinique poet's work, illustrated Césaire's fourth book, *Corps perdu*, in 1950.

While in Haiti during 1945, Breton declared the following to the poets of this Caribbean country:

> Surrealism is allied with the peoples of color, first because it has sided with them against all forms of imperialism and white brigandage . . . and secondly because of the profound affinities between Surrealism and 'primitive' thought . . . It is therefore no accident, but a *sign of the times* that the greatest impulses towards new paths for Surrealism have been furnished . . . by my greatest friends of color – Aimé Césaire in poetry and Wifredo Lam in painting.[53]

As James Clifford has pointed out in his exemplary discussion of 'Ethnographic surrealism', the Surrealist aesthetic was still in keeping, in several important respects, with what we have identified as the most fundamental characteristics of Rubén Darío's original conception of modernism, for they valued fragments, curious combinations and unexpected juxtapositions that were drawn from the domains of the erotic, the alien, the precolonial and the repressed. Furthermore, the progressive part of the Surrealist trajectory generally operated along a track that Clifford has identified as follows:

> Unlike the exoticism of the nineteenth century, which departed from a more-or-less confident cultural order in search of a temporary *frisson*, a circumscribed experience of the bizarre, modern surrealism and ethnography began with reality deeply in question . . . the 'primitive' societies of the planet were increasingly available as aesthetic, cosmological, and scientific resources. These possibilities drew on something more than an older orientalism; they required modern ethnography . . . For every local custom or

[national] truth there was always an exotic alternative, a possible juxta-position or incongruity . . . And it is important to understand their way of taking culture seriously, as a contested reality – a way that included the ridiculing and reshuffling of its orders . . . Another outgrowth of ethno-graphic surrealism . . . is its connection with Third World modernism and nascent anti-colonialism.[54]

CONCLUSION

A task not only of Darío's original concept of modernism as it has been developed and even transformed through these subsequent movements, but also of critical theory in the tradition of Marx, Benjamin and Adorno, was precisely to salvage for progressive purposes whatever was still worthwhile in the various class and ethnic legacies to which we are all heirs. Bertolt Brecht's advice of 'Use what you can' carried with it the critical corollary that what turns out to be reactionary in such lineages should be discarded without reluctance. One such concept that in some, but not all respects, remains valuable and emancipatory is *modernism*, or at least 'alternative modernism'.

* * *

To sum up this discussion of the progressive legacy of modernism, it would be very instructive to return briefly to the same country in which the term modernism originated, namely Nicaragua, to see how the lineage of Rubén Darío and *modernism* have fared in the last two decades. If we examine some of the notable artworks produced by the Sandinista Revolution of 1979–89, we shall see artworks that are anti-imperialist and non-Eurocentric (but *not* anti-western); artworks that are richly multicultural *and* that are unquestionably linked to modernism. One such work is Santos Medina's painting of 1982 entitled *La unidad revolucionaria de los Indoamericanos*, which is located quite justifi-ably within the tradition of Rubén Darío's *modernismo*. This painting combines intentional references to pre-Columbian ceramics, such as Nicoya ware, with allusions to European Cubism and an oblique recollection of Diego Rivera's contribution to modernism via 'Anáhuac Cubism'.[55] In this situation, as in others, modernism is not simply a regressive remnant of the colonial past, but a still viable *modus operandi* as well as raw material for reconstructing a postcolonial present in keeping with a more egalitarian future.

* * *

Reverse Appropriation as Nationalism in Modern African Art

OLU OGUIBE

One interesting theatre of nationalist struggle in Africa at the beginning of the twentieth century was the changing space of the visual arts. More interesting still was the nature of this struggle, which resided not in a direct confrontation with the structures of colonialism, nor in the tropes of imaging and representation, but was written through an appropriation of the forms of imperial culture.

In the second half of the nineteenth century, Christian missions began to establish schools in Africa. The missions needed interpreters and junior teachers, while growing colonial business concerns required cheap, semi-skilled labour and law enforcement cadres. This specific necessity determined the scope of the school curriculum. As A.D. Galloway has written, the 'early mission schools . . . [were] somewhat uninspired in their conception and excessively utilitarian in their concentration upon Reading, Writing and Arithmetic (the Catechism being printed alongside the multiplication tables in their text books)'.[1] In Nigeria, the Revd Birch Freeman's school timetable of 1848 departed slightly from this narrow scheme and included geography. Art education, however, was not considered necessary or indeed useful. In his history of art education in Nigeria, Uche Okeke concludes that with the colonial Christian mission, 'cultural and creative education was not considered important for the converts'.[2]

Beyond the logic of the functionalist argument, though, lay a more fundamental principle at the heart of colonial discourse, namely the perpetuation of the fictions of difference upon which the colonial project was constructed. A crucial device of colonial authority was to insert and institutionalize a corridor of slippage that granted the colonized only partial access to the possibility of transition and transformation to a modern identity. This boundary of possibility, identified by Sir Edward Cust as the cornerstone of colonial policy, allowed the colonized only a 'mimic representation' of imperial culture, such that the colonized was transformed from the extremities of backwardness which colonial discourse ascribed to her, into a partial presence, one that supposedly existed at the crossroads of barbary and civilization.[3] Behind this device, remarked Cust, lay a 'fundamental principle . . . in our system of colonial policy, that of colonial dependence'. For as long as the colonized were precluded from acquiring full mastery of colonial ways, for as long as difference was maintained, colonial dependence could be guaranteed.

Early colonial education was conceived, therefore, to ensure this dependence by restricting itself to the encouragement of specific skills for the service of empire, and certainly not those which ascribed unconditional humanity to the colonized by acknowledging full creative abilities in her. Within colonial discourse, art and the aesthetic sensibility were signifiers of the civilized station, and constituted the unbridgeable distance between savagery and culture. Like speech, art was seen either as a signifier or lack, the absence of which relegated the colonized in the hierarchy of the colonial text. It was into this territory of performance that the supposed primitivism, and thus inferiority, of the colonized was written. Writing in the *Blackwood Advertiser* of January 1918, for instance, the colonial governor of the Gold Coast, Sir Hugh Clifford, noted:

> The West African Negro has often been reproached with his failure to develop any high form of civilization. It has been pointed out *ad nauseam* that he has never sculptured a statue, painted a picture, produced a literature, or even invented a mechanical contrivance worthy of the name, all of which are perfectly true.[4]

This underprivileging fiction translated into a pedagogical principle which questioned the introduction of art into the colonial curriculum. As a certain George Fowler noted in the visitors' book of a Lagos artist in 1938, 'teaching an African the art of a white man is not only a waste of time but also a misplaced value . . .'[5] It was further argued that 'rather than impose on them [Africans] what will end up being a torturing load [i.e. art], they can be taught some aspects of European crafts which will be useful to various missions in the colony'.[6]

The substitution of crafts for art on the curriculum was projected as an act of philanthropy, when in truth it was part of a complex colonial strategy of the iterative exercise of hegemony, to assimilate the colonized into regulatory administration of colonial power. However, at a meeting of the staff of Achimota College, Gold Coast, in March 1928, G.A. Stevens, a colonial functionary, strongly deplored this policy and argued for the recognition of the equal creative and mental capabilities of Africans, and the acknowledgement of their rich creative heritage, by introducing meaningful and non-discriminatory art courses in schools in the colonies.[7] But in the general scheme of early colonial relations such arguments could only be dismissed as dangerous and not at all mindful of what Edward Cust further described as 'the folly of conferring such privileges on a condition of society that has no earthly claim to so exalted a position'.[8] It is against this background that Africans began to enter and appropriate cultural forms of modernity at the turn of the nineteenth century.

While the colonial curriculum ignored art education and discouraged the teaching of art to the colonized, the Christian missions engaged in the deprecation and destruction of existing artistic traditions. Artistic practice in traditional idioms was condemned as idolatry and was therefore violently combated, with tons of art objects seized and destroyed in bonfires. Converts were warned in damning language of the harsh and irrevocable consequences of either creating or keeping indigenous art forms.

It is easy to find the frustrating potentials of this strategy in the sermon of the Catholic apostate who cited African sculpture as the stumbling block to his mission in the colonies, describing the works as 'the wretched, irritating and grotesque woods . . . this annoying block . . . the shade that dims the light of faith that is already burning in the hearts of so many natives'.[9] The 'shade', however, was much more than the wood. It was the split in the colonizing mission that the persistence of these images inscribed, the germ of fragmentation and dissolution in the body of the colonial project their perpetuation symbolized. It signified the writing of colonialism as trespass, and represented the earliest instances of its rejection. The artist's persistence with tradition, or that of her clientele and society, became not merely an aesthetic or temporal act, but a contest of identities which signalled the beginnings of a new discourse of nationalism.

The scheme to obliterate colonial claims to culture was carried out through the combined devices of textual erasure, material vandalism and cultural protectionism that were carried out in Africa. The deracination of material cultures among the colonized on the one hand, and the prohibition of access to western/school art on the other, provided perfect conditions for the manufacture of the mimic man, the utilitarian craftsman with no traditions of great art and no access to imperial Enlightenment. At the same time, it created only two possibilities of resistance, two possibilities for its own negation. One was to persist with the indigenous forms which colonialism condemned and sought to obliterate. The other was to hack, to use a most appropriate colloquialism, into the exclusive space of the antipode, in other words to possess the contested territory by mastering the forms and techniques of western artistic expression in order to cross out the ideological principles resident in its exclusivity.

NATIONALISM AND MODERNITY

The advent in parts of Africa of a new artistic idiom akin to that of Europe in the late nineteenth century was not intended simply to prove the equal competence of the colonized as an end, but in so doing also to undermine the ideological foundations of the colonial project and overwrite, as it were, the colonial text. In West Africa the artist generally accepted as the earliest to draw and paint in a Western idiom began this practice without formal training.[10] While it is known that Aina Onabolu (1882–1963) was not the first West African to practise painting and the graphic arts in the tradition of Renaissance Europe,[11] he was the earliest recorded in colonial West Africa to defy the restriction of the colonized to crafts, and begin a fine art practice by teaching himself. Onabolu began to draw as a school boy in Ijebu Ode, Western

Nigeria, in the 1890s, copying illustrations from European religious and business literature.[13] Though formally educated in a mission school, Onabolu received no art instruction in school because the curriculum offered only training in crafts-making. Nor was he encouraged in his artistic interests by his teachers.[13] Between 1900 and 1906, when he finished school and took up a job with the colonial marine department in Lagos, Onabolu worked on his own, improving his skills in draughtsmanship and the use of watercolours. Using connections provided by his job, he channelled his earnings into obtaining materials from England, and applied his resources not only to art practice but also to teaching.[14] At the time, he was alone in the region in his peculiar fascination.

Onabolu described realism as the 'true art'. For him the canons and devices of realism, like the science of perspective for which he became widely known all over Lagos as 'Mr Perspective', were not only European inventions or ciphers of western civilization but part of a universal artistic idiom. It is important to note here that realism was also part of Onabolu's own artistic heritage, in the form of the traditions of classical Ife court art. In choosing realism over abstraction, therefore, Onabolu was not merely mimicking Europe, he was also beginning to define his idiom as a vehicle for translating and reinstating his own heritage into new forms in the context of the changing reality of Africa.

Although he did his best to draw public attention to his work, Onabolu was actively discouraged and on occasion subtly threatened by Europeans. Ola Oloidi observes that the colonial authorities failed to distinguish between the classical African forms, which they condemned as heathen, and Onabolu's work.[15] He further notes that this 'can be considered a deliberate action, for the Missionaries, especially, who did not want any artistic mode that could remind the Africans of the age-old traditional art which these missionaries rejected'. The problem with this explanation, of course, is that it fails to observe that contempt for Onabolu's realism was not extended to the very examples of European art which he used as models in his self-tuition. In other words, it does not account for the evident contradiction in European attitudes to like forms in the colony *vis-à-vis* their distaste for appropriation of European techniques, a contradiction that is predicated on a discourse of authorial identities, a contest over author-ity. Clearly, Onabolu's work, though produced in the same idiom of verisimilitude as most European art in the colonies at the time, was unacceptable for the simple but significant reason that it bore the authorial sign of a colonial. Rather than 'remind the Africans of the age-old traditional art which these missionaries rejected', it reminded the Europeans of the fallacy of their construction of the colonized as an incompetent savage. Within the frames of that construct, the ability to draw like the European, which Onabolu had acquired by the end of the century, signified civility beyond disputation. And the possibility of this acquisition outside the regulatory powers of colonial authority represented a crack in the scheme of Empire. It signalled the possibility of independence and foregrounded the dangers which Cust identified when he warned that a colony 'would not be a colony for a single hour if she could maintain an independent station'.[16] Thus, the veiled threat in this letter from a British acquaintance of Onabolu's, a J. Holloway of the Nigerian Railway, Lagos, to the artist in October 1910:

> I am happy you yourself realize the danger of going your forefather's way . . .
> by creating the type of art that our church can quarrel with . . . I came back
> from Abeokuta a few days ago, and I must here bring to your knowledge what
> the Revd in our church said. This Revd gentleman strongly rebuked the
> congregation for their stubborn devotion to their idols which he regarded as
> heathen objects. They were considered ungrateful people who could not
> appreciate what God had done in their lives . . . Though you once said that
> your own art is special . . . I am not trying to discourage your type of art for
> the colony, but knowing your potential very well, you may have to think well
> about its acceptance in the colony.[17]

Though the relationship between Onabolu's 'type of art for the colony' and the 'heathen forms' condemned and vehemently combated by the Christian missions was not apparent   ous, nevertheless, that the anxiety was not over the production of a p   ind of creative endeavour. It would not be overstretching the point to   nnection between the pseudo-ecclesiastical anxiety of the Church an   all colonialist desperation to deny the cre- ativity of the native.[18] Prot   s Mr Holloway's made Onabolu even more determined to prove that   of drawing and painting were not culture- specific and could not, b   ery nature, manifest the superiority of one culture or people to anotl   aw the practice and propagation of the new artistic tendency not only   pportunity to emphasize its universality but also as a chance to affirm   bilities of his people, and in so doing restate his equality with the Eurc   His intentions were not to achieve validation in the eyes of the white man, but to invalidate European assumptions upon which the civilizing mission in the colonies was founded. If the African could perform equally well in what Europe claims as its exclusive domain, then the former cancels out the tropes of ascendancy and puts Europe in its proper place.

Between 1900 and 1920 Onabolu made a consistent and relentless effort to persuade the colonial education department in Nigeria to introduce art in schools, but met with little or no enthusiasm, as is clear from his correspondence with the deputy director of the department in Lagos in 1919. However, on the advice of a few mission school head teachers, Onabolu wrote to the department asking permission to teach art in a number of schools in the Lagos area. In his letter, he pointed out the great advantages of introducing what he described as 'the prestigious art of drawing and painting', and referred to his already proven ability as a practitioner, enclosing commendations from highly placed figures in the colony. He also attached his curriculum vitae, as well as the names of three referees. However, in his reply of 3 April, 1919, the acting deputy director of education in the colony, Mr L. Richards, regretted that he was not disposed to grant the permission sought, referring Onabolu back to the head teachers, pointing out, with not a little touch of sarcasm, that it was doubtful that the head teachers would need Onabolu's services.[20]

Onabolu did not despair. Instead, he collected willing enthusiasts and began to give them private tuition. Eventually a number of the head teachers, contrary to the deputy director's pronouncement, finally engaged him, and at some point he was teaching in four schools around Lagos.

During several years of distinguished practice, Onabolu produced numerous drawings and portraits of the Lagos élite, including a number of colonial officials.[21] Among his portraits from this period is the 1906 watercolour, *Portrait of Mrs Spencer Savage*, considered by scholars to be a masterpiece of early modern Africa's realism. In 1920 Onabolu went to England to study art at St John's Wood College, London. According to his son, Dapo Onabolu, his mission in England was to acquire 'whatever he could of the sciences of painting, perspective, anatomy and the other specializations and ancillary disciplines which characterize European art education'.[22] Since he had already proven himself quite competent in these skills before his visit to England, a more logical reason for Onabolu's sojourn there would have been to obtain a teaching diploma with which he stood a better chance of gaining entry into the colonial education system and introducing art into schools.

Onabolu's example represents a phase in cultural nationalism in Africa when the regulated space of colonial education became a theatre in which the colonized might unravel the mystique of colonialism prior to its dislodgement. In his early novels Chinua Achebe details a narrative of differing strategies among the colonized which coalesce in the logic of confronting Europe on its own grounds by mastering it.[23] This has been qualified as anthropophagia, or the digestion of the West.[24] However, the mastery of Europe implies a tactic of overdub rather than cannibalism. The appropriation of the European realist tradition in painting and the graphic arts which Onabolu introduced was a significant part of a process of crossing out Europe's texts of exclusivity, rather than merely imbibing forms and surfaces.

AFRICAN QUEST FOR MODERNISM VS. COLONIAL CONSTRUCTION OF AUTHENTIC NATIVE

After his return from Europe in 1922, Onabolu eventually received official approval from the colonial administration to teach art in schools within Lagos and its environs. By 1926 the teaching load had become too heavy for one teacher, and Onabolu requested that another art teacher be appointed. With no candidates available in the colony, the administration brought in Kenneth C. Murray from England.[25] The young Murray had little art education, and no experience in studio practice. But the colonial administration, still ambivalent over the challenge which Onabolu represented, felt more comfortable with the new British art teacher. As Oloidi has observed, Murray was accorded 'an almost exclusive recognition [and given] many powerful responsibilities [as] art teacher, travelling teacher, art supervisor, education officer, and, though unofficially, preserver of Nigerian antiquities, all duties performed almost at the same time'.[26]

Murray's appearance signalled a new contest over modernity, a contest which was replicated eventually in other parts of Africa in an increasingly addled rhetoric of iteration. Murray admonished his students to ignore the formal concerns which Onabolu emphasized, and to occupy themselves only with portraying scenes from their rural lives as a means of preserving and perpetuating their own identity. He felt that Onabolu's themes and methods were too steeped in the European tradition, and taught his students to eschew what he considered alien to their natural sensibilities. Instead of life studies and a keen understanding of anatomy, chiaroscuro and the science of depth and perspective that Onabolu enjoined his students to acquire, Murray urged his own students to concentrate not on the acquisition of technical skills but on painting the subject matter of their daily life and environment. He encouraged them to produce romantic images of village life: fetching firewood, women going to the stream, children sweeping the yard or climbing trees. Such images, he contended, though naive and lacking in technical finesse, were more authentic, as they represented the natives' world more accurately than Onabolu's portraits, life drawings and exercises in perspectival representation.

Murray's understanding of what should constitute an appropriate response to Europe by the colonized thus differed markedly from Onabolu's. It also represented a shift in the colonialist stance, one that was both political and generational. The European was moving from complete denial of colonial creativity to constructing, and preserving, the *authentic* native. Recognizing a certain futility in its original regulatory strategies, the colonial project seemed to have progressed from attempts merely to efface or even erase the colonized or their claim to culture. Its new strategy, manifest in Murray's different understanding of and approach to the creative abilities of the natives, seemed to engage instead in the production of what Fanon describes as the 'palatable' Negro, the admired, authentic colonial.

Murray was dedicated to the preservation of his ideal of the cultures that he met. He failed to understand their predilection for change, and seemed to loathe their strategy of selective appropriation. This manifested itself in undue zealotry and colonialist fervour on his part – Murray was reputed to possess the energy and restlessness of five men[27] – and a pontifical conservationism. By opposing the acquisition of the skills of observation and representation that Onabolu insisted on, Murray produced a strange, new form of naive art which had little to do with the classical traditions of his pupils' backgrounds, or with the modern tendencies that were beginning to emerge as a result of the appropriation and domestication of European principles. For the next three decades, Onabolu's work was thus actively undermined.

During the same period, the discourse of authenticity which Murray's methods introduced was played out in other parts of the continent, particularly in South Africa. In his study of South African Art, Steven Sack notes in *The Neglected Tradition* that a 'kind of prescriptiveness, and a desire to keep the artist "tribal" and untainted by outside influence is reiterated time and time again'.[28] Quoting Tim Couzens, Sack recalls the experience of John Mohl, one of the earliest black South African landscape painters:

> Mohl was once approached by a white admirer and advised not to concentrate on landscape painting: but to paint figures of his people in poverty and misery. Landscape, he was advised, had become a field where Europeans had advanced very far in perfecting its painting.[29]

In response, Mohl brought the subtext of contested identities running through the above to the fore. He challenged the rhetoric of fixity and hierarchization, and the construction of the colonized as a lack by advancing a teleological argument which significantly prefigured postcolonial articulation of difference. 'But I am an African,' Mohl replied, 'and when God made Africa, He also created beautiful landscapes for Africans to admire and paint.' Mohl recognized the attempt to place him within the frames of palatability, whereby the hegemonic position of the European is acknowledged and upheld. To defy such stipulative borders, therefore, was to break free from this hegemony, and in Mohl's case it was landscape painting, remarkably, that emerged as the contested territory which he must possess to achieve this. Mohl verbalized his objectives in terms almost identical to Onabolu's:

> I wanted the world to realize that black people are human beings and that among them good workers can be found, good artists and in addition to that I wanted to lecture indirectly or directly to my people of the importance of this type of thing, which to them is just a thing.[30]

Though Mohl's rural and urban landscapes were in themselves hardly distinguished, they nevertheless articulated a clear discourse of cultural defiance. By painting landscapes, Mohl thus transgressed beyond the frame of imperial fiction and expectation of the native.

Gerard Bhengu, a contemporary of Mohl's and a particularly talented naturalist painter, could not match his evident talent with the skill that would be expected of a white artist of his endowment and creative dedication. Bhengu, according to Sack, 'was denied the chance to acquire formal training'.[31] Bhengu's story parallels those of many early artists in the post-traditional manner in different parts of Africa. Though his work benefited considerably from the patronage of European benefactors, Bhengu was nevertheless considered unfit to possess the same skills as a European. A recommendation that he be allowed access to formal training was rejected by the University of Natal on the grounds that he should 'work in his own way and develop his own technique'.[32] Unlike Mohl, however, Bhengu was unable to move his practice beyond pastoral illustrations that fell within the bounds of colonial acceptability.

Gerard Sekoto, on the other hand, left South Africa for France in 1947 in pursuit of his modernist aspirations. Whereas Onabolu identified European academicism as *the* visual signifier of colonial identity, Sekoto considered modern expressionism the proper space of contest for modernity in the 1940s. In his determination to occupy a space in modernity, he drew on Post-Impressionism and Fauvism for his urban landscapes and figure paintings, despite the disregard by white authorities and lack of patronage. In some of his early work, Sekoto referenced Van Gogh, and his undated *Girl with Orange*, probably from the same period, directly quotes from Gauguin. Although the extent of Sekoto's influence on art in South Africa is rather uncertain,[33] as he chose to spend the rest of his life in France in a private pursuit of modernist subjectivity, he is regarded as an important figure in the development of modernism in Africa. His *Self-Portrait* of 1943 stands as one of the remarkable examples of early modern art in Africa.

Sekoto belonged to a generation of black South African artists which would choose expatriation and relocation to the European centres of modernist practice as a way not only to escape the machinery of European supremacy at home but also to challenge and defy it. For a handful of artists of that generation, proving themselves in Europe, where opportunities supposedly exceeded those available in a white-dominated South Africa, was a more effective response to that dominance than remaining within its reaches to combat it.

Whereas African artists were considered only good enough for wood-crafts and other media such as clay, Sekoto and Mohl deliberately defied this limitation. Equally, they defied the subsequent extension of these limits to watercolour, the medium in which Bhengu did much of his work. Murray's students in Nigeria worked exclusively in craft or cheap watercolours and drawing materials, the same media that the authorities encouraged in art courses in South Africa. Mohl and Sekoto, however, both proceeded to work in oils as well, as Onabolu had done earlier.

The significance of artists like Onabolu, Mohl and Sekoto in the construction of modernity in Africa should be understood in the context of what was produced by the several 'workshops' and art centres that would later sprout up all over the continent under the direction of European art teachers. In every case, the art was predictably naive and unaccomplished, which for the colonialists represented the limits of African ability to represent what they saw as African reality. Only those artists who understood the ideological underpinnings of such art actively contested these underpinnings and produced work of an accomplished quality as part of Africa's aspirations for change through modernity.

It was the discourse of colonial authentication of the native, identified by David Koloane as 'the aesthetic barrier imposed between black and white artists' in South Africa, which was also carried on in Rhodesia under Frank

McEwen, a Fine Arts Representative of the British Council in Paris in the 1970s. McEwen was acquainted with the Cubist school in Paris, before he went to Rhodesia in 1954 on the advice of Herbert Read.[34] Having helped found the National Gallery of Rhodesia, McEwen became its director in 1955, and the next year instituted an 'informal gallery workshop' for museum staff and visitors,[35] the products of which he then began to promote vigorously through powerful, highly placed friends in the art world. Soon, McEwen had fostered an international clientele and he was able to move the workshop outside the gallery. This marked the beginning of contemporary 'Shona' stone sculpture.

A recent narrative of this very significant episode is quite revealing. According to Michael Shepherd, it was after McEwen had listened to folk-tales by Shona labourers at the site of the gallery in Salisbury that he 'infiltrated potential artists into the security and curatorial staff . . . [and gave] them crayons and paint . . .'[36] Shepherd maintains that after this, 'the urge to carve and sculpt – long forgotten in Zimbabwe and virtually without surviving traces – emerged again *spontaneously*, without his [McEwen's] planning it'.[37] This narrative of colonial 'spontaneity' nevertheless fails to explain how McEwen's rogue curators and security men came to entirely occupy their new sculptural tradition with the same folk-tales they related to McEwen, all without the latter's intervention. McEwen was more revealing, when he declared in 1968: 'Once again in the history of art, an umbrella of protection has allowed dormant genius to revive.'[38] But of greater importance to us is McEwen's obsession with 'purity and authenticity' in the tradition he fostered, and his exaltation of 'untutored craftsmanship' in 'an unspoilt people'.[39] McEwen's mission in Rhodesia was to produce a new noble savage, a reconstruction of the innocent colonized, the savage saviour of the world. The product of this reconstruction is a fetish, an object of European fantasy and containment of the Other, in which the anxiety of the loss of innocence is displaced but which remains an object of hegemonic regulation in the form of the alterity of the Other. Before he left Paris, McEwen was already convinced that 'a new wave of "Trivialism" was overtaking the world centre of creative art'.[40] He had come to the conclusion that if 'some vital new art exists or is about to exist . . . it may occur elsewhere, in a different walk of life with a different raison d'être: prompted by a new environment'.[41] It was this environment, and this new art, that he reified in Rhodesia. Having constructed his 'unspoiled' colonial, McEwen proceeded to fetishize *it*, and would spend the rest of his life defending its 'authenticity' and struggling to provide it with an 'umbrella of protection'.

In the 1960s, McEwen's experiment was repeated by the young British artist Georgina Betts in Oshogbo, Nigeria, where, beginning in 1964, she and her German partner Ulli Beier ran four-week workshops that drew participants from a travelling theatre in the little Yoruba town. As the claim goes, the previously untrained participants were instantly transformed into competent, professional artists by the workshops[42]. Writing about the experiments, Beier noted that the most significant feature of the 'short cut' artists from the work-shops was that they 'worked in a kind of euphoria. They did not have any conception of what an "artist" was and they did not agonise about the meaning of "art".'[43] Though Beier maintains that the relationship between Betts and her students was one of 'mutual trust [and] not authority', he nevertheless admits that she exercised discretion in 'spotting and pinpointing each artist's very own personal vision'.[44] We find the same processes of hegemonic replication, as were evident in McEwen's workshop, played out here in both the conceptualization of the Oshogbo experiment and the language and formula of its affirming narrative.

The McEwen workshop echoed Murray's methods in imaging the 'untutored' as the 'authentic'. The reiteration of this fiction of colonial dis-course provided a matrix of relevance for its fragmentation, for the continual disruption of colonialism's constructed identities. Similar workshops and centres sponsoring European ideals of the 'authentic' sprang up in several parts of Africa, and vigorously marketed the art they produced. In many such centres or their fringes, a tendency to adopt a mercantilist strategy emerged that split the fiction of identities and authenticities. This had little nationalist pretension. It was within the context of crossing out the manufactured identities mentioned above that a nationalist discourse sited itself, and it was there that the work of Onabolu, Mohl and Sekoto assumed its nationalist significance.

A NEW NATIONALISM

Of the pioneer South African modernists, one in particular deserves mention for representing a different strategy to those of Onabolu, Mohl and Sekoto. The new strategy, evident in the work of Ernest Mancoba from the mid-1930s, involved a redefinition of African modernism by electing classical African art as its model. It displaced the iconography of the European Enlightenment and chose African sculpture and forms as the source of inspiration, the point of departure and yet, the frame of reference. Its intent was a new aesthetic. Conceptually, this new aesthetic also effectively conflated European and African modernisms by writing African art as the common frame and subtext of all modernisms. Rather than quote premodernist western form, as did Onabolu and Mohl, or western modernism as had Sekoto, Mancoba referenced African sculpture on the specifically modernist principle of formalist articulation.

Ernest Mancoba received early instruction in wood sculpture, and although he eventually studied at the University of Fort Hare and the University of South Africa in the 1930s, received no further formal art training beyond this initial introduction. Eventually, he left South Africa and was later associated with the Cobra group in Europe. Mancoba, like most African artists in South Africa of the period, began by producing ecclesiastical pieces in wood, commissioned by the Christian missions. Around 1936, however, a noticeable change appeared in his sculpture. According to Steven Sack, Mancoba 'turned away from ecclesiastical and European sources in exchange for a keener interest in the sculptural tradition of Africa'.[45] Sack quotes a contemporary newspaper report on Mancoba's development: 'Recently he came upon a book of primitive African sculpture. He was deeply stirred . . . He was fascinated by the "pattern within the pattern", and the way in which the carvings nonetheless remained wholes.'[46]

Mancoba's *Musician* of 1936 abandoned the pseudo-realist finish of his earlier pieces, and of Makoanye, Bhengu and the others, for the planar surface of sculpture from the Congo basin. In *Musician*, Mancoba sought the peculiar dialect of the adze, phrasing his form in a staccato of cuts and geometric elements, a syncopation of surfaces. In place of academicist anatomy, he chose stylization, and thus was able to achieve a strength and affective presence that was similar to the quality that European modernism sought in African art.

Yet Mancoba was not a traditionalist. His approach to African sculpture was not one of iteration or even direct quotation. Instead, he employed the rhetoric of allusion. And other than the tactic of *reaction*, which the colonial regulation of the contest for modernity dictated, and which Mohl and Sekoto adopted, Mancoba identified a different site of practice outside the boundaries of colonialist intervention. Conceptually, if not formally, his new aesthetic seemed to parallel the Negritude aesthetic, then in its formative stages among African intellectuals and artists in France. At the centre of both was the relocation of colonial desire from the exclusivist and supremacist sites of Enlightenment aesthetics to the territory of African forms and paradigms. Negritude, of course, ultimately failed to extricate itself entirely from the enclosures of European contemporary thought and form. But the new aesthetic that Mancoba introduced existed outside those boundaries.

Mancoba's rejection of stipulated as well as preferred frames began a process of redefinition which would take nearly three decades to realize fully. It prefigured an important turn in nationalist response to colonial regulation in Nigeria in the late 1950s. By this period a group of young Nigerian artists began to question the praxis of reverse appropriation outlined by Onabolu, and to reassess strategies of response to colonialist hegemony. These artists felt it was no longer of paramount importance to disprove colonialist superiority, as other historical events had presented the colonized with opportunities to do so sufficiently and effectively. The period of rigorous contestations over modernity was gone, and the imperative of nationalism, whether political or cultural, was no longer to engage in a contest of sites with colonialism, but to dislodge it.

Where Onabolu and his contemporaries pursued a discourse of humanist universalism, the younger artists initiated what one might call a discourse of mapped difference, and set about defining and inscribing that difference. The formation in 1958 of the Zaria Art Society by a little group of students at the College of Arts, Science and Technology, Zaria, was precisely for this purpose: namely, to rethink and reformulate attitudes to European forms, and devise a new aesthetic akin to Mancoba's. This aesthetic would locate the nationalist imperative not in the reverse appropriation of Europe, but in the translation and foregrounding of colonized forms, and through this, the fabrication of new national cultures, and a new modernism.

———————————————

Displaying *Authenticity* and *Progress*

JOHAN LAGAE

AUTHENTICITY AND PROGRESS IN THE DISPLAY OF COLONIES

The representation of colonies was an intrinsic part of international exhibitions from their inception. The Universal Exhibition of 1867, however, introduced a change in these displays and sought to present a new spatial concept for the exhibition grounds. For the first time, separate pavilions were now also erected outside the main exhibition hall, and henceforth, the participants would present themselves increasingly by means of an individual section or pavilion, using its design to evoke their own identities. Consequently, a visit to the exhibition became an architectural *tour du monde*, in which colonial pavilions brought distant and exotic cultures into view. This *tour du monde* and the evocation of identity in these colonial sections were, of course, highly ambiguous and Eurocentric.[1] The display of colonies was, in fact, determined by a duality. The organizers of these settings claimed to offer an accurate, realistic representation of the colony's environment, the key notion in their discourse being the 'authenticity' of the display. Such 'authentic displays' are to be understood as architectural displays that refer, in one way or another, to the native architecture or material culture of the colony: colonial pavilions were sometimes designed as replicas of existing colonial buildings, but more often these so-called 'authentic displays' were hybrid mixtures of European and indigenous architectural languages, in which morphological elements selected from the native built environment were recombined according to western design rules. Often the section's claim of authenticity was enhanced by informal *mise-en-scènes*, like the 'Rue du Caire' (1889) or the 'Village Sénégalais' (1913). The presence of indigenous peoples, temporarily brought over for these events, was to secure the realistic character of the colonial setting in which the visitor was immersed. Because these authentic displays underscored precise ideological goals, they can be regarded as a translation into architecture of what Eric Hobsbawm has called the 'invention of tradition'.[2]

The colonial sections were also, of course, essentially a legitimization of

The 'African village' at the Congolese section in Tervuren, built for
the Brussels 'Exposition Universelle' of 1897. Photo courtesy of the
Africa Museum, Tervuren, Belgium.

colonialism itself. To convince visitors of the civilizing mission of colonialism,
particular emphasis was placed in the presentation on 'progress', progress as
imported into the colonies. Progress, as defined in the discourse accompanying
the colonial sections, encompassed the religious, educational and cultural
upheaval of the indigenous population, as was particularly emphasized in the
presentations of missionary congregations. But progress also stood for modernization, as implemented through technology, that mirrored, or even represented, the advance of the western world itself. It is in this particular sense that I
will refer to progress here, because the display of this modernization became
increasingly important in colonial sections from World War I onwards. An
exotic setting, however, remained crucial for appealing to the general public.
One can thus argue that at international exhibitions of the 1920s and 1930s the
main characteristic of the colonial sections, and of the architecture of their
main pavilions in particular, was the simultaneous display of authenticity and
progress.

Such a simultaneity profoundly marked the representation of the Belgian
Congo during the 1930s. In comparison with earlier exhibitions, the Congolese
sections of this era are notable for two reasons: first, the particular emphasis
placed on progress was stimulated by specific economic and political conditions.
In answer to the worldwide economic crisis that left its mark on both Belgium
and the Congo, trade possibilities with the colony were presented in Belgian
colonial propaganda as a solution to Belgium's financial difficulties as late as
1939, as politicians and industrialists had never been eager to invest in the
colonial project. During this decade, moreover, several other nations also tried
to claim parts of the immense territory in the Belgian colony, while in the
European political forum voices were raised in favour of a general international
control that would substitute the authority of all colonial powers. Within such a
context, the Belgian government was forced to present convincing demonstrations of its 'civilizing mission' in the Congo if it wanted to maintain its absolute

rule there. Therefore, technological progress in the Congo was given due attention in the presentations at international events, albeit accompanied by a philanthropic discourse emphasizing the efforts made in the realm of education and medical services.[3]

Second, designing an authentic setting to represent the Belgian colony had proven to be a problematic undertaking for Belgian architects, and it was not until 1931 that a Congo pavilion was built that was unmistakably inspired by the built forms of central Africa. Combining a convincing representation of Congolese culture with a display that evoked the modernized colony presented a specific architectural challenge. From 1930 onwards, architects addressed this challenge and proposed a wide range of divergent design solutions. A consideration of the Congolese sections from the 1930s sheds light not only on shifting interpretations of authenticity within the colonial milieu but also on issues closely linked with architectural practices at the time.

THE PROBLEMATIC DISPLAY OF AUTHENTICITY

Although the Congo only became a colony in the true sense of the word in 1908, there had been Congolese sections at international exhibitions since the 1885 Antwerp Universal Exhibition. The last event in which the Congo was presented as a colony was the Brussels World's Fair of 1958. Even though ethnographic research on Congolese peoples had received a great deal of attention in the colonial milieu as early as the end of the nineteenth century, colonial officials, architects and critics all agreed that the Congo lacked a proper native architecture worthy of attention. Central African building forms were considered unsuitable sources of inspiration for the design of the Belgian Congo exhibition pavilions at World's Fairs, as well as for the elaboration of a contemporary colonial architecture. The *Livre d'or* of the 1905 Liège Universal Exhibition, declaring why the Congo pavilion bore no reference to African built forms, gives us a telling example of the mainstream argument: 'Because no relic of an indigenous public building of importance is to be found anywhere in the Congo, it is meaningless to search for representative [morphological] elements amenable to transformation in a stylistic manner.'[4] As illustrated by Emile Bayard's popularizing book *l'Art de reconnaître les styles coloniaux de la France* of 1931, published as a kind of guidebook for the 'Exposition Coloniale Internationale', this argument applied to the whole of *l'Afrique noire*: its native built forms, '*les paillotes*', could not be described in terms of contemporary western architectural conceptions such as 'monumentality', 'durability' and 'history'.[5]

Not surprisingly, in the first Congolese sections, the authentic atmosphere had depended less on the architectural image of the pavilion itself than on the informal reconstructions of Congolese villages, crowded with natives in indigenous garb. Due to the difficulty of acclimatizing to the Belgian weather, several of these Congolese died during the 1897 Universal Exhibition in Tervuren – an incident which put an end to this practice at future exhibitions. As a result, the representation of the Belgian colony became wholly dependent on the architectural design of the section. Yet, precisely because of the preconception that the Congo did not possess a built environment that could qualify as architecture, there was no clear answer to the question as to what the nature of an exhibition architecture for representing the colony was to be. This was not so for the architects commissioned to design authentic displays for the north or west African colonies. The former could be inspired by the Islamic architectural tradition, resulting in what François Béguin has called *arabisances*;[6] the latter were most often modelled on the mosque architecture of Djenné and Tombouctou. A similar design strategy – inventing a native architecture by mixing indigenous and European architectural forms – was initially considered inapplicable for the representation of the Belgian colony. As a result, several formal approaches had been followed or proposed for the design of the Congo pavilions since 1885, ranging from Beaux-Arts classicism (Antwerp 1894, Brussels 1897 and 1910) and Art Nouveau (Brussels 1897, Paris 1900), to Vienna Secession (Liège 1905) and a bizarre form of classicist orientalism (Ghent 1913, Antwerp 1930).[7] Twice, the main pavilion was a replica of a building in the Congo, but significantly in both cases its source was not indigenous but Belgian/colonial in origin: at the 1885 Antwerp Exhibition, the sanatorium in Boma was reconstructed, while the pavilion at the 1905 World's Fair in Liège was modelled on the Governor General's residence in Boma, a pre-fabricated metal construction erected in 1888. Of all these design solutions, only Art Nouveau offered an evocation of the native culture that was truly successful among the visitors: due to the interior decoration of the 1897 Congolese section in Tervuren (a design by Paul Hankar, Henry Van de Velde and other representatives of the Art Nouveau movement), this style became popularly known as the '*style Congo*'. The Congo pavilion built at the 1930 'Exposition Coloniale, Maritime et d'Art Flamand' in Antwerp, however, leaves no doubt that until then the Congo was still not credited with an architecture of its own. Even in the *Rapport Général*, it was admitted that the pavilion was oriental, rather than Congolese, in appearance. The organizers relied on the architect's use of decorations based on indigenous patterns for their defence of the design; close analysis reveals this decoration to be superficial and mediocre.

INVENTING A CONGOLESE ARCHITECTURE

In 1931, just one year after the Antwerp World's Fair, France organized the 'Exposition Coloniale Internationale' in Paris (Vincennes). This event marked a turning point: for the first time (as was noticed in several contemporary commentaries) the visitor was confronted with an authentic architectural representation of the 'traditional Congo'. The architect Henri Lacoste had succeeded in inventing a native architecture by integrating a large number of elements from the Congo's material culture in the building's design. In the contemporary architectural and colonial press, the project was praised unanimously for its

The French West Africa pavilion at the 'Exposition Coloniale
Internationale' in Vincennes, 1931.

powerful and realistic impression. A French critic compared its effect to the
Cameroon section, suggesting that in both cases the architects 'proved that they
had understood the plain and instinctive grandeur of *art nègre* and had succeeded in interpreting it without deforming its essence'.[8] In historical studies,
however, the design has been harshly criticized. Jean-Claude Vigato writes of an
'overblown and regularized hut', while Peter Greenhalgh saw it as an example
of a 'mock African' exhibition architecture only serving as a stage set 'in an
attempt to mentally transport the visitor away from Europe' and lacking all
'serious architectural considerations'.[9] If there can be little doubt that the
essence of Lacoste's design was precisely such mental transportation, I would
like to counter some of these criticisms.

First of all, one has to remember that Henri Lacoste was the first architect
who did not *a priori* reject African built forms as a source of inspiration. If he
had not actually travelled in the Congo at the time he designed the project, he
did make a conscientious effort to study African and Congolese culture. Extensive research in museums and contemporary publications enabled him to
develop a profound knowledge of African art, as is proven by his use of rare
Congolese sources. Instead of using geometric *velours de Kasaï* motifs (which had
already become very popular in the decorative arts by the end of the 1920s),
Lacoste inserted animal motifs inspired by little-known Yombé textiles in the
mosaic floors of the main pavilion. But he also used motifs of non-Congolese
origin: references to the cave paintings recently discovered by Léo Frobenius in
Rhodesia and South Africa, as well as to artefacts from the Ivory Coast and
Gabon, can be traced in the decoration of the 1931 Congo pavilion, revealing
the influence of the 1930 Brussels exhibition 'L'Art nègre: les arts anciens de
l'Afrique noire' on its design. It is obvious that the artefacts used as sources of

inspiration were chosen according to aesthetic, rather than ethnological, principles, but this predominance of aesthetic criteria reflects the reception of indigenous art in Europe at the time. Louis Madeleine, a French architect and close friend of Lacoste's, wrote of the design that 'all [its] details are based on authentic indigenous sources, but have been applied according to a knowledge and approach that belongs only to Europe'.[10] Within the French ethnographic milieu, moreover, it was only at the time of the 'Exposition Coloniale Internationale' that the aesthetic presentation of indigenous objects began to be questioned.

In its use of decoration, Henri Lacoste's design also sheds light on the role of ornament in architecture, a fundamental theme of contemporary architectural debate in Belgium at the time as well as elsewhere. Jean-Claude Vigato has argued that, since the 1925 'Exposition des Arts Décoratifs' in Paris, architects had been seeking to 'reinstate the architectural symbol at the peak of social signification'. In his view the 'Exposition Coloniale Internationale' of 1931,

The Congolese section at the 'Exposition Coloniale Internationale', Vincennes, 1931 (architect: Henri Lacoste).

because of its particular ideological programme, offered an ideal context for implementing this ambition.[11] It is significant in this respect that Marcel Temporal, a critic who wrote a commentary on the exposition for *L'Architecture d'Aujourd'hui* in 1931, vehemently reacted against the empty formalism of many pavilions built in the 'modernist' style. The most contemporary designs, according to Temporal, were not the undecorated cubist constructions, but the pavilions 'uniting the spirit of the colonial style, which they should represent, with a formal logic resulting from functional demands'.[12] The examples he used to illustrate his statement were the pavilions of Madagascar, Togo/Cameroon, the Dutch Indies and the Belgian Congo – curiously enough all hybrid reinterpretations of native architectures. Within this selection, Lacoste's design is particularly interesting for its efficient combining of divergent design practices. On the one hand, through the accurate positioning of the three building parts, Lacoste created a visual symmetry from a privileged point of view, with cupolas marking the centre of the volumetric composition. This approach seems to coincide with what Vigato has described as colonizing the vocabulary of exotic architecture through the architectural principles of the Ecole des Beaux-Arts.[13] On the other hand, when one analyses the conception of the plans and structure of the pavilions, Lacoste's handling of the programme and the interior layout proves to be in tune with some of the major tenets of architectural functionalism, as suggested by Temporal.[14] Ingenious solutions for illuminating the pavilion were also applied, using new technologies for artificial, indirect lighting.

The apparent dichotomy between the interior and exterior of Lacoste's design – the stage set-like outer appearance versus the very functionally organized interior – is partly dissolved in the striking design of the cupolas, which clearly refer to native architecture. These cupolas consist of a structural wooden frame, left unconcealed on the inside and covered with straw on the outside. The frame is made of prefabricated elements, permitting easy assemblage on site and allowing large spans without secondary supports. At the time, this structural solution was regarded as highly innovative. In 1937, the leading periodical *l'Architecture d'Aujourd'hui* would still describe this *charpente à lamelles* as a totally new concept offering promising prospects for future constructions. Yet, as was already noted in 1931 by several critics, the frame simultaneously refers to the construction of indigenous building forms of what were still considered 'primitive' cultures.[15] In its duality – being both 'modern' and 'primitive' – this structural solution of the cupolas blurs preconceived notions of colonial imagery, and embodies the intriguing hybridity of Lacoste's design.[16]

OPPOSING CLAIMS OF AUTHENTICITY

If the Congo pavilion at the 1931 'Exposition Coloniale Internationale' was applauded as one of the most remarkable constructions of the event, it did not succeed in setting a standard for the representation of the Belgian colony in the years to come. Marcel Schmitz, an influential Belgian architect and critic, formulated a fundamental critique on this kind of 'authentic display'. In his opinion, colonial sections should function as laboratories for developing a contemporary colonial architecture, rather than as displays for evoking the native culture. Lacoste's design thus offered no solution for future events: 'The hut, used in a very pleasing decorative way indeed by the architect Lacoste in his design for the Belgian pavilion,' Schmitz argued, 'is for current [architectural] practice not an apt source of inspiration. Its essence is too indigenous in nature.'[17] Schmitz's critique was echoed in a letter addressed to the Minister of Colonies in 1933 by Raymond Cloquet, one of the few Belgian architects residing in the Congo at that time. If even as gifted an architect as Lacoste had failed to design a convincing display for the Congo, this was, according to Cloquet, because the documentation assembled in museums and catalogues remained 'empty of life, if one had not experienced it on the spot'.[18] Cloquet, and Schmitz also in a sense, thus suggested that claims of authenticity could only be made in reference to the contemporary situation in the Congo, not in reference to an invented past.

During the preparation of the 1935 Brussels World's Fair, two projects for the Congolese section were submitted to the Ministry of Colonies that reveal this shifting interpretation of authenticity. The first proposal had already been put forward at the end of 1931 by Raymond Moenaert, the architect who had won the competition for the construction of the new Governor General's residence in Leopoldville, without doubt *the* major public building commission in the Belgian colony. Moenaert regretted that the Belgian colony had until then always been represented by phantasmagoric images. In his view, a new concept was needed and he therefore proposed to build the Governor General's residence at the 1935 Brussels exhibition. Even if the economic crisis had temporarily halted the construction of the actual residence in Leopoldville, this proposal, in his view, was the most authentic display imaginable: by reconstructing his residence project, the Congolese section would become 'a [contemporary] part of Kinshasa, imported and implanted in Belgian soil'.[19] If Schmitz had known of this proposal, he would surely have supported it, because at various occasions he had praised Moenaert's residence project and its '*style hispano-colonial*' as a rare example of a truly contemporary colonial architecture for the Congo.

The contrast with the second proposal for the Congolese section in Brussels in 1935 could not have been more striking. Submitted by Henri Lacoste in 1933, the proposal consisted of a huge exhibition hall containing a *panorama atmosphérique* that would offer the visitor the experience of an expedition that crossed three climate zones in the Congo: the savannah, a tropical forest and the mountain range of the Ruwenzori.[20] Lacoste's proposal can be seen as a reinterpretation of the informal African villages at previous expositions, yet its claims of authenticity were even more emphatic: the latest engineering technologies, it was argued, would be used to replicate environmental conditions, and the panorama would generate visual, as well as tactile, olfactory and auditory sensations. Lacoste originally thought of masking the exhibition hall with an

Proposal for the Congolese section at the Brussels World's Fair of 1935 (architect: Henri Lacoste) – the *panorama atmosphérique*, second project for the façade. © Archives d'Architecture Moderne, Brussels, Belgium.

overblown version of his design for the 'Exposition Coloniale Internationale' of 1931. In the end, however, he changed the outer appearance completely and clad the gigantic hall with a striking modern façade. This change clearly reveals the ethnocentric character of the project. In fact, the *panorama atmosphérique* was based on the blunt confrontation of the so-called 'primitive' African regions, experienced inside, and the contemporary civilization of the West, as presented at the exit, where an impressive view over the city of Brussels was offered. Thus, the panorama legitimized the civilizing mission of Belgian colonialism in the same way as nineteenth-century colonial sections had done. Within only two years, Lacoste seems to have lost all the subtlety and productive ambivalence that had marked his design approach for the Congo pavilion of the 1931 exhibition.

CELEBRATING A CINQUANTENAIRE

The Brussels exhibition of 1935 marked the fiftieth birthday of Belgian colonialism.[21] It should have been a glorious event, but in reality, it was disillusioning. Because of the economic crisis, the colonial government made only a minor investment in the Congolese section. The proposals by Moenaert and Lacoste were rejected, and in the end the official Congo pavilion was built by an engineer-architect of the Ministry of Colonies, René Schoentjes. Schoentjes's design approach was an attempt to invent a native architecture, very similar to what Lacoste had done in 1931. Schoentjes used a wider range of references, however, combining sources from central African, Islamic and Egyptian

The front façade of the Congo pavilion at the Brussels World's Fair
of 1935 (architect: René Schoentjes).

material culture. This approach was reviewed very differently by his contemporaries. While a prominent connoisseur and promoter of African art,
Gaston-Denys Périer, was enthusiastic about the design, the Commissaire
Générale of the exhibition harshly criticized the fact that Schoentjes applied
decorative patterns from contemporary catalogues of commercial interior
design, which, in his view, completely undermined the harmony of the design.[22]
While Schoentjes's design shows several similarities with the 1931 Congo pavilion, a comparison of both projects quickly reveals the former's lack of subtlety
and skill in the formal treatment as well as in the handling of space.

Furthermore, the Congo's representation at the 1935 Brussels exhibition
lacked the unity that had been so characteristic of the Congolese section at the
'Exposition Coloniale Internationale'. This was partly because the several parts
of the Brussels section were designed by different architects. Two colonial pavilions flanking the official building were designed by Victor Bourgeois, the most
prominent figure among Belgian modernist architects. On close analysis, Bourgeois's designs did not really address the issue of representing the Congo in an
architectural manner. The Leopold II restaurant remained completely in tune
with the sober modernist style characteristic of Bourgeois's *œuvre* and, apart
from the food served, only the frescoes in the interior, depicting curious Congolese figures, reminded the visitor of its connection with the colony.[23] But it is in
the pavilion that housed the Congo's tourist industry displays that Bourgeois's
failure to create an architectural language capable of referring to the colonial
programme, while remaining in accordance with the tenets of modernism, is
most apparent. At one stage of the design process, Bourgeois even produced a
design solution for the entrance reminiscent of the three cupolas of the 1931
Congolese section, which fails to be more than an immature paraphrase.[24]

The Leopold II restaurant at the Brussels World's Fair of 1935
(architect: Victor Bourgeois). © Archives d'Architecture Moderne,
Brussels, Belgium.

REPRESENTING THE MODERN CONGO

For many visitors, the Congolese section at the Brussels exhibition of 1935 was
pervaded with a sense of *déjà-vu*, because of the reuse of exhibits and displays
from former exhibitions. Moreover, the section had not functioned as an architectural workshop in which a contemporary colonial architecture could be
developed. Interest in the topic, however, was minimal among Belgian architects, even if, from the late 1920s on, initiatives had been made to stimulate a
debate on colonial building. That colonial architecture was not a priority on the
political agenda of the government – a fact most clearly illustrated by its decision to abandon, albeit temporarily, all initiatives for building the new Governor
General's residence in Leopoldville in 1932 – was no doubt a major reason for
this lack of interest in the architectural milieu.[25] That the Ministry of Colonies
had resorted to the approach of an invented native architecture for the 1935
Congolese section was probably also due to the public success of the 1931
section and the conviction that most visitors were still enchanted by the exotic
exhibition architecture. Yet, Schoentjes's and Bourgeois's rather mediocre
designs made it clear that such a display was gradually becoming untenable, as
it was incapable of representing contemporary colonization in the Congo.

This was the reason, at least in part, why the organizers of the Congolese
section at the Paris 'Exposition des Arts et des Techniques dans la Vie Moderne'

of 1937 explicitly chose an opposite strategy. They claimed to give the visitor an impression of the modern way of life in the colony, suggesting at the same time that 'ideas of tradition and exoticism by no means have to stand in opposition to a sense of transformation and new conceptions'. The colony was presented by means of an elegantly designed bungalow with an encompassing veranda, representing the ideal home of a Belgian colonial.[26] The pavilion was modelled on the colonial bungalows that had been imported in the tropics since the late nineteenth century and which had provided Europeans with comfortable living conditions in this tormenting climate. At the time of the Paris exposition, however, such bungalows were no longer the most common type of housing for white colonizers in the Congo. Due to emerging urbanization in the colony, they had been replaced since the early 1920s by designs that were based on the middle-class villas of Belgian garden cities.[27]

The 1937 Congolese section thus cultivated the romantic image of the domestic life of colonial pioneers, rather than offering an accurate view of contemporary daily life in the Belgian colony. It failed to define an architectural image for the 'new Congo' that was characterized by gradual modernization. In fact, the section placed only a minor focus on technological progress; and the visitor was reminded only in a subtle way of the importance of the expanding industries in the Congo. Delicately arranged displays illustrated how many contemporary products were derived from raw materials of Congolese origin. In comparison, the display of technological progress in the Congolese section at the 'Exposition Coloniale Internationale' had been far more straightforward. In the interior of the pavilions of the 1931 section, the different infrastructural networks and mining exploitation in the colony had been presented through impressive stands that showed part of a bridge, for example, and an aeroplane. This interior display of the modernized Congo formed an ambivalent alliance with its exterior design that aimed at representing the Congo's native culture. In this sense, the Congolese section at the 'Exposition Coloniale Internationale' of 1931 exemplifies an 'architectural ambivalence' in the sense that the 'invented hybrid exterior acts as mediator between a prestigious western presence in the interior and an absent, native environment, considered not worth showing'.[28]

THE END OF AUTHENTIC DISPLAYS?

If representing the Belgian Congo by means of an authentic display of the colony's native culture had been a primary concern at the 1931 'Exposition Coloniale Internationale', by the end of the 1930s such concern for authenticity was no longer considered important. Colonial propaganda now almost exclusively focused on the modernization of the Congo – a shift in attention which can be illustrated by reviewing the two Congolese sections that were designed for international exhibitions in 1939. The first section was built at the New York World's Fair, organized on the theme 'The World of Tomorrow'. As the presence of the Belgian colony at this fair was primarily a marketing strategy

Fragment of a bas-relief on the outside of the Belgian pavilion that
marked the Congolese section at the New York World's Fair of
1939 (sculptor: A. Dupagne).

The Congolese section at the 'Exposition Internationale de la
Technique de l'Eau', Liège, 1939 (architect: Henri Lacoste), contemporary postcard (collection: Denys Lacoste).

to promote the Congolese diamond industry in the United States, the organizers
did not make any efforts to create an authentic display. The Congolese section
was not even housed in a separate building, but formed a part of the Belgian
pavilion. The architects, who included Victor Bourgeois, had avoided all
exotic formal vocabulary and used a modernist idiom. On the outside, only a

bas-relief revealed the presence of a Congolese section. In the luxurious but sober interior, elements referring to the Congo's native culture were restricted as much as possible.[29]

The representation of the Belgian colony in New York contrasted greatly with the Congolese section at the 'Exposition Internationale de la Technique de l'Eau', held in Liège the same year. At this event, the Congolese section was meant to promote Belgium's civilizing mission in the colony by displaying the progress made in hydraulic engineering, water purification and water supply. The overall architectural co-ordination of the exposition was given to a team of young architects who imposed strict design rules, based on a functionalist doctrine.[30] This did not, however, prevent Henri Lacoste, commissioned to design the Congolese section, from repeating his design approach of 1931. He submitted a proposal for a phantasmagoric Congolese setting, placing four gigantic golden elephants in the canal running in front of the pavilion.[31] Due to financial restrictions, the design was strongly simplified, and, in the end, the elephants were replaced by a huge, totem pole-like construction, decorated with Congolese masks and armoury. If such an approach had been apt for the 'Exposition Coloniale Internationale' in Vincennes – which, in the end, was the ultimate 'Théâtre des Colonies' – it was rather out of place at the Liège exhibition. Lacoste's design was not capable of grasping the essence of the 'Exposition de l'Eau', which was purely a celebration of technological progress, nor did it create a meaningful image of the emerging 'new Congo'.

In only a few years, the strategy of inventing a Congolese architecture had been outstripped. But the Congolese section at the New York World's Fair could hardly be regarded as a suitable alternative, as the mental connection with the colony's culture was established not through the architectural design but by purely decorative means. The architectural representation of the Belgian Congo thus remained problematic, all the more so because from 1945 onwards, the indigenous populations' struggles for independence could no longer be neglected. The Congolese section of the Brussels World's Fair of 1958, however, made it rather shamefully clear that this new situation was not yet fully understood.[32]

OPPORTUNITIES FOR CREATIVITY

One can legitimately criticize the various Congolese sections I have discussed here for their underlying ethnocentric preconceptions. The 'voice of the colonized' was totally absent in these representations of the Congo. Moreover, the general assumption that the Congo did not have a native architectural tradition worthy of attention was never questioned by architects, most of whom had never even been to the colony. Given his projects for the 1935 and 1939 expositions, not even Henri Lacoste fully deserves to be noted as an exception, despite the fact that his design for the 1931 'Exposition Coloniale Internationale', in my view, offers a rare glimpse of hybridity, capable of breaking open fixed notions of colonialist imagery. Because of the general acceptance that a native architectural tradition was non-existent in the Congo, there were no appropriate models available for the Belgian architects who were commissioned to design a Congo pavilion. But this situation should not necessarily be regarded as restrictive: it actually offered architects a rare opportunity for creativity and imagination. While the native architectures of north or west African colonies offered French architects ample inspiration, just as the built heritage in India provided models for the British, designing these pavilions could easily become a dangerous routine. Sylvianne Leprun has rightly blamed the '*déssèchement créatif*' in French colonial sections.[33] As the many divergent design solutions discussed here illustrate, in Congolese sections this 'desiccation of creativity' was much less to be feared. This is not to say that Belgian architects always succeeded in designing pavilions that were innovative from an architectural point of view, or that they offered that rare quality of hybridity. Still, I believe that analysing these colonial displays offers particular opportunities to reveal specific aspects of contemporaneous architectural practices. Through such analysis we might gain a more nuanced understanding of architecture as visual representation and as a discipline, as well as of the role of architecture in the realm of colonialism.

ACKNOWLEDGEMENTS

This article is an extended and reworked version of a paper presented at the 52nd Annual Meeting of Architectural Historians in Houston, Texas, 14–18 April 1999. I would like to thank Lisa Schrenk, Mil De Kooning and Jean-Luc Vellut for their comments during the various stages of this research. Unless otherwise noted, translations are my own.

Colonial/Postcolonial Intersections

ZEYNEP ÇELIK

Lieu de mémoire, a concept developed by historian Pierre Nora in order to help explain the construction of a nation or a community, offers a useful tool to architectural historians by emphasizing the importance of physical and conceptual sites. Nora associates the role played by memory with a 'symbolic typology' and identifies the sites where memory resides as *lieux de mémoire* (the place, the site, the realm of memory). A *lieu de mémoire* is thus 'any significant entity, whether material or non-material in nature, which, by dint of human will or the work of time, has become a symbolic element of the memorial heritage of any community'.[1] Pointing to the difference between history and memory, Nora claims that 'memory is life', whereas 'history is the reconstruction . . . of what is no longer'. Memory is subject to remembering and forgetting; it is vulnerable to appropriation and manipulation; and it can lie dormant for long periods, only to be reawakened suddenly. The *lieux de mémoire*, the material, symbolic and functional sites, are the products of the interaction between memory and history. They embody a will to remember (memory) and to record (history). They also display the exciting quality of being able to change, that is, to resurrect old meanings and generate new ones, along the way establishing unpredictable connections.[2] While focusing on the sites of memory that define France, Nora's concept pertains to all societies. Starting from this assertion, yet staying in part within French history, I hereby extend the concept to Algeria and show how the *lieux de mémoire* acted as catalysts in the imposition of power structure, as well as the definition and endurance of identity in a colonial context. The symbolic sites for the colonizer culture continued to maintain their significance in the postcolonial era as their capacity to change and acquire new meanings allowed them to act also as places of memory for the colonized.

My case studies are drawn from two different types of *lieux de mémoire* identified by Nora: the topographical, characterized by their specific location and their rootedness, and the portable.[3] The urban spaces of Algiers will serve as my topographical *lieux*; Eugène Delacroix's famous painting, *Les Femmes d'Alger*, and its various reincarnations, as the portable.

In a city with as turbulent a past as Algiers, the *lieux de mémoire* are many, but even here several stand out more prominently than others. Place d'Armes, opened in the heart of the city immediately following the French conquest in 1830, was undoubtedly the receptacle of the most charged meanings and memories. The initial gesture stemmed from practical necessities: the French army needed a large open space for gathering and manoeuvres, not accommodated by the tight urban fabric of precolonial Algiers. The first carving out took place in the months that followed the conquest and was randomly continued for the next two years. The Place d'Armes, explicitly associated with the French army and the military occupation, was an 'immense', if shapeless, void in front of the Palace of the Dey, the headquarters of the Ottoman governor of Algeria.[4] The symbolism of the authoritative presence of the Place d'Armes was blatant for both the conqueror and the conquered, but the new plaza was also imbued with the memory of what it was before the occupation. The army engineers had demolished an entire fabric that had harboured some of the city's most vital institutions – most prominently, the al-Sayyida mosque that stood in front of the Palace of the Dey and which was remembered as the most elegant of all religious buildings in Algiers. In addition, an extensive commercial tissue was torn down that had comprised the food markets, the specialized *suqs*, such as those of the jewellers, leather workers, weavers and booksellers, and in the centre, the Badestan. Several military barracks that belonged to janissaries and many houses were also taken down.[5]

The physical transformation did not erase the past for Algerians. The precolonial fabric of the Place d'Armes survived in memory and was passed from generation to generation. The following excerpt, from a much longer poem dating back to the time of the conquest, testifies to the persistence of the memory, as well as of the violence exerted on the place:

> O regrets for Algiers and for its stores,
> Their traces no longer exist!
> Such inequities committed by the accursed ones!
> Al-Qaisariya has been named Plaza
> And to think that holy books were sold and bound there.[6]

Within a couple of years after the occupation, the image of the Place d'Armes was not deemed fitting enough to reflect the grandeur of the French Empire. Innumerable projects were drafted to endow it with the appropriate glory. Order and regularity that contrasted with the precolonial urban forms of Algiers were taken as design guidelines to symbolize the new presence. In 1831, for example, Mr Luvini, the government architect, proposed a rectangular plaza, defined by monumental structures that represented France – among them a theatre and a Palais du Gouvernement; the seventeenth-century al-Djadid mosque, another major religious monument, would be demolished to make room for the new configuration.[7] The project encountered opposition from the Lieutenant-General Lemercier – beginning to acknowledge the initial errors committed by the army engineers, he made a call to show respect for 'the religious sentiments of the Moors'.[8] Lemercier's consideration of the Algerian society was not taken to heart immediately by the army engineers, as can be traced in another project for a rectangular plaza in 1833 that attempted to raze the al-Djadid mosque.[9] Nevertheless, his objection to the demolition of Islamic religious monuments found a response in a theoretical project for a rectangular plaza in 1834: the al-Djadid mosque was preserved, setting a precedent for further regularizations.[10]

Capitalizing on the damage caused by a fire to the Palace of the Dey in 1844, several projects attempted to readjust the plaza's overall shape in the following years. By mid-century, it had acquired its final hexagonal form, with arcaded buildings in the French style on three sides and the preserved al-Djadid mosque determining the irregularity of the east side. The edges of the plaza that bordered the steep hill descending to the harbour level were neatly defined by a balustrade. Most significantly, an imposing, 5-metre-high equestrian statue of the Duke of Orléans, the prince to the throne who had fought and was wounded in Algeria in 1836, was erected on the site in 1845 – in a gesture that complemented the nineteenth-century French 'statumania' at home. Monumental civic statues of great men had been incorporated as elements of modern urban design since the beginning of the century in mainland France and had dotted the public spaces of French cities as symbols of liberal and secular values.[11]

The placement of the statue of the Duke of Orléans by the sculptor Marochetti did not follow the rules set for similar gestures of celebration in the *métropole*, but was manipulated to respond to the colonial mission. It was strategically situated, not in the centre of the plaza as one might expect from the geometry-conscious army engineers, but to the side – right in front of the al-Djadid mosque. Elevated on a high base and contrasting with the serene mass of the white mosque in its blackness and dynamic shape, and with its back to the mosque, it conveyed a straightforward message about the power structure in Algeria. The Duke of Orléans' gaze, turned away from the plaza to face the casbah, underlined the statement about French control over the Algerian people. A public art form that was totally foreign to local norms, the statue dominated the major perspectives toward the plaza, thereby reiterating its message over and over.[12] The statue of the Duke of Orléans on horseback permanently constructed the following lines from the Algerian poem (quoted earlier) into the built fabric of the city:

O believers, the world has seen with its own eyes.
Their horses tied in our mosques,
They and their Jews rejoiced because of it
While we wept in our sadness.[13]

Statue of the Duke of Orléans with the al-Djadid mosque, close-up
view, *c.* 1900 (postcard).

The story of this statue as a *lieu de mémoire* was not restricted to the city of Algiers. As an act of transporting the memory of the Algerian occupation back to the home country, a replica was produced and placed in the court of honour in the Louvre. It did not enjoy great popularity in its Parisian setting, however, as it soon turned into a symbol associated with royal oppression in the eyes of the working classes. It was knocked down in a mass revolt during the 1848 revolution and transported to the Palace of Versailles to be placed at the foot of the great stairway in the courtyard. In this location, the memory of Algiers was dimmed and superseded by the memory of a major workers' revolution in Paris.[14]

Back in Algiers, the passage from the military regime to a civilian one in the 1870s, with the implication that France was here to stay, led to the renaming of the plaza as Place du Gouvernement, or Government Square. It was frequently referred to as the 'forum of the colony'. René Lespès, the author of a comprehensive monograph on Algiers,[15] described it as the site where 'the most passionate discussions on the colony took place', and where great historic events were acknowledged by public ceremonies that ranged from commemorative gatherings to funerary processions, proclamations of changes in the political regime and civic and patriotic banquets. The Place du Gouvernement was also deemed to be the heart of Algiers. Théophile Gautier, for example, wrote that it was 'the meeting point of the entire city', the place to give appointments, and through which 'entire Algiers passed inevitably three or four times a day'.[16]

The Place du Gouvernement embodied both the 'dominant' *lieux de mémoire* and the 'dominated' *lieux de mémoire*. To quote Nora, the former are 'imposing as well as generally imposed from above by the government', whereas the latter are 'the places of refuge, sanctuaries of instinctive devotion and hushed pilgrimages, where the living heart of memory still beats'.[17] The colonial interventions in the plaza sharpened the distinctions between the two types of memories, and their confrontational quality enhanced the preservation of the Algerian memory, with much help from the statue of the Duke of Orléans. To use Michel de Certeau's words, the square was imbued with 'inward-turning histories' and 'a sort of knowledge that remain[ed] silent'.[18]

Following independence in 1962, the plaza was renamed 'Place des Martyres' to honour those who died during the Algerian War. The statue was taken down and its location marked by an abstract memorial. No other changes were made, but the deletion of the statue turned the al-Djadid mosque into the unchallenged monument of the Place des Martyres. The appropriation of the public space superimposed a new symbolism on it, without radically transforming its formal character, namely its boundaries and the buildings surrounding it. Thus, the preservation of the colonial structure did not conceal the thirteen decades of French occupation, but underlined Algerian independence and the memory of the war. This was a 'shrewd comment . . . upon the realities of the colonial power' that recycled a European tradition (an urban form) while defining a new society.[19] The gesture reversed at the same time the 'dominant' and the 'dominated' *lieux de mémoire*.

Place des Martyres, view toward the al-Djadid mosque, 1990.
Photo: Zeynep Çelik.

In a curious twist, the memory of the colonial structure lives in the everyday vernacular of the city: forty years after independence, many residents of Algiers still refer to the square as 'Place al-Auod', or 'Place du Cheval' (Square of the Horse).[20] What remains from the statue in collective memory is not the Duke of Orléans, then, but his horse – for reasons that may have only tangential links to the original intentions, but which are also detached from the redefinition of the public space following independence. To refer to de Certeau's analysis of everyday spatial practices, the 'ordinary practitioners of the city' wrote their own urban text, allowing their alternative experience of space to 'slip into the clear text of the planned and readable city'.[21]

Other public spaces underwent similar transformations that interlocked the memory of the colonial and postcolonial eras. Place d'Isly, more commonly known as Place Bugeaud and named after Maréchal Bugeaud (made Duc d'Isly in 1843), was one of the major nodes in the 'European city' next to the old town. It was designed in the early 1850s after the demolition of the Ottoman walls and the construction of a new set of fortifications that significantly expanded the urban territory. The growth pattern of Algiers under the French was characterized by two distinct phases: the first interventions attempted to regularize the fabric of the old city by cutting through it in a Haussmannian manner some twenty years before Haussmann – as seen in the case of the Place du Gouvernement. The wide and straight arteries, lined with colonnades, made references to the public spaces of the *métropole*, among them the much-cherished Rue de Rivoli.[22] The second phase emerged with the realization that the original core could not accommodate the increase in the European population and its specific needs. The sixteenth-century fortifications were taken down and a new, European city began to be built next to the precolonial one. The dual structure that resulted on a trial-and-error basis in Algiers later became official

Statue of Maréchal Bugeaud, *c.* 1950 (postcard).

policy of urban design in French colonies as an effective tool to separate the colonizer from the colonized.[23]

Place Bugeaud was a square-shaped opening in the middle of the Rue d'Isly, the main artery of the new quarter. The starting point of the Rue d'Isly, the Bab al-Djadid, or the new gate, had special significance in terms of the French occupation, because it was the gate from which the French army had entered Algiers.[24] The perspective from Place Bugeaud toward the north was terminated by a view of the casbah on the hill beyond. European-style buildings framed the vista to the old city, etching another contrast onto the urban fabric of Algiers. In 1852, a statue of Maréchal Bugeaud was placed in the square. Bugeaud, a key figure in the conquest of Algeria, had fought against the Algerian leader Abdel Kader in the 1830s and was named Governor General of

Statue of Emir Abdel Kader, 1990. Photo: Zeynep Çelik.

Algeria in 1840. Like that of the Duke of Orléans, Bugeaud's gaze was fixed on
the casbah, in an act of permanent supervision. In the words of artist and writer
Eugène Fromentin, 'the statue of the Maréchal [was] placed there as a definitive
symbol of victory'.[25]

Lined by elegant structures with commercial spaces on the street level, Place
Bugeaud became one of the most popular centres of European life in the city.
For example, the Milk Bar, the gathering spot for the European youth, was
situated here in the late 1950s. Its bombing during the heat of the Algerian War
on 30 September 1956, planned by the National Liberation Front as part of a
series of attacks that followed each other within minutes throughout the city,
added another layer of memory to the square. The first of their kind in Algiers,
these attacks were undertaken by women fighters Zohra Drif, Samia Lakdari
and Djamila Bouhired.[26] After independence, the statue of Bugeaud was
replaced with a statue of Abdel Kader, on horseback and raising his sword,

finally reclaiming his victory over the French military. The name of the square was changed to Place Emir Abdel Kader. The memory of the war also lingers in the daily life of the square in more subtle ways – the Milk Bar is still intact and maintains its original name, but its sign is now only in Arabic letters, and Zohra Drif practises as an attorney from her office in one of the buildings that line the square.

Names of public spaces coalesce into a text and define the city on a semiological level. In her analysis of Paris as the site of revolution, Priscilla Parkhurst Ferguson observes that, together with other urban signs such as monuments and statues, the names of public spaces tell the history of a city and act as 'a system of representation through which the collective identity defines itself, to itself and to the world beyond'. The names are given in order to control the city in the symbolic realm and while they record and interpret the past, they affirm the present ideologically and politically. The 'urban text' (the nomination of public spaces) is thus not fixed, but changes in a continual process of interpreting and accommodating social transformations.[27] Daniel Milo's discussion of street names as *lieux de mémoire* also underlines their role in displaying a community's collective memory, as well as 'the *establishement*'s representation of the national memory'.[28] The text inscribed on Algiers during the 130 years of French rule celebrated the occupation and appropriation of the city, meanwhile displaying a flexibility to adapt to the shifting conditions at home and in the colony. In the aftermath of Algerian independence, it was rewritten by Algerians in order to claim the city back, to rebuild it metaphorically. While it was clear that the representational landscape of French power had to be erased, the authority of history had to be considered and the past had to be negotiated carefully for the postcolonial text to fulfil its promise.[29]

The renaming of Place Bugeaud as Place Abdel Kader marked an opposition that bound the past to the present. The post-independence names of many streets were similarly rooted in the history of the colonial era and were linked to the present by a corresponding memory that represented the struggle against French rule. For example, Rue d'Isly that bisected Place Bugeaud was renamed Rue Ben Mehidi Larbi after one of the six leaders of the National Liberation Front who had taken the historic decision to launch armed resistance against the French; Rue Bugeaud, in the same vicinity, took the name of another member of this group, Mustapha Ben Boulaid; Rue des Colons (Street of Settlers) became Rue de Libérés (Street of the Liberated) and Rue du Colonel Driant (of the French army) turned into Rue du Colonel Salah Zamoum, a National Liberation Army leader in charge of the Algerois region who was killed in 1961. Equal rank was not always an issue: a legendary resistance fighter from the streets of the casbah, Ali La Pointe, poor and illiterate as he was, could topple a prominent historic military figure, Général Randon, who was remembered for fighting against Abdel Kader and especially for his pacification of Kabylia.[30] Renaming public places after independence was, therefore, a systematic act of reappropriation, one that capitalized on the ideological and pedagogical potential of urban semantics. The names 'reflect the idea that a people holds

Eugène Delacroix, *Les Femmes d'Alger*, 1834. Collection and photo:
Musée du Louvre.

regarding its own history', to quote Leonard Kodjo, who examined the same
phenomenon in the Ivory Coast.[31]

   The private spaces of Algiers were also imbued with symbolism about power
structure and conquest. The dense and interlocked forms of the residential
fabric, photographed over and over by the French, stood as the physical
manifestation of the impenetrability of the Algerian society. The house, not
accessible to outsiders because it was the realm of women and the family, was
understood by the French as the key unit to be conquered. For Algerians, it
epitomized the 'inviolable space' that preserved Algerian identity and acted as a
buffer against the colonial society.[32] The political importance of the houses of
Algiers was recapitulated in a painting which itself became a symbol of French
colonialism and an enduring *lieu de mémoire*: *Les Femmes d'Alger dans leur appartement*
by Eugène Delacroix, painted in 1834. As a window into the harem of a Muslim
house in the casbah, Delacroix's painting alluded to entering the most private,
the most sacred part of Algerian society. An official commission from the French
government, hence blatant in its political meanings, it represented the conquest
of Algeria by entering the Algerian home. It corresponded chronologically to
the carving of the Place d'Armes and complemented metaphorically the physical gesture made by the public square. *Les Femmes d'Alger* carried a long-lasting
authority as a *lieu de mémoire*, intertwining the colonial and the postcolonial
periods.

   As a masterpiece, Delacroix's *Les Femmes d'Alger* (prominently displayed in
the Louvre) had always been a popular topic of study among artists, but its
importance as a political symbol was highlighted around 1930, the centennial
of Algeria's occupation. Earlier, from the 1880s on, the postcard industry

had capitalized upon the same image, popularizing and disseminating its innumerable versions throughout the empire – and the world – expanding the accessibility of this 'portable' *lieu de mémoire* way beyond 'high' art circles.[33]

In her renowned book, *Les Femmes d'Alger dans leur appartement* (published in 1979), Algerian writer Assia Djebar reads this painting in reference to Pablo Picasso's *Les Femmes d'Alger*. One marking the beginning of French colonization, the other the end, the paintings evoke divergent interpretations for Djebar, sparked by the differences in the visions of the two European artists, but more importantly, in the social and cultural transformations brought by the French occupation and the Algerian War. It is not Delacroix's 'superficial Orient' that Djebar cares to dissect, but the subtler implications of the painting, especially the fact that the scene makes the observer conscious of his unwarranted presence in the intimacy of this room which encloses upon the women, who are frozen in an act of waiting, passive and resigned.[34]

Picasso obsessively reworked Delacroix's theme during the first months of the Algerian War, producing fifteen paintings and two lithographs from December 1954 to February 1955.[35] As amply documented by the army photographers themselves, it is during the last years of their rule that the French finally pene- trated the casbah, from its streets to its rooftops, to the courtyards of the houses. Against the violence of this background, Djebar argues that in Picasso's work, the universe of the women of Algiers has been completely transformed from Delacroix's 'tragedy' into a 'new happiness' by means of a 'glorious liberation of space, an awakening of body in dance, energy, and free movement'. Their previous hermetic situation has been preserved, she tells us, but now reversed into a condition of serenity, at peace with the past and the future. Djebar associates the 'liberation' at home with the occupation of the city's public spaces by women resistance fighters taking part in the war. She establishes a meta- phorical relationship between fragments of women's bodies and the explosives they carried under their clothes. She also provides a critique of women's condi- tions in Algeria following independence by arguing that the grenades women hid under their clothes 'as if they were their own breasts' exploded against them.[36]

Djebar's reading of Delacroix's and Picasso's works to frame the dramatic change in women's lives during her country's *nuit coloniale* and its aftermath calls for continued debate and possibly disagreement, especially given Picasso's 'con- tinual struggle in the *Femmes d'Alger* series to reconcile distance with presence, possession, and watching' – in the words of Leo Steinberg.[37] What matters, however, is the fact that Djebar re-establishes the connection between domestic spaces and women's lives by relying on the authority of one of the most blatant symbols of French colonialism and the artistic tradition based on reproductions and reinterpretations of this symbol. She thus accentuates the entanglements of her message. Delacroix's painting becomes a place of memory that can be turned around and recharged with new meanings. Djebar's stand does not imply 'giving in' to the colonizer culture, but rather deploying it to broaden and underline her critique.

Djebar is not alone in reloading colonial cultural formations with new meanings and provoking complicated linkages between contemporary Algerian problems and the country's history. For example, in Kamal Dahane's 1992 documentary film, entitled again *Les Femmes d'Alger*, Delacroix's painting re-emerges: the famous setting is re-created in the last scene, but now is emptied of women. Following the issues raised in the film, Dahane suggests that the women have decided to leave Delacroix's symbolic realm in an act of resistance to present-day political and religious movements that attempt to ban them from public life and confine them to the domestic realm.

Novelist Leila Sebbar takes another leap and brings *Les Femmes d'Alger* back to present-day France, to the realities of postcoloniality in the former *métropole*. When she sees Delacroix's famous painting in the Louvre, Shérazade, the pro-tagonist of Sebbar's *Les Carnets de Shérazade*, associates Delacroix's women of Algiers with the Maghrebi women imprisoned in dismal, small apartments on the outskirts of French cities.[38]

Therefore, contemporary Algerian intellectuals deliberately maintain the colonial *lieux de mémoire*, but complicate their original implications. Twisted and turned, they are now used to provide a familiar platform of critique for today's realities. The *lieux de mémoire* intricately convolute their own themes in ways that define their significance. They act, in Pierre Nora's words, as 'distorting mirrors'.[39]

Whose Heritage?
Un-settling 'The Heritage', Re-imagining the Post-Nation

STUART HALL

This conference on 'Whose Heritage?' provides an opportunity to look critically at the whole concept of 'British Heritage' from the perspective of the multi-cultural Britain which has been emerging since the end of World War II. How is it being – and how should it be – transformed by the 'Black British' presence and the explosion of cultural diversity and difference which is everywhere our lived daily reality?

In preparing to say something useful on this topic, I was struck again – as many of you may have been – by the quaintness of the very term, 'Heritage'. It has slipped so innocently into everyday speech! I take it to refer to the whole complex of organizations, institutions and practices devoted to the preservation and presentation of culture and the arts – art galleries, specialist collections, public and private, museums of all kinds (general, survey or themed, historical or scientific, national or local) and sites of special historical interest.

What is curious in the British usage is the emphasis given to preservation and conservation: to keeping what already exists – as opposed to the production and circulations of new work in different media, which takes a very definite second place. The British have always seen 'culture' as a vaguely disquieting idea, as if to name it is to make self-conscious what well-bred folk absorb unconsciously with their mother's milk! Ministries of Culture are what those old, now dis-credited, Eastern European regimes used to have, which is altogether the wrong associations! Culture has therefore entered the nomenclature of modern British government only when sandwiched alongside the more acceptably populist terms, 'Media' and 'Sport'.

This gives the British idea of 'Heritage' a peculiar inflection. The works and artefacts so conserved appear to be 'of value' primarily in relation to the past. To be validated, they must take their place alongside what has been authorized as 'valuable' on already established grounds in relation to the unfolding of a 'national story' whose terms we already know. The Heritage thus becomes the material embodiment of the spirit of the nation, a collective representation of the British version of *tradition*, a concept pivotal to the lexicon of English virtues.

This retrospective, nation-alized and tradition-alized conception of culture will return to haunt our subsequent thoughts at different points. However, it may also serve as a warning that *my* emphasis does include the active production of culture and the arts as a living activity, alongside the conservation of the past.

We spend an increasing proportion of the national wealth – especially since The Lottery – on 'The Heritage'. But what is it *for*? Obviously, to preserve for posterity things of value, whether on aesthetic or historical criteria. But that is only a start. From its earliest history in western societies – in the heterogeneous assemblages of the 'cabinets of curiosity and wonder' – collections have adorned the position of people of power and influence – kings, princes, popes, landowners and merchants – whose wealth and status they amplified. They have always been related to the exercise of 'power' in another sense – the symbolic power to order knowledge, to rank, classify and arrange, and thus to give mean-ing to objects and things through the imposition of interpretative schemas, scholarship and the authority of connoisseurship. As Foucault observed, 'there is no power relation without the relative constitution of a field of knowledge nor any knowledge that does not presuppose and constitute . . . power relations'.[1]

Since the eighteenth century, collections of cultural artefacts and works of art have also been closely associated with informal public education. They have become part, not simply of 'governing', but of the broader practices of 'gov-ernmentality' – how the State indirectly and at a distance induces and solicits appropriate attitudes and forms of conduct from its citizens. The State is always, as Gramsci argued, 'educative'. Through its power to preserve and represent culture, the State has assumed some responsibility for educating the citizenry in those forms of 'really useful knowledge', as the Victorians put it, which would refine the sensibilities of the vulgar and enhance the capacities of the masses. This was the true test of their 'belongingness': culture as social incorporation.

It is important to remember that the nation-state is both a political and territorial entity, *and* what Benedict Anderson has called 'an imagined community'.[2] Though we are often strangers to one another, we form an 'imagined community' because we share an *idea* of the nation and what it stands for, which we can 'imagine' in our mind's eye. A shared national identity thus depends on the cultural meanings which bind each member individually into the larger national story. Even so-called 'civic' states, like Britain, are deeply embedded in specific 'ethnic' or cultural meanings which give the abstract idea of the nation its lived 'content'.

The National Heritage is a powerful source of such meanings. It follows that those who cannot see themselves reflected in its mirror cannot properly 'belong'. Even the museums and collections apparently devoted to surveying the universal, rather than the national, achievements of culture – like the British Museum, the Louvre, or the Metropolitan Museum in New York – are harnessed into the national story. Carol Duncan and Alan Wallach have argued that these institutions 'claim the heritage of the classical tradition for contemporary society and equate that tradition with the very notion of civilization itself'.[3] Much the same could be said about the museums of modern or contemporary art in terms of the way they have colonized the very idea of 'the modern', 'modernity' and 'modernism' as exclusively 'western' inventions.

Heritage is bound into the meaning of the nation through a double inscription. What the nation means is essentialized: 'the English seem unaware that anything fundamental has changed since 1066'.[4] Its essential meaning appears to have emerged at the very moment of its origin – a moment always lost in the myths, as well as the mists, of time – and then successively embodied as a distilled essence in the various arts and artefacts of the nation for which the Heritage provides the archive. In fact, what the nation 'means' is an ongoing project, under constant reconstruction. We come to know its meaning partly *through* the objects and artefacts which have been made to stand for and symbolize its essential values. Its meaning is constructed *within*, not above or outside representation. It is through identifying with these representations that we come to be its 'subjects' – by 'subjecting' ourselves to their dominant meanings. What would 'England' *mean* without its cathedrals, churches, castles and country houses, its gardens, thatched cottages and hedgerowed landscapes, its Trafalgars, Dunkirks and Mafekings, its Nelsons and its Churchills, its Elgars and its Benjamin Brittens?

We should think of the Heritage as a discursive practice. It is one of the ways in which the nation slowly constructs for itself a sort of collective social memory. Just as individuals and families construct their identities in part by 'storying' the various random incidents and contingent turning points of their lives into a single, coherent narrative, so nations construct identities by selectively binding their chosen high points and memorable achievements into an unfolding 'national story'. This story is what is called 'Tradition'. As the Jamaican anthropologist, David Scott, recently observed, 'A tradition . . . seeks to connect authoritatively, within the structure of its narrative, a relation among past, community, an identity.' He goes on to argue, however, that

> A tradition therefore is never neutral with respect to the values it embodies. Rather a tradition operates in and through the stakes it constructs – what is to count and what is not to count among its satisfactions, what the goods and excellences and virtues are that ought to be valued . . . On this view . . . if tradition presupposes 'a common possession' it does not presuppose uniformity or plain consensus. Rather it depends upon a play of conflict and contention. It is a space of dispute as much as of consensus, of discord as much as accord.[5]

The Heritage is also a classic example of the operation of what Raymond Williams called the 'selective tradition':

> Theoretically a period is recorded; in practice, this record is absorbed into a selective tradition; and both are different from the culture as lived . . . To some extent the selection begins within the period itself . . . though that does not mean that the values and emphases will later be confirmed.[6]

Like personal memory, social memory is also highly selective, it highlights and foregrounds, imposes beginnings, middles and ends on the random and contingent. Equally, it foreshortens, silences, disavows, forgets and elides many episodes which – from another perspective – could be the start of a different narrative. This process of selective 'canonization' confers authority and a material and institutional facticity on the selective tradition, making it extremely difficult to shift or revise. The institutions responsible for making the 'selective tradition' work develop a deep investment in their own 'truth'.

The Heritage inevitably reflects the governing assumptions of its time and context. It is always inflected by the power and authority of those who have colonized the past, whose versions of history matter. These assumptions and co-ordinates of power are inhabited as natural – given, timeless, true and inevitable. But it takes only the passage of time, the shift of circumstances or the reversals of history to reveal those assumptions as time- and context-bound, historically specific and thus open to contestation, renegotiation and revision.

This is therefore an appropriate moment to ask, then, who is the Heritage *for*? In the British case the answer is clear. It is intended for those who 'belong' – a society which is imagined as, in broad terms, culturally homogeneous and unified.

It is long past time to radically question this foundational assumption.

It is, of course, undeniable that Britain has been in recent times a relatively settled society and 'culture'. But as something approaching a nation-state, the United Kingdom of Great Britain and Ireland (subsequently 'and Northern

Ireland') is in fact a relatively recent historical construct, a product of the eighteenth, nineteenth and twentieth centuries. Britain itself was formed out of a series of earlier invasions, conquests and settlements – Celts, Romans, Saxons, Vikings, Normans, Angevins – whose 'traces' are evident in the palimpsest of the national language. The Act of Union linked Scotland, England and Wales into a united kingdom, but never on terms of cultural equality – a fact constantly obscured by the covert oscillations and surreptitious substitutions between the terms 'Britishness' and 'Englishness'.[7]

The Act of Settlement (1701) secured a Protestant ascendancy, drawing the critical symbolic boundary between the Celtic/Catholic and the Anglo-Saxon/ Protestant traditions. Between 1801 (the date of the Act of Union which brokered Ireland into the Union) and Partition in 1922, the national story proved incapable of incorporating 'Irishness' into 'Britishness' or of integrating Irish Catholic migrants into an imagined 'Englishness'. Their culture and presence remains marginalized today.

Though relatively stable, English society has always contained within it profound differences. There were always different ways of being 'English'. It was always fissured along class, gender and regional lines. What came to be known, misleadingly, as '*the* British way of life' is really another name for a particular settlement of structured social inequalities. Many of the great achievements which have been retrospectively written into the national lexicon as primordial English virtues – the rule of law, free speech, a fully representative franchise, the rights of combination, the National Health Service, the welfare state itself – were struggled for by some of the English and bitterly resisted by others. Where, one asks, is this deeply ruptured and fractured history, with its interweaving of stability and conflict, in the Heritage's version of the dominant national narrative?

The British Empire was the largest *imperium* of the modern world. The very notion of 'greatness' in Great Britain is inextricably bound up with its imperial destiny. For centuries, its wealth was underpinned, its urban development driven, its agriculture and industry revolutionized, its fortunes as a nation settled, its maritime and commercial hegemony secured, its thirst quenched, its teeth sweetened, its cloth spun, its food spiced, its carriages rubber-wheeled, its bodies adorned, through the imperial connection. Anyone who has seen the Channel 4 series on *The Slave Trade* or the 'hidden history' of the West India Regiment or the BBC's *The Boer War* will not need reminding how deeply intertwined were the facts of colonization, slavery and empire with the everyday daily life of all classes and conditions of English men and women. The emblems of Empire do, of course, fitfully appear in the Heritage. However, in general, 'Empire' is increasingly subject to a widespread selective amnesia and disavowal. And when it does appear, it is largely narrated from the viewpoint of the colonizers. Its master narrative is sustained in the scenes, images and the artefacts which testify to Britain's success in imposing its will, culture and institutions, and inscribing its civilizing mission across the world. This formative strand in the national culture is now re-presented as an external appendage, extrinsic and inorganic to the domestic history and culture of the English social formation.

Despite all this, the idea of Heritage *has* had to respond to at least two major challenges. The first we may call the democratization process. Increasingly, the lives, artefacts, houses, workplaces, tools, customs and oral memories of ordinary everyday British folk have slowly taken their subordinate place alongside the hegemonic presence of the great and the good. The inclusion of domestic vernacular architecture and the agrarian and industrial revolutions, together with the explosion of interest in 'history from below', the spread of local and family history, of personal memorabilia and the collection of oral histories – activities witnessed to in, for example, Raphael Samuel's memorable celebration of the 'popular heritage', *Theatres of Memory*[8] – have shifted and democratized our conception of value, of what is and is not worth preserving. A few courageous if controversial steps have been taken in our direction – the Transatlantic Slavery Gallery, the Liverpool Maritime Museum's rehang. However, by and large, this process has so far stopped short at the frontier defined by that great unspoken British value – 'whiteness'.

The second 'revolution' arises from the critique of the Enlightenment ideal of dispassionate universal knowledge, which drove and inspired so much of Heritage activity in the past. This has to be coupled with a rising cultural relativism which is part of the growing decentring of the West and western-oriented or Eurocentric grand-narratives. From the 'Magiciens de la terre' exhibition at the Pompidou Centre in Paris in the 1980s, on through the 'Te Maori' exhibition from New Zealand at the Metropolitan Museum of New York, the 'Paradise' exhibition from New Guinea at the Museum of Mankind, 'The Spirit Sings' exhibition of Canada's 'first peoples' at Calgary, the 'Perspectives: Angles on African Art' at the Centre for African Art in New York, and on and on, the exhibiting of 'other cultures' – often performed with the best of liberal intentions – has proved controversial. The questions – 'Who should control the power to represent?' 'Who has the authority to re-present the culture of others?' – have resounded through the museum corridors of the world, provoking a crisis of authority.

These two developments mark a major transformation in our relation to the activity of constructing a 'Heritage'. They in turn reflect a number of conceptual shifts in what we might loosely call the intellectual culture. A list of these shifts would have to include: a radical awareness by the marginalized of the symbolic power involved in the activity of representation; a growing sense of the centrality of culture and its relation to *identity*; the rise among the excluded of a 'politics of recognition' alongside the older politics of equality; a growing reflexivity about the constructed and thus contestable nature of the authority which some people acquire to 'write the culture' of others; a decline in the acceptance of the traditional authorities in authenticating the interpretative and analytic frameworks which classify, place, compare and evaluate culture; and the concomitant rise in the demand to re-appropriate control over the 'writing of one's own story' as part of a wider process of cultural liberation, or – as Frantz

Fanon and Amilcar Cabral once put it – 'the decolonization of the mind'. In short, a general relativization of 'truth', 'reason' and other abstract Enlighten-ment values, and an increasingly perspectival and context-related conception of truth-as-interpretation – of 'truth' as an aspect of what Michel Foucault calls the 'will to power' . . .

Each of these developments would take a whole lecture on their own to elaborate. But I take them here as together marking an unsettling and subver-sion of the foundational ground on which the process of Heritage-construction has until very recently proceeded. We see it reflected in different ways: in how the texts supporting artworks and framing exhibits are written by museums; in the attempts to make explicit the 'perspective' which has governed the selection and the interpretative contextualization, so as to make it more open to challenge and reinterpretation; in the exposing of underlying assumptions of value, mean-ing and connection as part of a more dialogic relationship between the cultural institutions and their audiences; and in the tentative efforts to involve the 'sub-jects' themselves in the exhibiting process which objectifies them. These are only some of the manifest signs of a deep slow-motion revolution in progress in the practices of cultural representation.

They have taken hold, but are certainly not yet extensively or ubiquitously deployed in the institutional complex of the British Heritage 'industry' as a whole. Their appearance is at best patchy, more honoured in the breach – in profession of good intentions – than actual practice. Nevertheless, the question 'Whose Heritage?', posed in the context of the current 'drift' towards a more multicultural Britain, has to be mounted on the back of this emerging 'turn'. I take the appearance of 'cultural diversity' as a key policy priority of the newly restructured Arts Council, its greater visibility in statements of intent by the government and the Ministry of Culture, Media and Sport, the recent efforts by the British Council to project a more 'diverse' image of British culture abroad, and even the much-delayed declaration of a 'Year of cultural diversity' – two years after Amsterdam, but much to be welcomed nevertheless – as potential but uncertain harbingers of change.

Suppose this *were* to turn out to be a propitious moment. What would those new constituencies who feel themselves woefully inadequately represented in the mirror of culture which the Heritage holds up to British society want out of it?

It goes without saying that we would need more money specifically targeted at this objective. The corners of the government's mouth tend to droop signifi-cantly when the money and material resources required to meet objectives are mentioned, and the weary muttering about 'not simply throwing money at the problem' rises to a quiet crescendo. However, the idea that a major culture-change – nothing short of a cultural revolution – could take place in the way the nation represents the diversity of itself and its 'subject-citizens' without a major redirection of resources is to reveal oneself as vacantly trivial about the whole question.

In fact, however, money really *is* not enough. For if my arguments are correct, then an equally powerful obstacle to change is the deep institutional investment which the key organizations have in going on doing things in the ways in which they have always been done; and the operational inertia militating against key professionals re-examining their criteria of judgement and their gatekeeping practices from scratch and trying to shift the habits of a professional lifetime. It will require a substantially enhanced programme of training and recruitment for curators, professionals and artists from the 'minority' communities, so that they can bring their knowledge and expertise to bear on transforming dominant curatorial and exhibitory habits. It also will take the massive leverage of a state and government committed to producing, *in reality rather than in name*, a more culturally diverse, socially just, equal and inclusive society and culture, and *holding its cultural institutions to account.* There are some straws in the wind and a lot of wordage, but so far no consistent sign of this.

Nevertheless, it seems to me that *we* have here an opportunity to clarify our own minds and to refine our agendas so that we can seize every opportunity to challenge institutions, shift resources, change priorities, move practices strategically in the right direction. The rest of my talk is devoted to this task of clarification.

First, we need a better idea of who the 'we' are in whose name these changes are being articulated. Principally, we have in mind the so-called 'ethnic minority communities' from the Caribbean and Indian subcontinent, whose presence in large numbers since the 1950s has transformed Britain into a multicultural society, together with other groups from Africa, the Middle East, China and the Far East, Latin America and the poorer parts of Europe. Their impact on diversifying British society and culture has been immediate and significant. It may therefore surprise you to hear me say that it is really very complex to understand how appropriately these communities should now be culturally represented in mainstream British cultural and artistic institutions. Our picture of them is defined primarily by their 'otherness' – their *minority* relationship to something vaguely identified as 'the majority', their cultural difference from European norms, their non-whiteness, their 'marking' by ethnicity, religion and 'race'. This is a negative figuration, reductive and simplistic.

These are people who have formed communities in Britain which are both distinctively marked, culturally, and yet have never been separatist or exclusive. Some traditional cultural practices are maintained – in varied ways – and carry respect. At the same time, the degrees and forms of attachment are fluid and changing – constantly negotiated, especially between men and women, within and across groups, and above all, across the generations. Traditions coexist with the emergence of new, hybrid and crossover cultural forms of tremendous vitality and innovation. These communities are in touch with their differences, without being saturated by tradition. They are actively involved with every aspect of life around them, without the illusion of assimilation and identity. This is a new kind of difference – the difference which is not binary (either–or) but whose '*différances*' (as Jacques Derrida has put it) will not be erased, or traded.[9]

Their lives and experiences have been shaped by traditions of thought,

religious and moral values, very different from the Judaeo-Christian and classical traditions whose 'traces' still shape 'western' culture; and by the historical
experience of oppression and marginalization. Many are in touch with cultures
and languages which predate those of 'The West'. Nevertheless, colonization
long ago convened these cultural differences under the 'canopy' of a sort of
imperial empty 'global' time, without ever effectively erasing the disjunctures
and dislocations of time, place and culture by its ruptural intrusion into their
'worlds'. This is the palimpsest of the postcolonial world. These communities
are, as C.L.R. James once put it, 'in but not of Europe'.[10] Nevertheless, they
have known 'Europe' for three or four centuries as what Ashis Nandy, in his
unforgettable phrase, calls 'intimate enemies'.[11] They are what David Scott has
called 'conscripts of modernity'. They have dwelled for many years, and long
before migration, in the double or triple time of colonization, and now occupy
the multiple frames, the in-between or 'third' spaces – the homes-away-from-
homes – of the postcolonial metropolis.

No single programme or agenda could adequately represent this cultural
complexity – especially their 'impossible' desire to be treated and represented
with justice (that is, as 'the same') simultaneously with the demand for the
recognition of 'difference'. The agenda will itself have to be open and diverse,
representing a situation which is already cross-cut by new and old lateral connections and reciprocal global influences and which refuses to stand still or
stabilize. We ourselves should recognize that there will be many complementary
but different ways of being represented, just as there are many different ways of
'being black'.

Without becoming too specific, what would be the basic elements or building
blocks of such an agenda?

First, there is the demand that the majority, mainstream versions of the
Heritage should revise their own self-conceptions and rewrite the margins into
the centre, the outside into the inside. This is not so much a matter of representing 'us' as of representing more adequately the degree to which 'their'
history entails and has always implicated 'us', across the centuries, and vice
versa. The African presence in Britain since the sixteenth century, the Asian
since the seventeenth and the Chinese, Jewish and Irish in the nineteenth have
long required to be made the subjects of their own dedicated heritage spaces,
as well as integrated into a much more 'global' version of 'our island story'.
Across the great cities and ports, in the making of fortunes, in the construction
of great houses and estates, across the lineages of families, across the plunder
and display of the wealth of the world as an adjunct to the imperial enterprise, across the hidden histories of statued heroes, in the secrecy of private
diaries, even at the centre of the great master-narratives of 'Englishness' like
the two world wars falls the unscripted shadow of the forgotten 'Other'. The
first task, then, is redefining the nation, re-imagining 'Britishness' or 'Englishness' itself in a more profoundly inclusive manner. The Brits owe this, not
only to us, but to themselves: for to prepare their own people for success in a
global and decentred world by continuing to misrepresent Britain as a closed,

embattled, self-sufficient, defensive, 'tight little island' would be fatally to disable them.

This is not only a matter of history. London and other major cities have been, throughout this century, 'world cities', drawing to themselves the creative talents of nations far and wide, and standing at the centre of tremendously varied cross-cultural flows and lateral artistic influences. Many distinguished practitioners who chose to live and work in Britain – Ronald Moody, Aubrey Williams, Francis Souza, Avinash Chandra, Anwar Jalal Shemza, David Medalla, Li Yuan Chia, Frank Bowling and many others – have been quietly written out of the record. Not British enough for the Tate, not International enough for Bankside, I guess. The ways in which the 'modernist' impulse in western art drew inspiration from what it defined as 'primitive' is now an art-historical cliché. But the numbers of non-European artists who played a central part in European, and especially British, modernism, is far less widely acknowledged – what Rasheed Araeen called, in his historic retrospective, 'The [largely untold] Other Story' (1989). The existence of major 'other modernisms', with their own indigenous roots elsewhere, passes without serious attention. The incontestable truth of the observation that 'The search for a new identity expressed in modern forms has been the common denominator of most contemporary art movements in Africa'[12] is, for western curators and art historians, still a well-kept secret.

Then, second, there is the enormous, unprecedented, creative explosion by contemporary practitioners from the so-called 'minority' communities in all the arts (painting, visual arts, photography, film, theatre, literature, dance, music, multimedia) which has marked the last three decades. Unless this work is funded and exhibited, young talent and promise will simply dribble away. And it needs to be said loud and clear that this is not work which is likely immediately to appeal to the new culture-heroes of the art world – the corporate sponsors – who are already in search of their next Monet outing at some prestigious venue. For a time, the work of contemporary artists from the minority communities was patronizingly secured within an 'ethnic' enclave, as if only non-European work reflected the cultural idioms in which they were composed – as if only 'we' had 'ethnicities'. However, the movement has long ago breached its boundaries and flooded – but only when permitted by the cultural gatekeepers – into the mainstream. Its visibility has depended largely on a few pioneering figures and the efforts of a whole fleet of small, local and community-based galleries.

Like the rainbow, this work comes and goes. Major practitioners surface and pass quietly from view into an early and undeserved obscurity. Their work occasionally surfaces in mainstream venues – and has an innovative vitality which much 'indigenous' work lacks. But they cannot be properly 'heritaged'. The critical records, catalogues and memorabilia of this great tide of creative work in the visual arts since the 1980s, for example – from which, one day, the histories and critical studies of black diaspora visual culture will be written – existed for many years in boxes in a filing cabinet in Eddie Chambers's bedroom in Bristol before they found a resting place – in AAVAA, the Asian and African

Visual Arts Archive, courtesy of The University of East London. No proper archive, no regular exhibitions, no critical apparatus (apart from a few key journals like *Third Text* and the now-defunct *Ten 8*), no definitive histories, no reference books, no comparative materials, no developing scholarship, no passing-on of a tradition of work to younger practitioners and curators, no recognition of achievement among the relevant communities . . . Heritage-less.

Third, there is the record of the migrant experience itself. This is a precious record of the historical formation of a black diaspora in the heart of Europe – probably a once-in-a-lifetime event – still *just* within living memory of its participants. Anyone who watched the *Windrush* programmes and listened to their moving and articulate interviews, or saw the images which Autograph (The Association of Black Photographers) helped to research and mount at the Pitshanger Gallery in Ealing or read the first-hand evidence of the political struggles of the period 1940–90 being put together by the unfunded George Padmore series – edited by a veteran figure, John LaRose, whose autobiography we await – will know the rich evidence in visual imagery and oral testimonies which is waiting to be consolidated into a major archive.

It needs, of course, to be supplemented by extensive oral histories, personal accounts, documents and artefacts, from which, alone, 'the black experience' in Britain since the 1950s could be re-created. We know, from a few bold efforts to build the everyday concerns of migrant people into 'daily life' local exhibitions (for example, by the adventurous Walsall Museum and Art Gallery), of the rich and complex details – customs, cuisine, daily habits, family photographs and records, household and religious objects – which remain to be documented in these domestic settings, poised as they are on the edge of and constantly negotiating between different 'worlds'. There is no such systematic work in progress, though the Black Cultural Archives with its recent Lottery grant *may* at last be able to make a small start on oral histories. Some selective attempts have been made to do this for some Afro-Caribbean communities. So far as I know, there is very little comparable work as yet on the Asian experience(s). Heritage? *Which Heritage?*

Fourth, there is the question of those 'traditions of origin', so often deployed to represent minority communities as immured in their 'ethnicity' or differentiated into another species altogether by their 'racialized difference'. These 'traditions' are occasionally on view in performances by visiting companies, framed as an exotic entertainment. But in general terms, the public is deeply uninformed about them. The complexities of practice, interpretation and belief of Hinduism or Islam as world systems of religious belief are virtually a closed book, even to the intelligentsia. The long, highly complex and refined traditions of Indian music or dance, the key texts, poets and novelists of these great civilizations, the extraordinarily varied cultural history of the Indian subcontinent itself, are beyond the reach of even the well-educated. Equally obscure are the complexities of tribe, language and ethnicity in sub-Saharan Africa.

These basic building blocks of the new global universe we inhabit confront a blank and uncomprehending provincial 'Englishness' as if fitfully glimpsed from outer space. Beyond sea, sun, sand, reggae and ganja, the fantastic intricacies of the 'transculturation' of European, African and Indian elements over centuries, which have produced the variety and vibrancy of Caribbean 'creole' cultures, is another Great Unknown. Latin America, with its highly evolved Hispanic and Amerindian cultures, may well be less familiar than the surface of Mars. The 'peculiarity' of Afro-Caribbeans – that they are simultaneously deeply familiar because they have lived with the British for so long, and ineradicably different because they are black – is regarded by most of the British (who have never been asked by their 'Heritage' to spare it a thought) as culturally inexplicable. Here, the National Curriculum and the truncated remnant of history as a discipline which remains, with only its most simplistic relationship to notions of 'Heritage' intact, has done irreparable damage.

And yet many of the creative talents of these communities are still 'framed' within a familiarity with the practices of these richly traditional arts, so deeply are they interwoven with the textures of a lived culture itself; and even new and experimental work draws on their repertoires, idioms and languages of representation. Unless the younger generation has access to these cultural repertoires and can understand and practise them, to some extent at least, from the inside, they will lack the resources – the cultural capital – of their own 'heritage', as a base from which to engage other traditions. They will, in effect, be culturally 'monolingual' if not silenced – literally, deprived of the capacity to speak – in a world which requires us all to be or become culturally bi- if not multilingual.

There is no intrinsic contradiction between the preservation and presentation of 'other cultures' and my fifth point – the engagement with the production of new diasporic forms. The popular culture of our society especially has been transformed by the rich profusion of contemporary hybrid or 'cross-over' cultural forms – in music, dance, street-style, fashion, film, multimedia . . . which mark the production of 'the new' and the transgressive alongside the traditional and the 'preservation of the past'. Here, 'modernity' (or postmodernity) is not waiting on some authority to 'permit' or sanction this exploration of creativity in contemporary media and form. This is the leading-edge cultural phenomenon of our time – the 'multi' in multicultural, the 'Cool' in 'Cool Britannia'. For a time, black Afro-Caribbeans were in the vanguard of these avant-garde cultural practices, like cultural navigators crossing without passports between ragga, jungle, scratch, rap and electro-funk. In recent years, they have been decisively joined by the 'disorienting rhythms' of Asian youth. Perhaps this aspect of cultural production needs no 'archive' or 'heritage'. But it is proceeding unrecorded and unanalysed, consigned to the ephemera of its day – expendable. Yet it represents one of the most important cultural developments of our time: the stakes which 'the margins' have in modernity, the local-in-the-global, the pioneering of a new cosmopolitan, vernacular, post-national, global sensibility.

What I have offered is a wholly inadequate sketch – leaving out whole tracts of activity and countless examples aside. The account is inevitably skewed by my own interests and preoccupations. The detail does not matter. What matters is some greater clarity about 'the big picture'. I have tried to suggest not only *what* but *why* the question of 'The Heritage' is of such timely and critical importance for our folks at this time. 'British' most of us were, at one time, but that was long ago and, besides, as Shakespeare said, 'the wench is dead'. 'English' we cannot be. But tied in our fates and fortunes with 'the others' – while steadfastly refusing to have to *become* 'other' to belong – we do, after all, have a stake, an investment, in this phase of globalization, in what I might call 'the post-nation'. But only if it can be re-imagined – re-invented – to include us. That is the bet, the wager, the gamble we are here to discuss.

Representation

Introduction

ANNIE E. COOMBES

'The practices of representation', Stuart Hall tells us, involve 'the embodying of concepts, ideas and emotions in a symbolic form which can be transmitted and meaningfully interpreted.' Meaning must enter the domain of these practices, if it is to circulate effectively within a culture. Language, then, is the property of neither the sender nor the receiver of meanings. It is 'the shared cultural "space" in which the production of meanings through language – that is, representation – takes place'.[1] The essays in this section all argue in different ways that an acknowledgement of the historical legacy of colonialism, new forms of global capital, together with processes of decolonization and resistance, operate in productive ways to complicate this definition and that a recognition of these processes is fundamental to an understanding of how representation works in society.

Cultural difference has historically provided some of the most provocative challenges to the fantasy of a stable and continuous Subject. The resultant anxieties frequently circulate through the narrative form of myth as a means of embodying but also of managing the terror invoked by the prospect of a destabilized identity/Subject. Roger Bartra's essay traces the trajectory of one such pervasive myth in his analysis of the recurrence of the image of the 'wild man' in early European narratives of 'discovery' and exploration, and in the scientific treatises which sought to 'explain' these encounters in terms that would 'rationalize' the relations between colonizer and colonized. His objective is not just to chart the myth's repetition but also to demonstrate how the lived experience of the colonial encounter often ran counter to the expectations produced by the circulation of such 'wild man' myths. Part of the work of this essay is to insist on contingency and on the necessity of recognizing how the particularities of social and political relations at any given historical moment transform the nature of persistent myths in ways which usefully tell us more about those who rehearse and rehearsed them than (in this case) the colonial subjects who were their putative objects.

As a way of further elaborating the centrality of historical contingency, it is worth returning to Gayatri Spivak's analysis of the impact of Salman Rushdie's novel *The Satanic Verses* which first appeared in *Third Text*. 'The case of *The Satanic Verses*', she argues, 'is a case of the global *Lebenswelt* – the praxis and politics of life – intercepting an aesthetic object so that a mere reading of it has become impossible.'[2] Our understanding of the hiatus created by Rushdie's novel requires that we take account of both the fact of its existence as a

narrative fiction – and thus already circumscribed by its relation to a 'tradition' of writing governed by its own forms of representation – and the
complex political context that gave rise to the multiplicity of conflicting
critical attention generated by the book, which also inevitably produces its own
body of contradictory meanings for the novel. Such an intellectual project
necessarily challenges the authorial voice and throws into question the way
the reader might credit this with a legitimizing presence. It also further
complicates the issue of whether moral and ethical imperatives should be laid at
the door of the author/artist. If a contributing factor to the hiatus around
Rushdie's novel was created by the volatile cultural and political status of
Islam in the wider world, it was also due to the particular forms of marginalization experienced by the various South Asian Muslim communities in
Britain in the 1980s. In such a climate, questions regarding who speaks for
whom and who has access to and/or controls the means of representation are
crucial considerations.

   Where Spivak focuses on the ways in which any meaning derived from
Rushdie's novel is irrevocably embedded in the significance it acquired as a
stake in the competing political agendas of a number of different constituencies, Kobena Mercer focuses on the ways in which art institutions and the art
market can similarly circumscribe various cultural practices and lend them
meanings beyond the intentions of their producers. He explores two institutions of the 1980s, the Young British Artists and inIVA, as countervailing
tendencies of contradictory responses to globalization as a new phase of capitalist modernization. Mercer analyses the intersection of local, national and
international interests vested in the promotion and production of the late-
1980s phenomenon known as the Young British Artists (yBas). His argument
turns on the limited definition of 'Britishness' which circulated through the
marketing of this group of young artists and the implications such a notion of
'Britishness' had for what Mercer calls 'diaspora' artists in Britain. In particular,
he argues that the insistence on the 'local' (almost parochial) as an aggressive
marketing strategy, pushed as the intrinsic appeal of the yBas in an international
arena, was a regressive response to the bewildering effects of globalization.[3]
Crucial to his argument is that, simultaneously, a number of important exhibitions at key art venues nationally and internationally had begun to assert the
centrality of cultural difference as a problem-solving response to criticisms of
ethnocentric exclusion, subsequently transforming it into a fashionable concept
and robbing cultural difference of its potential to engage critical political issues.
Artists, relieved of the 'burden of representation' (to use Mercer's own term
from an earlier essay) in which they felt obliged to produce work addressing
their status and condition as 'black' artists working in Britain, now felt able
to explore other themes. However, in a context where 'Britishness' is represented by the yBas' pastiche of the local, there is a new dilemma for
'diaspora' artists who are also British. What space is available for them within
this exclusive definition of 'Britishness'? Mercer posits the Caribbean
Artists' Movement (active in London between 1966 and 1972) as an alternative

manifestation of cultural difference where 'the worlding of the ethnic signifier may take forms other than prevailing trends towards market-based multicultural normalization', and which might provide a different 'British' tradition and tell a more cosmopolitan London story to the version promoted through the yBas.

Jimmie Durham's essay develops this analysis of institutional practices and their effects on possible representational practices. He offers a riposte to Marx's infamous statement in the *Eighteenth Brumaire of Louis Bonaparte*, 'They cannot represent themselves, they must be represented', not by simply filling in the gaps left by institutionalized absences but by problematizing the ensuing silence and investigating the available options open to the self-representation of marginal-ized populations. Durham's analysis of this dilemma is an interesting one which foregrounds the complexities of appropriation in relation to what is often pre-sented as 'Native American' culture in the United States and the difficulties this poses in terms of strategies for self-representation. He argues that the problems stem from the particularities of 'settler' colonialism in the United States – a condition shared with Australia, Latin America, South Africa, Palestine and Canada:

> For the peoples of Europe the 'Other' may be a foreigner, the person from another place. For those Europeans who have established permanent colonies . . . it cannot follow that the 'Other' is the colonized person 'here at home', because that would call into question the very legitimacy of the colonial state. In these states the 'Other' must be denied one way or another.

He recalls the familiar tropes of colonial expansion, encounters with those produced as non-people – the 'wild man' (another reincarnation of Bartra's myth), the 'savage' – and the constant contradictory refrain of the 'empty land' made habitable by the indomitable spirit of the pioneer-civilizer. The pioneer-settler so frequently invoked as the hero of a now-lost 'innocence' is, Durham argues, a myth founded on a denial of invasion and murder. It is a denial which necessitates the *visibility* of Indians in the United States as guardians of the ecological order and spiritual guides for the 'lost' souls of inner-city America, and which ensures their *invisibility* as agents for political and social change and advocates for land and human rights, since *this* Indian necessarily challenges the very basis of the foundational myth of the United States. In the context of the American states' celebration of multicultural diversity as the condition of 'American-ness', this structural denial works to contain and limit the available forms of self-representation open to 'American Indian' cultural producers. Either they enter into the 'Indian arts and crafts' market, which guarantees personal success for some individual artists but only in a limited specialized commercial arena; or adopt

> some strategy or another for presenting the 'plight of the Indian', that is, using art to attempt to show our situation to the USA or to show our view of

the USA to itself . . . but it is an error, because such attempts are expected and accepted within the narrative. 'Indian' suffering is part of the entertainment. Finally, though, to accept any idea of ourselves as the subject matter for our art is a trap, potentially.

The emergence of new 'hybrid' cultural forms derived from apparently mutual 'borrowings' and intersections across ethnic and national boundaries is another complication of the debate raised by Durham's essay and has been the focus of much contemporary cultural criticism in recent years. Indeed, the contemporary art market thrives on the commodification of the results of these supposedly cross-cultural and inter-ethnic exchanges. Most of the centres of contemporary art in western Europe, North America, Canada and Australia have hosted large exhibitions foregrounding such cultural products, and many smaller organizations have been launched on the basis of such an enterprise. Commentators have variously lambasted such attempts as bare-faced appropriation by entrepreneurial capitalists or as the dawning of a new era of mutual respect which moves the old liberal rhetoric of cultural relativism onto a more concrete and material footing. Other research has sought to analyse the more contradictory and complex trade-offs and negotiations that may take place in such instances.[4] The controversial production and marketing of Australian Aboriginal art is a case in point, where the creation of a thriving market for acrylic painting and prints from desert communities in rural areas has been criticized by Anne-Marie Willis and Tony Fry (among others) as a profitable ploy, highly controlled and directed by those who manage the production and sale of the work, even while it might also be acknowledged that the funds from the work have facilitated different kinds of projects which have been highly beneficial for the communities involved.[5] It is also the case that such liberal pluralist strategies in Australia, the United States and South Africa have had evidently progressive repurcussions by providing a certain (circumscribed) visibility which autochtonous peoples have used strategically to support claims for both land rights and political enfranchisement more generally. Nevertheless, a contradiction remains in the use of Aboriginal work, for example, as an international icon of Australianess (as in the 2000 Sydney Olympic Games), while such a recognition remains painfully incommensurate with the abysmal state of Aboriginal civil rights compounded by a long history of persecution and marginalization. This contradiction is also at the heart of Durham's ruminations on the possibilities and impossibilities of 'visibility'. Ultimately, however, all these texts remind us that the terms of the language that makes the 'shared cultural "space"' of representation intelligible is constantly being contested and, as Kobena Mercer (drawing on William Bryce Gallie) points out, 'what matters are the strategies and tactics by which you play the game as the winners and losers of yesterday can easily change places today and tomorrow'.[6]

Discovering the European Wild Men

ROGER BARTRA

For many centuries European wild men[1] lived almost exclusively in the mythical consciousness of the popular classes and were scorned by theology and science. It seems strange, therefore, that the wild man should reappear in the political and natural sciences of the eighteenth century in the form of Rousseau's noble savage and Linnaeus's *homo ferus*. The thought patterns of the Enlightenment clearly had their origins in the literary traditions of the Renaissance, in the works of Montaigne, Cervantes and Shakespeare who kept the myth of the wild man alive in characters such as the cannibal, Cardenio and Caliban. However, the main force behind the myth of the wild man in Enlightenment thinking cannot just be explained by focusing upon the persistence of folklore in literature: we need to search for other bridges which link the medieval myth to the modern one, for dark historical ties such as these can elucidate both the trajectory behind the continuity of the myth of the wild man and some new characteristics it begins to acquire.

One of those bridges has been curiously ignored by the few historians who have attended to the myth of the wild man, although it was frequently traversed by Romantic writers of the nineteenth century. Here I refer to the only treatise I know which has attempted to explain and define the existence of these strange prodigious men unconnected to Adam's stock. I refer to *Liber de nymphis, sylphis, pigmaeis et salamandris et de caeteris spiritibus*, written by Paracelsus in the first half of the sixteenth century, where an explanation is elaborated of the nature of nymphs, sylphs or sylvani, pygmies, vulcans or salamanders.[2] The interpretation of this audacious Swiss physician is interesting precisely because it acknowledges the presence of wild men as an authentic phenomenon rather than as a diabolical invention or a pagan idolatrous fiction. Such a vision was clearly unacceptable to orthodox theology, which viewed any approximation of man to beast with abject horror. This aversion is well illustrated in the sermons of Geiler von Kaysersberg (1445–1510) published under the general title of *Die Emeis* (The Ant): in sermon twenty he presents a classification of wild men who, like demonic creatures, are placed into five distinct categories: 1. the solitary (*solitarii*, hermits like Mary Magdalene, Mary the Egyptian and Onophrius); 2. the wild men proper (*sacchani*, identified as satyrs); 3. the hispanics (*hispani*, wild men of foreign lands); 4. the pygmies (*piginini*); 5. the devils (*diaboli*).[3]

In his study, Paracelsus establishes the existence of four types of strange beings, which are very similar to man: nymphs (undines, sirens or melusines), sylphs (silvani or woodland folk), pygmies (gnomes or mountain people) and salamanders (vulcans or Etneans). But they are creatures of God not creatures of the devil and are 'living proof that we are not alone',[4] for God created these wild beings in the image and the likeness of man:

> Just as we say that man is the image and likeness of God, that is, an imitation of his form, we might also say that these people are the image and likeness of man, construed in his form. Man is not God but in appearance, though he was created similar to him. Similarly, these are not men, even though they are created in the image and likeness of man . . . they cannot boast of possessing a soul like that of men, though they are like him. Just as man does not boast of being God, in spite of being made in his image and likeness as a reflection of him. In other words, man refrains from being God and wild men renounce the soul, and therefore cannot be called men.[5]

It emerges clearly from this hallucinating logic, that the presence of an intermediary space between man and beast was a very thorny issue. Paracelsus recognizes their human habits, though unrefined and coarser than man's, their flesh and blood, their mortality and their human feeding habits, as well as their wisdom to govern and to respect justice. Clearly, for Paracelsus, the wild man is redeemed, released from the disdain which appears in tales of medieval knights: they are endowed, he says, 'with human reason, though they possess no soul'.[6] Therefore, he reasons, they are naturally inclined to pursue personal justice in the course of their lives, and are the wisest of living creatures:

> Just as man's talents and knowledge make him the closest creature to God, they are the closest and most approximate creature to man, which is why they are called people and men, and are viewed and respected as such. Consequently they are indistinguishable from men, save for their spirit and lack of soul. They are strange and marvellous creatures, and merit contemplation above all others.[7]

It is plausible that Paracelsus conceived the inhabitants of the new American colonies when he reflected on the wild man. But he was primarily concerned with achieving a better understanding of the characters which inhabited the waters, forests and mountains of Europe and formed part of its pagan folkloric tradition; by accepting the credibility of popular beliefs about wild men, nymphs and gnomes, Paracelsus was adopting the same rebellious attitude he had done as a physician, when he sought in popular cures the path towards a new science radically opposed to the Galenic tradition founded upon the four humours. We might say that Paracelsus was a genuine wild doctor: 'Universities', he would say, 'do not teach everything, which is why a physician should turn to old widows, gypsies, witches, wandering tribes, old thieves, and others who operate outside the law, and attempt to learn from them.'[8] Though his ideas about wild men could have been used to justify the bestial nature of the American Indians, this did not apparently occur. It is true that in 1520 Paracelsus

The wild man, transformed into a harmless element of heraldic semiotics, symbolically transfers his virility to the owner of the coat of arms. Engraving by Martin Schongauer (Germany, 1480–90). The Metropolitan Museum of Art, New York, Harris Brisbane Dick Fund, 28.26.7.

expressed his incredulity at the possibility that the people discovered in those 'remote islands' might be descendants of Adam and Eve: 'It is more likely that they are descended from another Adam, since one can hardly prove that they have consanguineous ties with us.' He goes on to say that these figures were born 'after the great flood, and probably possess no soul: they talk like parrots . . .'[9] These were fundamentally gradualist notions, which never attained the atrabilious attitude of classifying the American Indians along with insects, as has been mistakenly suggested;[10] on the contrary, the gradualism implicit in the theories of Paracelsus, Caesalpinus or Bruno represented an early scientific spirit in the investigation of the relationship between man and animal. Indeed, notions that attributed a bestial nature to Americans constituted a myth rather than an important trend of thought.[11]

However, Paracelsus's vision was considered a blasphemy, since it undermined Christian dogma about salvation by acknowledging the existence of a figure made up of two parts: man and spirit; a mortal creature of flesh and blood who could nevertheless pass through walls without incurring damage; since this hybrid monster lacked a soul he had no cause to serve God.[12] Yet, Paracelsus does not define these beings as pernicious or harmful. He classifies them according to his own idiosyncratic and stoical vision of the cosmos, based upon the idea of a universe composed of four fundamental elements: air, earth, water and fire. Pagan folklore contained plenty of examples of fictional beings which corresponded to these elements, with the exception of the last one, fire, which Paracelsus attributed to the strange figures partially inspired by the Christian myth of Satan and Vulcan in Greek mythology.[13] The pygmies corresponded to earth, the silvani and sylphs to air, the nymphs to water. For Paracelsus, the true wild men were the sylphs (*Sylphen*), silvani (*Sylvestres*) or woodland folk (*Waldleut*), who were extraordinarily similar to man, since they breathed the same air, were burned by fire, drowned in water and suffocated under the earth.[14] These wild men 'are coarser, rougher, taller and stronger' than the nymphs, the water folk.[15] Moreover, in contrast to nymphs and pygmies, the wild men of the woods 'do not speak, that is to say, they cannot speak, in spite of having a tongue and all the faculties of speech', and in spite of 'possessing a great capacity for learning'; 'the woodland folk', he adds, 'are like men, but more timid and fickle.'[16] Sylphs can be possessed by the devil, especially the females, and consequently, 'those who dare to couple with these women of the woods – not an uncommon occurrence – shall become mangy and scabby like lepers, and shall be eternally beyond human help.'[17] Paradoxically, marriages between men and nymphs are possible, for they represent the means by which aquatic women and their children may obtain a soul and eternal salvation. Thus by embracing such a hope, all of marvellous stock but not of Adam's kin are able to find human love: 'They are so like humans', asserts Paracelsus, 'that they ought to be considered as wild men [*Wilden Menschen*], for although we say that a wolf is a wild dog and a mountain goat is a wild billy, none of these is able to marry a man.'[18]

As a typical Renaissance man, Paracelsus accepts a popular ancient tradition that does not clearly distinguish man from nature, thereby contributing to the creation of a *natural history* in which humanity could form a link. Medieval Christianity either satanized the wild man by adapting him to the powerful image of the incubi and succubi who rabidly fornicated with sleeping humans, or else regarded him as an instrument of the devil employed to trick man's senses.[19] But Paracelsus, in contrast, attempts one of the first scientific explanations of wild men still immersed in the mists of medieval theology: he accepts the presence of an intermediary link between man and beast as contained in popular mythology to be an incontestable fact, although he does not believe, of course, in the notion of an evolutionary process linking the two.

Therefore, the first contact between the wild man and the modern scientific spirit of the Renaissance resulted in a restoration of the ancient myth, contrary to what could be expected. But whether or not this constituted the beginning of the end of a myth, destined to be shattered by the progress of science and anthropology, is questionable. Could modern rationalism and humanism terminate a myth which had survived the brunt of half a millennium of Christian theology? There was a marked interest during the sixteenth century for what Linnaeus called *homo ferus* (isolated humans raised since infancy by woodland beasts), for anthropomorphic beings from Asia and Africa depicted by travellers (gorillas, chimpanzees, etc.), as well as for monstrous children occasionally born to normal women. Gesner cites the astonishing case of a quadruped captured in the forest of Hanesbergium in the diocese of Salzburg:

> Of a reddish colour verging on blond; of a marked savagery, fleeing from men, and when able hiding in darkness. Because keeping him in captivity was not feasible because of his need to eat, he died a few days later. His back feet were different to his front ones and considerably longer . . . he was captured in the year of grace 1531.[20]

The account is illustrated with a curious print. Gesner also included descriptions and prints of other humanoid beings, like the sphinx, the satyr, the aegopithecus and the cercopythecus. The latter is illustrated in a print taken from Bernard of Breidenbach's *Journey to the Holy Land*, published in 1486. He depicts a strange animal standing before a salamander, a stick in one hand and a camel's rein in the other; the complete print, which features a giraffe, a unicorn, a crocodile and an Indian goat, represents a medieval vision of the great chain of being.[21] According to Gesner, the animal, 'with legs, a virile phallus, and a face of human shape and proportions, could be regarded as a wild man' (although in the print it is clearly female).[22] Of interest is not just the fact that Gesner readopts the Breidenbach print, but that three centuries after the publication of *Journey to the Holy Land*, a copy of the same print should be used by Hoppius in his famous thesis to his teacher Linnaeus, to portray *homo caudatus hirsutus*, or Lucifer standing next to a satyr, a pygmy and a troglodyte, all of which were classified as forms of *homo monstruosus* within the *homo sapiens* species.[23]

This remarkable example of the pervasiveness of a graphic representation of the wild man from the fifteenth to the eighteenth centuries shows how the myth could survive the brunt of modern rationalism in scientific iconography. In fact, it was able to slip into the very heart of science and adopt new forms of expression.

The persistence of the myth was fostered by the scientific pursuit of explanations of monstrous or prodigious phenomena which were not based upon divine will or Satanic illusion. In his famous treatise, the surgeon Ambroise Paré (1509–90) established a series of explanations for the existence of monsters, including those believed to be of divine or diabolical origin: excess, insufficiency, mix or decay of semen, the narrowness of the womb, knocks to the abdomen or the incorrect posture of a mother, hereditary or accidental illnesses and – inevitably – the imagination.[24] Paré exhibits a miscellaneous gallery of monstrosities in which cases of crosses between humans and animals attributed to a mix of semen abound: 'These are the products of sodomites and atheists who mate unnaturally with the beasts, and create all manner of monsters repugnant and horrible to the eye or to conversation.'[25] One hairy maiden, in particular, is construed as typical of a monster of the imagination, since the mother imagines or fixedly contemplates some weird thing during conception or while the child is still unformed; he quotes Damascene, who knew of 'a woman, as hairy as a bear, deformed and repulsive at birth, owing to the fact that her mother stared

Carl von Linné and C.E. Hoppius included the myths of wild men
in their celebrated classification of species (*Amoenitates Academicae*,
Vol. 6, 1789, p. 76). The same wild female being reappeared from
a drawing of 1486, illustrating the astonishing iconographic
persistence of the myth.

too hard at an effigy of Saint John covered in untanned furs, an image of which
lay bound to the legs of her bed while she conceived.'[26] Thus, an erotic imagination was potentially lethal, an awesome Pandora's Box.

Ambroise Paré's detailed explanations started to narrow the gap separating
man from natural beast with real flesh-and-bone monsters: nature seemed to go
berserk when women gave birth to serpents, dogs or bicephalous children; when
the human-like figures of mermaids and Nile Tritons grew out of the water; and
when pigs and mares mated with anthropocephalous animals. In contrast to
Paracelsus, Paré did not believe that these beings belonged to a species parallel
to Adam and Eve's line: these were deviations from the normal course of nature
or counter-natural phenomena.[27]

Daily coexistence with monstrous beings of different sorts must have surely
provoked misgivings and conjecture regarding the causal link between natural
phenomena and human identity. Cross-breeds often led to notions of individuality in crisis, as was the case with the bicephalous beings. In 1605, the French
anatomist Jean Riolan – known, among other things, for his opposition to
Harvey's theses on the circulation of blood – published his collection of case
studies of double monsters who lived at the turn of the thirteenth century, of
which the following is an example:

He was joined at the stomach, and possessed two heads and four hands with
common lower parts. The king ensured it was carefully brought up and
educated, and was especially keen it learn music; not only was marvellous
progress made, but it also learnt many languages. These two bodies did not

act in concord, and had different wills, and often fought when one disliked
what was liked by the other; sometimes one would listen to the advice of the
other. Most interesting was the fact that when their thighs and kidneys hurt
them, both felt it; but when one of them was pinched, or hurt in the upper
half, only one would feel it. This difference was further evident at the time of
death, when one of the bodies died several days before the other, and the
survivor was left to languish slowly while the other half rotted away. This
monster lived 28 years and died under the reign of John, a Scottish earl.[28]

Ambroise Paré, who considered excessive semen to be responsible for cases of
two bodies joined together, followed Aristotle in determining the number of
individuals inside the body of a monster by counting the number of hearts.[29]
The cercopithecus cited above also posed problems of identity:

He loves women and children just like his countrymen, and when he can
escape from his shackles, he tries to be reunited with them. He is nevertheless
a fierce beast, but of such intelligence that one might say that in this regard
men are inferior to him: certainly not our fellow citizens, but perhaps the
barbarians who inhabit the hostile climes, like the Ethiopians, the Numids,
and Lapps.[30]

Also worth mentioning here is Aristotle's explanation that simians, baboons
and cinocephales 'possess a nature, shared by both men and quadrupeds'.[31]
The colonization of America was also a great part of the medieval theological effort to recover those spaces lost to modernization; and in many ways,

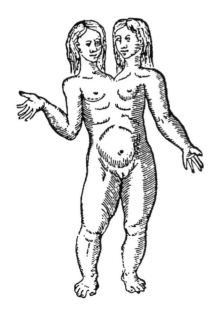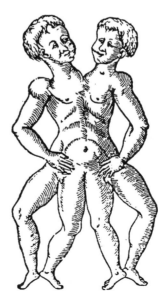

Ambroise Paré, *Des monsters et prodiges*, Paris 1573.

too, recognition of the new American land and culture was a highly favourable sign of the modern age for the Europeans. Columbus fanatically believed that his venture was a vital part of the universal expansion of Christianity and, when describing the American man, he had in mind the kind of questions that his contemporaries posed: 'In these islands I have not discovered monstrous men, as many believed, but instead a people of a very pleasant deference . . .'[32] The myth of the wild man was shattered before the reality of the real American wild man: they were not hairy, but intelligent and beautiful. However, it must be added that the images brought to us by Columbus are contradictory, for his descriptions also leave room for a wild man resurrecting the long and rich mythical tradition of Caliban, the Caribbean cannibal. Columbus says: 'Thus I have not found a trace of monsters, except on a Caribbean island . . .' The Caribbeans were ferocious cannibals, 'no less ill-proportioned than the rest, except that they are accustomed to wearing their hair long like women'.[33] In spite of all the medieval imagery that the American colonizers carried in their heads – peopled with lost paradises, mermaids, amazons, giants – the daily reality of a life shared with the men and women of the New World gradually imposed itself. The adventure of a gentleman from Savona which occurred during Columbus's second voyage is very illustrative:

> having captured an extremely pretty Caribbean woman, which the Admiral had offered me, and – after having taken her to my cabin in a state of nakedness as was her custom – I was overcome with the desire to satisfy my pleasure. When I wanted to come on to her, she refused and scratched me in such a way that I almost wished I had never started. But upon seeing this (to tell the story to its end), I took a rope and gave her such a hiding that she let out some extraordinary shrieks, which you had to hear to believe. Finally we reached such an understanding that I can say it seemed as if she had been brought up in a school for prostitutes.[34]

The wild woman was basically nothing other than a lustful creature: one had to know how to treat her with measured violence – as a master and as a man – to discover in her heart the human sweetness of a profane love. The monster of the Caribbean melted in the arms of the Conquistador.

The main tendency was to assimilate American humanity into the concept of barbarity, rather than that of wild men, although there was clearly a great confusion over the two terms.[35] Bartolomé de las Casas, for example, considers wild men as one of four species of barbarian (the third kind):

> The first, taking the general meaning of the word, denotes any kind of people with an oddness about their opinions or customs, yet who require neither policing nor prudence for guidance. The second kind are lacking the class of appropriate languages that can be expressed with characters and letters, as the English once did . . . The third kind of barbarian, owing to their perverse customs, the coarseness of their wit, and their brutal inclinations are like the

Medieval wild folk evolve to exemplify natural and original tenderness, and furthermore, they appear as a happy family in a paradisiac land. Engraving by Master BXG (Germany, 1470–90), Albertina, Vienna.

wild beasts that inhabit the fields, lacking cities, houses, police, laws, and rites and tracts of *iure gentium*, but go about as *palantes*, as is said in Latin, which means that they rob and use force, as the Goths and the Alani once did, and now say there are those whom in Asia we call Arabs and who in Africa we call Alarabs. And from these we can understand the words of Aristotle, that since it is lawful to hunt wild beasts, so it is lawful to make war with them defending ourselves from those who harm us, procuring their submission to the human police.[36]

These assertions form part of the complex discussion over the supposed incapacity of the Indian, which provoked the confrontation between las Casas and Sepúlveda, and which has been intensely studied.[37] What I wish to point out here is not the widely documented way European notions of wildness and barbarity were employed to qualify the American people; I am rather interested in the reverse process: the solvent quality of the American reality (and, in general, the mass of information proceeding from travellers of the Renaissance) in the myth of the wild man. One could say that, while Europe colonized American 'savages', these in turn colonized the European myth of the wild man and contributed to its transformation. During the fifteenth and sixteenth centuries, an important transition took place, not in the structure of the myth of the wild man so much as in the space which it occupied. As travellers' accounts and anatomists' studies limited the conditions for the veridical existence of sylphs and nymphs, so these wild men were obliged to migrate, and change *habitat*. At the same time, by undermining the traditional foundations of theology, the Renaissance opened a new ideological and theoretical domain for them. Theology, as we have seen, did not admit a space for the wild man, only the invocation of whom threatened a human community which drew its cohesion from a promise of eternal salvation. Consequently, the *homo sylvestris* remained imprisoned inside the camp of popular imagery, literary adventures and art, where he was kept alive in the figure of a natural human being, an inhabitant of the woods and of earth's unexplored corners. This wild medieval man survived as a tangible and physical reality; in contrast to the wild man who takes form in the Renaissance and evolves until it reaches – in the Enlightenment – a completely spiritual, ideal and ghostly character, whose true existence is no longer credible. The twist is interesting: medieval wild men were, just like monsters, considered to be real and threatening realities. Modern science and travellers at the dawn of the colonial era, by revealing the inexistence of these beings, opened a new space, one which was totally and consciously imaginary and fabulous. Why believe that a demythification of the wild man took place? The fact remains that the Renaissance wild man who ended in enlightened rationalism is far more fabulous than the medieval *homo sylvestris*. Although modernity believed increasingly less in its physical existence, its ideal and spiritual reality influenced western culture far more than had it been made of flesh and bone.

Paracelsus's attitude provides us with various clues for understanding this strange transition of the myth: the Renaissance doctor acknowledges the empirical existence of wild beings in the mythological tradition, but at the same time is opening a theoretical and rational space for them within modern thought. The opposition between *mythos* and *logos* is not as simplistic as has been sometimes claimed, neither is the course marking the shift from the clouds of mythology to rational thought so clearly drawn. In reality, the contrast between *mythos* and *logos* is quite deceptive: a careful look at the evolution of certain myths shows us how easily they are able to adopt a rational form and to shed religious and ritual wrappings, not unlike Schelling's demand for 'a mythology of reason'.[38] The history of the myth of the wild man of the sixteenth century shows us not his decadence but, on the contrary, his revitalization and relocation. The myth of the wild man found a niche in the very kernel of new forms of humanist thought, for which some form of representing *otherness* – in a modern world more inclined towards defining the individual identity of the modern man – became indispensable. This complex tradition cannot but help remind us of one of the earliest classical forms in which the problem was circumscribed: when Plato, talking through Socrates in *Phaedo*, jeers at the rhetorical seers who claimed to have found the rational codes of myths. Socrates purposely satirizes the frivolity of those who, having deciphered the mythologem of Boreas and Oreithya (she is thrown headlong by the North wind and her death becomes a kidnapping), attempted to unravel the phantasmagories of 'the hypocentaurs and the chimera, the throng of gorgons and pegasus, and the multitude of strange and terrifying monsters'. Socrates – who revered the traditional forms of myths – then warned that 'it will be a long time before the incredulous can unfold his *wild knowledge* and provide a credible version' (author's emphasis).[39] This *agroikos sofia*, this wild thought of the incredulous, contrasted with the precept of the famous delphic inscription which advised one to *know oneself*. Therefore, Socrates prefers – instead of worrying about distant and faraway monsters – to contemplate himself: 'I want to know if I am a more complex and furious monster than Typhon, or a creature simpler and sweeter with a part of divine nature . . .'[40] History has shown that the explanation of monsters and myths is intrinsically linked to the definition and the wisdom of oneself: the I and the Other are inseparable. The ancient sophists and Greek rhetoricians with their wild knowledge, their *agroikos sofia*, were correct: explaining myths is not a useless task.

Cowboys and . . .

JIMMIE DURHAM

the exploring party returned to England with such good accounts of the new country that Queen Elizabeth called it Virginia in honor of herself.[1]

Wilbur F. Gordy

I recollected seeing a boy who was shot down near the house. His arm and thigh were broken, and he was so near the burning house that the grease was stewing out of him. In this situation he was still trying to crawl along; but not a murmur escaped him, though he was only about twelve years old. So sullen is the Indian, when his dander is up, that he had sooner die than make a noise, or ask quarter. The number that we took prisoner, being added to the number we killed amounted to a hundred and eighty-six.[2]

Davey Crockett

For the other remains to be discovered. The fact is worthy of astonishment . . .[3]

Tzvetan Todorov

In an installation piece in California's Museum of Man, Luiseño Indian artist James Luna put himself in a display case. Viewing 'the body', an American white woman said to her husband, 'Dear, I think he is alive.' The husband replied, 'Don't be silly; they don't put live ones in museums.'

Luna makes other installations wherein 'American Indian' people are represented by only a few articles of clothing, sometimes by cowboy boots and hats which are typical 'Indian' dress today.

In New York much of my own work has dealt with what Jean Fisher has called 'the necrophilous codes of the museum',[4] and of misrepresentation and misidentification of 'American Indians' by the colonizers. But Luna and I did not know each other's work. At opposite ends of the USA we worked on similar problems, because, I believe, the problems are so intolerably before us.

This essay is concerned with the invisibility of 'American Indians' in the Americas; not to plead a case for more visibility, but to attempt a tentative investigation into the ramifications of the 'presence of the absence/absented Indian body'[5] in American discourse.

This solid vacuum is a special case. I feel, therefore, that I must relate anecdotes to convince readers that the situation actually exists. Certainly for readers from the Americas, it is necessary (at least from my experiences) to approach the subject obliquely. The following few anecdotes, then, are related only by the invisible theme of invisible 'American Indians'.

The great Shawnee resistance leader Tecumseh was killed around 1810 in Ohio Territory. One of the most famous generals in the American Civil War, William Tecumseh Sherman was born in Ohio surely not much more than ten years later. How is it that Sherman was named after the most hated and feared man of the time while the Indian wars were still, further west and south, in full bloom?

Naomi Bliven, reviewing Nirad Chaudhuri's autobiography in *The New Yorker* magazine,[6] compares England's colonization of India not to its colonization of 'American Indians' but of American whites. Regarding herself and her country as fellow-colonized persons, she has a sympathy with Chaudhuri and India.

In V.S. Naipaul's book about the American South, Anne Siddons, a white novelist from Georgia, states, 'We [Southern whites] were a conquered and occupied people, the only people in the United States to be like that.'[7]

At a recent convention of the College Art Association (CAA) in New York a Brazilian woman showed slides of Brazilian paintings. The paintings were traditional in form, done on stretched canvas or linen in oils or acrylics. Her thesis was to show, by the styles of paintings, that, as she put it, 'the Brazilian people are truly a new people'. If Europeans are then the 'Old People', who are the 'Indians' of Brazil? Obviously, they are considered either as a special kind of property of the 'new people', or not at all.

In the USA people phrase their questions about 'Indians' in the past tense, not only to me or other individual 'Indians' but also to groups. It is not unusual for us to answer in the past tense. Once in South Dakota a white man asked, 'What did the Indians eat?' One of our elders replied without irony, 'We ate corn, beans and squash.' (That is the standard answer in US school books.)

There is in the USA (and to a lesser extent in Chile and Argentina) a curious phenomenon that is seldom given intellectual *consideration*: whites claiming to be 'part-Indian', and even more, whites who claim to *be* 'Indian'. Surely there is not another part of the world where members of the racist oppressor society claim to be members of the oppressed group. (The Americans do not, of course, claim any of the concomitant disadvantages.)

It seems also necessary to state that 'Indians' of the Americas *are* colonized peoples; that the colonization is not simply the language of some political rhetoric of past decades. Europe may be passing through a postcolonial time, but we in the Americas still live in a colonial period. Our countries were invaded, genocide was and is committed against us, and our lands and lives are taken over for the profit of the colonizer.

Although I do not want to express a moral outrage, since the investigation is about American discourse and not of an 'Indian' problem, I ask you to imagine my state of mind when once more I say that we are *colonized* peoples. We are not 'primitives' who suffer under a culture shock by contact with 'more developed societies'. Yet in my experience if I were addressing a live audience someone would question the simple facts, 'But didn't you at first welcome the settlers?' Or, 'Weren't relationships friendly at first?'

For the peoples of Europe the 'Other' may be a foreigner, the person from another place. For those Europeans who have established permanent colonies, such as the USA, Australia, South Africa or the Latin American countries, it cannot follow that the 'Other' is the colonized person 'here at home', because that would call into question the very legitimacy of the colonial state. In these states the 'Other' must be denied one way or another. Golda Meir said that there were no Palestinians, and South Africa has always claimed that there were no Africans in the area until after the arrival of the settlers. 'Aboriginals' have only recently been included in Australia's census, and of course the American pioneers tamed a 'wilderness'.

There is something unique about the USA; it was the first settler colony to establish itself *against* and through the *denial* of its original inhabitants. It developed thereby a narrative which was more complete, more satisfying, than similar narratives in Canada and Latin America. That narrative has generated new cultural and political behaviour which has been a main influence in the modern world. When, as a political activist in the 1970s, I attempted to present our case to the United Nations, I was more than intimidated by the tenacity with which other countries upheld the American narrative. And that was in the most obvious and unsubtle political discourses. The economic power of the USA does not seem reason enough for the propagation of the myth, because the myth was expanding its influence long before the USA obtained its majority.

The narrative has its origins in Europe, of course. But the USA refined, that is, coarsened, the European premise of the 'primitive' so that it was made more operable for industrial expansionism.

The USA's narrative about itself centres, has as its operational centre, a hidden text concerning its relationship with 'American Indians'. That central text *must* be hidden, and sublimated, and acted out. 'American Indian' artists, as artists and as persons responsible to our people, have traditionally attempted intervention, but even our attempts are seen as quite minor entertainment. As we approach the 500th anniversary of Columbus, many people throughout the Americas are renewing certain superficial discourses about their history. *That* seems to be for the purpose of reassuring known propositions. In the USA we 'Indians' are now called upon to speak within this framework. The difficulty is not so much that we are expected to say known things as that our speaking at such a time *is* a known thing. Coming just at the period when institutions in the USA are already celebrating a 'multicultural'-ism, I suspect that this new development in fact makes intervention on our part more difficult.

The USA, because of its actual guilt (instead of some thought-out or not thought-out perception of guilt) has had a nostalgia for itself since its beginnings. Even now one may read editorials almost daily about 'America's loss of innocence' at some point or other, and about some time in the past when the USA was truly good. That self-righteousness and insistence upon innocence began as the USA began, with invasion and murder.

The master-narrative of the USA has not (cannot be) changed. It has been broadened. It has been broadcast. This narrative is only superficially concerned with 'taming the wilderness' and 'crossing new frontiers'. The USA has developed a concept and a reality of the state, I might say of 'state-ism', because US culture is so completely ideological.

The profound operative concept has to do with a specifically American premise of the 'Other'. Any poll taken in the USA would show, I believe, that Americans imagine that the Ohio Valley mentioned earlier has always in some way belonged to the USA, and that in fact what is now the continent-wide state was always the proper property of the USA. It is a country which may continually expand (and as a state, not as a 'commonwealth' or 'empire') but which cannot give up territory even if, as in the case of Puerto Rico, the territory has been proven to be held illegally.

There is an unbroken line between the first American Thanksgiving Day, celebrating the slaughter of an entire 'Indian' village, and the overwhelming popularity of Bush's slaughter of thousands in the 1989 invasion of Panama.

Whether from the right or the left, whether the topic is Panama or Mapplethorpe, criticism in the USA must ultimately depend upon the 'American'-ness

Jimmy Durham, 1987.

or 'Un-American'-ness of the project being criticized; it must *rely* on ideology and state-ism.

Can we assume from that that there *is no* USA except its ideological and expansionist state-ism? The question is not meant spitefully. I once explained 'American Indian' legal rights and the consequent demands of the American Indian Movement to a member of the Institute for Policy Studies. His response was: 'That would mean the break up of the United States.'

Suppose Germany had *begun* with the Holocaust and its denial. The intellectual or political admission of the situation might cause a breaking up of the state. But the comparison is a little silly. The USA is a continual and movable holocaust.

In 1914 the US navy was slaughtering Yaqui 'Indians' in the centre of Mexico for the 'protection' of European settlers. (After Mexico had consolidated its revolutions in the 1920s, it too recommended the killing of Yaquis and Apaches.) The last battle between US troops and my own people was in 1923. The USA has been continuously at war, continuously invading and killing since the Jamestown and Plymouth colonies. Supposedly, it had an 'age of expansion-ism' beginning in 1898 with the invasions of the Philippines, Puerto Rico and Cuba, just after the last 'Indian' wars(!)

If 'Indians' are not considered as victims of colonial aggression, how are we considered? I am tempted to write the question twice, for emphasis. It implies a second question, however: why are we not considered as colonized? For any 'Indian' person the questions are subjective and quotidian: 'How might I exist?'

The master-narrative of the USA proclaims that there were no 'Indians' in the country, simply wilderness. Then, that the 'Indians' were savages *in need of* the USA. Then, that the 'Indians' all died, unfortunately. Then, that 'Indians' today are (a) basically happy with the situation, and (b) not the real 'Indians'. Then, most importantly, that that is the complete story. Nothing contrary can be heard. Europeans might at least search for 'authenticity' among the primitives, but Americans already know the complete story. The narrative is complete and known and not important. The settlers claim the discourse on 'Indians' as their own special expertise, yet the expertise is of such a familial, at-home nature that it is not worthy of explanation. Husbands know their wives very well, of course, but the wives, as known property, cannot be the subjects of serious discussions among husbands; less so can they speak on their own behalf to the husbands. Americans believe themselves to be cowboys (frontiersmen, pioneers). So, they believe that if, in fact, there might be 'Indians', those 'Indians' would be their silent partners in wilderness-taming activities – that is, like wives.

This is the state's idea and scheme. It is its scheme for existence. How might it otherwise exist? The US scheme has always been, necessarily, both 'biggest' and 'best'. Because of its atrocities it must be the *most* innocent and the *most* just, and it must expand. If the USA's notion of itself has seemed to fit so well the times we call modern, isn't it because that notion created these times? What I am calling an American notion is a European project, except the European states could not themselves carry out the project efficiently. They are intertwined with what we say are countries. The state called 'France' is connected to something like a country, also called 'France'. The state called 'America' is connected to an independent settler colony. At the end of its 'empire' Great Britain must return to that island in Europe. The economic power of the USA is losing its grip in much of the world, but at the end, to where might it return? It is *only* a state, *only* a political entity, so its ideological base and its narrative can be absolute.

If someone imagines otherwise, at the end of America's 'external' empire it would follow that there is a country that is America. Would *my* country become free of the USA? If so, where is America? If not, do I really not come from any place? Is the country of my people really only a story in the Great American Story?

The denial of 'American Indians' in American discourse requires a lengthy investigation and what I have presented so far is only a rough outline. We may, however, consider some curiosities as brief evidence.

First, there is little intellectual interest in the situation. The existing discourse on 'American Indians' is always sentimentally moral. Edmund Wilson's least-known book, *Apology to the Iroquois*, is properly seen as no more than an apology. It contains no analysis of the conditions of US society which make the apology seem necessary to him. Aside from Roy Harvey Pierce's *Savagism and Civilization*, ahead of its time and academically sequestered, and Leslie Fiedler's *The Vanishing Indian in American Literature*, more a literary reportage, there has been no serious treatment of the USA's relation to 'its indigenous populations'. Instead there has been a stunning silence.

The settlers must consume us. There is no one to challenge their ownership of us except ourselves, which of course cannot be allowed. In American literature the 'Indian' is always a passive witness to the cowboy's action. Neither Queequag in *Moby Dick* nor Tonto nor the Indian in Ken Kesey's *One Flew over the Cuckoo's Nest* have speaking parts. There is a vast difference between Tonto and Gunga Din. Gunga Din, as the good Indian fighting the bad Indians on behalf of the Empire, is capable of heroic deeds. In the USA a good 'Indian' is necessarily passive; like Cochise in the films, his role is to 'allow the settlers in'.

It is in film that we can most easily see that the myth of the USA remains intellectually unchallenged. The Lone Ranger is always alone in the wilderness he does not quite call home. (His home might be named 'travelling the earth and protecting the settlers'.) It is amazing that he can be quite so alone: I mean, without any of us at all. At first, John Wayne, as the Lone Ranger in films such as *Wagonmaster* and *The Searchers*, saved innocents from the savages. In the last great wave of Hollywood westerns – *Shane*, *High Noon*, etc. – the hero and the settlers are all by themselves on the endless prairies. They cannot remember when they last had to kill 'Indians'. At some point late at night by the campfire, presumably, the Lone Ranger ate Tonto. By the time Alan Ladd becomes the Lone Ranger in *Shane* he has consumed his Indian companion. Now the Lone Ranger is himself the stoic, silent Noble Savage, so much neater and more suitable for the job.

In the 1970s, films such as *Soldier Blue* used 'Indians' as the backdrop for the USA's coming to terms with its war against Vietnam. Nothing, though, has had the impact of the earlier films. At any rate, film critics from James Agee to Pauline Kael have seen nothing noteworthy about the USA's image of itself as seen through the camera's not looking at the situation with 'Indians'. Every other part of the American myth may now be critically examined. The central, operational part remains sacred. Americans retain the right to be the pioneers.

'American Indians' cannot have a Sidney Poitier or Harry Belafonte, much less an Eddie Murphy. We still cannot be trusted to portray ourselves.

A second curiosity emerges in the political arena. The civil rights movement of the 1960s (and even as far back as the debates before the Civil War) created a situation wherein the struggles of American blacks are seen as an agenda item for the entire country, not exclusively a concern of black people. Something of the sort has also happened concerning Chicanos and Japanese Americans; but no such perception has evolved in relation to 'American Indians'.

The African peoples are seen to have legitimate political struggles, as part of an important concept called 'human rights'. Africans may be called Africans. 'American Indians' obviously cannot be called 'Americans'; we cannot, therefore, be 'considered' politically. We must be spoken of mythically – 'American Indians' – or anthropologically – 'Native Americans'. We are removed from the political arena. Instead of human rights we have the more specialized and esoteric 'Rights of Indigenous People'. It is a set of rights which precludes intellectual consideration and substitutes sentimental feeling. Colonization of Africa and even the USA's repression of Latin America are seen as 'outrageous' and 'intolerable'. It is merely a shame about us!

The USA takes pride in describing its government as one 'of laws, not men'. According to the American Civil Liberties Union and other institutions, any breach of the US Constitution is a breach of that valuable constitutionality by which the people are protected from despotic tyranny. Yet we 'American Indians' are continually and consistently denied our legal and constitutional rights. The denial causes alienation and poverty. (We are the poorest people in the USA.) But Congress and the courts pretend that our legal rights are too mysterious to decipher.

The blatant racism that allows comic-strip characters with exaggerated facial features and names such as 'Leapin' Lizard', sports teams called, for example, the 'Washington Redskins' and the use of 'American Indian' names and images to sell every sort of product, in the face of the actual suffering of 'Indian' people, passes unmentioned by the American public.

I once thought of making an installation using the more obviously racist images of 'Indians', juxtaposed with the Noble Savage-type portrayal such as one sees with Cherokee clothing and Big Chief writing tablets. The title would have been 'Which is the Correct Way to Portray Indians?' But I didn't, because it seemed to me that even the most perceptive American viewers would be able to smile and remove themselves from any involvement in the situation.

Jimmy Durham, 1992 (detail).

The Master said, 'What is necessary is to rectify names – If names be not correct, language is not in accordance with the truth of things. If language is not in accordance with the truth of things, affairs cannot be carried on to success.'[8]

We divide the world into North and South. It is understood that the concept 'Third World' is in large part concerned with the southern hemisphere *versus* the northern. In that simplistic scenario 'American Indians' in the USA and Canada are once more negated, and 'Indians' in Latin America are negated by being made part of a Latin American project. But intellectuals of the Third World, perhaps even more so than those of the First World, have often accepted a monolithic idea of some Third World of which they are proudly part, or which they must overcome.

I have written that the USA is unique, yet its narrative as a colonial power differs from those of Latin American countries only by degree of completeness. In a way, Latin American culture remains more closely tied to Europe; it remains colonial in a more traditional European sense. For that reason the US narrative has 'won' over those of Latin America. The mythical plains 'Indian' of the US West has become the prototype for 'Indianness', has become the 'red Indian', even for Latin America's 'Indians'.

Once again, it may be useful to relate some anecdotal curiosities:

The Latin Americans do not know what an 'Indian' looks like. Even in countries such as Bolivia and Peru, a man with typically 'Indian' features is nicknamed *Chino* (Chinese). A man who is large, robust and with features typical of southern Spain will be called *El Indio* (The Indian).

One knows a 'real Indian' by his 'Indian' suit. Quite often a person who is obviously racially 'Indian' but culturally alienated will have no awareness of 'Indian' ancestry. One can also find obviously European members of the Latin bourgeoisie boasting of their 'Indianness', and even of Latin America's 'Indianness'. (Paul Gauguin learned to adopt that attitude as his own.[9])

The literature of Latin America, as in the North, chronicles very well the alienation of the settlers *sans* 'Indians'. Colombian novelist Garcia Marquez lived part of his childhood in the countryside; at that time, and at the time he was writing his novels, and at the time in which the novels are set, 'Indians' in Colombia had been politically organized and were hunted down and slaughtered. There are no 'Indians' in Garcia Marquez's Colombia.

Juan Rulfo, the Mexican writer who is cited as an aspiration for so many Latin American writers, could not produce even the ghost of an 'Indian' in his Mexican village.

Miguel Asturias's novel, *Men of Maize*, so mythologized Guatemala's 'Indians' that they seem more like exotic animals than humans. Later, Asturias became an official in the government which razed 'Indian' villages.

In Isabelle Allende's recent novel of the Allende years in Chile, *House of the Spirits*, which attempts to give some sort of overview of the conditions in Chile at the time, the only Indians present are so placidly evil and inscrutable that the author cannot maintain an interest in them herself. One is described as having 'tiny oriental eyes', and later in the book what the author calls 'mongoloid' (Down's syndrome) children are also described as having 'tiny oriental eyes'. Allende's 'Indians', like virtually all Latin American 'Indians', do not speak languages – they speak 'dialects'. (In Latin America *lengua*, language, is reserved for European languages. 'Indians' speak *dialectos*.)

While the USA advertises itself as a 'nation of immigrants', Mexico claims that the battle between Cortez and the Aztecs 'was neither a victory nor a defeat, but the birth pains of a new race and a new nation – Mexico',[10] nullifying the existence of hundreds of 'tribes' who today still fight for enough land to stand on.

In Brazil, 'Indians' are still 'wards of the state', neither adult human beings nor children in the legal system.

Uruguay makes a contradictory boast. It captured and killed the last 'Indian' within its borders in 1926. Uruguayans are prone to consider themselves *gauchos*, 'Indian'-European mestizo cowboys. Along with Chile, at various times, it has also claimed to be 'the Switzerland of South America', just as Costa Rica has called itself 'the Switzerland of Central America'. Here, one may see American insanity at its most simple. Even discounting the 'Indians' from other countries who must surely wait tables and carry garbage in Montevideo, Uruguay cannot be 'Indian-less'. They must have the twisted discourse which first programmed them running on an endless cassette, the convoluted American pathology well in place.

The Europeans who make up the countries of the Americas have never left Europe. They brought it along with them. They are always and obviously never at home here. Their true feelings about the actual land are ones of fear and contempt. In their minds they still live on the 'frontier', and are perfectly willing to 'pull up stakes' and move on. After 500 years they still know very little about the local flora and fauna (many Latin Americans believe that armadillos, like vultures, eat dead things), and they seem to think that our 'Indian' knowledge of such things is either occult or some sort of animal cunning. The difference in *look* and *feel* between the cities and developed countrysides of Europe and those of the Americas is striking. Europeans seem to feel at home in Europe. Americans do not feel at home.

The *Patria* from which springs their exaggerated patriotism – 'The American Way', 'Our great Mexican heritage', etc. – is a combination of the political state and defensive bravado. It is not based on land. In no other countries have both the people and the governments had such a will for the despoliation of the natural habitat. It is the despoliation done by colonizers pretending to be native, without even the most simple concern for the actual native peoples.

The settlers feel that they must consume us. They feel that they have a historic right to us, and often that they *are* us.

In the American countries where we are no longer a significant percentage of the population, we have a deep fear of populism. The 'populace', whether picturesque peasants or radical students, is always a ready lynch mob against 'Indians', either by direct action or programmatically.

In Latin America as in the USA, schemes for 'progress' are always against 'Indians', and the various nationalisms are anti-'Indian'. Both Peru and Brazil are well-known examples of that, but Panama might be a more instructive case. The USA invented Panama from a piece of Colombia. Its interest, and then the interest of the Panamanian government, was the canal zone. 'Indians' in Panama's southern forests were thereby protected by disinterest. The same 'tribe' in northern Colombia is hunted down. When the canal is returned to Panama, the Panamanian government might well develop an interest in the entire country. The 'Indians' of the south will then face the same problems they face in Colombia.

The governments of Latin America often develop a sense of selfhood and unity for their countries and regions by appearing to oppose US imperialism. The USA may then be seen as a benefactor of nationalist sentiment; in any case, it is clear that Argentina, Brazil, Chile, etc. would be willing to fill an imperialist vacuum should the USA disappear.

The settler colonies most often tied their sentiments for independence from European fatherlands to a perceived softness toward 'savages' on the part of the parent countries.

The progressive intelligentsia of Latin America have adopted the pose, 'we are all the same people'. They take our land, our music, our clothes and our history; in turn they insist we take up their struggles, but they will not call a truce. Geronimo, the Apache leader, said in his surrender speech to the US army, 'So you have captured me; the Mexicans would have killed me.'

I have tried to present the outrageous idea that the profound division in the Americas is between 'Indians' and settlers. As the hidden operant for all American narratives, its discourse is not a product of US imperialism but its instructor. The concealment and its methods have served to take away from 'Indians' a reality in the world, and therefore our voices in the world. I began this section with a quotation from Confucius about names. The false terminology used against us is so pervasive that any of its words call up the (false) idea of 'Indian'-ness. The word 'tribe' comes from the three peoples who originally founded Rome ('tribunal', based on the number three, comes from the same root). It is not a descriptive word, nor a scientific one. Its use in anthropology has been completely discredited, and came from the European concept of human progress at the pinnacle of which were the capitals of Europe. 'Tribe', 'chief' and similar words do not describe a part of reality for any peoples; they are descriptive within the discourse of enclosure and concealment, for the purpose of showing primitiveness.

Yet these words must be used. In the USA an 'Indian' reservation is governed by a Tribal Council (controlled by the US Bureau of Indian Affairs). Those opposed to the Tribal Council usually organize themselves under a system of 'chiefs'. We cannot insist that the world learn the terms for leaders in our own languages (almost 300 languages in the USA alone), nor can we realistically insist that the terminology of modern states be applied, such as 'President' or 'Prime Minister'. At best, one ends up with

'Tribal President', 'Tribal Chairman', or in the case of my own people, 'President of the Cherokee Nation'. In the last example the use of the word 'nation' has become synonymous with 'tribe' (one does not say 'the President of the French Nation').

It is not understood that we are colonized but it is well understood that we are *not* nations, in the sense of independent modern states; therefore, any insistence on our part for a different terminology is perceived as sensitivity to racism, as in the American blacks' insistence against the term 'negro'.

The world knows very well who we are, how we look, what we do and what we say – from the narrative of the oppressor. The knowledge is false, but it is known.

We, then, are left somewhere else (nowhere else). By the very act of speaking we contribute to the silence, the nullification, laid upon us.

It is not as though we ourselves are attempting to speak from within some pristine state of savage grace. Colonization is not external to the colonized, and it makes for neither wisdom nor clarity among the colonized. Made to feel unreal, inauthentic, we often participate in our own oppression by assuming identities or attitudes from within the colonization structure.

The twentieth century began with 'Indian' people attempting more individual efforts (as opposed to communal efforts) at intervention. Among artists today, those efforts are still usually made with constant re-enforcement of the individual's identity and authenticity by employing parts of the stereotype. One's 'Indian' community cannot authenticate or designate a position in the world of art, because that world *is* of the colonizer. One must approach the colonizer for the space and licence to make art. The colonizer, of course, will not grant the licence but will pretend to in certain circumstances.

In different ways, Guayasamin from Ecuador, Tamayo in Mexico, Houser, Howe and C.N. Gorman in the USA produced what Blaise Tobias has called 'Indian-flavoured art'. Tobias means art within the European tradition but with recognizable signs of 'Indian'-ness. No matter how foolishly (or wisely) or cynically those efforts have been conducted, they *were* attempts to intervene in the Americas' master-narrative. Conversely, no matter how successful the individual artist became, the attempts cancelled themselves because of the nature of the narrative.

In the 1960s and 1970s there was a veritable explosion of 'American Indian' art in the USA and Canada. The sociological reasons for it, I believe, are connected with the American settlers' anxiety about themselves at the time. With the civil rights movement, the feminist movement, the counterculture, the war, the assassinations, and culminating in the Watergate scandal, the USA needed to adjust its self-image without admitting any new images. The hippies had already adopted their ideals of our ways and dress to suit their self-image (a variation on the cowboy-as-Indian theme), so the idea needed only to be expanded and cleaned up.

I do not believe that we necessarily produced more, or more talented,

Jimmy Durham, 1992 (detail).

artists during that time, although it may be true simply because suddenly a larger market existed. What seems more pertinent is the fact that the market arrived. But the market has never been the 'art market'; it is always a sub-outlet – the 'Indian art market'. It did not come about because of our demands but because of America's needs. Therefore, the subject matter of 'Indian' art was the 'Indian' face, the 'Indian' body romanticized; not us but their image of us.

The three most successful 'Indian' artists at the time were Fritz Scholder, R.C. Gorman and T.C. Cannon. Scholder painted 'Indian chiefs' in full regalia, using brilliant magentas, greens and oranges. The facial features and bodily forms were blurred, indistinct, as though part of the painterly landscape. Gorman painted and drew 'Indian' women wrapped in blankets, placed like stones in decorative Southwest desert landscapes. Cannon gave his painted 'Indian chiefs' a little Oklahoma Pow Wow glitz: metallic paints and contemporary trappings in settings that were always clearly the past.

We had begun our 'new' political activism in New York State and in Oklahoma in the 1950s. Our resistance became nationally visible in 1967–8 with the take-over of Alcatraz Island. After the massive resistance at the village of Wounded Knee in 1973, I became a full-time activist in the American Indian Movement (AIM).

I was continuously incredulous at the way the American public seemed to welcome our struggle. (I was never surprised at their ignorance of what we were struggling for.) Completely passive, even complacent, people felt that the 'Indian' struggle was one they knew. It was one they had sympathy with, *as though it were their own*, and they *knew* that we did not threaten them. We would not ask for a seat anywhere.

In public addresses, no matter what situation or atrocity we described, we received the same audience responses: standing ovations and then the questions: 'What did the Indians eat?' 'How can I find out about my Cherokee grandmother?' etc. As our situation worsened, America loved us more.

By 1980 white men were already teaching 'Indian' shamanism in universities. White students were participating in Sun Dances and Peyote ceremonies. Every shopping mall in the country had a store which sold Cherokee magic quartz crystals, and every airport had a boutique which sold 'Indian' dress and arte-facts along with cowboy gear. As Ralph Lauren's television commercial has it, 'the Spirit of the West that is everywhere today'.

Our lives, and our rights, continue to deteriorate. The 'Indian' art market continues to expand, but it has never been ours. It has served to isolate 'Indian' artists through commercial success in a specialized area. James Luna has said, 'What should be foremost in the intent of American Indian artists is the opportunity to say, not to be spoken for or about . . . it is truly unfortunate that there are so few Indian artists who address current issues of Indian communities or those of contemporary American art.'[11]

Those of us who have considered ourselves as militant or traditional (in the 'Indian' sense of that term) have often relied on some strategy or another for presenting the 'plight of the Indian', that is, using art to attempt to show our situation to the USA or to show our view of the USA to itself. It is natural, probably, or understandable, given the situation, that we make that error; but it is an error, because such attempts are expected and accepted within the narrative. 'Indian' suffering is part of the entertainment.

Finally, though, to accept any idea of ourselves as the subject matter for our art is a trap, potentially.

Today we have non-'Indian' artists using us as subject matter once more. It is a phenomenon that seems exactly connected to the special American discourse about 'primitives' and 'primitivism'. Brazilian photographer Claudia Andujar has taken the Yanomami people in the Amazon as her exclusive property. Her photos of abstracted parts of 'Indian' bodies with arranged exotic flora have made her reputation. She has founded a committee to create a 'Park' for the Yanomami.

German artist Lother Baumgarten has also made a reputation using 'Indians' as subject matter, but in a more sophisticated way. According to a mutual friend, Baumgarten's intention is (in part) to address a new, more committed, concept of anthropology, yet the anthropology remains a science of the Other. (If anthropology were truly the 'study of mankind', why are European men not studied?) Although I sometimes use the Cherokee writing system in my own work, when I saw that Baumgarten had used it as the principle element in an installation in Pittsburgh I felt appropriated and sort of cancelled out.

Mexico has a history of portraying 'its Indians' in art at least since Diego Rivera, so much so that Mexican art is often perceived as mainly those portrayals. The sculptor Zuñiga makes large bronzes of groups of 'Indian' women, in a style that recalls Henry Moore. How are we expected to look at those placid and elemental giant bodies? Were the models friends with Zuñiga? Did they appreciate the likeness he achieved? Did they cook beans and tortillas for him?

Francisco Toledo is probably Mexico's most important contemporary artist. He comes from the Zapotec city of Juchitan in southern Mexico, and has remained close to the community and committed to the people's struggles. In the early 1980s, Toledo, along with Gloria and Victor de la Cruz, published a magazine, *Guchachi' Reza*, in Juchitan. It had poems in Spanish and Zapotec, with artwork by well-known artists such as Cuevas, Gallegos and Rius; and included letters about the area by D.H. Lawrence, Edward Weston and others. Besides presenting explanations of Zapotec language by anthropologists, the magazine chronicled the history of the struggles. But to present such a collection to the very Spanish art world of Mexico City, a bastion of settler 'Indianitude', without challenging that system, is to volunteer for appropriation.

'Indianicity' is an actual and employed term in Latin America. In Colombia Antonio Caro has been doing installations using the signature of Quintin Lamé, an 'Indian' leader in the early part of the century. (Lamé's signature was a kind of calligraphic design.) Caro is not 'Indian' but he is dedicated to producing art that is socially oriented. In an interview in *Arte en Colombia*[12] he stated that his work about Lamé 'combines art, sociology and ethnology', and that he has allied himself with 'indigenism' (*indigenismo*). Quintin Lamé's kinsman Justiniano Lamé was assassinated in the 1970s by Colombian troops. I expect I would not really like to see documents of Justiniano's life hanging in an art gallery, but Caro's selection of a man from a more distant past, who happened to have an artistic signature, seems insulting.

As America becomes more comfortable in re-employing its 'Indian' myths, the more invisible we become, even if (or probably especially if) we are allowed to participate.

One wants, of course, to develop ideas for effective strategies for intervention in the American narrative. It is not a narrative about us, it is a narrative absolutely *not* about us. There is nothing to correct, no footnotes to add. The negation of 'Indians' informs every facet of American culture. It is most obvious in the language: US businessmen speak of 'shooting their way out of the thicket', 'circling the wagon train', 'sending out scouts' and 'scalping'. The most destitute section of the Bronx has a police station called 'Fort Apache', and American children act like 'wild Indians'. That is just the surface.

Americans have the reputation of 'moving on'; not only physically but intellectually as well. Culturally, in art, literature, daily life, not simply in academical circles, knowledge is reduced to facts which are to be assimilated *so that* one may move on. The public is rightly called 'consumers'. The energy and vitality for which the New World is famous comes from vampirical activities.

Americans must always be at the height of their empire. It is a nice empire, and democratic. Much of Europe has been forced to accommodate a token of receptivity to interventions in its myths. As America pretends to copy that model, it becomes more closed, but 'kinder and gentler'.

I continue to think that this tightness might show itself as a potential weakness of the system, so I continue to experiment.

Ethnicity and Internationality
New British Art and Diaspora-based Blackness

KOBENA MERCER

Now that the 'young British artist' (yBa) phenomenon is mostly tired and expired, it seems timely to ask: what was all that about? To tell the story as a simple sequence that starts with the 1988 'Freeze' exhibition, organized by Damien Hirst and other Goldsmiths' students in a Docklands warehouse, and that ends with the Royal Academy of Art's 1998 'Sensation' exhibition of Charles Saatchi's collection, is to collude with mythology. Taking account of the aesthetic, cultural and, above all, ideological aspects of 'the myth of the young British artist',[1] this article considers the curious position(s) of diaspora artists amidst the contradictory forces of art world globalization and regressive localism which, I shall argue, are the key factors in critically understanding recent shifts around cultural identity.

* * *

MULTICULTURAL NORMALIZATION

Amidst the uneven coexistence of corporate internationalism and regressive localism, the 1990s generation of black British artists were neither invisible nor excluded from the hyper-ironic 'attitude' in which the yBa was immersed, but enjoyed access to an art world in which ethnicity was admitted through an unspoken policy of integrated casting.

Like their transatlantic counterparts, such as Kara Walker, Michael Ray Charles and Ellen Gallagher, they arrived into a habitus in which the de-funding of public subsidy gave the market a greater role in distributing opportunities for hitherto 'minority' artists. Whereas Howardena Pindell's late-1980s research found that few New York galleries and museums represented Latino, Asian, Native or African-American artists,[2] today one would be hard pressed to find a commercial gallery or public museum that did not represent at least one or two 'artists of colour'. Diversity is now normal, not 'special'.

Taking stock of this unprecedented turnaround in art world attitudes, Jean Fisher argues that 'cultural marginality [is] no longer a problem of invisibility but one of excess visibility in terms of a reading of cultural difference that is too easily marketable'.[3] Cultural difference appears more visibly integrated into mainstream markets than ever before, but it is accompanied by a privatized ethos in which it is no longer an 'issue' for public debate. How have these changes influenced the choices diaspora artists make? To explore this question it is necessary to take account of parallel changes in black popular culture, not only because some artists take it as source material for conceptual inquiry, but because the visible integration of cultural difference into the global spheres of postmodern capitalism, whether Benetton, Nike or Coca-Cola, informs the cultural horizon against which diaspora art practices are widely interpreted.

Taking account of hip-hop in the music industry, of black-themed cinema in Hollywood and the plethora of African-American images on US network television, especially Rupert Murdoch's Fox channel, Herman Gray observed that 'given the level of saturation of the media with representations of blackness, the mediascape can no longer be characterized using terms such as invisibility. Rather, we might well describe ours as a moment of *hyperblackness*.'[4] The marked degree of concurrence between the observations of Gray and Fisher allows us to suggest that US-centred globalization has moved the goalposts around the rights and wrongs of 'black representation' so profoundly that we now have a scenario in which the long-standing metaphor of minority 'invisibility' has given way to a new and wholly unanticipated predicament of 'hypervisibility'.

Associated with Ralph Ellison's modernist classic, *Invisible Man* (1952), the trope of invisibility addressed the demand for recognition that Frantz Fanon articulated in *Peau noir, masques blanc* (1952). Voiced in relation to the clear-cut political boundaries of colonial domination or supremacist racism, the metaphor posited an equivalence between political empowerment and public visibility. While this overarching equation was held together during late modernity, such that struggles for voice and for visibility meant that blackness embodied a diacritical 'difference' as a source of protest or resistance in relation to the culturally dominant, the era of postmodernity has given rise to the post-civil rights predicament which has torn such equivalences apart. Visibility has been won, in the African-American world, through complicity with the compromise formation of cultural substitutionism. 'Hyperblackness' in the media and entertainment industries serves not to critique social injustice, but to cover over and conceal increasingly sharp inequalities that are most polarized *within* black society itself, namely between a so-called urban underclass and an expanded middle class that benefited from affirmative action.

The sociological dimension in black Britain is quite distinct, although the underlying discrepancy whereby media-visible figures like Ian Wright coexist with the Stephen Lawrence inquiry points to similar turmoil. Henry Louis Gates observed, 'there you have the central contradictions of post-Thatcherite England: the growing cultural prominence of black culture doesn't mean that racism itself has much abated'.[5] In the realm of the visual arts, the highly vocal dissidence of 1980s artists and arts activists like Keith Piper and Eddie Chambers sought visibility against exclusionary boundaries that regulated access to the art world such that black artists were burdened with the responsibility of speaking on behalf of the socially excluded. Although Fisher regards their efforts as a 'limited success',[6] I would argue that it was the *institutional response* to the agenda, during the late-1980s moment that brought about a sea-change in the 'relations of representation',[7] that created the scenario in which 1990s black artists sought distance from the hyper-politicization of difference.

Seemingly released from the 'burden of representation', black artists now enjoy a sense of permission that contrasts with the gravitas associated with the frontier-effects of institutional racism fifteen years ago. However, having won such individual freedom of expression (which was always normative for Euro-American modernisms), the pendulum swung to the opposite extreme, such that difference was almost unmentionable. What arose was a trade-off whereby the 'excess visibility' associated with both multicultural exhibitionism, and its sublation into corporate internationalism, was offset by a mute or evasive positioning on the part of younger artists who no longer felt 'responsible' for a blackness that was itself increasingly hypervisible in the global market of multicultural commodity fetishism.

Despite the variety of individual artistic concerns, the generational shift was of a piece with the overall loss of direction consequent upon the collapse of clear-cut frontiers in cultural politics. The neo-black subject of the 1990s, born under a bad sign of global risk and uncertainty, faced the false choice of three new identity options: neo-assimilationist, closet resegregationist or genuinely confused! Moreover, when so-called Generation X fully embraced the mass consumption of ironic and parodic hyperblackness in gangsta rap, club culture or designer-label clothing, all common currency in global youth culture, the ground was pulled from under the diacritical or even 'oppositional' positioning of blackness. It was this gradual decoupling of political empowerment and cultural visibility that ushered in a new regime of *multicultural normalization*.

Norms are slippery things. Not as formal as rules or laws, they require social consent and psychic investment in order to regulate structural contradictions and social antagonisms. But what happens when hitherto contested notions of cultural difference become socially normative? Be as visibly different as you want to be, says the all-inclusive idiom of free-market enterprise, but woe betide you if you try and make any critical or dissident claim on the basis of your pathetic little identity, says the social authoritarianism of neo-liberal managerialism. The art world mirrors this Janus-like constellation. Its growing informality among younger audiences is said to have overcome modernism's great divide between fine art and everyday life, although the production of such we-feeling is nonetheless accompanied by the managerialist rhetoric of making 'tough choices'. Under such circumstances, the now-you-see-it, now-you-don't equivocation around difference, often employed in framing the projects of contemporary diaspora artists, is understandable as a response to another inter-related process. To the extent that diversity is increasingly administered as a social and cultural norm of postmodernity, it has become part of the establish-ment. Artists have therefore sought to slip out of its tendency towards fixity in the visual management of cultural difference.

In neo-conceptualist installations using wax-print fabric, such as *Double Dutch* (1994), Yinka Shonibare eludes the heavy-handed approach to ethnic authen-ticity in official multiculturalism by unravelling the intercultural story woven into the threads of his found object. Seen as exotically 'African', the material originated in Indonesian batik, was reinvested for mass manufacture by Dutch and English textile industries, was exported to West and Central African mar-kets as luxury goods, and then appropriated by Afro-Americans as a badge of counter-modern blackness.[8]

Chris Ofili's paintings, such as the *Captain Shit* series (1997–8), are engorged upon a carnivalesque repertoire of art-historical allusions, all of which are embedded in a self-deprecating take on the foibles of black macho in gangsta nihilism or blaxploitation hyperbole. Whereas Shonibare is happy to describe his outlook as that of a 'postcolonial hybrid',[9] the story of Ofili's scholarship year in Zimbabwe, and his discovery of elephant dung, did the rounds so often as to become a bit of a joke, although it alludes to David Hammons's *arte povera* of unwanted 'waste' materials.[10] The subtle interplay of sacred and profane in Ofili's devotion to decorative beauty[11] is covered over by the artist's willingness to play along with the jokey yBa demeanour. When adjectives like 'funkadelic' arise in critics' responses, on the other hand, one wonders whether, rather than engage with Ofili's interests, the concern lies with conveying a post-boomer whiteness that is *au fait* with the black vernacular – a whiteness of the sort Quentin Tarantino enacted in *Pulp Fiction* (1993) in a frenzy of over-identification with the abjected 'nigga'.

Steve McQueen's early trilogy, *Bear* (1993), *Five Easy Pieces* (1994) and *Stage* (1996), seemed to offer critical distance by creating subtle provocation around the intimacy and anxiety of bodies in the spatial cube of a video installation. Taking up the much-debated fears and fantasies around the black male body – which today, in the form of Nike's Michael Jordan jump-man logo, makes hyperblackness a visual cliché as lame as Linford's lunchbox – McQueen's post-Minimalist approach emptied the image of such stereotypical investments. Arousing intense yet undefinable feeling, the work called for careful critical response; but when asked, in a broadly sympathetic interview, whether *Just Above My Head* (1997) dealt with 'questions of visibility', McQueen seemed irritated at the mere mention of the idea and replied, 'When I walk out into the street or go to the toilet, I don't think of myself as black. Of course, other people think of me as black when I walk into a pub. Obviously being black is part of me like being a woman is part of you.'[12] An equally tetchy tone came across when he announced, 'Just like everyone else I want people to think beyond race, nationality and all that kind of crap. This debate is tired, ugly and beat up . . . it is boring.'[13]

'Playing dumb . . . and taking your knickers down has become an attractive move in the face of the institutionalization of critical theory,' quips John Roberts,[14] whose neo-populist reading of New British Art, although intrinsically problematic, nonetheless pinpoints some possible reasons for McQueen's boredom and spleen. Roberts perceives the yBa's dumb pose as a knowingly 'philistine' rejection of the textualist 'politics of representation' associated with the impact of poststructuralist theory over the past twenty years. The rapid incorporation of cultural studies into 1990s higher education both neutralized its critical ambitions and made it a target for the 'cynical reason' of the short-lived British journal *The Modern Review*. Relatedly, to the extent that the postcolonial vocabulary, characterized by such terms as diaspora, ethnicity and hybridity, has successfully displaced earlier immigration narratives of assimilation, adaptation and integration, its broad influence has extended to the apparatus of 'bureaucratic multiculturalism' it once sought to critique.

For diaspora artists engaged in neo- or postconceptualist practices, an impasse had arisen in art's relationship to (postcolonial) theory. Renée Green mused, 'There's a certain power dynamic that occurs in terms of how the artists are positioned that disturbs me. I would like to restructure this dynamic so that it doesn't feel like art is merely a decorative element – something which is tagged on to the 'heavier ideas'.[15] When art is reduced to visualizing theory, or worse, when the aesthetic encounter is over-determined in advance, McQueen's annoyance is intelligible as an attempt to evade ideological capture. Arising from both the institutional incorporation of critical theory's once adversarial idiom, and the market's preferred solution, which is to imply that the way to a race-free future is to simply stop talking about divisive matters of 'difference', these hidden pressures call for a more empathic understanding of McQueen's post-identitarian predicament when he says:

> I'm in a position I am because of what other people have done and I'm grateful, for sure. But at the same time, I am black, yes. I am British as well. But as Miles Davis said, 'So what?' I don't say that flippantly but like anyone else I deal with certain things in my work because of who I am. I make work in order to make people think.[16]

COSMOPOLITAN LOCALES

Precariously poised between the art market's corporate transnationalism and the inward provincialism of the London 'scene', diaspora artists inhabit the contradictory conditions of post-Empire Britain. 'Capitalism only advances, as it were, on contradictory terrain. It is the contradictions which it has to overcome that produce its own forms of expansion,' Stuart Hall has said on the subject of globalization and ethnicity.[17] The particularities of Britain's skewed insertion into the world system of modernity enable the contradictory coexistence of regressive neo-nationalism and multicultural normalization within its art world.

In his insightfully wide-ranging story of 'the pop cultural constitution of Englishness', Michael Bracewell evokes British modernity as a century-long 'retreat from Arcady', which engendered a quintessential ambivalence best encapsulated when Noël Coward quipped, 'I am England, and England is me. We have a love-hate relationship with each other.'[18] Revealingly, Bracewell depicts New British Art as a loser in an either/or play-off between such ambivalent ironies of Englishness and the bland multiculti-commodification of 'difference' in US-centred global capitalism:

> With . . . the replacement of Englishness, as a current cultural term, with the multiculturalism of Britishness, the baton in the cultural relay race between fine art, literature, music, film and drama could be said to have been exchanged for a basketball and a pair of Nikes.[19]

While sympathetic towards 'the creative marriage' of African-American-originated dance culture and the legacy of 1960s psychedelia which he hears in Goldie's drum 'n bass (whose coexistence alongside BritPop's retro-centric ironies echoes the art world tensions we have examined), Bracewell's telling distinction between Britishness and Englishness is left symptomatically unresolved. In his ambivalently open-ended conclusions, Morrissey's 'Hang the DJ', which 'sings of England and something black, absurd and hateful at its heart'[20] allows the *sotto voce* suggestion that multicultural otherness is an obstacle to the completion of English ethnicity. Although it stops short of Enoch Powell's discourse on 'alien cultures', what we see acknowledged in this irresolution is the open wound of whiteness otherwise fetishistically covered over and smoothed out by the managerial feel-good factor of Cool Britannia.

In an art world habitus shot through with these simmering tensions, we may understand inIVA's (Institute of International Visual Arts) unpopularity as an outcome of its association with the bureaucratic institutionalization of cultural theory. By virtue of its free-floating placelessness, or rather its reluctance to author a distinct curatorial signature, inIVA effectively withdrew from a public debate about misperceptions of minority artists. The Roundhouse project failed because black artists could not agree on a common purpose for it. Commenting that, among arts administrators, 'The resounding response was "whatever you do, don't build a black art gallery",' inIVA's director Gilane Tawadros disclosed the reasoning behind the organization's obedience. She states:

> There was a time when it was important to make black artists visible in the same way that women artists were making themselves visible, but that time has passed. You cannot differentiate black art history from white. These things come together and both their currencies are intimately intertwined.[21]

While entirely valid and necessary as a starting point for a more inclusive account of contemporary art which assumes cultural mixing, or hybridity, as a cornerstone feature of modernism and modernity, the problem is that the story of how 'that time has passed', and the whys and wherefores of its passing, were not opened up for public discussion. By retreating from the challenge of examining why nobody likes 'black art' as a classificatory or curatorial category, Tawadros's evasive positioning reciprocally mirrors and inverts Steve McQueen's, suggesting that inIVA too was vulnerable to hidden pressures. Whereas one tactic sought resolution by simply not talking about 'it', another tactic was to talk about 'it' all too much, using the language of postcolonial theory to cover over and conceal unresolved tensions in the art world's management of cultural difference. In this way, inIVA went along with the decoupling of aesthetic interests and social responsibility that made matters of representation crucial to the counter-modern traditions of the various Caribbean, African and Asian diasporas for whom Britain was also a place called home, whose cold comforts Perminder Kaur evoked in her *Cot* (1993).

While the subversive potential once invested in concepts of hybridity has been tempered by pre-millennial downsizing, the grey area of complicity that Nikos Papastergiadis perceives between identity-driven demands for minority representation and market-based adaptation to diversity suggests that the outcomes of social agonism over norms can never be guaranteed in advance.[22] Such inIVA exhibitions as 'Aubrey Williams' (1998) have drawn attention to the Caribbean Artists' Movement (CAM), a loose network of artists, writers, students and teachers who met at the West Indian Students' Centre in London between 1966 and 1972. Although primarily literary in orientation, with Edward Kamau Brathwaite, Andrew Salkey and John LaRose as its organizers, CAM articulated an 'outernationalist' outlook among the post-independence generation. While some participants returned to the Caribbean to influence cultural policy, others re-migrated to North America, and yet others stayed on to shape the black British arts sector in the 1970s.

The CAM story was simultaneously culturally nationalist, exilically internationalist and Black Atlanticist, and as such it offers a vivid example of Homi Bhabha's 'vernacular cosmopolitanism',[23] although the modest localism of the narrative might not fulfil the more bombastic claims that postcolonial theory sometimes aspires to. For me, the value of Ann Walmsley's lucid documentation lies in its provision of a genealogy of the mixed times and spaces inhabited by diaspora artists.[24] This is a starting point for the 'homework' which visual studies has yet to catch up with in terms of researching the distinct art-historical milieux out of which Asian, African and Caribbean artists in Britain criss-crossed paths with various critical modernisms.

Jean Fisher is an important contemporary art critic who has given time and trouble to these genealogical matters that form part of the unexplored historical context of black British visual practices.[25] However, the proposed distinction between hybridity and syncretism misleadingly contrasts different colonial attitudes to cultural mixing, without recognizing that the mix among Anglophone,

Francophone and Hispanic dispositions is precisely what makes 'the Caribbean' a diasporic location where the encounter with difference is a regulating convention of everyday life, i.e. a norm. To regard 'the Caribbean' as the name of a habitus in which hybridity is normal is not to say that everywhere else is like that now, but that the worlding of the ethnic signifier may take forms other than prevailing trends towards market-based multicultural normalization.

What I liked about the trans-localism of the CAM story was that it was made possible by London's cosmopolitan status as a world city, which in my view makes CAM the site of a specifically British vernacular modernism. To the extent that this would imply that a certain Britishness was *always already* hybridized in the encounter with Asian, African and Caribbean diasporas, it confirms Stuart Hall's account of the postcolonial as the time of a double inscription, in which elements hitherto banished to the constitutive outside of society return through the gaps in the signifying chain of cultural identity to decentre its symbolic authority.[26]

Doing our 'homework' means opening out such stories so that they 'belong' not just to British artists and audiences, but to anyone interested in art's ability to survive the wreckage of modernity. Telling these stories reactivates ideas of syncretism, creolite and metissage which are all conceptually hybrid. To paraphrase Johnny Rotten, one might say that such postcolonial hybrids are the flowers in the dustbin of art's history.

Art as Ethnocide[1]
The Case of Australia

ANNE-MARIE WILLIS AND TONY FRY

BEGINNING WITH REFUSALS

We need to begin by refusing to enter the art world debate on Aboriginal art on its own terms. This world asks questions framed within the art discourse like: How can we talk about Aboriginal art? How can it be understood within the discourses of art? How can productive, non-exploitive exchanges occur between Aboriginal and non-Aboriginal artists, gallery owners, curators? Such questions are subtended by an ethnocentric assumption that it is Aboriginal people and their culture that are 'the problem' and that the art world has to find ways of dealing with it. The crucial shift that has to be made is from seeing 'them' as a problem for authority and institutions to seeing the forces of power (in its hard and soft forms) as *their* problem. In other words, overt or covert, structural and institutional racism needs to be the main focus rather than 'Aboriginal art'. What we must first address then is the consequences of *our own practices* and their impact on Aboriginal culture. The issue of 'Aboriginal art' then falls into place as a secondary, rather than primary pathway into the political field.

The refusal to centre 'Aboriginal art' is of course linked to another necessity. This is to refuse to disarticulate Aboriginal culture from the crucial political agenda of social justice, including land rights, health, housing and employment. In doing this it becomes impossible to view the claimed artistic 'achievement' (viewed in white terms) of a few as a marker of progress of the position of Aboriginal people in Australian society. We must ask, for instance, just how significant is the fact that more Aboriginals are having their work bought and displayed in mainstream art museums and galleries in and beyond Australia, when there are still an alarming number of deaths of Aboriginals in police custody, when levels of health, education, life expectancy are all dramatically lower than the national average, and when rates of infant mortality and unemployment are much higher? As will be argued later, much of what is named as 'progress' is the assimilation of signs of difference into a homogenizing system, the art market.

* * *

INTERNAL ART WORLD DEBATES ON ABORIGINAL ART

Having put in place these overarching considerations, we will now turn to more specific and localized debates around Aboriginal art, focusing on the claims made about 'progress' and 'progressiveness'. Much attention has been given in Australia to the art of the Western desert, particularly of Papunya, to the art of Ramingining and to urban Aboriginal art. Artists in scattered communities around Australia are seen to be reviving or re-appropriating traditional cultural practices using modern forms and materials. There has been much anguish by curators around the art/kitsch divide; at first only the most traditional artefacts – in terms of their iconography and materials – were accepted as authentic. 'Transitional' forms – traditional motifs painted on canvas using acrylic paints or the work of urban artists who use traditional stories and motifs and recent Aboriginal history, reworking these through various conventions of western painting – have now found acceptance in the marketplace and in survey exhibitions of contemporary art. The claimed progress is that such works are now considered as legitimate cultural forms. Aboriginal artists are able to move forward, to enter the art world on terms beginning to approach those of non-Aboriginal artists (that the cultural and economic roles of the artists in their respective cultures do not correspond simply gets overlooked).

What needs to be recognized is that this kind of overview – which can see the arts of Papunya, Ramingining and the work of urban artists existing as part of a totality – is, once again, one that can only be made through the deployment of the categories of curatorship and art history.[2] The power of the Eurocentric view and how it structures perceptions is essential to identify. An artist from Papunya, for example, and a 'cultured' Anglo-Australian are not looking at the same textual object, and more obviously, not from the same place/point of view. They occupy different historico-aesthetic space as well as geographic, cultural, social space. The artist moves out to perceive the world of art through the passage of his/her artwork; for the few, this can mean seeing it as an exhibit within a Biennale or a Perspecta (biannual national exhibitions of contemporary art), in a state or national collection, which for most will mean seeing it in a milieu of visual incoherence (because the narrative that makes sense of the disparate objects is not in place). The 'cultured' viewer, however, is able, almost automatically, to place the object within that ordered hierarchical field of visual discrimination that constitutes the history of art – before its symbolic content is even recognized – thus the object is categorized, placed and qualified as a genre within a remade, contemporary primitivism.

And so Aboriginal art has moved from an artefact of anthropological concern to an art of curatorial interest and public display. 'Aboriginal art' is a product of western culture; as has already been indicated, the very category of art is specifically western; this is not to deny a rich Aboriginal material culture, but to recognize that the function of objects in those cultures is not as signs of disinterested aesthetic speculation. The fact that Aboriginal management may be inducted into this activity through trainee curatorship programmes and the like does not alter the ethnocentric character of this assimilation exercise. Again, we affirm that domination is not simply a figure of the past. In fact, there is double damage done: in addition to the 'usual' process of assimilation (the imposition of new logics/practices and the displacement of a cultural system), there is a process occurring in relation to what was once *their* culture. First their visual culture was taken from them and next they are told how it should be managed. Such 'reforms' neglect to recognize that any cultural or political self-determination must include the freedom to name, to classify as part of its *own* logic. To do anything else is to carry out acts of ethnocide through the action of deliberate cultural destruction.

Contemporary Aboriginal art is, of course, not a totality. 'Papunya', the place, signifies very differently according to who speaks the proper noun. White writers may speak optimistically of the art-making communities of Papunya and Ramingining and give an impression of groups of people in charge of their own destinies using art as a form of intervention, 'a counter-offensive' to 'cultural colonialism'.[3]

But in the art market 'Papunya' and 'Ramingining' are names of commodities, and furthermore they are names that would never have circulated anywhere beyond the local had not the process of commodification inserted them into the system of exchange. Commodification is the *motor* which drives the revival of Aboriginal arts and it ushers in irreversible changes. What we are

witnessing is the partially comprehended induction of often fringe-dwelling
Aboriginals into the political economy of art. In addition, Aboriginal art
has become, as said, an international commodity (in fact, it was popular with
American art investors long before it was taken up by local collectors) and its
meanings/functions in that context are no doubt even more remote to the
producers. Talk of 'self-determination' and 'intervention' are hollow indeed, in
this context.

Some have argued that because the meanings of Aboriginal culture are
vested in individuals and clan groups rather than the objects themselves, the sale
and display of objects in art galleries does not take away from their functioning
in Aboriginal culture. For example, Vivien Johnson claims:

> the authenticity of Aboriginal art persists notwithstanding the all-too-obvious
> consequences of insertion into a Western context ... For traditionally
> oriented communities like Papunya and Ramingining [authenticity] consists
> in having fulfilled one's obligations as custodian of certain Dreaming sites
> and tracks and the stories associated with them. Regular materialization and
> appropriate ritual practice are part of this process, in the Art Gallery of NSW
> or the Tanami Desert.[4]

We need to ask, however, for whom is authenticity an issue? It is clear that the
claim is being directed at a white audience, that liberal audience for whom the
idea of gazing upon an inauthentic cultural activity would be unacceptable. Yet
the context of that authenticity is ultimately unknowable to that audience; it
may be crudely presented with accompanying catalogue notes outlining mythological stories, but given that the explanatory power of those narratives is
incommensurable with western logic the stories can do no more than function
as *signs* of content.

Similarly, promoters of Aboriginal art point to the rich meanings encoded
into Papunya paintings concerning dreaming sites, sacred places, mythological
beings. But how do the variants of western rational consciousness position such
meanings? To be told that a particular set of lines represents a snake, or a series
of circles, waterholes, may at best generate a generalized respect for the complexity of an unfamiliar cultural system, at worst function as signs of an exotic
modern primitive. Either way, what is not faced directly is that that belief system
and the way of acting in the world it represents has become increasingly inoper-
able with the ongoing process of colonization (particularly in its 'neo' form of
cultural and economic imposition). It no longer exists in a pure state. Viewers of
Aboriginal art are being asked to 'appreciate' signs of a living culture, when in
fact what they are actually gazing on is the power of their own culture to
appropriate signs of otherness. The fact that people from Ramingining may
perform their ritual ceremonies in the Art Gallery of NSW is testimony to that
institution's power rather than a demonstration of the 'power' of Aboriginal
culture; the only power it would seem to have is to 'move' an audience, but this
too simply reflects back the power of western art institutions, which have pro-

gressively been able to accommodate difference under the levelling mechanism of the aesthetic emotion. So it is nonsense for Vivien Johnson to claim that it is 'profoundly shocking' for the art world to discover that 'not they but the gentle victims of the tyranny they dispense hold the purchase on truth *and* beauty'.[5] This is no more than the power of the primitive – as an aesthetic category of western invention.

PAPUNYA AND THE ART OF ASSIMILATION

To 'progressive' sections of the art world Papunya represents a success story – dispossessed tribal Aboriginals reclaiming their traditional culture and giving it a modern visual form in acrylic on canvas, gaining a measure of economic independence and control over their products in addition. This is claimed as progress because Aboriginals are no longer locked into producing the 'authentic artefact' from traditional materials such as ochres and barks. But this progress was only possible through a re-designation of the hybrid art object from kitsch to high art – a shift which has little to do with Aboriginal initiatives. A change in taste has been made to occur in the art market, one which has been consciously engineered by enthusiastic collectors and curators who have striven to present Papunya paintings in 'favourable' circumstances – professionally lit museums and galleries, high-quality colour catalogues – as opposed to tourist and craft shops. The objects have been re-coded through relocation. This is not to suggest that Papunya paintings travelled a smooth path through the art institutions – in early days individual curators battled conservative boards of trustees and gallery directors, but this intra-institutional struggle must *never* be conflated with Aboriginal resistance. It was a battle over objects which was won at the level of taste (one major gallery director who was resistant for a long time now permits Papunya art to be collected and displayed because he regards it as a superior form of abstract painting, which, after all, is not a contradictory position to hold within the logic of the art museum). And it might be added, that once won at the level of taste, it was irretrievably lost at the level of the complexity of the political.

So, it appears that members of a fringe-dwelling community are now making decent incomes out of the sale of their art, they have their own company protecting their rights, there is control over the use of sacred designs, their work is not sold as anonymous craft objects but as individual, signed authored works with due recognition for outstanding talent (a survey of the work of Clifford Possum Tjapaltjari, for example, was shown at the Institute of Contemporary Art in London as part of their focus on Australia in its bicentennial year). These developments may mean a great deal to individuals in that community – we are not in a position to know exactly what it means to them. But such developments can only be seen as 'progress' within the discourses of hierarchy of the art world, in which the acceptance of what one produces as high art is the assumed goal of artists. Yet the world of operation, the art world, is not in fact viewable in the community of the artists (or it has an existence only as differentially mediated, fragmentary, second- and third-hand reports, as stories and 'travellers' tales'). So, 'success' exists in an invisible space.

Looking at the art of fringe-dwelling Aboriginals outside this system of valorization, and viewing it instead through the discourses of race politics, it can be concluded that what has been achieved is not cultural intervention or resistance, or a place from which to speak 'their' cause, but rather, moderately successful assimilation. A shift has taken place from overt racism to cultural ethnocide. And control still rests ultimately with 'white' institutions.

As a number of writers have pointed out, Papunya was an artificial settlement created by bureaucracy,[6] in which a number of disparate tribal groups were collected together, an act of administration which took on particular urgency with the testing at Woomera rocket range in the 1950s and early 1960s (*Settle Down Country Pmere Arlaltyewele* records Aboriginal experiences of being rounded up and dumped at Papunya, the subsequent illnesses and deaths due to being cut off from traditional foods, and memories of Papunya as an 'unhappy place'[7]). Art-making, the production of portable painted objects whose primary function is aesthetic contemplation, was at the time of inception an alien, western concept introduced by white art teachers. The people of Papunya are barely a generation away from a life of hunting and gathering in the desert; few of them would have visited the city galleries and museums that display their work; even fewer would be cogniscent with the cultural strategies available to cosmopolitan white and Aboriginal artists. The rhetoric of 'interventionism' (which is consistently claimed by white voices) needs to be heard in this context.

Similarly, arguments have been put that Aboriginal artists travelling overseas with exhibitions of their work can act as 'ambassadors' for land rights and liberation. But this claim needs to be seen in relation to the constraining practices (via selection, close monitoring and coercion) of the State when it is funding overseas appearances of 'Australian culture'. As activist Michael Mansell remarked in the press in January 1988, there are often more strings attached to money given by the Commonwealth government than by regimes such as Libya.

Additionally, the closures of the art world to political discourses are well maintained internationally (it is not so much that such concerns are denied a voice, but that they are consistently positioned as peripheral to the 'real business' of art).

So, rather than 'cultural intervention', the production of paintings at Papunya (and other fringe settlements) can be seen as a culturally problematic form of economic activity in an economically deprived region, something that may offer slightly more independence than welfare payments, but a form of economic activity that has become 'necessary' because white uses of the land have rendered the traditional hunting and gathering life increasingly less viable. The presence of Aboriginal arts and crafts advisers to settlements involved in art production does not automatically guarantee Aboriginal control either. Black voices speak as mediating agents for white domination when they talk of quality control, deadlines and the need to promote individual artists (which is not to say the market economy can be avoided, but rather that control of exchange relations is inseparable from the issue of self-determination).

What the success of the arts of Papunya and Ramingining represents is the shift of Aboriginal work from craft to art status (two of the biggest Australian collectors are Alan Bond and Robert Holmes à Court), its packaging according to the norms of the art market – with regionally distinct styles ('schools') and increasing prominence of selected individuals – and in the process, the induction of certain members of remote Aboriginal communities into the value system and social relations of the art market. To claim that traditional values encoded in the works remain intact while this process goes on is to be blind to the inevitable restructuring of social relations ushered in by commodification within conditions of extreme uneven development. Dreaming stories, mytho- logical sites ('the past') may be present in the imagery as traces, but what happens to the cultural tradition of *relations between people* in the present and in the future? What is significant is that this question is not being asked by 'progressives' in the art world, who remain locked into the culturalist myth of art as an agency of resistance and radicality *in and of itself.*

A recent tragic incident can serve as one answer to this question. Six mem- bers of a single family were victims of a mass killing in Arnhem Land in the Northern Territory in September 1988. One of the victims was Dick Murru- murra, a well-known bark painter whose work is in the Australian National Gallery. The incident has been attributed to a fight over the distribution of income from the sale of a painting. A cultural economy of ownership, artistic identity and property collided with a cultural economy of common goods. In the weighted movement from one system of exchange to another, the ethnocidal impetus gained momentum.[8]

* * *

The plight of Aboriginals is, as Adrian Marrie made clear earlier, a constant reminder that the country has not transcended colonialism, that ethnocide is not just history and the past, but also of the present. Certainly, it is inappropri- ate to talk, as Vivien Johnson does, of 'the art of decolonization' – the art of recolonization is actually a more apt term.

Frequently, there is a latching onto and celebration of the slightest signs of 'progress'. There is also the promotion of token 'successful' figures. When the argument is put that the production of Aboriginal art represents little more than a subsidization of welfare, the answer sometimes is, 'Well, isn't that better than nothing?' Here, the limited and reformist character of the enterprise becomes clear; what such a statement reveals is that the dominant culture and those who speak from and for it desire no more than the appearance of material progress. They want a cleaned-up version of Aboriginal culture – no children with flies crawling in their eyes, healthy-looking people producing healthy-looking art, assimilation into our system of values and exchange relations, but with the retention of surface appearance of difference – in the form of the good-looking commodity and spectacularized culture (the latter is also of great value to the burgeoning economy of tourism). What they are not at all concerned with,

beyond sentimentality, are continuing structural inequalities. Fears exist of a
real transfer of resources and power, and even of power being taken by force.
Similarly threatening is the potential of the challenge to dominant values made
by a new Aboriginal culture. Such fears exist, usually unspoken, certainly they
are held silently by many a progressive poseur.

Many Australian cultural institutions and their spokespeople have been at the
forefront of the development of policies that have a surface appearance of
progress while leaving structural inequalities in place. The whole debate around
museums and cultural property is one example: the woolly concepts of 'world'
and 'national' heritage are deployed in order to assert the necessity of the
continuation of the museum's right over cultural objects. John Mulvaney has
written a carefully worded article, 'Museums and cultural property', in which he
strains to show how sympathetic he is to indigenous peoples' rights to their
cultural heritage, yet ends up suggesting that objects only be returned to those
peoples if they agree to certain conditions set by museums![9] Unconditional
transfer of power, the opportunity to exercise fundamental cultural difference, is
consistently shied away from by white liberals. It often appears that an insidious
game is played out across policy areas concerning Aboriginal people – a kind of
'let's see how progressive we can appear to be, without really risking anything'.
A great deal of the politics, then, is rhetorical play. The rationale of these
practices is that the preservation of cultural objects takes precedence over the
cultural rights of the dispossessed and the uses of these objects to them *now*, a
point poignantly observed by Henrietta Fourmile:

> My people around home who want to paint Aboriginal designs borrow from
> those designs which belong to the people of Arnhem Land and the Kimber-
> leys, or copy them off DAA posters, because they have never seen the designs
> which are their birthright, until last year when I took back an album of
> photographs of our artefacts in the South Australian Museum; things they
> never knew existed. And why was last year so important? Because it was last
> year that I found out about the existence and whereabouts of my heritage
> through my own efforts, not through the efforts of the individual institutions
> which hold our cultural property.
>
> It hurts me deeply to think that I was 30 years old before I saw artefacts
> bearing the totemic emblems of my ancestors and yet the staff and students
> of one particular institution have been making detailed studies of the
> material culture from my country for the past seven or eight years, benefiting
> from the museum collections which we did not know about.[10]

Similarly, for non-Aboriginals to support 'Aboriginal art', for all the reasons
already cited, is to risk nothing; it is to be involved in the production of the
appearance of progress. An illusion of cultural autonomy and a cultural politics
is being put in place where the basic prerequisites for that do not exist (e.g.
substantial land rights, a treaty recognizing Aboriginal occupation of Australia
prior to white invasion with appropriate compensation and reconciliation).

While art is continued to be claimed as a vanguard site for the advancement of Aboriginal interests, the more fundamental bases for change will remain obscured. The danger is that while the myth of art as progress remains in place, it has the capacity to induct and subsequently deactivate people (both Aboriginal and non-Aboriginal) who have a genuine interest in countering racism in Australia today.

As indicated earlier, the romantic interpretation of 'cultural survival' needs to be challenged. Yes, it is a culture which has survived a very long time, and that must be a source of Aboriginal pride. At the same time, it is a terribly damaged culture in both its past two hundred years and in its contemporary forms.

FROM ABORIGINAL ART TO THE POLITICAL ECONOMY OF ABORIGINALITY

While a rejection of what has been constituted as 'Aboriginal art' is being advocated, this does not in any way mean a complete turning away from issues of culture and visual representation in relation to Aboriginal politics. As stated at the outset, the task should be to counter racism, to view the cultures of domination as the problem; this requires the development of a complex under-standing of the functionings of racism, the ethnocentric/logocentric bases of dominant cultures, an understanding of power and institutions, the functioning of the art system and culture industries.

What also needs to be understood is the function of the sign 'Aboriginal art' within the social text. It is increasingly becoming a driving force in a sign system of commodification that seeks to claim 'Australian-ness'. And here there is a continuity, rather than a separation, between the museum and the street. From the 'Ancestors and Spirits' exhibition at the Australian National Gallery, to Clifford Possum, Tim Johnson, Imants Tillers (both the artists' names and what they produce function as signs), to the down-market souvenir shops that sell Aboriginal design(ed) T-shirts with swing tickets naming artist and clan group (signs of the authentic commodity), to department stores' displays of Aboriginal-style designer fashions, to the journal *Bulletin/Newsweek* with its declaration that in the bicentennial year of 1988, Aboriginal art is 'in' (but the writers don't see the irony) – all these signs proliferate claiming an updated, remade culturally sophisticated Australian-ness (no more unauthorized, anonymous rock carving designs on tea towels), which in addition circulates internationally in step with the middle-market commodification of post-McClaren, post-Jean Paul Goude neo-primitivism. And, in contradiction to the recentness of their production/coding as commodities, cultural depth is claimed for these signs ('the oldest living culture in the world', as the tourist brochures state). The dominant culture desperately needs these kind of 'appealing' appearances of Aboriginality – as signs of distinctiveness and depth which its two hundred years of second-hand Euro-American culture cannot claim.

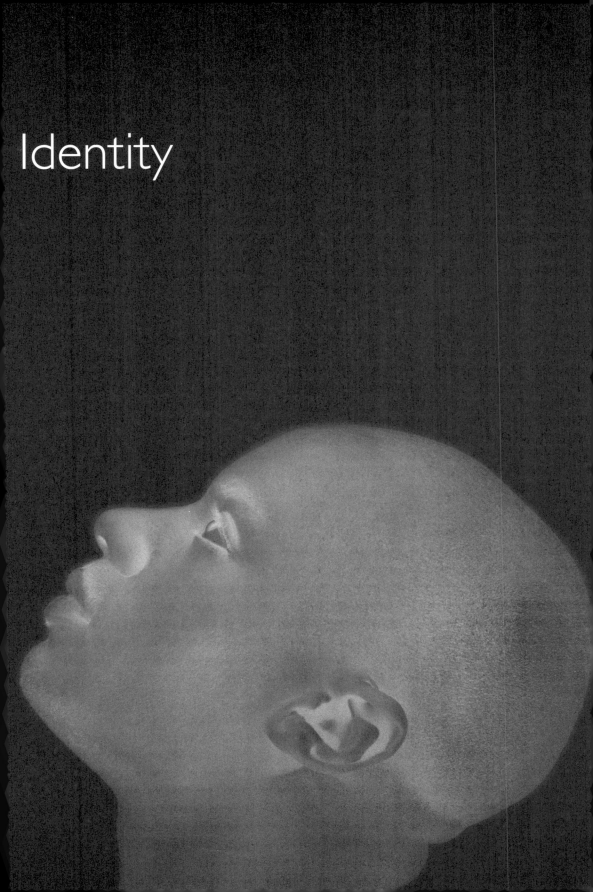

Identity

Introduction

JORELLA ANDREWS

In *The Absent Body,* Drew Leder suggests that while our bodies are 'the most abiding and inescapable presence in our lives', it is primarily in periods or contexts of dysfunction that they become a thematic object of experience.[1] Something similar might be said concerning questions of identity. For when such questions arise, pertinent and troublesome, they are inevitably symptomatic of some disorder, dis-ease or desire. On the one hand, they point to certain discontinuities, struggles, anxieties and needs, whether of a sociopolitical or a psychological/soulish nature, in which individuals and groups are variously implicated. On the other hand, they indicate certain insufficiencies within the cultural realms of language, thought and representation. Thus, approaches to questions of identity must be multifaceted. It is necessary to engage with critical debates concerning the meaning, implications, and indeed viability, of the term itself. And it is crucial also to attend to this topic with a diagnostic eye: to consider the specific, lived conditions in which questions of identity become manifest; to regard them as the effects of certain causes, and consequentially as markers of quite specific social, political and cultural urgencies. As Sebastián López suggests, we must consider 'who is now invoking identity, and to what purpose?'

'Identity: Reality or Fiction?' was first presented by López at a conference entitled 'Cultural Identity: Fiction or Necessity' held in Maastricht in 1991. One context for this conference, and thus for López's contribution to it, were the ongoing talks occurring in the city in preparation for the establishment of the Maastricht Treaty (1993) and the European Parliament and the questions concerning national and cultural identity that were being forced, across the continent, by this movement towards greater economic, legislative and political unity. As López points out, however, questions concerning European national and cultural identities had also been provoked by the permanent presence, within this territory, of some sixteen million people of non-western ancestry. 'If some people are discussing Dutch identity,' he writes, 'it is because we are here.' The continuing rise of racism and fascism in Europe during this period was another related issue. López starts by juxtaposing current debates around Dutch identity with those concerning Latin American identity with which he had been actively involved during the 1970s. In so doing, he emphasizes the radically different political and hegemonic scenarios at issue in each case. Then, having identified the 'problem' of the non-European foreigner as central to European debates, he elaborates upon the various strategies whereby this 'enemy within' is consistently excluded from social, cultural and economic mainstreams. Particular attention is directed towards the restrictions placed upon artists of non-European origin living and working in Holland.

In contrast to López, Ticio Escobar is interested in questions of methodology. How, he asks in his contribution to this section, can identity be discussed in a contemporary world in which 'the great mythical concepts that serve as its [identity's] foundations – People, Nation, Community, Class, Territory, etc. – are placed in doubt'? He discusses three competing models according to which, historically, identity has been thought: an ontological (essentializing) model, an oppositional model and one – taken to mark 'our present concept of culture' – in which a concept of identity as necessarily plural and shifting is proposed. Elaborating upon the last, Escobar argues that the uncertain atmosphere of 'migrating signs' at issue here is one also marked by remarkable resilience, strength and productivity. 'Indigenous peoples understand all this,' he writes, 'for they face national society from situations that differ greatly, yet are all disadvantageous. They know that to preserve their image they must wear several masks and reinvent their profiles in many different ways.' Ultimately, though, such engagement with dissimulation does not obviate the need, at certain times and in certain conditions, to invent and adopt (possibly provisional) myths of collective identity – for strategic purposes, for survival and in order to facilitate the discovery of new social, cultural and political possibilities.

The plural approach to identity described by Escobar is also characteristic of Edward Said's 'The Voice of a Palestinian in Exile'. This autobiographical photo-text is based on a BBC2 television programme (part of the series *The Exiles*, broadcast in 1988) dedicated to the renowned American-Arab cultural theorist. By foregrounding the problem of exile – exile in general, and from the Israeli Occupied Territory in particular – Said opens up matters of displacement and discontinuity from a different critical perspective. For at issue here is the pain of a forced leaving, and the impossibility of return. Among several key issues raised by Said is that of his own problematic negotiation of a national identity generally perceived as unfavourable in the West, and invariably demonized. He also reflects upon Israeli/Zionist attempts to forge a national identity against a background of diaspora and holocaust (again, forms of exiles) – but by means of the dangerous fantasy of starting over in 'virgin territory', a colonial/imperialist orientation of long-standing which requires, whether through physical violence or legislative means, the erasure of indigenous peoples.

The scene shifts in James Clifford's 'The Others: Beyond the "Salvage" Paradigm' to issues of collecting, taxonomy and museology. Clifford provides an analysis and critique of a 'redemptive' anthropological model which, problematically, still tends to organize western practices of 'art-and-culture-collecting' from non-western sources. At issue here is the attempted preservation of supposedly 'authentic' and 'timeless' cultural traditions perceived as being at risk of corruption/eradication through contact with western modernity in its various forms. This is, of course, a western projection. Though apparently beneficial in orientation, it stages non-western cultures as 'without historical consciousness' and therefore as lacking the resources 'for processing and innovating historical change'. Once again, we are forced to ask ourselves why? And to what purpose?[2] Clifford presents counter-positions to this reductive and prejudiced attempt at engaging with otherness, turning to more recent (western) anthropological research and to the testimonies of indigenous peoples themselves.

The final text in this section deals with one of the most discussed terms in the identity field: hybridity. From the mid-1980s onwards, hybridity has a near-ubiquitous presence in debates around cultural identity, where it was understood not (as had traditionally been the case) as a negative marker of impurity and degradation but in positive and productive terms. Nikos Papastergiadis provides an evaluative historical account of the trajectory of hybridity as a theoretical concept. Papastergiadis considers the critical contributions of such thinkers as Gilberto Freyre, Ashis Nandy, Mikhail Bakhtin, Yuri Lotman, Michel Serres, Stuart Hall and Homi Bhabha, first considering those models in which issues of correspondence are central and then (with Bakhtin and Lotman) those in which it is difference instead that is foregrounded. With respect to Bakhtin's studies of textuality, for instance, he writes that 'the "doubleness" of the hybrid voices' at issue 'is composed not through the integration of differences but via a series of dialogical counterpoints, each set against the other, allowing the language to be both the same and different'. Papastergiadis's text ends with words of caution, however. Following cultural theorist Gayatri Spivak, he warns that although it is certainly the case that all human beings are 'hybridized subjects' (and always have been), it is vital we remember that not all forms or articulations of hybridity are equally valued within the societies in which they occur. Because our encounters with otherness and our flexing of translation are not equal, we may well need to return to a theory of ideology to demonstrate how the gaps and slants of representation have various effects on the subject. However elliptically, theoretically or creatively we may wish to approach questions of identity, specified, diagnostic explorations of the politics and plays of power at issue cannot be pushed aside.

Identity: Reality or Fiction?

SEBASTIÁN LÓPEZ

When I heard it for the first time I couldn't believe it. I thought: 'Is that possible? I must be dreaming, here, in the Netherlands.' The newspaper was in front of me. I checked it once more. I called up a Brazilian friend and he confirmed the news; and he laughed. Mariano, a Mexican photographer, also confirmed it, but he did not have much time to discuss the matter, excited as he was by an invitation to participate in the next Havana Biennial. A Chilean artist I called didn't pay much attention to it; he was packing. I thought, let's get out of the Latino circle. Bushaip, a Moroccan friend who is a painter, had known about it for some time. His encounter with it was so painful that he couldn't sleep for some days; and now he only wanted to forget it. My neighbour, also from Morocco, who works for Dutch TV, was preparing a TV programme. Although she makes specifically Moroccan programmes, she said: 'Maybe I can squeeze it in.' Anny, a British friend (together we founded the Falklands-Malvinas Association: once a week we get together to dance tango and drink tea, the following week to play cricket and drink wine, that is the deal), said, 'Oh no, don't worry about it.' But Ana, my Argentinian friend, a writer who is trying very hard to get her second novel published (she even offered to have it translated into Dutch, but was told that they only want something from 'over there'), said exactly what I felt: 'What, here? It gives me a feeling of déjà-vu.' These small comments, amazements and surprises were expressed by a group of friends in Amsterdam.

What had actually happened, you may ask.

At the intellectually prestigious theatre De Balie in Amsterdam, a discussion was organized by the history magazine *Script* on Saturday, 6 April 1991. The participants were: Mr Hofland, writer and journalist; Professor Cauwenberg; the historian Van Deursen; Mr Briels; the Director of the Moluccan Museum, Mr Manahuttu; the social anthropologist De Harting; and the writer Astrid Roemer. The title of the afternoon talk was 'Over Holland' (About Holland), and the purpose was to discuss Dutch Identity. I know it sounds like a joke, but it really happened. I couldn't be there that day, but the newspaper *De Volkskrant* reported in a long article the seriousness with which all the speakers addressed the subject. Maybe it is important to recall some of the things they talked about: the Dutch Golden Age in painting; Roemer, the writer, discussed the problems of young Moroccan girls; Professor Cauwenberg urged the assimilation of foreigners and stressed how important it was that everybody spoke Dutch. Above all, every one of them, under the topic of 'Colonial Heritage', discussed the problem of foreigners in the Netherlands. So, be aware that, while we are spending these three days together talking about 'Cultural Identity', some people in this country are organizing other symposia concerning different kinds of identity. And that is not a joke. If some people are discussing Dutch identity it is because we are here.

If I am looking with surprise and amazement at the development of this debate in Europe, and particularly in the Netherlands, it is because I was actively involved in the early 1970s in Argentina in discussions concerning Latin American identity. Those discussions took place under very different circumstances. For us in Latin America, living under cultural, economic and political dominance, to ask questions about identity was not only serious but also risky. It was risky because, as you probably know, many lost their lives, not only in Argentina but also in Chile, Uruguay, Brazil and elsewhere in Latin America, for simply daring to think about their identities, or to express them in public. In fact, many journalists, writers, workers, visual artists, film workers and performers were imprisoned or taken to concentration camps in many Latin American countries.

Confronted with the daily menace of imperialism, and the different dictatorships this imperialism helped to create in Latin America, visual artists who tried to deal with the question of identity could not do otherwise than answer it politically. But there was no single answer. There were various perspectives representing different political and cultural groups, together with different artistic points of view: some proposed the recuperation of an Indian past; some wanted to change radically the aesthetic object – making 'conceptual art' surprisingly *avant la lettre*; there were those whose painting and prints had taken a painful and satirical look at the national clichés and symbols; some engaged in joint projects with workers; and there were those who believed in the autonomy of the art object and gave their work over to the interests of the national bourgeoisie.

But the discussions concerning Latin American identity already had a history that went back to the 1920s and 1930s. In fact, during those years Mexicans, Brazilians, Uruguayans, Argentinians and Peruvians, to name only some of those who made the more remarkable statements, had tried already to deal, politically and artistically, with the problems of the continent. In Europe, whose cultural and political involvement had helped to create our own idea of modernity, these efforts remained unnoticed.

It may be important to point out that references to other cultures have been among the recurrent patterns within European modernism. These references were, in practice, the use of motifs, forms, colours, thoughts, ways of working and stories coming from non-European countries, which helped European artists to sustain their work in such a way that their production could not be possible without them. Artists since Gauguin and throughout Fauvism, Cubism, Expressionism and Surrealism – a large part of the development of modern art in Europe – have defined themselves in relation to non-European cultures.

At the same time, some non-European countries have, in turn, also made use of their national or regional culture in order to establish their own modernity programme. If we look again to Latin America, we can see that during the 1920s and 1930s, artists' groups from countries like Uruguay, Argentina, Peru, Brazil, Cuba and Mexico incorporated into their artistic production a large range of iconographic motifs, stories, descriptions and references to do with their own past and present. Artists as different as Tarcila do Amaral, Torrés García, Diego Rivera, Wifredo Lam and Pelaez, among others, were engaged in the recuperation of their past: not only that which belonged to the Spanish and Portuguese colonizers but also that of their victims – American aboriginal peoples and black slaves. These visual artists recognized the richness of their past and of their mestizo present. Their intentions, and their artistic significances, were quite different from those of the Europeans. First, in Latin America the use of their artistic past was both an aesthetic and a political statement. Those artists were engaged in drawing a new map in which a new social and economic order was going to be born, together with a new and rich cultural activity. Many of them recognized at the same time that Europe was culturally finished, a point made by Torrés García in his writing, and by the Mexican Siqueiros in his open denunciation of the Europeans' use of 'primitive motifs'.

In our time the situation is very different. In fact, the 'others' and their artistic production, which Europeans were seeking in faraway countries at the beginning of the twentieth century, are now among us and have come here to stay. As a result of the postcolonial situation, economic migrations – or 'importation' in the case of the Netherlands – and of the political situation in various parts of the world, many visual artists have established themselves in Europe. They are not visitors, or simply here to make contact with the avant-garde, as at the beginning of the twentieth century, but permanent residents.

If the rise of European fascism and Nazism, resulting in the persecution of artists and intellectuals (a situation which definitely marked modernism), pushed many of them to the Americas, over the past twenty-five years many Latin American as well as Asian and African artists have come to Europe in search of a better political situation. But if the emigration of European intellectuals was seen in the Americas as a welcome phenomenon, this has not been the case for non-European artists in Europe. They have been disregarded and misunderstood. They brought with them other artistic and political ideas which were considered by Europeans to be either dated or not what was expected of them. The lack of information about their cultural backgrounds was covered over by the surfeit of information about their economic backgrounds. Coming from countries seen only as the source of raw materials, it is not surprising that their artistic and cultural contributions were neglected by the Europeans.

It is important that we now focus on the particular situation of foreign artists living in the Netherlands, and to recall briefly some points concerning their activities. The late 1960s and early 1970s saw an increasing presence of foreign artists living and working here. Although some were practising traditional media such as painting, many were involved in what has come to be known as the 'dematerialization of the art object': performance, installation, video, mail-art, film and photography. Foreign artists opened one of the very first alternative artists' spaces in Europe. Called the 'In-Out Centre', it opened its doors in Amsterdam in 1972 under the initiative of the Colombian artist Michel Cardena, but received no response from the Dutch daily or specialized art press. To date, the achievements and activities of that period have continued to be met with silence from many quarters, and still have not been completely documented. In that early group were Colombians Cardena and Raul Marroquín, the Mexican Ulises Carrión, Icelanders Friednisson and Gudmunson, working together with Dutch artists like Peter Laurens Mol.[1] As in the early days of the avant-garde, there was no separation here based on nationality or cultural background but a collective artists' venture. It was not a question of the Dutch cultural climate of the 1970s being of interest to foreign artists, as is stated in the catalogue of *Het Klimaat*, because, thanks to the BKR system[2], they could be easily subsidized. To say this is not only to consider foreign artists as economic migrants, as did the neo-conservative ideology which emerged during the 1980s, but also to accuse them of profiting from state welfare. This ignores the fact that many came here for political reasons and for the cultural freedom that was unique in Europe in those early days.

Subsequently, the artists' space 'Agora', and this very same Academy here in Maastricht, played an important role, as was also the case of the Academy of Fine Arts (AKI) in Enschede and 'Atelier '63' in Haarlem as a meeting place for foreign students and teachers. In Amsterdam, 'Other Books and So' was opened in 1975. It was a shop and art centre created by Ulises Carrión to sell art books, art journals, artists' newspapers and posters, and to show visual poetry and other forms of production like mail-art, stamp-art, new photography, performance. It may be said that one of the mottoes of those days, later used by Carrión in one of his works, was 'Personal world, or cultural strategies?' In fact, we understood, at the beginning of the 1970s, that if we as artists were to play a role, it must be played in a wide cultural framework; and that framework was the media.

During those early days no one talked about foreign artists; or better, no one emphasized their foreignness. It was in the second half of the 1970s that the term *gasterbeiders* (guest workers) was used for the first time. But this was applied mostly to the Turkish and Moroccan communities who had been 'invited' to work here to enable Dutch economic growth through their cheap labour. Even though this categorization did not initially apply to artists, it was to have consequences for the subsequent roles foreign artists were to play in cultural and political decisions. At the end of the 1970s and the beginning of the 1980s, there was a schizophrenic series of categories for naming foreigners: *etnische minderheden* (ethnic minorities), *migranten* (migrants) and most recently, *allochtonen*. This last word, the opposite of 'autochthonous' and in many languages the name for foreigners, is given an interesting definition in the standard Dutch dictionary Van Dale: '*allochtonen: van elders aangevoerd*' (transported from elsewhere), an almost literal description of the original 'guest workers'. The choice of this last term needs to be taken into consideration because it came into usage in the Netherlands at the time when a project to repatriate foreigners – mostly Moroccans and Turks, who together made up a large minority community in the Netherlands – to their countries of origin was discussed.

What is important for us in this symposium is to recognize that these definitions, with the exception of the term 'guest workers', were used by the Ministry of Culture in different moments to develop projects and legislation concerning the work of foreign artists. When the term *allochtonen* was established at the beginning of the 1980s, this covered, for official agencies, not only already recognized groups like the Surinamese, Antilleans, Turks, Moroccans and Moluccans but also Latin Americans and so on. In the report 'De kunst van het artisjokken eten . . .' ('The Art of Eating Artichokes'), Hortence Sermaat pointed out that the Arts Council considers *allochtonen* to be 'those who have emigrated to the Netherlands, as well as their children and grandchildren; those who have Dutch nationality and those who do not'.[3] It is surprising that the Arts Council and the Ministry of Culture do not take into consideration that, under Dutch law, not only are the children of foreigners automatically Dutch, but also that *allochtonen* does not cover all foreigners but only those of a particular kind. It has become synonymous for non-Europeans geographically, for non-whites racially and for those outside the mainstream culturally.

Allochtonen as a definition was established in the Netherlands at the official level in a period of strong political, cultural and racial polarization. It was a period of intense but hidden racism, a period in which the extreme right political party, Centrum Partij, made its way into parliament and municipalities by campaigning for the expulsion of foreigners. Culturally, it was a period which saw the end of the BKR system, and the beginning of a discussion around the concept of 'artistic quality', which curators and officials have been using as an effective weapon to legitimize their policies.

It is important to analyse this concept of quality, because it has to do with the judgements that are made regarding foreign artists' work. The notion of quality has been one of the more effective strategies for levelling artistic production in modern as well as in postmodern times. This phenomenon has also taken place in the United States; I want to recall what Lucy Lippard has pointed out recently, since it can also be applied to the Dutch situation:

> Ethnocentrism in the arts is balanced on the notion of Quality that 'transcends boundaries' – and is identifiable only by those in power. According to this lofty view, racism has nothing to do with art; Quality will prevail; so-called minorities just haven't got it yet . . . The conventional notion of good taste with which many of us were raised and educated was based on an illusion of social order that is no longer possible (or desirable) to believe in. We now look at art within the context of disorder – a far more difficult task than following institutionalized regulations. Time and again, artists of color and women determined to revise the notion of Quality into something more open, with more integrity, have been fended off from the mainstream strongholds by this garlic-and-cross strategy . . . Such sheeplike fidelity to a single criterion for good art – and such ignorant resistance to the fact that criteria can differ hugely among classes, cultures, even genders – remains firmly embedded in education and artistic circles, producing audiences who are afraid to think for themselves.[4]

We also need to consider this question in relation to artists themselves. Although a separation was established during the 1980s between *allochtonen kunst* and *kunst* (interestingly enough the production of Dutch artists has never been called *autochtonen kunst*, a subtle but important difference), many 'foreign/ethnic' artists did not want their work to be submitted to this regime for recognition. They continued as artists to try to interest art galleries and museums in their work but without any success. Their work was considered too idiosyncratic or, again, as something lacking quality. Many artists dared not ask ministries and municipalities for special subsidies, because that would put them in a complicated political position regarding the conditions for showing work. They found themselves trapped in a paternalistic system which provided them with subsidies on the one hand, but on the other hand denied them participation in Dutch cultural life. Those who accepted their ethnicity and official definition could only show in alternative art circuits and marginal exhibition spaces. The issue here is that while European artists are allowed to look into other cultures and enrich their own work and perspectives, artists coming from other cultures are expected to deal only with that background and those artistic traditions in which they were born (even though many Dutch policy-makers, curators and art dealers are ignorant of these artistic traditions and their contemporary manifestations). If foreign artists do not conform to this separation, they are regarded as inauthentic, westernized and as just followers or mere copyists of what 'we do'. Universality is on 'our side', particularity is on 'theirs'.

The only institutions that have shown interest in the contemporary work of non-European countries and of foreign artists living in the Netherlands have been a few museums of anthropology. In fact, at the Volkenkunde Museum in Rotterdam and at the Tropenmuseum (Tropical Museum) in Amsterdam, there have been regular exhibitions of contemporary art. In 1985, the former organized a meeting for representatives of Dutch museums and cultural institutions. The goal was to interest them in, and to inform them about, the modern artistic production of non-western countries and of non-western artists living in the Netherlands. None of the museums of contemporary art invited to the meeting showed any interest. The series of lectures given by different researchers and scholars in the field did not impress them. Their response remained negative.

Since 1982, while all this was happening, some of us tried to write, to curate exhibitions and to build up a space for non-Dutch artists in cultural centres, foreigners' associations and in squatters' galleries. But these activities often passed unnoticed. They are not even now mentioned in the catalogue of *Het Klimaat*, the 'manifestatie' which has brought us together today. Let me recall some of them: 'Vulkaan van Handen' (Volcano of Hands) in Amsterdam; the exhibition of Surinamese artists at the Niuwe Kerk in Amsterdam; the numerous shows at the Chilean Centre in Rotterdam; the shows at the José Martí Foundation in Amsterdam; 'Op Papier' (On Paper) at the Tropenmuseum in Amsterdam; 'Light and Shadow' at De Balie in Amsterdam, etc. And now there are some organizations in this country which, because Paris and New York have shown that ethnic artists are OK, are trying to champion them and to use the new product – very selectively, of course, and always with 'quality' as the criterion for judgement.

So when we are brought together, as now in this symposium, to talk about 'identity' in relation to artists coming from so-called ethnic minorities, I must ask: whose reality and whose fiction? Who is asking about identity, and to what purpose?

Polysemy, the capacity of the same word to mean different things, such differences ranging from nuance to antithesis, characterizes the language of ideology. George Steiner pointed this out, and went on to say that Machiavelli had already noted that meaning could be distorted in popular speech so as to produce political confusion. Political ideologies rarely create new terminologies, as Kenneth Burke and George Orwell have shown regarding the vocabulary of Nazism and Stalinism. They pilfer and decompose popular speech. In the new idiom of fascism and communism, 'peace', 'freedom', 'progress' and 'popular will' are as prominent as in the language of representative democracies. But they have fiercely disparate meanings. The words of the adversary are appropriated and hurled against him. When antithetical meanings are forced upon the same word (Orwell's Newspeak), when the conceptual reach and valuation of the word can be altered by political decree, language loses credibility.

Therefore I ask: who is now invoking identity, and to what purpose? What kind of discourses are now being created in Europe when confronted with the possibility that in 1992 we are all to be one, together and for ever?

Translation: Anno Voorhoeve.

Identity and Myth Today

TICIO ESCOBAR

The issue of identity poses a serious challenge. So many words have been said and so many dreams have vanished since those heroic times when, nervous and compliant, Latin America discovered the right to express itself and be defined differently, that today it seems almost naive to speak of the identity of Latin American art.

But that is precisely why this issue becomes interesting, and to deal with it poses a challenge when those major concepts protecting it may be considered bankrupt or lost. Who dares speak today about the nation, the people or the tribe: terms that accurately represent identity in a contemporary world that disowns great homogenizing speeches and thinks in a code of fragments and remnants? When terms like 'cultural dependency' or 'counterculture' are more nostalgic than operational concepts, we realize that the time has come to look for the foundation of identity in new locations.

The issue of the identity of Latin American art was first addressed in the 1920s, and since then it has been a topic of continuous interest for artists and, especially, critics. This is a reasonable obsession. Latin American cultures, self-defined as dependent, had to define constantly their specificity and justify their image *vis-à-vis* powerful foreign models. The 'national being', conceived as a compact and homogeneous element, and 'latinoamericano', its projection on a continental scale, served as effective substitutions for local identities. Each national culture was understood as the specific difference of a supra-identity emerging from a similar indigenous and colonial past, from similar conditions of dependency and seeking the same dream. On the one hand, brown America, identical to itself, striving to imagine its deepest essence; on the other, an abstract conqueror who unceasingly modernizes his harquebuses and greeds.

THE IDENTITY OF THE MYTH

Unfortunately, we must today deride utopias that at other times were fruitful. Culture is ungrateful; it must desecrate its myths to renew them.

Modernity is stubborn: it refuses to admit that to guarantee the triumph of *logos* over *mythos* it needs new myths. The 'national being', the 'Latin American essence', the homogeneous people, the bronze-skinned Indian and Identity in capital letters – as much as 'motherland' and reference were useful as imperishable ideas, for some time at least. Every society needs comprehensive explanations intended to avert chaos, to which it is always vulnerable, and what it cannot explain by reason it explains by myths.

Problems ensue when these myths, intended to work within a given society, sector, institution or group, are extrapolated to other groups, institutions, sectors, society as a whole or other societies (for example, when the military establishment or the Church or the metropolis try to enforce their myth – of a circumscribed validity – on everyone). Hegemony has reasons that Reason knows only too well and it turns us into heirs apparent of often beautiful alien forms.

Another problem emerges when the myth becomes obsolete: mysterious atmospheres of history, which may be born any day, dissolve a mask or blur an essential mirror. The spell disappears and the solution of sacred metaphors obscenely appears.

For enlightened thought, 'demythicizing' and 'demystifying' are one and the same. Against this attitude, a trend has emerged that considers fiction not as a falsehood that must be unmasked, but as a roundabout way of discovering new approaches. Thus, when we speak of 'demythicizing', what we are really doing is renewing fictions: we denounce the mythical status of a great Discourse, which has become obsolete, to create new images and other symbols that will take its place, in an effort to give a name to what is inaccessible to discourse.

This approach may make us understand that our brand-new truths may really be the myths of tomorrow. Moreover, the democracy we strive for today and the tolerance we call for may be our most recent utopias; perhaps the confused mixtures and fragments that we all love may be the pieces that cover and camouflage new totalities. Yet we shouldn't be too anxious in demystifying for better or for worse; myths vanish by themselves when the time is ripe and, punctually, the new masks appear in some other place on the stage. Meanwhile, no culture runs the risk of calling by their names the myths it still needs.

THE MYTH OF IDENTITY

We are moving too far away from the issue of identity, but there are obscure matters which are better approached in a roundabout fashion. Moreover, identity to a large extent forms part of a dark underground where the struggle between reality and symbolism is waged; the backroom where the play is plotted, the backstage area where myths will be performed.

Let's link these issues. What happens with 'identity' when the great mythical concepts that serve as its foundations – People, Nation, Community, Class, Territory, etc. – are placed in doubt? As a unifying metaconcept it loses all support, but the very fact that these comprehensive totalities are questioned forces contemporary culture to be once again obsessed by the concept of Otherness. It is then necessary to go back to the issues of otherness and diversity, individuality and subjectivity, collective imagination and representations, the contour of the other face in part invented by itself and in part drawn by myself. In brief, these are the issues that have to do with identity.

Do we need here new myths to fill the imaginary void left by former myths? Let's be cautious and leave that question aside. For the moment, we need to redefine concepts so they will be operational and contribute to the elaboration of our new concerns.

A brief summary and, as such, the necessary arbitrariness and simplification of several concepts of identity may help towards this redefinition:

Identity

A first concept of identity, which we may call 'ontological', sees it as built around some essential elements: a community is specifically defined by certain given traits which produce in its members an awareness of uniqueness.

Group identity is characterized by its language, territorial location, class position in the social fabric, common history and so on. This set of elements, which the group elaborates internally through representations, are the symbolic correlations of its sets of objective positions. According to this point of view, what is Latin American is usually understood as the product of geographic, social, economic and political situations that standardize its history, protect it and give rise to a single cultural style. For example, the presence of indigenous cultures as well as shared colonial patterns and similar mechanisms of cultural dependency would have produced as a result an unmistakable family likeness in artistic production (a trend towards Baroque exuberance or, at the other end, towards geometrism, intense colours, spatial simplification, expressive vehemence, preference for social and indigenous subjects, etc.).

We have used this example because, as already mentioned, the first systematic attempt to underline the identity of Latin American culture took place in the sphere of art. Renovation, impelled by modernist movements translating or imitating the positions of European avant-gardes, advocated the breach with traditional forms and the right to local specificity with the same conviction. Paradoxically, this nascent modernity resorted to images and arguments that were already obsolete. On the one hand, strict modern standards, decreeing the rapid obsolescence of all 'isms', must be continually violated by the historical circumstance that demands the retention of variegated elements, whether they are in vogue or not in their original metropolis. (This fact has already made some critics speak about a specifically Latin American postmodernism.) On the other hand, the concept of identity being used was frankly premodern. The truth is that the ontological principle underlying the discourse on the issue had not varied too much from Parmenides's premises of identificatory reason, that plain statement sacrificing all plurality for the sake of the identical.

This holocaust freezes all opposition and prevents all resolution. (The principles of Non-Contradiction and of the Exclusion of the Third are indissolubly linked to that of Identity.) Thus, the theory of Latin American art frequently found itself up a blind alley of absolute disjunctions. Pressed to choose between cultural dependency and backwardness, this theory has hesitated in the face of too many false alternatives, leaving it with more feelings of guilt and recrimination than concrete results.

Inverted Identities

The concept of identity could not solve pressing problems in its time and thus had to be renewed. Substantial identity was therefore denounced as a myth, condemned and executed.

The new model of identity seems based not on the stable essence of the term but rather on its dynamic confrontation with another term. Identity is defined by its opposition: one's own image is presented and represented from the unescapably roundabout way of otherness. Contradictions are not now separated by the incompatible art of metaphysics, but solved through dialectical processes. Latin American artists can now resort to their history without reducing it to a huge stock of universal forms; they can be up to date and not be renegade.

Moreover, assuming the game of oppositions and understanding the logic of resolutions that foresee a meaning for the former allows us to place in binary order realities hitherto ill-defined. Thus, for example, folk culture is opposed to scholarly culture (or, rather, the dominated culture to the dominant culture) within a unidirectional, rationally oriented scheme. That is, each identity is not considered statically, but in an antagonistic relationship to another, and this confrontation will necessarily lead to another perfected identity which surpasses and redeems them both. Between the forms of Latin American art and those of metropolitan art – as much as between the terms of other discordant pairs, art and society, art and life, art and reason, and so on – there is an essential dispute that must be settled. But the happy ending has already been written: if things are approached well, a synthesis that in a better moment will include both poles will emerge. And so on and so forth.

We know what happened on realizing that this better moment had never arrived: each movement began pushing ahead relentlessly until they disqualified their own vanguards, lost belief in their own utopias and arrived at the conclusion that evolutionary history, the self-regulated Idea and the Great All were just pure myths of obsolete modernists.

Plural Identities

It is now more fruitful to understand identity as a result of variable positions rather than as a basic and definite opposition. Thus, identity is portrayed on many fronts: it is an unstable notion formed (and deformed) through confrontations that simultaneously take place in different settings.

Thus, the position of each one of the many cultural (id)entities proliferating in Latin America is not established once and for all *vis-à-vis* a predetermined adversary. It takes shape in relation to other cultural forces with which it clashes, joins or crosses, trading metaphors and concepts, establishing ambiguous boundaries and sharing hybrid territories.

Now there is no definite script for this story: the conquest of identity always presupposes risks; it can end anywhere, it can be solved or not, it can have a happy ending on one level and an unfortunate one on another.

There are no longer winners or losers. Neither are there actors with fixed roles, nor is the necessary omnipotence of the master or the envisaged impotence of the slave taken for granted. This uncertainty guarantees relief and wields a threat: in the same way that an occupied culture can strengthen its identity feeding it with the symbols of the invader, any hegemonic position can become bloated with the forms it has usurped. Cultural systems that have apparently been devastated by modernity survive healthily in spite of the bleak forecasts of apocalyptically minded and integrated persons, while other imperial images, which are deemed all-powerful, languish, worn out by the boredom of satiated societies.

There are no longer categorical boundaries separating the sphere of folk culture from that of scholarly or mass culture. Migrating signs, born in no-man's land, wander aimlessly through several regions randomly crossing over absent boundaries. The well-guarded kingdom of the Genius and of the form is desecrated by spurious images. This virginal abode, sanctuary of authentic traditions and pure essences, is polluted by imposed signs and stolen memories.

This fruitful mixture marks our present concept of culture. Identity takes different shapes today to break loose from its noisy and monotonous conditioning background. At times you must appeal to all your memories to retain the feeling of yourself in the presence of someone else; at times it is enough to enunciate an exact accent, recognize a small signal or remember the short-lived existence of some shared taste.

Indigenous peoples understand all this, for they face national society from situations that differ greatly, yet are all disadvantageous. They know that to preserve their image they must wear several masks and reinvent their profiles in many different ways. The Guarani widen or narrow the concept of identity by changing the range of the pronoun 'we'; the Andé include the person they address; while the Oré excludes him or her. This is the starting point: each term has such a strong presence that rules are defined from the outset. A Guarani *Chiripá*, from Acaray-mi (a village near Ciudad del Este, that capitalist Babel in which a thousand nations merge), included me when facing a Korean or a Brazilian, but excluded me before a *Mbyá*. At times, he linked his identity with part of the Guarani-speaking mestizos to remain apart from the Chaco natives, who speak other languages; at other times, he felt an identification towards them by opposition to 'the Paraguayan', a term including rural metissage. ('You white men', an old *Chiripá shaman* good-naturedly told me once. I replied by comparing my skin with his, both equally brown. He smiled politely and changed the subject.)

The Chiriguan is a Guarani group that has lived in the Paraguayan Chaco region since colonial times, a territory quite different from that of their original settlements. Their major annual celebration, the *Areté Guasú*, based on a number of propitiatory agricultural ceremonies and including complex ancestor cult rituals, summarizes several Guarani, colonial and Andean traditions. The *Areté Guasú* held at a village two kilometres from Mariscal Estigarribia, a powerful military post surrounded by missionaries, farmstead owners, foreign natives, foremen, hunters and diverse adventurers, without lessening either its expressive potential or its ancient magic, has become a great festival of differences. The *Smahu* wooden masks, or masks made with the skins of wild animals and sacred feathers, compete with dark sunglasses, motorcyclist gloves, posters of political candidates by famous artists; the high, conical bonnets, taken from Spanish religious plays, display rattlesnake tails, Catholic medals and scapulars, military badges, deer hooves, decals, shaman amulets, patriotic insigniae and ferocious fangs. But in the *Areté Guasú* there are also new people entering the rite in search of different goals: those who find in it a similarity with the carnival look for fun; postconcillium priests look for new ways of preaching the Gospel; prostitutes, contractors and peddlers look for business; scholars look for trophies and themes; military men look for excuses to increase their control. In the end, this dusty scene of disguises and shadows offers everyone the opportunity to mask their own desires with the face of another person; and each person lives the rites in his own way. Chiriguans know it and during the three days it now lasts, the participants call it *ñandé Areté Guasú*, whether they be Indians, Paraguayans, Mennonites or Bolivians. Masks are thrown away in the cemetery at night. The following day the stage is taken down and the identity it represents will be closed again and everyone will take the badge they want.

A POSSIBLE CONCLUSION

Our times boast a certain cynicism (inherited from the Enlightenment, like it or not). Perhaps that attitude is the result of the confusing malaise characterizing every moment that comes after another moment. Perhaps the very ambiguity of the present allows this attitude to mask other positions, like the modesty that prevents the naming of new utopias or the understandable fear of speaking about our own myths. The truth is that today we enjoy the right to a healthy opportunism which allows us, without feeling too guilty, to collect scraps, plunder ruins, cancel commitments to history, drink from remote dark wells and inhabit locked presents. Of course, this bricolage, this patient process of trying to reorganize new identities with refuse and relics, is a task of every culture. But we are at the end of a century and of a millennium – and, for some, at the end of ozone and of green areas – and we must make the prescribed major balances and inventories. This task demands enormous efforts: an extraordinary storing of clarity that ends up by leaving us watchful and sleepless; a perverse awareness of cultural processes that should be more natural is prey to a critical inertia that can hardly be stopped. (Thus, many believe that if the last resort of modernity is criticism, postmodernism would be a kind of self-criticism, an enlightened reason turned on itself.) All this situation justifies, or at least explains, the opportunism we have been talking about.

One of the most powerful criticisms of modern culture stems from its purpose of homogenizing all symbols in our planet in the single mould of its own desire. This argument assumes the defence of otherness, of identities. And opportunism appears here again; the constitution of identities is not a matter of anthological bases or ethical imperatives, but a strategic issue. To affirm itself as such, each culture, immersed in a multitude of symbols and power forces, must strive to survive and get hold of all its resources to grow. Their protean nature helps them. They can assume different shapes, disguise themselves, disintegrate and unite as they see fit.

Therefore, despite their enormous differences, if certain cultural sectors in Latin America deem it advantageous, they should stress their similarities, look for consensus, combine common problems, plan joint projects and even – because of epistemological or political factors – create a common front when it would seem useful to strengthen positions or protect our newly born myths.

Ancient Chamacocos obtained the title of *palota* (chief) when they had collected the necessary identities to lead a nomad horde successfully. A good chief had to be a skilled hunter, a courageous warrior, a convincing speaker and a wise negotiator. Today, the new chiefs need to assume other identities. Bruno Barras, present *palota* of the Chamacoco group, speaks five languages besides his own, has several names he has won in the forests, villages and cities and says with great pride that, besides the strict ritual initiation in his community, he has been baptized according to Catholic, Protestant and Mennonite rites. He knows that to maintain his identity and that of his people he must carry today several passports. His people, descendants of ancient nomad hunters, are today mostly farmers and day labourers. The Chamacocos he leads listen to radios and tape recorders, walk to Bahía Negra to make phone calls and dream of having their own motorcycles. But when the night falls, they tell, whispering and staring at the fire, stories that took place before the beginning of time. Then, at an invisible signal, they enter the jungle looking for their deepest identity, erase their faces with masks, cover themselves with paint, feathers and cries, shed their identities and become gods and strange birds.

The Voice of a Palestinian in Exile

EDWARD SAID

This photo-text is based on BBC 2's programme on Edward Said, as part of the series The Exiles, *broadcast on 23 June 1988. The photographs are taken directly from the broadcast and the text is our own edited version of Said's spoken words.*

We are grateful to BBC 2 and Edward Said for the permission to make use of their material for this article.

Right from the moment I arrived in the West in the early 1950s until the present, there has always been a sense in which, as an Arab, and obviously as a Palestinian, you feel in some way criminalized or delinquent. So powerful is the definition of you as somebody who is outside the pale, whose sole purpose in life is to kill Jews.

I don't have any Arab colleagues. Most of my colleagues are in fact Jews or Americans who have no connection with the Middle East, and with them my relationships on the whole, I would say, are thoroughly normal and perfectly pleasant. I think there is a general way of being in the academic world that tends to reduce conflict; so that with Jewish colleagues who may feel strongly about [the situation in the Middle East], we simply never talk about it. The worst aspect of it is, of course, the occasional threat of violence. I mean, my office has been raided and vandalized. I receive death threats and phone messages that are, you know, quite unpleasant. So there is that . . . hint of violence around there. And I suppose in general I do feel, given the atmosphere surrounding Palestine and Palestinians, in New York in particular, whether anything is said or not, as if I am a delinquent. Before anything gets going I am somehow guilty as charged.

I think, to be honest with you, my first inclination is to be vaguely amused by this. As a group that is supposed to be the enemy of Israel we seem, to me anyway, not to be a very formidable enemy. But then you get angry because it is obviously meant to be intimidating and to threaten you and, obviously, to smear

Said as a young boy with his sister.

your reputation. There is always something suggestive about it: that you are in the pay of somebody else or that you are really a terrorist, you are an agent for terrorism. I've been called that, actually quite frequently, by polemicists and even other scholars who prefer to do that rather than try to engage with my ideas. But the overall feeling that I have, when I think about it for any length of time, is one of astonishment at the injustice of it. Here I am, a child of a people that's been kicked out of its own land, forbidden to return, and there are the authors of books, sometimes students, who are employed by these agencies to spy on me. And if they are Jewish just by the fact of being Jewish, born in New York of Jewish parents, they are entitled to go to Israel or Palestine as I call it, become Israeli citizens at any time they wish. I was born there, my father was born there, my grandfather, great-grandfather . . . and I can't return. I don't have the same right. The law of return somehow covers them, and my people, my family, were kicked out of there, and there are books accusing me of terrorism. The enormity of the whole thing just baffles me at the same time as it strikes me very strongly.

My mother was born and lived in Nazareth and married my father there in 1932. My father came from Jerusalem. And it wasn't really until about, I would say maybe ten or fifteen years ago, that she told me – it's quite an extraordinary experience that she had – that when she married my father they had to register at the wedding and together they went to the Palestine government mandatory office. The official there was an Englishman and my mother said that she watched him rip up her passport and, in amazement, my mother said, 'Why are you doing this?' He said, 'Well now you'll travel on your husband's passport.' She said, 'Yes, but I mean, why did I have to lose mine in that way?' And he said,

Said's mother.

'Well, because your place and this card is going to be given to a Jewish emigrant to Palestine.' Her identity was, just by the simple act of tearing a piece of paper, taken away from her by a foreigner. And she lived through the consequences of that for thirty years and then she became, in the late 1950s, a Lebanese citizen. Of course, she is not Lebanese. She is Palestinian.

There is a place on the application where it says 'place of birth', so I put on Jerusalem, Palestine. Then I get a passport back saying Jerusalem, Israel. I then go into the passport office and say, 'Look, I wasn't born in Israel.' They said, 'Where were you born?' 'Palestine.' 'Palestine doesn't exist any more.' I say, 'Yes, but I was born there and Israel didn't exist when I was born.' So, back and forth until finally I get a passport which just says: place of birth, Jerusalem, without any country. I don't think it would work for any other city, because Jerusalem is, I suppose, a rather special place.

Palestine is not an ordinary place. I am sure we are oppressed and accursed like South Africa or Chile. Those are not ordinary places either, but Palestine I think has something more. It's the place where religions were manufactured and all kinds of revelations are alleged to have occurred. And it has a kind of density and resonance that virtually no other place in the world has. And it is also a very small place and very crowded. And that criss-crossing, that fabric of claims and counterclaims interests me a great deal. The political and even philosophical question is, why is it that visions of community in a land that is as dense as this have tended not to triumph, and what has triumphed instead are visions of exclusiveness?

It has been very important for me to try to understand the tremendous appeal of Zionism to the European mind, and I would say that there are really two very powerful and compelling reasons for that appeal. One of them, the first reason, is that Zionism appears to be a movement and an ideology that gathered together the remnants and the remains of a shattered community of people who had historically been oppressed, abused, discriminated against and persecuted in the West, and gathered them together into a very powerful movement which created a new country. It had all the elements of a kind of phoenix rising from the ashes. It also had the appeal of the creation of a new state which is, I think, very central to the European consciousness: for example, Europe sending out people to America to create a new country. And, obviously, it explains the peculiarly close connection between America and Israel. There is this tremendously attractive idea of starting out afresh, of starting with a clean slate, of building a new country, of making the desert bloom. It also has all the elements of a miracle, and that's very appealing.

The really dramatic change was in 1967, the war of '67 when the entire map of the Arab world changed. For the first time Israel, which had been confined largely to the small boundaries of the state, had overflowed into Jordan taking the West Bank, and also taking Gaza, the Sinai and the Golan Heights. Reading about this in America, watching it on the television, almost entirely from the viewpoint of a horrified and shamed victim, it was perfectly clear that I was an Arab. I couldn't go on simply being an undergraduate with this strange cachet

Said's father.

of being somehow from the Arab world, maybe from Egypt. The whole idea
of being an Arab and then beginning to discover what that meant, being a
Palestinian, that all really came to the fore in 1967. That was, I would say, the
great explosion and it had a tremendous effect on my psychological and even
intellectual processes, because I discovered then that I had to rethink my life and
my identity, even though it had been so sheltered and built up in this completely
artificial way. I had to rethink it from the start, and that was a process that really
is continuing. It hasn't ended for me.

The great problem that we face as a people is that we are being told by the
Israelis that in a certain sense we don't really exist, that the continuity of our
existence in Palestine, that our history, our identity, is manageable by Israeli
historians, by propagandists, by politicians, is manageable as something else.
Begin used to call us two-legged beasts, terrorists, everything, but not Palestinians. We were there! You can't do more than that. But it's so indecent and
humiliating an exercise to have to say that *we do exist*. There were Palestinian
villages, there were Palestinian cities, there was a Palestinian society. There were
Palestinian people before 1948 who formed a society – underdeveloped, whatever you want to call it, but it was there – which abruptly and dramatically in the
middle part of 1948 was shattered, dismantled, destroyed by the Zionists.

It's very hard for the Palestinian who feels himself or herself to have been the
victim of injustice by Jews, Israeli Jews, to sympathize or imaginatively
incorporate the history of the Holocaust and say: well, we forgive them for what
they did because after all they have suffered this enormous, this colossal historical tragedy, and the fact that they are evicting us from our territory, that they

are placing us under occupation, that they are treating us like third-class citizens, that they are killing our people, that they are confining us to camps, etc., etc., we understand. Look, nobody can understand that. You can grasp the first fact, the fact of the Holocaust, but you can't translate that into your own doom, I mean as another person, the doom that is visited on you by those people. It's very, very hard to do that. On the other hand, I really genuinely believe that it is incredibly important for the Palestinians to try to understand what force it is that we are dealing with. I made a great effort to see *Shoa*, you know the Lanzmann film about the Holocaust which was shown recently in New York. It's nine and a half to ten hours, and I am certain that my wife and I were the only two Arabs in the audience. I could feel it all and I understood the enormous horror, and I was devastated, because I understood as a kind of European or westerner the Holocaust for what it was. But then, when I came to the point of saying what does this mean to me, it means that this is the legitimization of what has happened to us as a people, the Palestinians. And then it's a paradox. You can call it an antinomy, you can call it a tragedy, but it doesn't lessen one's will, it doesn't lessen your will to struggle against it.

I've always felt that the emphasis on armed struggle, as it has been called, has been indiscriminate and sometimes foolishly and, in a political sense, stupidly relied on; but I will never, never concede that the essence of the Palestinian struggle is, as the Israelis say, terrorism. I think that the Palestinians, by and large to a fantastic degree, have waged a war against a merciless occupier, a state, an army, an enemy that has dispossessed them and has done far far worse to Palestinians than anything Palestinians have done to Israelis. I think one must always make the distinction between terrorism – which is, as I say, random, stupid and unpolitical – and the struggle against an oppressor. In that particular distinction, I am obviously for the latter and totally against the former. At the same time, as I said, I myself have always been made uncomfortable by the use of arms in this very ugly and long-standing struggle. I certainly must say that I have been much more, much much more, impressed by the cruelty and, above all, the extent of Palestinian suffering at the hands of the Israelis, than the other way round. The ratio is infinitely greater. The Israelis have made no secret of it: that they have always killed Palestinian civilians, sometimes at the rate of a hundred to one Israeli death.

I have grown up in an area which has had more than its share of violence in my lifetime. Certainly, the Zionists have used it and in fact brought it to the area. Terrorism as we know it today – the planting of bombs in marketplaces, etc. – was, in fact, introduced to the Middle East by the Zionists in the 1920s. Some people will say that it advances a political cause. I myself don't feel that it does. I think in this way it simply attracts attention. The net result of Zionist terrorism and violence in the first third of the twentieth century has brought forth, to my mind, the anomaly, the horrific and unacceptable status in the Middle East today of the state of Israel, which is in fact an armed garrison state which now exports more arms and distributes violence all around the world, vastly disproportionate to its size. In that respect, I think it's a horrible cycle of violence, but in it the Palestinians are the victims. There is no question about that.

In August 1982 I was in, of all places, Chicago. My family, my mother, my sisters, my wife's family, many many friends, were all in Beirut. So, the actual end of the war was symbolized by the Palestinians, the PLO fighters, leaving Beirut by sea, and it meant a number of very different things. One obviously saw the irony of the situation in which Palestinians were put out to sea in boats. For years we have heard it said that we were the ones who would drive the Jews into the sea and here, before the world's eyes, could be seen the spectacle of Palestinians being sent out into the sea, further away from the land that they came from. The second significance to me, watching it again at a great distance, was that I knew instinctively that this was the end of a very important phase of Palestinian life and that it would never be the same again. The Palestinian presence in Beirut, from the early 1970s for about a decade, was the first time in our existence when we have in fact constituted a kind of substitute or *Ersatz* Palestine in, alas, a sovereign country – Lebanon – and have led a kind of relatively independent existence, with institutions and so on. It was the first time that we have in fact constructed a kind of Palestine for ourselves, but everyone knew it wasn't in Palestine. It was somewhere else and I'd say that's the quintessential Palestinian irony, that we are always doing things that we would like to have done in Palestine, but couldn't. We are doing them somewhere else at the wrong time, causing a lot of trouble for others. That's got to be said too. Of course, the main significance beyond those two other things is that tremendous sadness and uncertainty of what was to come afterwards. Knowing that not one of the Arab countries – Arab friends, if you like – came, with a very few individual exceptions, to our aid, I thought it quite heroic that a small force of people, who had no heavy arms to speak of, no air force, no navy, no tanks, none of that stuff, fought off this immense Israeli concentration, which depended on Phantoms and cluster bombs and remote-control devices to kill, just kill, large concentrations of Palestinians.

Beirut really became the last of the places – Palestine, Egypt and Lebanon – of my early years to which I can no longer return, and its disappearance was of immense and terribly sad significance for me. It was also the loss of a place that had been immensely generous and hospitable to a whole generation of Arab exiles, not only Palestinians but Iraqis, Syrians and Egyptians and so on. It was the expatriate capital of the Arab world and it was over. In that respect Beirut really now represents a kind of nostalgia, for that period of intellectual, political and personal development which is really utterly closed, shut off in a way that is so sad. It is not as if it happened and it was over. The news from Beirut as we hear it – since my mother still lives in Beirut – is that of a city that is sort of chopping itself and bleeding to death.

The state of exile is a pretty serious and unpleasant experience. Somebody has been sent away, banished, severed from his or her native place. This was traditionally considered one of the worst fates. You could never return to your *patria*, to your place of origin, to your country, your native soil. I think it's right to concentrate therefore on the dispossessions, on the diminutions and the unhappiness of all that, the impermanence, the loss and so on. On the other hand, you could say: well, since exile is, as I believe it is, a permanent state, something that cannot be got over, that cannot be restored, you can't restore yourself to a state. It's like the Fall from paradise. You can't really go back. In that case, what is it that exile affords you that wouldn't be the case for somebody who always stayed at home, went through the daily routine? I think the essential privilege of exile is to have, not just one set of eyes but half a dozen, each of them corresponding to the places you have been. Therefore, instead of looking at an experience as a single unitary thing, it's always got at least two aspects: the aspect of the person who is looking at it and has always seen it, looking at it now and seeing it now, and then as you are looking at it now you can remember what it would have been like to look at something similar in that other place from which you came. So you can bring the two experiences together. There is always a kind of doubleness to that experience, and the more places you have been the more displacements you've gone through, as every exile does. As every situation is a new one, you start out each day anew; the more experiences seem to be multiple and complex and composite and interesting for that reason.

You become incapable of reacting further [to the news of violence against Palestinians in camps]. You just take it in and say: that's where we are. But I think it encourages in me and, I think, in most Palestinians who have watched or heard about this, the will to resist for ever. We mustn't simply let this take place and these people be effaced. We must continue to fight and to struggle towards something that will take us out of this. Bourj el-Brajneh and Shatila and Sabra, all the others, Tel el-Zaatar, there is a whole string of these catastrophes in our histories, and we have to end up somewhere that isn't just another catastrophe.

I have no doubt, it is the Palestinians' 'fault' that they exist. And wherever they exist, whether they exist in the former Palestine – now Israeli-occupied territories – Jordan, Syria, Lebanon, Egypt and elsewhere, they are a reminder, because they are extremely, politically conscious. They are people who are simply not going to go back on their national demand, which is self-determination, a society in a place of their own, so that by their very existence, they are a provocation to all the societies and all the states in the region and in the world elsewhere. We try to eliminate them or say that these people should be settled elsewhere, that they should be giving up on this. We now have Israel, we now have Lebanon, we now have Jordan, let's not have another state. So, the stubborn resistance of the Palestinian to say, 'No, I was the one who was driven off the land and dispossessed and dislocated', and just that very fact to say that you are a Palestinian in Lebanon or elsewhere is really to incur the wrath of your 'host' or whoever thinks of you as a problem. I think it's as simple as that. This is not a war to prevent Yasar Arafat or the PLO from establishing a base, this is a war to exterminate the Palestinian national identity. It's as simple as that.

I sense [commenting on recent Israeli brutalities, especially breaking the arms of Palestinian youths caught throwing stones], as one of the people in Gaza said, that fear has been forbidden, nobody seems to be afraid of armed Israelis and the subsequent beatings. And the brutality of it, that has been on the screen, has not deterred Palestinians from a rather disciplined and intelligent mass action of one sort or another. You know, throwing stones is only part of it, which is just endlessly disrupting the occupation in one way or another. So they never know what's coming next and they can never rest assured that they have got control over the territory. There is that for us, I mean for me as a Palestinian. There is a tremendous amount of attention focused on the Palestinians, who they are, what they are doing, etc., while we have always been secondary and shadowy figures. We still are to a certain degree faceless people, but still there is some sense in which somebody like myself is now called upon frequently to talk about this, to express, to explain, to interpret in a way that hadn't been true before. There is a kind of heroism here which has communicated itself to us all so that everybody feels he or she is willing to make sacrifices. I was prepared to go [to lecture at Bir Zeit University in the Israeli-occupied West Bank]. We were all going. I was going with my wife and two children. We had reserved seats on British Airways to London and then from London to Tel Aviv. About ten days ago I started to get signals that I better not come; and then, three or four days ago in mid-March, I got a clipping sent to me from *Davar*, which is an Israeli newspaper, in which it was suggested by the Prime Minister's office that, should I appear at the airport, I would not be admitted. So, in the circumstances it seemed to me rather quixotic to try, because it would probably mean being sent back; so I just didn't. But it was a blow because we had looked forward to it and I had wanted my children, who had never been there, to see it. I particularly wanted my son, who is named after my father, to go to the school where I and my father both went, St Georges, and see his grandfather's name on the first eleven for cricket and football in 1906 or whenever it was, but it didn't work out. Maybe we'll go at some later date, but it doesn't look too probable now.

Exile. The facts of my birth are so distant and strange. It has to be about someone I have heard of rather than about someone I know. Nazareth, my mother's town, Jerusalem, my father's. Pictures I see of these places today display the same produce, presented in the same carelessly plentiful way, in the same rough wooden cases, the same people walk by looking at the same posters and trinkets, concealing the same secrets, searching for the same pleasures, profits and goals. The same as what? The little that I can truly remember about Jerusalem and Nazareth, little that is specific, little that has the irreducible durability of tactile or visual or auditory memories, that concede nothing to time. Little that is not confused with pictures I have seen or scenes I have glimpsed elsewhere in the Arab world. Palestine is exile, dispossession, the inaccurate memories of one place slipping into vague memories of another. The story of Palestine cannot be told smoothly. Instead, the past like the present, offers only occurrences and coincidences – random.

The Others
Beyond the 'Salvage' Paradigm

JAMES CLIFFORD

The subtitle of this essay, 'Beyond the "Salvage" Paradigm', may seem cryptic. To some of you it will recall early twentieth-century anthropology, the 'salvage ethnography' of Franz Boas's generation, A.L. Kroeber and his Berkeley colleagues recording the languages and lore of 'disappearing' California Indians or Bronislaw Malinowski suggesting that authentic Trobriand Island culture (saved in his texts) was not long for this earth.

In academic anthropology 'the salvage paradigm' has an old-fashioned ring about it. Still, many ethnographies and travel accounts continue to be written in the style of *après moi le déluge*, with the exotic culture in question inevitably undergoing 'fatal' changes. We still regularly encounter 'the last traditional Indian beadworker', or the last 'stone age people'. The salvage paradigm, reflecting a desire to rescue something 'authentic' out of destructive historical changes, is alive and well. It is found in ethnographic writing, in the connoisseurship and collections of the art world, in a range of familiar nostalgias.

My essay's subtitle names a geopolitical, historical paradigm that has organized western practices I'd like to call 'art – and culture – collecting'. Seen in this light, it denotes a pervasive ideological complex. I'll sketch some of the paradigm's underlying conceptions of *history* and *authenticity*, conceptions that need to be cleared away if we are to account for the multiple *histories* and *inventions* at work in the late twentieth century. What's at issue is a particular global arrangement of time and space.

TIME/space. The dominant temporal sense is historical, assumed to be linear and non-repeatable. There is no going back, no return, at least in the realm of the real. Endless imaginary redemptions – religious, pastoral, retro/nostalgic – are produced; archives, museums and collections preserve (construct) an authentic past; a selective domain of value is maintained in a present relentlessly careering forward.

SPACE/time. A dominant 'theatre of memory' organizing the world's diversities and destinies has been described in Johannes Fabian's *Time and the Other: How Anthropology Makes Its Object* (1984). Speaking very schematically, in the global vision of nineteenth-century evolutionism the world's societies were ordered in linear sequence (the standard progression from savage to barbarian to civilized, with various, now arcane, complications). In the twentieth century, relativist anthropology – our current 'common sense' – emerged. Human differences would be redistributed as separate, functioning 'cultures'. The most 'primitive' or 'tribal' groups (the bottom rungs of the evolutionary ladder) could now be given a special, ambiguous, temporal status: call it the 'ethnographic present'.

In western taxonomy and memory the various non-western 'ethnographic presents' are actually pasts. They represent culturally distinct times ('tradition') always about to undergo the impact of disruptive changes associated with the influence of trade, media, missionaries, commodities, ethnographers, tourists, the exotic art market, the 'world system', etc. A relatively recent period of authenticity is repeatedly followed by a deluge of corruption, transformation, modernization.

This historical scenario, replayed with local variations, generally falls within the 'pastoral' structure anatomized by Raymond Williams in *The Country and the City* (Chatto and Windus, London, 1973). A 'good country' is perpetually ruined and lamented by each successive period, producing an unbroken chain of losses leading ultimately to . . . Eden.

In a salvage/pastoral set-up, most non-western peoples are marginal to the advancing world-system. Authenticity in culture or art exists just prior to the present (but not so distant or eroded as to make collection or salvage impossible). Marginal, non-western groups constantly, as the saying goes, 'enter the modern world'. And whether this entry is celebrated or lamented, the price is always that local, distinctive paths through modernity vanish. These historicities are swept up in a destiny dominated by the capitalist West and by various technologically advanced socialisms. What's *different* about peoples seen to be moving out of 'tradition' into 'the modern world' remains tied to inherited structures that either resist or yield to the new but cannot *produce* it.

In American anthropology a growing body of recent work has begun to unravel the assumptions about tradition, history and authenticity that underlie 'the salvage paradigm'. The result has been to displace global dichotomies long 'orienting' geopolitical visions in the Occident. One of these dichotomies sorts the world's societies into people *with* or *without history*. The inheritors of Thucydides, Gibbon, Marx, Darwin, etc. are endowed with 'historical consciousness', others have 'mythic consciousness'. This dichotomy is reinforced by other oppositions: literate/non-literate; developed/underdeveloped; hot/cold. The last pair, coined by Lévi-Strauss, assumed that, for good or ill, western societies are dynamic and oriented toward change, whereas non-western societies seek equilibrium and the reproduction of inherited forms. Whatever truth this sort of general contrast may contain, it becomes rigid and oppressive when ranges of difference – both within and between societies – become frozen as essential oppositions. The history of anthropology is littered with such oppositions: 'we' have history, 'they' have myth, etc.

Anthropologists now challenge the assumption that non-western (even small-scale 'tribal') peoples are without historical consciousness, that their cultures have scant resources for processing and innovating historical change. I'll quickly list a few important recent works. In *llongot Headhunting, 1883–1974: A Study in Society and History* (Stanford University Press, Stanford, CA, 1986), Renato Rosaldo discovers a distinctive historical idiom among non-literate Philippine highlanders, a concrete way of narrating real past events and of using the landscape as a kind of archive. Richard Price's *First Time: The Historical Vision of an Afro-American People* (Johns Hopkins University Press, Baltimore, 1983) probes an elaborate local historical memory and discourse among the descendants of escaped slaves in Surinam. A strong historical sense is crucial to the group's identity and its continuing resistance to outside powers. In *Islands of History* (University of Chicago Press, Chicago, 1985), Marshall Sahlins argues that eighteenth-century Hawaiian mythic and ritual structures, far from being time-less and unchanging, were concrete forms through which forces of historical change (like the arrival of Captain Cook) could be locally processed. Work by sociologists like Anthony Giddens and Pierre Bourdieu has introduced an increased awareness of process and inventive agency into formerly synchronic and holistic theories of culture. A seminal work of the mid-1970s by Roy Wagner, a work deeply influenced by Melanesian processual styles, gives its title to a whole new perspective: *The Invention of Culture* (Prentice-Hall, Englewood Cliffs, NJ, 1975).

Of course, I'm painting with a broom here, glossing over a number of important debates. Suffice it to say that, for me, the importance of the new anthropological attention to historical process has been to reconceive 'cultures' as arenas not merely of structural order and symbolic pattern but also of con-flict, disorder and emergence. Several of the essentializing, global dichotomies I've mentioned are complicated. For example, Sahlins has spoken of 'hot' and 'cold' sectors within specific societies: people may, in fact, be willing rapidly to discard or change whole areas of traditional life, while guarding and reproducing others.

Another dichotomy is displaced by Trinh T. Minh-ha in the special issue of the review *Discourse* she has edited (No. 8, Fall–Winter 1987: 'She, the Inappropriate/d Other'). She writes in her introduction: 'There is a Third World in every First World, and vice versa.' (A walk in many neighbourhoods of greater New York easily confirms the first part of her statement!) Old geopolitical oppositions are transformed into sectors within western and non-western societies. Hot/cold, historical/mythic, modern/traditional, literate/oral, country/city, centre/periphery, first/third . . . are subject to local mix and match, contextual/tactical shifting, syncretic recombination, import/export. Culture is migration as well as rooting – within and between groups, within and between individual persons.

A significant provocation for these changes of orientation has clearly been the emergence of non-western and feminist subjects whose works and discourses are different, strong and complex, but clearly not 'authentic' in conventional ways. These emergent subjects can no longer be marginalized. They speak not only for endangered 'traditions' but also for crucial human futures. New def-initions of authenticity (cultural, personal, artistic) are making themselves felt, definitions no longer centred on a salvaged past. Rather, authenticity is re-conceived as hybrid, creative activity in a local present-becoming-future. Non-western cultural and artistic works are implicated by an interconnected world cultural system without necessarily being swamped by it. Local structures produce *histories* rather than simply yielding to *History*.

What kinds of cultural and artistic histories are being produced? I'll end with a few examples drawn from the ongoing invention of Native American culture and art.

Anne Vitart-Fardoulis, a curator at the Musée de l'Homme, recently published a sensitive account of the aesthetic, historical and cultural discourses routinely used to explicate individual museum objects. (See the new journal *Gradhiva*, No. 1, 1986, published by the Archives Division of the Musée de l'Homme.) Vitart-Fardoulis discusses a famous, intricately painted animal skin (its present name: M.H. 34.33.5), probably originating among the Fox Indians of North America. The skin turned up in western collecting systems some time ago in a Cabinet of Curiosities; it was used to educate aristocratic children and was much admired for its aesthetic qualities. Vitart-Fardoulis tells us that now the skin can be decoded ethnographically in terms of its combined 'masculine' and 'feminine' graphic styles and understood in the context of a probable role in specific ceremonies. But the meaningful contexts are not exhausted. The story takes a new turn:

> The grandson of one of the Indians who came to Paris with Buffalo Bill was searching for the [painted skin] tunic his grandfather had been forced to sell to pay his way back to the United States when the circus collapsed. I showed him all the tunics in our collection, and he paused before one of them. Controlling his emotion he spoke. He told the meaning of this lock of hair, of that design, why this color had been used, the meaning of that feather . . . And this garment, formerly beautiful and interesting but passive and indifferent, little by little became meaningful, active testimony to a living moment through the mediation of someone who did not observe and analyze but who lived the object and for whom the object lived. It scarcely matters whether the tunic is really his grandfather's.

I don't know what's going on in this encounter. But I'm pretty sure two things are *not* happening: First, the grandson is not replacing the object in its original or 'authentic' cultural context. That is long past. His encounter with the painted skin is part of a modern recollection. Second, the painted tunic is not being appreciated as art, an aesthetic object. The encounter is too specific, too enmeshed in family history and ethnic memory. Some aspects of 'cultural' and 'aesthetic' appropriation are certainly at work. But they occur within a current tribal history, a different temporality (and authenticity) from that governed by 'the salvage paradigm'. The old painted tunic becomes *newly*, *traditionally*, meaningful in the context of a present-becoming-future.

This currency of 'tribal' artefacts is becoming increasingly visible to non-Indians. Many new tribal recognition claims are pending at the Bureau of the Interior. And whether or not they are formally successful matters less than what they make manifest: the historical and political reality of Indian survival and resurgence, a force that impinges on western art-and-culture collections. The 'proper' place of many objects in museums is now subject to contest. The Zuni who prevented the loan of a war god from Berlin to the Museum of Modern Art in 1984 were challenging the dominant art-culture system. For in traditional Zuni belief, war god figures are sacred and dangerous. They are not ethnographic artefacts, and they are certainly not 'art'. Zuni claims on these objects specifically reject their 'promotion' (in all senses of the term) to the status of aesthetic or scientific treasures.

I'm not arguing that the only true home for the objects in question is in 'the tribe' – a location that, in many cases, is far from obvious. My point is only that the dominant, interlocking contexts of art and anthropology are no longer self-evident and uncontested. There are other contexts, histories and futures in which non-western objects and cultural records may 'belong'. The rare Maori artefacts that recently toured museums in the United States normally reside in New Zealand museums. But they are controlled by the traditional Maori authorities whose permission was required for them to leave the country. Here and elsewhere the circulation of museum collections is significantly influenced by resurgent indigenous communities.

This current disturbance of western collecting systems is reflected in a new book by Ralph Coe, *Lost and Found Traditions. Native American Art: 1965–1985* (1986). It is a coffee-table book: we have not transcended collecting or appropriation. And once again, a white authority 'discovers' true tribal art – but this time with significant differences. The hundreds of photographs in Coe's collection document recent works, some made for local use, some for sale to Indians or white outsiders. Beautiful objects – many formerly classified as 'curios', 'folk art' or 'tourist art' – are located in ongoing, inventive traditions. Coe effectively questions the widespread assumption that fine tribal work is disappearing. And he throws doubt on common criteria for judging purity and authenticity. In his collection, among recognizably traditional katchinas, totem poles, blankets and plaited baskets we find skilfully beaded tennis shoes and baseball caps, articles developed for the curio trade, quilts and decorated leather cases (peyote kits modelled on old-fashioned toolboxes).

Since the Native American Church, in whose ceremonies the peyote kits are used, did not exist in the nineteenth century, their claim to traditional status cannot be based on age. A stronger historical claim can, in fact, be made for many productions of the 'curio trade', for the beaded 'fancys' (hanging birds, mirror frames) made by Matilda Hill, a Tuscarora who sells at Niagara Falls:

> 'Just try telling Matilda Hill that her "fancies" are tourist curios,' said Mohawk Rick Hill, author of an unpublished paper on the subject. 'The Tuscarora have been able to trade pieces like that bird or beaded frame at Niagara since the end of the war of 1812, when they were granted exclusive rights, and she wouldn't take kindly to anyone slighting her culture!'

'Surely,' Coe adds, 'a trade privilege established at Niagara Falls in 1816 should be acceptable as tradition by now.'

Coe does not hesitate to commission new 'traditional' works. And he spends considerable time eliciting the specific meaning of objects, as individual possessions and as tribal art. We see and hear particular artists; the coexistence of spiritual, aesthetic and commercial forces is always visible. Overall, Coe's collecting project represents and advocates ongoing art forms that are both related to and separate from dominant systems of aesthetic-ethnographic value. In *Lost and Found Traditions*, authenticity is something produced not salvaged. Coe's collection, for all its love of the past, gathers future.

A long chapter on 'tradition' resists summary. For the diverse statements quoted from practising Native American artists, old and young, do not reproduce prevailing western definitions. Let me end with a few quotations. They suggest to me a concrete, non-linear sense of history – forms of memory and invention, recollection and emergence that offer a different temporality for art – and cultural collecting.

> Whites think of our experience as the past. We know it is right here with us.

> We always begin our summer dances with a song that repeats only four words, over and over. They don't mean much of anything in English, 'Young chiefs stand up.' To us those words demonstrate our pride in our lineage and our happiness in always remembering it. It is a happy song. Tradition is not something you gab about . . . It's in the doing . . .

> Your tradition is 'there' always. You're flexible enough to make of it what you want. It's always with you. I pray to the old pots at the ruins and dream about making pottery. I tell them I want to learn it. We live for today, but never forget the past . . .

> Our job as artists is to go beyond, which implies a love of change, [always accomplished with] traditions in mind, by talking to the elders of the tribe and by being with your grandparents. The stories they tell are just amazing. When you become exposed to them, everything becomes a reflection of those events. There's a great deal of satisfaction being an artist of traditions.

> We've always had charms; everything that's new is old with us.

A slightly longer version of this article was published in English in *Discussions in Contemporary Culture*, No. 1, ed. Hal Foster, Dia Art Foundation. Bay Press, New York and Seattle, 1987.

Restless Hybrids

NIKOS PAPASTERGIADIS

In the last decade there has been barely a debate on cultural theory that has not acknowledged the productive side of hybridity, and almost every discussion on cultural identity is now an evocation of the hybrid state. The return of hybridity to academic respectability carries the promise of a reformed cultural sensibility and the emergence of a new theoretical concept. I am not sure how to test the former, but it is possible to trace the peculiar historical trajectory of hybridity. For as long as the concepts of purity and exclusivity have been central to a racialized theory of identity, hybridity has, in one way or another, served as a threat to the fullness of selfhood. The hybrid has often been positioned within or beside modern theories of human origin and social development, mostly appearing as the moral marker of contamination, failure or regression. Yet, one of the 'achievements' of poststructuralist theory was to liberate the subject from notions of fixity and purity in origin. And in a social context, the political structures for mobilizing and integrating emancipatory projects were also fragmenting; it was almost a form of succour to remind ourselves of our 'decentred selves' and 'multiple subjectivities'. Can we now have the confidence that hybridity has been moved out from the loaded discourse of 'race', and situated within a more neutral zone of identity?

A quick glance at the history of hybridity reveals a bizarre array of ideas. Hybridity has shadowed every organic theory of identity. Whether it has focused on either the physiological or the cultural constitution of the subject, it has primarily served as a metaphor for the negative consequences of racial encounters. These metaphors are mercurial. For even when the scientific basis of racism had been discredited, the racist practices were not abandoned but rehoused in the discourse of social types. The enigmatic 'nature' of the hybrid may still lurk within the contemporary uses of hybridity as a model for cultural identity.

CULTURAL HYBRIDS AND NATIONAL RECONCILIATIONS

The history of the hybrid must be at least as old as the narratives of origin and encounter. Whenever the process of identity formation is premised on an exclusive boundary between 'us' and 'them', the hybrid, which is born out of the transgression of this boundary, will be figured as a form of danger, loss and degeneration. However, if the boundary is marked positively – to solicit exchange and inclusion – then the hybrid may yield strength and vitality. The value of the hybrid is always positioned in relation to purity and along the axes of inclusion and exclusion. In some circumstances, the 'curse' of hybridity was seen as a mixed blessing.

Racialized classifications and the mythology of white supremacy reached their zenith in the justifications of slavery and imperial conquest. Notions of superiority were often premised on alterity, exclusivity and purity. The comforts of ideology, however, rarely constrained the parallel ideology of conquest through sexual penetration. Hence, the paradox of conquest was in both distanciation and penetration. Desire and disavowal was most palpably embodied by the presence of hybrids in Latin America. In Brazil, the hybrid was from the outset the basis of its culture, but it took time before the name was not spoken as a curse. Gilberto Freyre's celebrated account of Brazilian culture, *The Masters and the Slaves*, begins with the confession, 'of all the problems confronting Brazil there was none that gave me so much anxiety as that of miscegenation'.[1]

In the early records of the colonial encounters the hybrid was wrapped in ambivalence. On the one hand, hybridity was blamed for causing bad health: the symptoms included fatigue and indolence. Economic inertia, moral decadence and even syphilis were also effects that hybrids supposedly brought to the New World. For Freyre, the negative associations given to hybridity were not the result of a deeply internalized ideology of purity, but rather a confusion of subject positions. The disastrous consequences of the first contact had been falsely projected onto the offspring. Once the genuine causes of disease and disorder were identified, Freyre believed that the hybrid's advantage would be restored and establish a firm grounding for a 'racial democracy'. Moral repugnance would dissolve as the society was enlightened by its own potentialities. In this new celebratory myth, which was defined in opposition to the polarities of race relations in the USA, hybrids were conceived as lubricants in the clashes of culture, they were the negotiators that would secure a future free of xenophobia.

Freyre had found a resolution to his anxiety over miscegenation and became convinced that a hybrid society creates a new social order through the principle of synthesis and combination of differences. However, the hierarchy that privileged the white race through its positive association along the axes of public and private, culture and nature, masculine and feminine was nevertheless uncritically retained throughout his celebration of hybridity. Freyre's Eurocentrism prohibited him from questioning the paradigms of savagery and primitivism. The conceptual world of the other was rarely entertained, it was simply their virility and domesticity that was embraced, and in this sense his account bears a disturbing resemblance to the current integrationist discourse which promotes otherness in terms of 'black macho' and 'ethnic cuisine'. This is no coincidence, for the model that Freyre is expounding is drawn from European modernism.

The limitations in Freyre's model of hybridity can be exposed by considering his acknowledgement of being methodologically influenced by Picasso. The ambivalence of hybridity in early modernism is seldom examined in terms other than a celebration of the western capacity for integrating the 'raw' forms of the other into the dynamic body of metropolitan culture. The difficulties of conceptualizing hybridity can be witnessed in an essay by Max Raphael where he sets out to examine the means by which Picasso contributed to the 'break' in the European tradition.[2] Raphael argues that Picasso's affinity for 'Negro' art was a potential trespass of the border between reason and non-reason, and also signified a reversal in the exchange of cultural influence between the centre and the periphery. While Raphael's representation of 'Negro' art and other forms of non-European art merely repeats all the stereotypes of primitivist corporeality or orientalist exotica, his account of the process of its incorporation reveals a particular principle for the incorporation of difference.

Raphael's critique of the utilization of non-western elements in Picasso's art gives us an indication of an underlying pathos in the motivation to incorporate foreign elements, and also a surprising insight into the crudity of the process for translating foreign elements into the familiar discourse of western civilization. I say that this revelation is surprising because most critics associate the concept of modernity with an increasing complexity in the structures of everyday life, and assume that the cultural processes that accompany such structures are equally sophisticated. As Don Miller wryly observed, 'an idea like "simple modernity" would be seen as a blatant contradiction'.[3] But this is precisely what we do witness in the cultural dynamics that Raphael traces. He argues that the West's success in material production was achieved at the expense of hollowing out western spiritual values. Thus, the turn to primitivism in modern art was not a wholesale critique of material production, but simply another extension of the prevailing logic of appropriation and displacement. In primitivism we witness not only the commodification of other spiritual values but also the domestication of this otherness as it is translated back into the familiar western forms of 'corporeality' and 'mysticism'.

By demonstrating Picasso's paradoxical appeal to western reason and the appeal of non-western spirituality to abstraction, Raphael was able to probe at the very flaws in modern rationality as well as address the unresolved paradoxes between form and content in modernism. With Raphael we can witness the instability in the foundations and at the borders of modernity. Raphael's argument reveals a model of assimilation which regulates the reception and the conception of 'new' products. For the other to be domesticated it must also be doubled, it must have one face that turns inwards conveying a sense of belonging, and the other face that turns to the exterior, pointing to the beyond. It is this duality which secures a sense of extension and bridging, thus for every foreign element to be accepted there must be both a centrifugal and a centripetal force; a narcissistic sense of inclusion and a transgressive sense of extension. For the non-western to enter the West it must do so in the guise of the cultural hybrid: the non-western westerner.

HYBRIDITY IN COLONIALISM

The clash of cultures that colonialism invariably provoked not only produced a neat bifurcation between the colonizer and the colonized, but encouraged the formation of new cultural hybrids. Ashis Nandy's account of the levels of consciousness that at first sustained and then undermined the colonizing project stresses that the conventional binarism which represented the colonized as victim and the colonizer as victor overlooks the fact that both were caught up as players and counter-players in the dominant model of universalism. Shifting his attention away from the obvious sites of conflict and violence, Nandy focuses on the actual interfaces and processes of negotiation between opposing groups. With great subtlety Nandy notes the means of resistance expressed by urban westernized Indians and the degrees of degradation experienced by the Anglo colonizer. Agency is never the monopoly of one player, for both are locked in a dyadic relationship.[4]

Colonialism produced new losses and gains, allowed new forms of identity to ascend and debased or crushed others. This trajectory was always, at least, dual. It was one of the peculiar features of British colonialism that the subjects that induced the greatest discomfort and were the victims of the most bitter attacks were the hybrids. The repulsion that was genuinely felt towards the hybrids a was, according to Nandy, deeply connected to the repression of the antonyms and dualisms that jostled for position in the colonizer's sexual identity and political ideology.

The conflict of interests between the colonizer and the colonized was also a conflict between the parts and processes of identity. It promoted a self-image and form of consciousness that was defined in opposition to the putative characteristics of the 'Eastern man' and exaggerated the qualities of hardness, distanciation and responsibility. A self was fashioned that was not only more congruent to the needs of the colonial machine but intolerant of the inherent mixtures in one's self and in others.

For Nandy all encounters produce change. The perversity of colonialism is thus measured not just in terms of the extreme exploitation of the other but also in the contortion and constrictions of the self that were necessary to enforce such a relationship. Nandy explains this process of cultural co-optation in two ways. First, by demonstrating the homology between sexual repression and political dominance which led to an internalization of self-images of hardness and detachment as the appropriate 'manly' modes of colonial rule. Second, by revealing that the initial identification with the aggressor was not just an attempt to seek salvation by means of mimicry, but a resurrection of latent self-images which could be made compatible with the ideology of colonialism. A version of Indian hypermasculinism would thus not only mirror back the ruler's wishes but also serve as a 'new, nearly exclusive indicator of authentic Indianness'.[5] Under colonialism both the ruler and the ruled produced new self-images which were selectively drawn from earlier forms of social consciousness. Colonialism found legitimacy because it established a set of codes that were common to both cultures, and because it was thereby able to manipulate the importance of components that were previously subordinate or recessive in these cultures. The seeds for the founding colonialism were already contained in the consciousness of both parties, and central to its legitimacy was the valorization of the pure and the denigration of the hybrid.

Nandy's account of the colonial modes of exchange through the psychic mechanisms of projections and introjections, and his celebration of the 'superior' resilience of hybridity, leaves one central question unanswered: does the encounter with the other require a form of replaying of old identities or the invention of new ones? Nandy systematically elaborates the principles of exchange as a rupture in the prevailing codes and priorities and the establishment of new modes of self-presentation and social management. The rupture is not seen as a total upheaval but as a shift of emphasis, like highlighting aspects of the self which had been kept dark and a promotion of previously recessive components of culture. Although there is no explicit theory of hybridity in Nandy's narrative, this process of rupture and re-grounding outlines the dynamism of exchange. Nandy is able to link the denials and repressions in, say, Rudyard Kipling's consciousness to an inability to keep in play the contradictory forces and a tendency to create a distorted and untenable self-image. Similarly, he praises the Indian's humble capacity to include aspects of the other without losing his original cultural checks and balances. However, in order to consolidate the argument that distanciation inevitably leads to atrophy and identification secures survival, one also needs a closer theory of the dynamics of exchange.

Nandy demonstrates how colonialism was legitimized as it found cultural correspondences between the rulers and the ruled. Clearly, there are common elements which lurk and lurch between the two cultures. However, to understand both the disturbing anxiety generated by cultural hybrids and the productive and enabling force of hybridity there needs to be a closer scrutiny of the creation of differences, precisely when there is a renewed circulation of equivalences, or an exaggerated outburst of hostility towards the 'intimate enemy'. For this theorization of difference we must turn elsewhere. We must move on from the history of culture and consider the semiotics of culture.

THE SEMIOTICS OF HYBRIDITY

Robert Young has stressed the significance of Bakhtin's theory of hybridity.[6] Bakhtin's attention to the mixture of languages within a text, which both ironizes and unmasks authority, demonstrates a new level of linking the concept of hybridity to the politics of representation. The language of hybridity becomes a means for critique and resistance to the monological language of authority. The hybrid text always undoes the priorities and disrupts the singular order by which the dominant code categorizes the other. In Bakhtin's schema the 'doubleness' of the hybrid voices is composed not through the integration of differences but via a series of dialogical counterpoints, each set against the other, allowing the language to be both the same and different. This clearly constitutes a turning point in the debates on hybridity. However, an even more ambitious project was elaborated by Yuri Lotman, who drew attention to the dynamics of hybridity in the semiotics of culture.

Lotman's approach goes beyond the conventional concerns with the uses of signs for the communication of content, as he extends the role of language to representing a system of signs which organizes and structures relationships to produce specific forms. This approach requires a methodological convergence between the studying of signs in contemporary meanings and the historical reconstruction of their trajectories. Culture is thus defined as a system that mediates the individual's relationship to their context. It is the mechanism for processing and organizing the surrounding signs. The way we deal with inputs, how decisions are made, priorities established, behaviour regulated, models envisaged and questions are posed in the 'communicating dialogue' with the outside world is all expressive of a particular sense of culture.

This dialogue always comprises relatively individualized languages which are in a state of interdependence and are transformed by their specific historical conditions. Lotman stresses this interdependence and avoids any movement towards analytical abstraction, for culture is never a mere summation of separate and discrete languages. Therefore, the formation of a cultural system cannot be seen to resemble the overlapping leaves of an onion. The form of culture is to be found through a sense of motion rather than by comparison to a static object. Hence, it is seen to be more like a river with a number of currents moving at different rates and intensities. The aim is to see how culture functions as a whole, in a state of constant 'creolization', or what he calls the 'semiotic physiology' as opposed to the 'atomistic approach'.

The name he gives to this dynamic process of influence, transformation and coexistence within the space of culture is the 'semiosphere'.[7] The semiosphere is the totality of semiotic acts, from squeaks to sonatas, from blips on the radar to burps at the dinner table. The semiosphere also includes all acts past and present: 'It possesses memory which transforms the history of the system into its actually functioning mechanism, this includes the mass of texts ever created and . . . the programme for generating future texts.'[8] While the value and position of elements within a language shift and change, and the set of languages within a cultural field intersect, fragment, diversify or realign, the whole of the semiotic space remains constant. Thus, the semiosphere refers to the totality of the cultural system and also the condition for the development of culture.

To illustrate the heterogeneity of elements and the diversity of functions within the semiosphere, Lotman uses the example of the museum as a model for the possibility of representing and containing difference within a system. The museum, he argues, is a single space containing exhibits from different periods, each exhibit bearing inscriptions in languages which may or may not be decipherable; there are instructions, explanations, guides, rules and plans which, to some degree, regulate the responses of visitors and staff. Within this single space, Lotman stresses, we have to remember that all the elements are dynamic, not static, and that the correlations between terms are constantly changing. In a context where the construction of the museum as an encyclopaedic repository of culture's diversity is deeply contested this may seem a flawed example; however, it is nevertheless a paradigmatic example of staging difference.

Within the model of the museum we can at least see how Lotman's conception of the semiosphere recognizes oppositions and tension, for it does not presuppose that this binarism either leads to a single point of antagonism, or that positions are mutually exclusive and immutable. His representation of the system of communication recognizes that binarisms constantly undo their own fixity. It describes a system in which there is a constant conflict between resolute, opaque and contradictory codes. The relationship between centre and periphery in the semiosphere is not explained by either the functionalist paradigm of mechanical interaction, or the dialectical model for the overcoming of antagonisms, but rather by contestation over the fit between the language of the code and the language of practice. At one stage he tries to evoke the incalculable flux of intellectual energy within the semiosphere by saying that it 'seethes like the sun'.[9] However, with this metaphor, which suggests both organic thrust and chaotic dispersal, there is the sense that the principle of power cannot be contained neatly in the acts of cultural exchange. In some sense the energy of transmission passes over the political questions of power and overrides the moral co-ordinates of ethics.

The structure of the semiosphere is thus crowded with languages with different levels and forms of representation. Lotman consciously idealizes the opposition between centre and periphery in terms of codification and indeterminacy in order to articulate the constant tension in the definition of norms, customs and laws which are generated to legitimize the extension of one language over the whole semiosphere. He is astutely conscious of the counterproductive consequences of a hegemonic language. In the semiosphere, the expansion of one language is only achieved by its rigidification and its severance from the milieu of dynamic interaction. To expand in a unified manner is to become more and more prone to disintegration. For the periphery never passively accepts conversion and it is this tension between the code of the centre and its (in)ability to reflect the practices in the periphery that produces a dissenting language.[10]

This uneven terrain of cultural production and the stochastic distribution or multi-vectorial transmission of culture is also stressed by Michel Serres. In his complex analyses of cultural dynamics he persistently questioned the transparency of the laws of determinism and challenged the conventional passage from the local to the global.[11] The productive tension between local and global, noise and dialect that Serres notes is similar to Lotman's tracking of the flux of energy that follows every criss-crossing of a boundary. For Lotman, the semiosphere is in a constant state of hybridity. It always oscillates between identity and alterity, and this tension is most evident at its boundaries:

Paradoxically, the internal space of a semiosphere is at the same time unequal yet unified, asymmetrical yet uniform. Composed as it is of conflicting structures, it nonetheless is also marked by individuation. Its self-description implies a first-person pronoun. One of the primary mechanisms of semiotic individuation is the boundary, and the boundary can be defined as the outer limit of a first-person form. This space is 'ours', 'my own', it is 'cultured', 'safe', 'harmoniously organised', and so on. By contrast 'their space' is 'other', 'hostile', 'dangerous', 'chaotic'.

Every culture begins by dividing the world into 'its own' internal space and 'their' external space. How this binary division is interpreted depends on the typology of the culture.[12]

An archetypical example of this type of differentiation between US and THEM, a relationship of non-relationship whereby the exterior other is defined by the logic of the inversion, is the designation of the other as Barbarian, and as we all know a Barbarian is simply the person who does not speak Greek. However, the other that is within the semiosphere is not perceived by such an *a priori* categorization, but is identified through the processes of translation. The construction of the exterior other by the logic of inversion is designed to preclude dialogue, whereas the presence of the other who speaks different languages within the semiosphere interacts through translation and thus facilitates both dialogue and transformation. Because the different languages within the semiosphere do not have mutual semantic correspondences, translation presupposes asymmetry. But, as Lotman emphasizes, this difference has to be perceived as both necessary and desirable, for the precondition for dialogue is the mutual attraction of the participants. Lotman outlines the mechanisms by which dialogue occurs in the context of difference, that is, how information is generated from the tension between a language and its contact with a foreign text, as he describes this process of interaction in five stages.

First, a text arrives from the outside, it appears in its original form, in its own language, its strangeness is intact, it is not considered a threat or a problem because it is presumed to be superior and therefore will offer a positive contribution.

Second, a transformation at both ends begins to occur, that is, the imported text and the receiving culture begin to restructure each other. The foreign text is idealized because it offers the local culture the opportunity to break with the past. Here the foreign text is imbued with salvific qualities. However, there also emerges a counter-tendency whereby the foreign text is linked to a submerged element in the receiving culture, the foreign thus activates a dormant component and is therefore interpreted as an organic continuation or a rehabilitation of the familiar culture.

Third, there emerges the tendency to deprecate the source of origin from which the text came and an emphasis that the true potential of the text is only realized by being integrated into the receiving culture. Reception has led not only to transformation but is also a form of transcendence. Before it was debased and distorted, now it has the grace of truth and universality.

Fourth, after the imported text has been fully assimilated, its distinctive presence has been dissolved and has led to the production of a new model, the receiver having internalized the text and restructured its own axioms and values, the local becomes producer of the new and original texts.

Fifth, the receiver is now a transmitter, or in Lotman's words it 'issues forth a flood of texts directed to other, peripheral areas of the semiosphere'.[13]

Lotman was conscious that this dialogue, or what he calls this process of 'infection', could only be realized under favourable historical, social and psychological conditions. Where Lotman defines the semiosphere as the result and the condition of possibility of the system of communication, Serres invokes the third man, the parasite, the demon and the clinamen.[14] Both theorists are intensely conscious of the role of the hybrid and creolization and draw attention to the splitting, interference in the dissemination of languages, leading us towards a re-evaluation of the position, role and function of the migrant, yet both theories say little about the precondition of desire in mutual attraction or the disposition to delegate the third man. Are these structural questions simply left as the bias history?

The problem with the semiosphere is that it does not address the politics in the distinctions between language and silence, between coherence and babble, between comprehension and confusion. It does not distinguish between the patterns of selections that influence which languages will be learned and what thresholds between the axioms of transparency and opaqueness in language will be sustained in order to stimulate particular forms of knowledge and to permit the emergence of particular claims. In other words, it does not address the politics by which the margin is appropriated, tokenized or fetishized in order to serve the interests and maintain the hierarchical order constructed by the centre. For all his attention to the fluid dynamics of the semiosphere, Lotman appears to have overlooked the specific forces of access and exclusion. The levels of travelling and the process of transmission discount any degree of loss or mutation in the course of the journey. Meaning only begins once the text enters the space of the semiosphere, but what traces are there of the meanings prior to this encounter? The arrival of a foreign text is never a perfect isomorph of another culture, it too is formed by the hybrid journeys, both within one context and another.

From this perspective it appears that the primary tendency within the semiosphere is toward the acculturation of the foreign text and subtle modification of the dominant language. However, to witness the innovative potential of the foreign text, or the restructuring of the dominant language according to the laws of the other, we will have to measure the degree to which the memory of the foreign code has been preserved and examine the impact resulting from the insertion of the foreign text. It is the interruptive force of hybridity which seems to be ultimately smoothed over, as it is incorporated into the fundamental flux of the semiosphere. For as Stuart Hall argues, the emergence of 'other histories' in contemporary discourse is synchronous with the radicalization of the notions of identity, history and language. When such fundamental concepts are in crisis the position of the margin is paradoxically empowered. With the revelation of the multiple others in the self, or rather the understanding that the history of the self 'is composed always across the silence of the other',[15] and when language is framed by a broader politics of articulation, embedded within 'an infinite semiosis of meaning',[16] then, this opens the space for the process of re-identification and re-territorialization by which the margin comes into representation. Hall describes this re-articulation of the symbolic order through the Gramscian theory of hegemony and counter-politics. The margin speaks with a three-pronged strategy: first, through an opposition to the given order; second, via recovery of broken histories and the invention of appropriate narrative forms; and third, through the definition of a position and a language from which speech will re-emerge.[17]

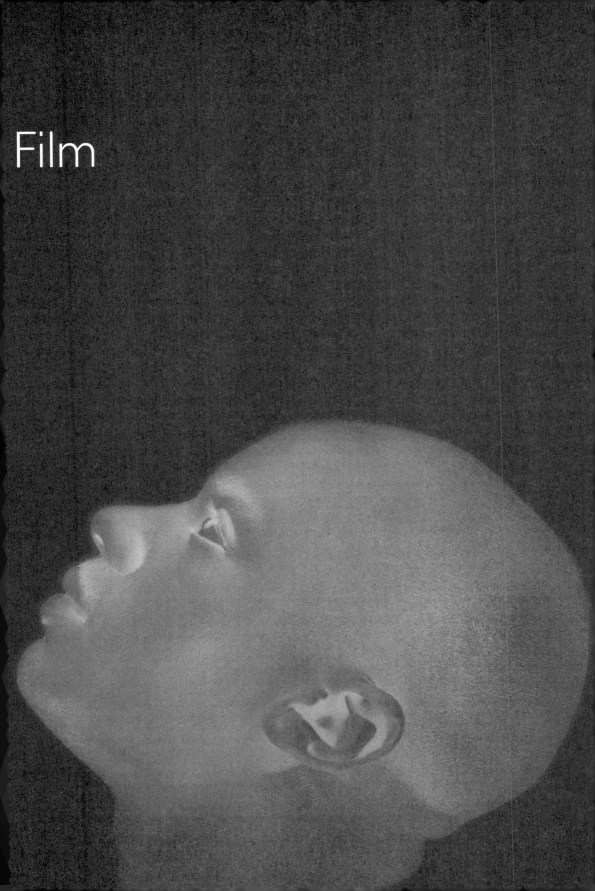

Film

Introduction

MERRYL WYN DAVIES

In darkened spaces, stories are projected and illuminated, myths re-created, epic sagas refashioned. Cinema is the medium of structured narrative and relation, in all senses of the word. Cinema makes, reforges and enframes history as it advances the ideology of global popular culture. Multiplex cinema complexes are a global domain where a multiplex global popular culture is disseminated. The history of cinema is a retelling of the history of dominance that serves as an engine of production of a new phase in the globalization of dominance. Hollywood is the ultimate terminus of western civilization, the place where it reaches the apotheosis of its manifest destiny.

The manifest destiny of cinema is the civilizing mission, the grand project of western civilization. The moguls who made Hollywood consciously conceived of cinema as a medium of assimilation into the culture of dominance. They sought to cater to a disparate audience of new immigrants, from among whom the moguls themselves were drawn, and provide them with the vital rudiments – shared language, stories, myths, imagery and ethos – for incorporation within Americana. The immigrants, however, were not merely domestic; the huddled masses yearning and fit for Americana were to be found globally, even in the early days of cinema. Charlie Chaplin, Mary Pickford and Douglas Fairbanks Sr were modernity's first genuine global popular icons.

Hollywood gives us enscribing narratives of dominance, the relation of the sustaining myths, the depiction and imagery of self-justificatory epic dramas, heroes who are the pioneers and pathfinders of civilization. Hollywood's cinema takes up the project of Pax Romana, Pax Christi, Pax Britannica and is the mouthpiece of Pax Americana. It neatly charts the westward march of the illumination of civilization. Appropriately, it finds its most potent and characteristic product in the genre of the western: the encounter of homesteaders, cowboys and the cavalry with the irreducible Other – the Indians – on the last frontier.

The first two articles presented here explore aspects of Indianology, which is not merely a genre of cinema but also one of the basic disciplines of western thought. Indianology as a discipline and discourse is a principal construction site where the Other has been fabled and made available to be enframed. Jean Fisher's essay on Kevin Costner's multi-Oscared film *Dances with Wolves* explores the inseparable relationship between the rhetoric of American democracy and its contemporaneous constructs of Indianology as an example of a relationship that constantly undergoes subtle reordering to ensure it remains essentially unchanged.

Fisher argues that the project of American history is accomplished through romantic literary conceits, with Indianology at its heart. *Dances with Wolves* uses the device of a diary to underscore its central theme, the privileging of white America as the only author of American history, including the superior right to represent and appropriate the Indian. The film's mythic saga concerns the redemption of its central white character through his encounter with native American life. Though heralded for its supposed sympathetic portrayal of Native Americans, in fact this is just another literary conceit to once again silence and marginalize the real Americans in the service of peddling a new vision of redemptive self-justification for the tyranny of American democracy.

The historic longevity of this practice is the subject of Ziauddin Sardar's essay on the Disney animated film *Pocahontas*. Historically, Pocahontas was the original appropriated Indian, mythologized to justify the right and rightness of white settlers in dispossessing the native inhabitants of America. As Sardar shows, Disney's reworking of the myth draws in all the iconic strands that have become the conventions of representation of the Other. But the ideological message of this cartoon is the latest expression of Pax Americana: the Other, in the character of Pocahontas, is represented as incomplete, dissatisfied with Otherness and yearning for a fulfilment that can only be found by assimilation within Pax Americana. Globalization is not only good for the Other, it is exactly what they want.

The next two essays take up the other side of the story, the multiplex of cinema within, of and about the Third World. Filipino cinema demonstrates further multiplex aspects of cinema in the dynamics of globalization. The assimilationist ideology of cinema is to be found in the way popular cinema can be used to entertain the objectives of totalitarian regimes and to contain and divert class antagonisms that endure within liberalizing regimes, argues Jonathan L. Beller. Beller provides an analysis of Lino Brocka's film *Orapronobis*, in which the media, its censorship and sensibility play a central role. The film explores the way television and newspapers, as well as cinema, operate as *the mode of the dominant*, serving the interests of global capital. But Brocka uses cinema with 'responsibility to the audience'. His work explicitly suggests that cinema, the very agent conceived for the assimilation of the masses within the mode of the dominant, can be subverted and used to unfree minds, to make them aware of the oppressions within which they live. In which case, Filipino cinema is not merely addressing a local audience, but it is signalling future alternative possibilities to a global audience, should such an audience have access to its work.

The organization and control of global media foregrounds popular culture and restricts the circulation of anything that is not mainstream popular culture, expressions of the culture of dominance. Who gets to see Third World Cinema and how it is seen are further aspects of the multiplex that would have to be considered in developing the concept of Third Cinema, the subject of Michael Wayne's essay. The three cinemas are: mainstream popular/populist cinema, art cinema and third cinema, cinema that is committed to political and cultural emancipation. Brocka, and filmmakers like Ousmane Sembene, director of the highly regarded *Xala* (1976), are not only Third World filmmakers, they are also part of Third Cinema. This leads to an easy conflation of Third World cinema as Third Cinema. But this is to mistake the nature of cinema, globalization and the inherent assimilationist agenda of the culture of dominance. If globalization is to exist as a new dispensation it will do so by becoming internal to the organization, structure and operation of each country and people. Just as colonialism produced its 'brown sahibs' and modernity its co-opted local élites, so globalization generates mass consumers tied to the dictates of the global marketplace. Consumers are as powerless and consumed in the First as the Third World. Third World cinema can be an agent of globalization, of assimilation practised on Third World audiences by indigenous filmmakers.

Third Cinema is a very different analytic category, an alternative global domain, an alternative ideology of cultural production. It is not geographically defined but defined by institutional structures, working practices, aesthetic strategies and cultural politics. The objective of Third Cinema is transformation, a dialectic that develops the means for grasping history as process, change, contradiction and conflict. As such it can be made by First as well as Third World filmmakers. Wayne's article provides an analysis of Gillo Pontecorvo's 1966 film *The Battle of Algiers*. This raises one of the most interesting questions of all: how far Third Cinema can operate within the mainstream, be popular without being popular cinema. If it succeeds in being made within the confines of popular cinema, does it do so by becoming such a multiplex text, sufficiently ambiguous that it can be all things to all people?

To conceive of a cinema with an alternative ideology of assimilation would indeed be something quite Other in a whole new definition of the term.

Dancing with Words and Speaking with Forked Tongues

JEAN FISHER

Dances with Wolves,[1] heralded as a breakthrough for the sympathetic portrayal of nineteenth-century American Indian life, opened in London shortly after President Bush's State of the Union Address on 29 January. 'We are Americans . . .', claimed Bush. 'Our cause is just, our cause is moral, our cause is right.' Following the defeat of the Iraqi army, Bush was inspired to describe the US military success as an exorcism of the spectre of the Vietnam War, as if these conflicts involved the same homogeneous horde. In true Hollywood spirit, a rhetorical manoeuvre reclaims and rewrites US history, while inducing the Iraqis to take the rap for America's prior fall from grace.

Western democracy's much-cited narratives of 'emancipation', 'moral virtue' and 'justice' have, in practice, been highly discriminatory. As Jimmie Durham said, within the Americas, the very people to whom the term 'American' does not apply are the first peoples themselves,[2] for whom democracy has meant political surveillance, social control and an economically crippling and malevolent paternalism. Moreover, more often than not, the abrogation of native rights has been justified, not by objective reason, the cornerstone of Enlightenment thought, but by subjective assertions bordering on the superstitious. To take one example, the Governor of Georgia claimed possession of Cherokee lands on the basis that

> Treaties were expedients by which ignorant, intractable, and savage people were induced without bloodshed to yield up what civilized people had the right to possess by virtue of that command of the Creator delivered to man upon his formation – be fruitful, multiply, and replenish the earth, and subdue it.[3]

That support for such assertions is sought in divine right – a tradition to which Reagan, Thatcher and Bush have fondly adhered – shows us how little 'reason' has progressed since the seventeenth century, when the Puritans convinced themselves that 'Indians' died of European diseases by divine providence to make way for God's Chosen.

Anglo-American democracy is a moral contradiction: the 'two centuries America has served the world as an inspiring example of freedom and democracy'[4] appears to ignore its 'inspiring' record towards the 'life, liberty and the pursuit of Happiness' of indigenous peoples and 'imported' Africans. Repeatedly, behind the façade of democracy, western imperialism has precipitated chaos, misery and barbarism in the very place it has claimed to liberate.

The wide disparity between democratic principle and conduct leads us to the somewhat cynical view that the rhetoric of democracy lacks consciousness of both history and the realities of the present; that 'democracy' is, perhaps, a *myth* of modernity, the most recent in a history of self-serving 'theologies', among which can also be numbered manifest destiny and evolutionism's racial superiority.

We cannot, however, regard the capitalist state's pious claim to global copyright over democratic virtue as simply a case of boldface hypocrisy. Rather, it is the symptom of a profound lack in meaning at the core of Anglo-American thought, which Max Horkheimer attributed to the displacement of objective theories of reason as embodying some higher purpose by subjective ones, leading to the 'formalization' of reason and its relegation to the forces of expediency:

Reason was supposed to regulate our preferences and our relations with other human beings and with nature. It was thought of as an entity, a spiritual power living in each man ... If the subjectivist view holds true, thinking cannot be of any help in determining the desirability of any goal in itself. The acceptability of ideals, the criteria for our actions and beliefs, the leading principles of ethics and politics, all our ultimate decisions are made to depend upon factors other than reason.[5]

What we need to ask, therefore, is how the modern western state rationalizes the concept and values of democracy, and how principle is reconciled with what appears, on the face of it, to be a contradiction in practice. I want to introduce these questions by way of an examination of *Dances with Wolves*, since a nation's popular culture often presents, in allegorical form, a clearer sense of its aims, fears and aspirations than the duplicity and mystification of political rhetoric.

Arbitrary though this juxtaposition of *Dances with Wolves* and ruminations about democracy may appear to be, it nevertheless has a certain ideological piquancy. The Western, as a genre capable of inspiring popular national identi-fication with settler 'heroicism', died in the early 1970s following a number of films 'sympathetic' to Native America's historical struggle against the brutal advance of so-called western civilization. *Dances with Wolves* is, in fact, the latest in a long but sporadic history of 'liberal' Westerns, of which *Broken Arrow* (1950), *Cheyenne Autumn* (1964), *Soldier Blue* and *Little Big Man* (both 1970) are among the most familiar examples. The tendency in these films simply to invert

Poster for *Dances with Wolves*, January/February 1991.

conventional stereotypes – 'good' Indians/'bad' Anglos – which we again find in
Dances with Wolves, does not, however, throw much light on the underlying
structures that establish these configurations in the first instance, except to
confirm that we are still trapped in a reductive binarism.

Posed as an alternative to the 'justifiable genocide' narrative of white westward expansion (which was re-enacted in Westerns of the 1940s and 1950s,
under the motto of the well-known humanitarian, General 'The only good
Indians I ever saw were dead' Sheridan), by contrast, the 'liberal' film purports
to show the 'truth' of how the West was 'won', focusing on what Herman
Melville once called 'the metaphysics of Indian-hating' among US military and
land- and mineral-hungry settlers. Nonetheless, it has been amply demonstrated
that the conflict played out on the so-called 'frontier' was not simply the work of
forces beyond the control of federal government but the consequence of its
territorial ambitions, which were themselves intimately linked to implicit or
explicit 'assimilate or exterminate' directives against native peoples.[6]

It has been persuasively argued, however, that irrespective of their
nineteenth-century setting, 'sympathetic' Westerns are primarily an expression
of 1960s and 1970s countercultural protest by America's more liberal conscience.[7] So I hope you will forgive me, Dear Reader, if, bearing in mind Bush's
exoneration of the Vietnam enterprise by way of the Gulf adventure, I ask what
underlies the popular success of *Dances with Wolves*, and the apparent revival of
interest in Native Americans.

THE ALL-AMERICAN HERO

In the history of American cinema, there are but a handful of fiction films that
seriously attempt a Native American perspective. Of these, few give leading
Indian roles to native actors, and even fewer allow the character to survive to the
end of the final reel. This is particularly true of those films with more contemporary settings, such as *Jim Thorpe, All American*, (1951), *Tell Them Willie Boy Is
Here* (1969), *Run, Simon, Run* (1970) or the recent *War Party* (1989), which,
although they attempt to present the difficulties Native Americans have experienced in accommodating white culture, end up confirming the popular but
nonetheless premature view that 'Indians' are an ill-fated race. Berkhofer is
probably correct in his analysis that the situations of the 'Indians' in films such as
Little Big Man and *Soldier Blue*, which refer to the US military's unconscienable
massacres of native villages during the nineteenth century – or even the non-
Western *One Flew over the Cuckoo's Nest* (1975), where Will Sampson's Indian is the
sole escapee from the mental asylum – are really *incidental* to a contemporary
unease about the legitimacy of America's involvement in Southeast Asia and
civil rights unrest at home.

Like the 1970s films, *Dances with Wolves* is set in the past, begging the question
as to whether we are dealing with another allegory of the present. Indeed, the
film has been described as a New Age Western, meaning, I presume, a response

to the 'green' and countercultural yearnings of those disillusioned by postindustrial Anglo-American society. Much is made in the film of unspoiled spacious landscape and intelligent nature (which is to say, the wolf and horse are the hero's allies). Kevin Costner, its star and director, in a televised interview, reinforced this reading by emphasizing his sympathy with Native America's traditional harmonious relationship to nature.[8] But as Rudy Martin of the American Indian Community House in New York pointed out, 'They want to deal with that image – that spiritual image of us – and tap into it to fulfil themselves. And yet, on the other hand, they ignore all the real issues that affect us.'[9] America's discovery of native harmony and spirituality introduces the 'green' Indian, a revamped version of the 'red' Indian as noble savage, and the latest obfuscation of the material realities, the desires and aspirations of native peoples themselves.

Critical approbation has also been given to the village of personable Lakota Sioux, whose sense of community is a major force in the film. The depiction of humour is more ambivalent; that Native Americans possess a sense of humour probably comes as a shock to Protestant America, which has hitherto preferred to image the 'Indian' as much like itself: dour, stoical and humourless. But the slapstick tendency in the film is a little too reminiscent of the Hollywood Indian buffoon. Unfortunately, this humanizing of the 'Indian' does not extend to the Pawnees, whom we see in the familiar demonized role of marauding savage. Their speech, unlike Lakota, is not translated through subtitles, and consequently Pawnee motives remain obscure.

The film's use of the Lakota language, and its meticulous attention to historical details of dress, social and ceremonial practice, like Eliot Silverstein's *A Man Called Horse* (1970), rely heavily on the nineteenth-century drawings and notes of George Catlin and Carl Bodmer, and the less hysterical of those testimonials known as 'captivity' narratives. In fact, one magazine presented publicity photographs of the Native American cast, posed in their costumes in the manner of Catlin.[10]

It is worth noting here that *A Man Called Horse* occupies an ambiguous position in the Western genre, approaching what might be called 'dramatized ethnography'. Presenting the Sioux as neither *irrationally* savage nor sentimentally noble, the earlier film manages to convey some sense of a people whose *difference* from modern Euro-American ideals includes a value system alien to *humanism*.

It is the trap of the latter into which *Dances* falls, since the film's narrative is articulated wholly through the actions and voice-over narration of Costner's Union officer, Lieutenant Dunbar, who acquires his 'Indian' name after he has elected to join the village in preference to his solitary 'frontier' outpost. *A Man Called Horse* presents no such fantasy: the film's eponymous captive hero is treated like a beast of burden until he can prove his worth as a human being. Moreover, he is an English aristocrat, a character who would hardly entertain relinquishing the privileges of a class assured of its position in the semi-feudal world of 'civilized' England, and whose actions throughout the film – motivated towards escape from his captors, despite his growing respect for them – are wholly consistent with this position.

Dunbar, however, exhibits all the symptoms of late modern middle-class man with a liberal conscience, whose sense of dislocation in time and place, and whose search for the passing 'frontier' (an arcadian space without memory), compels him to 'go native'. Such a move has historically been untenable to the Puritanical and essentially bourgeois Anglo-American mind, obsessed as it has always been with the righteous and proper (property and the work ethic), racial and class purity. To 'go native' is tantamount to treason: a descent into savagery and the horror of miscegenation (while the 'Indianized' Dunbar is punished for the first treasonable offence when the army finally catches up with him, he does not commit the second, having married a white woman adopted by the Sioux).

Penetration and exploitation of the so-called wilderness could only be accomplished, however, by men prepared to forego the niceties of 'civilized' society, which led to the popular assumption that frontiersmen had become, at least in part, 'Indianized' savages or children of nature. But bearing no allegiance to the moral or social restraints of either culture, frontiersmen must surely have existed in a moral and social vacuum. This, however, provokes a representational paradox. If the independent individual was to be the American ideal, how could this hero, lacking 'virtue' yet essential to the myth of advancing civilization, be accommodated with America's desire for a moral and ordered society, except by a series of romantic literary conceits,[11] whose most recent avatar is the patinated outsiderism of *Dances*.

If *Dances* at least presents the Lakota as possessing a civilization, it also touches briefly on a rather less popularized 'frontier' syndrome concerning the confrontation of whites with this plain of (for them) incoherent signifiers – the psycho-pathology, insecurity, suicide, irrational fears and superstitions among whites unable to adjust to a territory without familiar co-ordinates and border controls. Consequently, the 'Indianization' of the white man, and the *cultural degeneracy* that this implies, can have popular currency only if the native host possesses values that the Anglo-American can both recognize and desire – in other words, that the native culture is not so much alien as an *idealized* Other.

Although *Dances* attempts to explore the misunderstandings in language that ensue in the confrontation between mutually antagonistic cultures, it can resolve difference only by incorporating both sides to liberal humanism, a manoeuvre which also entails, however, the expiation of a guilty past. While Costner deliberately spares us the spectacle of bloody massacres, in favour of 'spiriting' the Indians away from the path of advancing troops, we are nevertheless left with the false illusion that Native America somehow escaped genocide. This is in marked contrast to *Powwow Highway*,[12] a film which bravely attempted to reconcile the problems and aspirations of *contemporary* reservation-based Native Americans, drawing on cultural configurations poorly understood by whites, and which, not surprisingly, received little public attention. *War Party*, using the contemporary Blackfoot Reservation and Glacier National Park in Montana, pulled no punches on the racism that makes for uneasy coexistence between

Anglos and Native Americans in the redneck Mid-western states. Made in 1989 and released in Britain only after *Dances, War Party* has had no publicity and poor audience response.[13] All of this suggests that, despite its sophisticated signs of 'Indianicity' and historical Lakota Sioux culture – a history nonetheless documented by whites – the 'Indians' of *Dances* remain the backdrop against which the problem of the white male individual is articulated.

The theme of the heroized individual operates both inside and outside the text of *Dances with Wolves*. Considerable advance publicity gave accounts of the difficulties encountered by Costner in raising interest and money for the project in the Hollywood industry, and the negative press during the shooting of the film. Following the film's public vindication – its box-office success, and the Golden Bear and Academy Awards – Costner's trajectory has now followed the trial-and-redemption of the classic hero, as well as confirming, on a less altruistic level, the popular American myth that individualism has its [just] reward.

In 1864 one man went in search of the frontier . . . And found himself: so declares the byline on the poster for *Dances with Wolves*. Superceded only by the star's name, it succinctly sums up the film's narrative plot as a conventional Hollywood hero quest. The white man is the subject of knowledge, while the 'Indians', rather than being full subjects in their own right, remain the *instruments* of his search for self-identity, revealing the self-interest at the core of American liberalism. Nothing illustrates the film's privileging of the western individual more decisively than the recurrent appearance of Dunbar's illustrated *diary*. This, then, is not the ambivalent hero caught between civilization and savagery of earlier Western genres; neither illiterate backwoodsman nor aristocratic tourist, nor violent gunman, he is liberalism's 'artist and author' – the bourgeois *historical* subject. By contrast, and despite the film's claim to ethnographic authenticity, we are given no insight into Lakota understanding of time and history, nor the means by which it recorded events (as, for instance, the 'winter counts' on tepee hides). This monological writing has a dual function: it circumscribes the other such that it cannot answer to the truthfulness of the account; and it legitimizes the white man as the author of American history. As one of the 'warriors' in *Harold of Orange*[14] stated, there were no 'Indians' before the arrival of the European; and for the European, there was no American history before he wrote it.

During the course of the narrative – while, in fact, he is resident with the Sioux whose traditions privilege the oral rather than the scriptural – Dunbar 'forgets' and 'loses' his diary, the evidence of his (white) identity as historical subject, and also the marker of time. In the absence of this book, space and its Indian occupants appear and disappear with the timelessness of a hallucination. Yet, significantly, it is returned to him as he leaves the community by the youth who recovered it, as if to suggest that it has the approbation of future generations of Native Americans as a True and Honest Account.

The *written record* overrides the legitimacy of the oral account, and is reminiscent of the Puritans' obsessive reliance on The Book. Indeed, that *Dances* is a redemptive narrative of Christian proportions is exposed at the outset in the crucified gesture with which Costner's Yankee officer makes his suicidal ride in front of the firing line of Southern troops; and later, by the beating and repudiation he receives from his own 'race'. Lieutenant Dunbar indeed 'dies', to be born again as a fringed and beaded latter-day hippie, having internalized white America's Indian Other.[15]

A SOCIETY OF STRANGERS

When, a couple of years ago, Mrs Thatcher claimed that 'there was no such thing as society, only individuals', she was restating the primacy of the sovereign subject underlying Anglo-American liberalist interpretations of democracy, and confirming the extent to which the ideology of the state-capitalist system is against society. A theory of the human subject that does not take account of its communal dimensions posits a society of strangers in which moral judgement and the conduct of justice are left to a contingent goodwill. It is its redemption of this (modernist) liberal individual's estrangement from both nature and community that, I believe, accounts for the popular appeal of *Dances with Wolves*. In this respect, it operates in reverse of Coppola's epic *The Godfather* (1972), which thematically charts the progressive breakdown of American community, and the social isolation and moral disintegration of the autonomous individual.

Democracy is a concept of government through the sovereignty of the people, and is embodied in the US Declaration of Independence, whose 'self-evident truths' are that all men are created equal with 'the inalienable rights of Life, Liberty and the pursuit of Happiness'. Agnes Heller identifies two interpretations of freedom: the 'democratic', which demands equal rights of participation in the decisions of the body politic, including the right and possibility of so doing; and the 'liberal', which claims everyone has the right to decide their fate and way of life, provided it is not detrimental to others, including the possibility of exercising such right.[16] Successive American governments have persistently failed to acknowledge these basic rights for Native Americans. For instance, the Indian Citizenship Act of 1924, unilaterally implemented by Congress, offered the former right only on condition that Native Americans relinquished the second – the right to traditional beliefs and lifestyles. Since then, in both Canada and the USA, native peoples have had to *prove* their identity as 'Indians' (by blood quantum) in the face of bureaucracies who have vested interests in proving that Native Americans no longer 'exist' – a form of legitimation not demanded of any other ethnic group. The most recent of such laws insists that Indian artists give documentary proof of their 'Indian' identity, a law which is less about securing the status of native artists against white impostors than protecting the white collector of Indian art.[17] The aim of US assimilation policies toward the Native American has been to incorporate him into the capitalist economy – 'to awaken in him wants . . . and a pocket that aches to be filled with dollars'[18] – while denying his right to freedom of choice.

The second principle of democracy derives from utilitarianism in which social organization is based on John Stuart Mills's concept of 'the greatest good for the greatest number'. It is clear, however, that in a modern pluralistic society, defining the common good demands an impossible-to-realize consensus, and a homogeneous constituency in which heterogeneity can have no place. The rights of one constituency are invariably in conflict with the utility of another. Hence, the social engineering necessary to achieve the aims of utilitarianism must be *coercive* for someone.

Utilitarianism found a convenient ally in twentieth-century pragmatism, described by Horkheimer as 'the opinion that an idea, a concept, or a theory is nothing but a scheme or plan of action, and therefore truth is nothing but the successfulness of the idea'.[19]

> In face of the idea that truth might afford the opposite of satisfaction and turn out to be completely shocking to humanity at a given historical moment and thus be repudiated by anybody, the fathers of pragmatism made the satisfaction of the subject the criterion of truth.[20]

It is at this juncture that democratic principles of moral right and justice dissolve into the murky waters of capitalist expediency. Given that, under modernity, 'good' has been defined (by Benjamin Franklin and Mrs Thatcher, among others) as individual wealth and private property,[21] one can see that this concept is open to abuse by self-interested majorities at the expense of more general humanitarian values. The 1980s under Reagan and Thatcher were perhaps the most intensive exploitation of this philosophy since the unfettered greed that characterized white westward expansion following President Andrew Jackson's Indian Removal policy in the 1830s: a genocidal policy whose melancholic 'vicissitudes', according to Jackson, 'true philanthropy' is nevertheless able to 'reconcile'.[22]

Defining the rights of the individual through rights of property has presented the greatest ideological conflict between European and Native American societies. When native communities were forced to accept the philosophy of land ownership, they soon found that legally binding treaties made to ensure native community land rights, 'which they shall possess as long as Grass grows or water runs',[23] could be invalidated when deemed incommensurate with private ownership and privileged white forms of land usage. Hence, the Dawes Allotment Act of 1887, which forced many Native Americans onto small privately owned plots of specified acreage, effectively caused the loss to white speculators of two-thirds of reservation lands by the 1930s. The remaining reservations are largely administered 'in trust' by the Bureau of Indian Affairs. Widely acknowledged to be one of the most inefficient and corrupt federal agencies, it operates a hierarchical system of local government, antagonistic to the ways Native Americans traditionally ran their affairs, as part of a panoptical policy of surveillance and control that stems directly from utilitarianism.[24]

The efficiency of the penitentiary/panopticon derives from its containment of the observed under the unseen eye of the observer, in such a way as to enable the latter to see only when and what he wishes to see, and to deprive the former of the right to look or represent himself. As a panoptical system, the reservation effectively 'criminalizes' native difference, and places it outside the protection of the institutional law of the dominant centre, operating a penal system of punishment and reward while at the same time claiming to impose a benevolent dependency. Thus, Native American societies are faced with irreconcilable contradictions because, far from emancipating them from what Reagan still likes to think of as a 'primitive' existence, democratic principles in themselves violate not only constitutional rights of the individual but also the sovereignty of Indian Nations.

What, then, has happened to democracy's emancipatory narratives of 'justice', 'moral truth' and 'freedom'? Horkheimer seems to suggest that they fail to find expression in practical conduct through the debasement of reason to the pragmatic demands of technocracy – in the age of multinational corporations, 'democracy' is most often identified with 'free-market forces' and communications/information, controlled, nonetheless, by corporations. This view accords in principle with that of the moral philosopher Alasdair MacIntyre, who claims that the contradictions of modernity are inherited from Enlightenment thought which, although it freed western man from feudal restraints, failed to provide him with a coherent *telos* (an inherent meaning or prior moral order). Our present language of morality and justice consists of fragments of a secularized conceptual scheme 'parts of which now lack those contexts from which their significance derived'.[25] What has taken the place of *telos* is *individualism*: the Kantian concept of a transcendental subject who exercises 'free will', exists prior to society and the state, and whose rights have come to be defined above all in terms of private satisfaction. Such a sovereign subject, however, is distanced from the social body, and therefore lacks a narrative that would provide him with a *social identity*. As Michael Sandel points out, this sovereign self is without morality, since a moral sense derives from interrelationship with others.[26] Sandel claims, moreover, that it is community which precedes and defines the individual. Self-identity is more than private will or desires; it is shaped by the shared histories and beliefs, bonds of kinship and friendship, which constitute community, and within which justice and moral values have practical and historical meaning.

But the modern view of moral agency has been precisely that one could stand back from any situation and judge from a purely abstract, ahistorical and universal point of view. That there can be no such 'God's eye view' is self-evident; and yet, since Andrew Jackson's assumption of guardianship over Indian Nations, it has been vested in the figure of the president in the form of a *paternal* metaphor; state-capitalism assumes the role of benevolent paternalism, but, in practice, infantilizes its citizens through an oral dependency (demand for private satisfaction through consumerism), and the myth of homogeneous nationhood – 'we are Americans'. With the increasing entry of multinational corporations into the structures of power, government is conducted less by the *elected* representatives of 'the people' than by a faceless bureaucracy without public accountability, whose principle demand is not justice or moral truth but efficient performance of an (increasingly paranoid) system – what the poststructuralists presumably mean when they characterize our experience as a time not of ends but only of means. The consequence is that, far from being 'autonomous' the individual under multinational capitalism is subtly *disempowered*.

We have no clear epistemes that can reconcile the contradictions of the western self, desiring, yet estranged from, both nature and social identity, or that can fill his lack of a coherent moral and just universe. MacIntyre prescribes a return to Aristotelian virtues which privilege the social role of the individual, advocating 'local forms of community within which civility and the intellectual and moral life can be sustained through the new dark ages which are already upon us'.[27] While his diagnosis of the situation may be accurate, he gives no account of how such a reformation of local communities and the re-empowerment of a social self can take place, given the continuing power of the state to atomize society; nor does he address the diversity of often conflicting subject-positions in late twentieth-century experience.

It is not surprising, therefore, that Anglo-America sees in its native neighbours only evidence of what it feels itself to have lost: the community of *Dances with Wolves* in 'harmony' with itself and with a non-threatening nature. But to seriously take on the values of traditional native societies entails a seemingly impossible shift in its concept of selfhood. Since Native American social practice gives priority to communal over private ownership, and to consensus over hierarchy, white America has assumed that native cultures traditionally lacked a concept of the individual. To conclude thereby that Native Americans were slaves to tribal law is thoroughly to misunderstand the status of *individuality* within the community, and to ignore the care with which an individual's natural aptitudes were identified and nurtured. That indigenous North American societies tended not to develop power hierarchies is attributable in part to the *equal* value assigned to individual roles and skills, and the shared responsibility to the well-being of the group accepted by every member.[28] Moreover, Pierre Clastres has argued forcibly that the distribution of power into non-hierarchical structures in such societies stems from their sophisticated understanding that power is always coercive and works against the interests of culture as a dynamic force.[29] Hence, in a society in which people identify themselves fully with their social roles – which is the presumed case for pre-contact North American societies – the possibility of understanding moral value and justice as expressions of individual approval would not exist. This being so, it would be what Fredric Jameson calls a 'category-mistake'[30] to read Native American societies through Eurocentric concepts of morality and justice. Similarly, Native American 'harmony with nature' is based considerably more in common sense (as science might now agree) than the term 'spiritual' would suggest, and, likewise, is inappropriate to western value-laden moral categories. Science, perhaps, gives us the possibility of a common ground. But a true epistemological change cannot take place where the western concept of the sovereign subject remains empowered to write the narrative. Costner's assertion that his intention was 'not to set the record straight' nevertheless leaves us with the semblance of a Native American subject without changing the terms of the relations of power, which disbars the possibility of equal cultural exchange. By contrast, the 'trickster' of *Harold of Orange*, conscious of the paradoxes that exist in the processes of transcription between contemporary Anglo and Native cultures, represents a truly radical departure from the privileged western protagonist.

Dances with Wolves expresses the desire for spirit and meaning beyond mere utility, but, trapped in the tyranny of sign, it presents a dehistoricized and fantasmic *image* of a culture now penetrated, however imperfectly, by the very structures that brought forth the image in the first instance. The view the film presents is one of mutual respect between white and red man, a romantic fiction bearing little relation to inter-cultural realities – as was demonstrated last year by the Mohawks on the Canadian and US border. *War Party* understands all this more clearly; and, in attempting a dialectic between the past and the present, offers a commentary on the kind of commodification of both Native cultures and history that *Dances* represents.

The popularity of *Dances with Wolves*, however, suggests that US self-flagellation over the public disgrace of Vietnam has given way to redemption through the packaged fantasy of multiculturalism and racial harmony – another subterfuge by the workings of cultural imperialism. The contradictions between the principles and conduct of morality and justice, between the individual and community, become reconciled in the passage to self-discovery of the liberal hero, who has internalized the 'ideal' elements of the Native world without having to deal with any of its contradictions. It is a supremely seductive illusion which finds its echo in the protestations of justice, morality and truth that punctuate the rhetoric of Bush's State of the Union Address. And if Bush can claim that for 'two centuries America has served the world as an inspiring example of freedom and democracy', against all evidence to the contrary, it is because in the 'cultural logic of late capitalism', to borrow Jameson's phrase, anything can be said as long as it says nothing.

Walt Disney and the Double Victimization of Pocahontas

ZIAUDDIN SARDAR

The 'Virginia born lady'[1] lived for a time at a London tavern called the Bell Savage just off the traditional home of the popular British press, Fleet Street. Perhaps it should not come as a surprise that she should end up in the clutches of media hype; one can never be too careful where one chooses to lay one's head. And for laying her head she has indeed become famous, a postmodern icon painted with all the lurid colours in Walt Disney's palette to whisk away the winds of history. The truth is otherwise, though truth has a limited role in the recorded history of the life of Matoaka, or as marquees around the world have proclaimed her, *Pocahontas*.

Walt Disney has conspicuously consumed history to provide a subtle, sophisticated reading for the old story, re-propagandizing a tale that gained currency precisely as polemic propaganda masquerading as history. In a television documentary made to promote their film, all the participants – the animators, the musicians, those who provided the voice-overs, the producers, the director – stress how they sought to be true to history, in a streamlined, digestible way that allowed them to concentrate on this wonderful love story at the heart of history.[2] What we are presented with is a neatly assembled cast of stereotypes. Pocahontas is the natural, idyllically in harmony with nature, peace and bounty, but she is also a restless spirit looking for something more in her world, according to the Disney production department. Her father, Powhatan, is the very embodiment of the noble savage, not the first time this character type has appeared on film, or had the voice of the ex-AIM leader, Russell Means. Disney's new history is a subtle selection, highly significant in how it chooses to paraphrase, collapse and conflate the details from the contemporary sources and repertoire of historic interpretation of the legend that goes before them and constitutes western civilization's colonial/colonizing history. To compound their new stereotypes, Disney is deeply indebted to old, familiar stereotypes which root their postmodern refurbishment in a continuing tradition.

The first and the most obvious selection is the character of Pocahontas herself. The earliest iconography of the new continent depicted America as a nubile, available maiden with long, loose tresses. It has been argued that the representation betokens a woman ripe for rape; certainly, the languor of the sexually charged figure of America was intended to suggest she was at the very least ready to be husbanded by Europe.[3] The drawing of Pocahontas in the cartoon version makes her the most sexually endowed of all the female forms that appear. Or as Mel Gibson puts it in the Disney television documentary: 'I mean, Pocahontas is a babe, isn't she, you've got to say it.'[4] Her costume, a figure-hugging little number, is obviously informed by the famous series of John White's drawings that he made at Roanoake, which owed their inspiration to ancient Greece, not the lithe tradition of vase painting but the solidity and ampleness of statuary.[5] Within the family viewing conventions of Disney, there is no doubt that the lusty manhood of John Smith is aroused by his first glimpse of this icon of America. How easily supposed political correctness betrays its origins and ends up redeploying the oldest stereotypes of all! In the early representations, America, while sexually charged and available, is always a passive figure, resting in a hammock, lying in a languid pose (not unlike all those famous harem postcards of Arab maidens). It was a conception of colonial womanhood that was widely diffused, a long-standing tradition, a conventional, stereotypical notion.[6] But Disney's Pocahontas is something new – she is entranced by John Smith even before he is aware of her presence. By this twist of the palette, Disney confirms its own statement in the television documentary: Pocahontas is looking for heightened experience, something more than her world offers. So it is that native America stalks the animus it desires – all that is embodied and represented by John Smith. In today's postmodern refashioning, instead of the passive, tractable native awaiting the colonizer, the native is yearning to make herself sexually available to her destiny: the colonizer.

Even in the concept of strange portents that trouble Pocahontas's dreams, Disney is selecting from another well-known trope. Popular history books are full of the legend that the Aztec permitted a bedraggled band of Spaniards to penetrate to the heart of their empire because they believed them to be the white gods which mythology foretold would come from the West. Peter Schaffer's famous play, and the movie thereof, *Royal Hunt of the Sun*, uses a similar convention, this time concerning the Inca, who supposedly took Pizarro and his tiny band for gods, thus enabling the latter to slaughter thousands of unarmed natives and take Atahualpa captive. Schaffer had a much more complex reading of first encounters to explore and is certainly right in pointing to the infinite attractiveness to European colonizers of being taken as gods by simple benighted savages, a feature of so many travellers' tales and representations that it is the hoariest old cliché in the books, cartoons and movies – think of the Rudyard Kipling story made into the John Huston film, *The Man Who Would Be King*, or the adventures of Indiana Jones in the Temple of Doom, or almost any adventure that sets off into Darkest Africa. Disney does not go for that cliché, it authors another: Pocahontas, of her own volition and needs, wants John Smith, is waiting for John Smith and ogles him as any susceptible teenager would Mel Gibson (who provides his voice-over). The convention of the available maiden, the portents of European coming – these are not disinterested reports but artefacts, consciously deploying ideology to explain the innate superiority of Europe in all parts of the European psyche, including the sexual libido. The white man as god is first the white man as missionary bringing the Christian message; then he becomes the god of scientific wonder and superior technology.

For Disney, he is merely a super-handsome hunk, but he is a true descendant of the genre with a new twist: Pocahontas's love at first sight is the exact equivalent of the god from afar.

Indigenous women have always been libidinous in the western convention, from Amerigo Vespucci's accounts to Margaret Mead's now discredited reports of sexual licence among Samoan girls. The Disney animators who made Pocahontas this vision of sexually explicit girlhood – their characterization is definitely adolescent – also explain that they wanted to express an animality in her movements. Once more Disney evokes a much older and redolent tradition linked to some very powerful colonizing ideas. Within the conventions of early modern Europe, when the first settlers wrote their travellers' tales – and the process of writing first reports went on for centuries, and is still not dead yet – and described the natives as scantily clad with long flowing hair who used bows and clubs and inhabited the forests, what they meant and were understood to be saying was very explicit: it was a highly stereotyped representation of a barbarian, a wild man and wild woman, people who lived within nature, who operated on natural law in a sense quite other from the existence of redeemed European Christian humanity.[7]

Pocahontas's feline movements have another powerful connection: the wild woman was conceived to have a store of learning about the natural world; just as Pocahontas demonstrates in her musical peroration to John Smith, the wild woman was skilled with herbs and potions, and she was conventionally conceived to have a familiar, a cat, for company. In short, the wild woman of the Middle Ages was the origin of the concept of the witch, exactly the concept Disney deployed in its very first full-length animated cartoon, *Snow White and the Seven Dwarfs*: 'Mirror, mirror on the wall, who is the fairest of them all?' The beautiful woman/old crone who tempts Snow White is the libidinous woman on the outside and the gnarled evil old crone inside. Living off the fruits nature offered, as feral creatures who modelled themselves on animals in whose skins they dressed themselves, the natives were not possessors of 'dominium', actual real property rights in the land they inhabited, or as the early settlers of Virginia explicitly stated, they had no 'meum and teum' (mine and yours): no private property, hierarchy, hereditary principles, religion, 'but all is common'. These descriptions had very precise meaning within the terms of European law and the self-interested rationalization it gave to the colonizing enterprise: those who had no property except in common could commonly have everything taken from them, justly, according to the law.

Disney is not merely trying to be historically accurate by the profuse use of the term 'savage' that it puts into the mouth of its European characters. It has built upon a tradition of representation that ties its supposedly politically correct, improved, postmodern vision of the Native American to some potent, familiar old ideas that are so widespread within western culture that they can only be refashioned and refurbished, not overturned or dispensed with. Walt Disney's postmodern revision has added to the old mix the Native American lust after the icon of the spirit of the settlers: John Smith. Pocahontas wants the newness that European settlement brought. The Other now, naturally, must be depicted as actively seeking out the postmodern dispensation, western domination in its new incarnation. All the earliest reports speak of the 'tractability' of the natives, how they seemed a blank page ready to follow the European way; however, once there was a hint of conflict with the desires of the colonizers, the natives became 'inconstant savages'. Opposition to the colonial dominating authority reflects the innate hostility and savagery of the savage, which according to the conventions of European law justifies the expropriation of all their property, life, liberty and pursuit of happiness – which one might be justified in recognizing as the origins of the Other as demon terrorist, a conception which firmly adheres to some Others today.

The very selection of the tale of Pocahontas for refashioning as a postmodern American icon is merely a return to the original. Despite the feisty banter with which she takes the assurance of John Smith down a peg, despite the truncation of the story of Pocahontas herself, the reason she is available for postmodern manufacture and conspicuous consumption is what it always was. Pocahontas was the first documented convert. Of course, Disney is not telling the story of Pocahontas; for all that they make her an icon, they are not telling her history. The 'new' history Disney authors is the history of the origins of the United States of America, to which Pocahontas has been appropriated. Just as *Dances with Wolves* took Lieutenant Dunbar off among the Indians to find renewed self-realization and then left the Indians to 'vanish', the details of which departure need not trouble the audience, though they may implicitly invoke a sadness and a tragic sense, so *Pocahontas* leaves out all the actual experience of the colonial Other. It deals only with a two-year span of time, defined by the presence in Jamestown of John Smith. It does not entertain the experience of the Powhatan, which included the familiar fate of decimation through illness, a genuine holocaust which the settlers praised as a providential act of God to clear the country for their domination, a proof of the rightness of their election and mission. It does not deal with the decimation from the unremitting warfare that began during John Smith's sojourn in Jamestown and continued for decades until only a handful of Powhatan were left. New history stops historical narrative at the point convenient to its own ideological needs. *Pocahontas* ends with the Indians bringing offerings of corn to the settlers who will remain when John Smith leaves, an allusion to the tradition and meaning of Thanksgiving Day. In the repository of the American mind, the Indian is the dead, trussed, cooked turkey offered up on Thanksgiving to ensure the survival of American Family Values.

What *Pocahontas* is permitted to say of the Native American worldview is a postmodern convention, the shorthand for New Ageism, that speaks of an animate universe, spiritually alive and interconnected. The spiritual power of native peoples is psychic power, an acuity to the irrational rationality that modernity drove out of the western mind through its dedication to scientific rationality. Of course, in modernist terms, the irrationality of routine recourse to psychic power was not deemed rational, it was the negative antithesis of scientific rationality: magic, or, in Levy-Bruhl's term, the 'pre-logical'. In the postmodern vision, it is psychic acuity that is the attraction of Others, the property common to all that is to be, and can be, appropriated. It is psychic spirituality, the being in touch with their inner premodern natural world, that adds nobility to the Other and gives it the last laugh on modern dispensation, the scientific, technological and polluted world in which western postmodernism resides. Furthermore, there is an innate linkage between this psychic/ spiritual acuity and peaceableness, the willingness to be first to lay down their arms. Not quite the outlook of a superpower nation that conceived first-strike capacity and the Star Wars option, that makes peace by carrying a big stick and is busy, in the new Republican backlash, worrying about the unpreparedness of its over-abundant armed forces.[8]

Innumerable films in recent years depict the whole 'spiritual' panoply used and evoked in *Pocahontas*: from Chief Dan George in *Little Big Man* (1976), who 'sees' through dreams and visions and therefore knows what happens to Little Big Man when he is living in white society, to Russell Means in *Windwalker* (1980) as the reincarnated spirit of Olympic champion Jim Thorpe, who becomes the wise old Indian mysteriously attaching himself to a young white boy to counsel and teach him through his difficult adolescence and then mystically departs from the world. A further example is Lou Diamond Phillips's unreconstructed character in *Avenging Lance* (aka *Renegades*, 1989), where the lance in question is a sacred object stolen from a museum exhibition that must be tracked down and retrieved by Phillips and his white sidekick (played by Kiefer Sutherland). The tracking takes in much visionary seeing and knowing, plus the 'magical' revenge of the lance itself, which eventually engulfs its thief in flames. Sutherland's sceptical character incredulously asks 'You don't believe all that Indian shit do you?'; to which Phillips responds, 'I am that shit.' Whereas the postmodern eclectic can make judicious selection of the useful and potent aspects of the Other's insights and psychic spirituality, the Other has no alternative definition even of Self. Native American psychic spirituality can have beauty and inform, fill in some of the increasingly obvious gaps in postmodern perfection, but it could never have produced a washing machine. Other spirituality and psychic power serve the ends of the postmodern consumer, opening new directions in the development of science and technology, not their abolition. Native peoples are the last repository of the psychic/spirituality that has been forsaken in the technological progress of western civilization. *Pocahontas* is in the mainstream of the postmodern project of domination of the Other through appropriation of the eco-dream, and like all postmodern expressions of this process, it is the dominant society that interprets, reports, analyses, selects and determines this Other psychic/spirituality. So bad has the situation become in the USA that Native Americans are banding together to prevent this new pillage of their culture. A pillage that is aptly represented in the satiric film *The New Age* (1994). The alternative settlements and communes that are being established using Native American design, motif and technique to author a more environmentally and psychically sound lifestyle at the height of western affluence are not inhabited or indeed frequented by Native Americans. This New

Age eco-learning taken from the indigenous past is irrelevant to the contemporary concerns of native peoples within the Americas still fighting for land rights, jobs, healthcare, education; Native Americas continue to occupy the lower rungs by all measures of social well-being. The only contemporary film that seeks to demonstrate this pathology is Michael Apted's *Thunderheart* (1992), which gives some representative voice to contemporary Native American experience.

Even the appropriation of Other spirituality is not a departure from the norms of western civilization. In large part, the selection from the religious perspectives of the Other that dwell upon an animate universe and the interconnectedness of man and nature answer the agenda of western romanticism born, at the end of the eighteenth century, as industrialization took its inhabitants further from the natural world. Postmodernism's eco-dream of the Other is nothing more than the utilization of Other systems of ideas to enable internal reform of the dominant, colonizing convention. This is an old familiar function the Other has been performing within western philosophy and social critique since Thomas More wrote *Utopia* in 1561, supposedly basing his dialogue, a virulent denunciation of European corruption, on the experiences of a traveller who had sailed with Vespucci.

But what voice does Disney's new history give to white America? The explicit purpose of Disney's new postmodern history is to wrest the USA from the calumny of European origin. The character it uses for this ideological purpose is John Smith, and the elements it deploys, appropriately enough, were provided by none other than the historic John Smith himself.

An explicit dichotomy is drawn between the respective representations of John Smith and John Ratcliffe. Ratcliffe is the villain; he is also the man who wields the Union Jack and plants it on the soil of America where, of course, honest, God-fearing and liberty-loving republican Americans will not, in the not too distant future, permit it to remain. Ratcliffe's character expresses colonialism in all its unremitting, naked greed and exploitation. He insists that Spain has had its way in the New World for too long and now it is his turn to reap the gold, implying that all the profits of the colony will belong exclusively to himself. Thus, Ratcliffe is the personification of the Virginia Company. He distracts the colonists from building homes and planting crops, sending them on a mad, futile and eco-destructive search for gold, a sequence that offers a rationale for the 'starving times' experienced by the early English colonies in North America. While Ratcliffe is the evil genius sending others forth to despoil this new land, he himself hardly moves from the fort he has constructed on the seashore alongside his ship, his lifeline back to England. And the only reason Ratcliffe wants to be in the New World is to make his fortune and thus establish his position back home at the Court of St James. On cue, at the end of the film, he is wrestled to the ground by the simple, salt-of-the-earth colonists to be sent off in disgrace, prefiguring the War of American Independence.

By way of complete contrast stands the representation of John Smith, the light to Ratcliffe's darkness. Smith is clearly weary of the Old World, though he

Engraving after Simon de Passe's portrait of John Smith, *c.* 1617. Photo courtesy of the National Portrait Gallery, Smithsonian Institution, Washington, DC/Bridgeman Art Library.

can wax lyrical about its achievements, but it is through his eyes and experience that the wonder of this new world of America is revealed to the audience. It is John Smith who appreciates the true and enduring significance of the kind of life and society that can be built in America; who, fearless and unconstrained by fanciful imagination, sets off alone to explore the new land and falls in love with it before he ever meets its embodiment, Pocahontas. John Smith is not bound by ties to England and is sufficiently open-minded to embrace, not merely the physical form of Pocahontas, but her challenge of relative pluralism.

Far from being the footloose freebooter, the historical John Smith was clearly in the favour of the Virginia Company. Smith may have arrived in Jamestown in disgrace, but he was one of the names in the sealed envelope brought from London containing nominated members of the Council of Jamestown, as was Ratcliffe. First President of that Council was Edward Maria Wingfield, a London merchant who was one of the original petitioners for the Letter Patent

James I issued to the Virginia Company. There had been considerable debate in England over the nature of this company, because the Virginia project was never intended to be a get-rich-quick venture but a long-term settlement to develop the trading possibilities of North America before any other European nation established itself there. True, no one would object if they found another Potosí, the mountain of silver, or Walter Raleigh's desperately sought Eldorado, the city of gold. The Virginia Company was the seventeenth venturing company formed in England, and experience had already taught that there was profit even where there was no gold, and that it would be a long time and require considerable investment and support from the home country before it turned a profit. The Charter of the Virginia Company assured all colonists that their status in the New World would be 'to all intents and purposes as if they had been abiding within this our realm of England'.[9] And their purpose would obviously be to propagate the Christian religion to such people who as yet live in darkness and ignorance, and bring 'infidels and savages living in those parts to humane civility, and to a settled and quite [*sic*] government'.[10] To that end the Instructions of the London Council of the Virginia Company that were issued in December 1606 ordered the captains and company to 'have great care not to offend the naturals, if you can eschew it; and employ some few of your company to trade with them for corn, and other lasting victuals'.[11] They were also warned to be eternally vigilant of the native inhabitants, never to let them get their hands on the guns, or get to know if any of the Englishmen were killed or sick, lest they should conclude the colonists are but 'common men' – it seems the arriving god scenario was very much in the thoughts of the Virginia Company.

It is true that for one mad month, the new settlers did go searching for gold. None of the mineral samples sent back to London proved to be worth anything. As one contemporary put it, 'our new discovery is more likely to prove the land of Canaan than the land of Ophir'.[12] And the earliest writings in and of Virginia use this motif: the Promised Land of Canaan, covenanted by God to his chosen people. The first of such references – the hope that Virginia would 'flow with milk and honey' – occurs in a letter written from Jamestown on 22 June 1607, just five weeks after its foundation. If the characterizations in any drama have to be distilled from the many, John Smith stands for the many, for the openly declared aspirations of a national undertaking. However, there is little to choose among the minds of any of the settlers to the Americas, as evidenced by contemporary records. They were all products of the European worldview and self-justification of its legal right to the land, its inherent superiority over all Others, and their Christian duty to convert them, even if that meant, in St Augustine's terms, they had to 'force them to come in'. Only conversion, indoctrination and submission could make the natives real people, predictable and reliable, and hence serviceable to the ends of the dominant order. There were debates in England, just as there had been in Spain, about the ill-treatment of the native peoples. The criticisms did not come from those who opposed the project of colonialism or business – no one stood for that impossible option – but voiced a conscience on the practice of dominance. Incidentally, the settlement of Virginia was properly a European, not just an English, venture. Within two years, the Virginia Company was despatching Poles, Germans, French and Italian settlers to Jamestown. As Thomas Paine noted at the time of the War of Independence, only about 65 per cent of Americans were of English derivation. But then as any analysis of Spanish, Portuguese, Dutch, British, French or Danish (the Danes were a flag of convenience for enterprising independent ventures) colonialism demonstrates, the ideology of domination was common to all, part of a shared literature, law and cultural predilection.

So why does Disney work so hard to manufacture such a stark contrast between Ratcliffe and John Smith? The characterizations evoke and depend upon a specifically American hagiography of its own history, and in particular certain notions introduced into American thinking by John Smith himself. Smith wrote copiously about the project of colonialism, and one of his most consistent themes was the need for humble artisans, fitted for the task of building and servicing a new society, to be sent out to the colonies. When he was President of the Council of Jamestown, a post he held for a year before an injury forced him to sail to England, he was vitriolic about the unsuitability of gentlemen settlers in getting on with the job in hand. These references have spawned a great tradition in the USA. On the one hand, there is the notion that Virginia, a southern state, derives from English gentlemen who were unwilling to roll up their sleeves, and hence the ease with which the 'peculiar institution' – slavery to everyone else – came to be adopted in that region. Information on the first slaves, or 'servants' as they were euphemistically referred to at the time, comes, incidentally, in a letter written by John Rolfe (whom Pocahontas did marry). He says some twenty odd were bought 'at the best and easiest rate' from a Dutch ship that put into Jamestown in August 1619. That August also saw the first meeting of the General Assembly at Jamestown, the transference of the traditions of Westminster to Virginia. It seems that it was not just artisans who would serve the ends of colonialism, even in the mind of John Smith. In a book published in 1616, he drew a telling distinction between the serviceability of the 'poor savage' of Virginia and the 'black, brutish Negers of Africa'. But what has passed most trenchantly into the self-image of the USA is John Smith's clarion call for honest artisans. What he argued for is summed up in the hagiography of the northern settlements, also under Letter Patent to the Virginia Company, that became the home of the Pilgrim Fathers of the 1620 *Mayflower* expedition. Here were honest ordinary people yearning to be free of the yoke of Church and State, willed into the conscience and concerns of the individual who set off to build a new society, a city on the hill in a new land by the sweat of their brow, with courage, determination and beholden to none: the imagery of the pioneer and the frontier evoked in the setting evoked by Disney and the characterization of John Smith.

Disney's portrayal of Smith and Ratcliffe, their new history, must conform to the script of US self-description and sensibility. From the 'city on the hill' shines forth a very special light. Western tradition, derived originally from Rome and

Engraving after Simon de Passe's portrait of Pocahontas, 1616.
Pocahontas (Matoaka) married John Rolfe and was baptized
Rebecca in 1613. She died on board ship at the outset of her return
journey to the Americas and was buried at Gravesend. Photo
courtesy of a private collection/Bridgeman Art Library.

transmitted through the ideas of Vico and Herder, has it that the light of
civilization continually passes westward. The USA sees itself not as a repository
of European heritage, but as a new distillation, a new civilization arising out of
the wreckage and decay of the old. From the founding of the Republic, the
United States of America, with its Declaration of Independence, self-

consciously sees its standards as universal, and the practice of the best universal principles as summed up in the workings of its own constitutional processes and, by extension, all of its social and economic mores. In his approach to the work of domination, through his relations with Pocahontas, as the object of her love and desire as much as through the courage by which he makes the Indians tractable and serviceable to the new colony – this is what John Smith symbolizes and must be understood to symbolize in Disney's new history, that is the most important point of political correctness they must endorse. The subtext of the characterization of Smith and Ratcliffe is the confirmation of the rightness of the Pax Americana, because the USA is the desire of all peoples, not just the huddled masses yearning to be free who, lured by the Statue of Liberty, come from the Old World, but of all Others too, as represented by Disney's Pocahontas herself.

Directing the Real
Orapronobis Against Philippine Totalitarianism

JONATHAN L. BELLER

THE INVISIBLE OF TELEVISION

Orapronobis (*Fight For Us*, 1989) opens in October 1985 with the gruesome murder of rebel sympathizer Father Jeff (Gerard Bernschein) by right-wing vigilante leader Kumander Kontra (Bembol Roco). Temporally, the film passes through the 1986 EDSA revolution and into the present tracing the release of political prisoner, liberation theologist and former priest, Jimmy Cordero (Philip Salvador). The film splits Jimmy between his two families, one which is post-EDSA and bourgeois and the other which is pre-EDSA and provincial. Following his post-EDSA liberation from incarceration he marries Trixie (Dina Bonnevie), the media liaison officer for the Free Jimmy Cordero Committee of the Alliance for Human Rights. However, upon seeing his pre-EDSA girlfriend Esper (Gina Alajar) on television, her silhouetted figure giving testimony about a massacre outside of Manila in which her husband was killed, he renews his acquaintance with her and hence moves closer to the rebels with whom she is associated. While on a fact-finding mission to gather testimony of human rights abuses by Kumander Kontra and his vigilantes, Jimmy discovers that he has a son with Esper. Thus Jimmy's politicization is framed by two forms of family life and two disparate futures, a post-EDSA one of self-protective bourgeois forgetting and a pre-EDSA one of continued struggle. In the climactic scenes, both Esper and her son are killed by Kontra. The aftermath, in which Jimmy lifts his murdered son's body away from press photographers and right-wing politicos and slowly carries it into a church, is utterly devastating – a *pietà* of incredible pathos. When Jimmy returns home to Trixie and their newborn child, he retrieves a gun left by a friend and makes a phone call to join the underground.[1] The film thus effectively intertwines elements of necessity (intolerable outrage), faith (the terrible sanctuary of the church in the mourning scene) and struggle (the underground movement) so that history (its transformation) becomes the only medium of salvation.

Immediately after the point-blank shooting of Father Jeff in the opening sequence, *Orapronobis* cuts to February 1986 footage of the EDSA uprising. Poetically, it is here, amidst the people, that Brocka places the credits. The EDSA footage is also accompanied by helicopter noise and a soundbite from the US media coverage: 'in constant contact with Ms Aquino, as you know there has been no split in the ranks between Cory Aquino and Enrile and Ramos . . .' This voice-over immediately raises questions as to who has been in constant contact with Aquino and at the same time introduces the surveying presence of world (US) media. The fact that EDSA is a global media event also implies that the US-Global has had a hand in it. Following this dialectic, which immediately problematizes news 'coverage' as reporting and shows that it is a part of making, the film will investigate less publicized workings of this global hand.

Other mediations are quickly taken up. In a barren room, men watch the last Marcos television broadcast. As a stony-faced Marcos cautions civilians to stay out of the line of fire and fields questions from US reporters about press censorship, one of the audience members points an imaginary hand-gun at the screen and asserts, 'You're dead, old boy.' Pulling the trigger he shouts 'Bang', and the TV screen suddenly goes to static. Thinking the television just conked out, his friend comments, 'You're a good shot,' but all at once everyone realizes that Marcos may be off the air. We, as Brocka's audience, have seen that this broadcast is watched by another audience within the film, *who, though absent from the television, are here represented during and indeed in the fall of Marcos.* The dictator is not an autonomous power but a social relation. Imagining his downfall is part of bringing him down. Brocka takes aim at the television from the point of view of the people, people who challenge mediated control in both conscious and unconscious ways; although in a highly mediated way, the imaginary shot fired at the television does indeed destroy Marcos. This network of mediations – its foreclosures and potentialities – is the epistemological subject of the film.

The television audience shown during the credits demonstrates a role of alternative media of the kind which Brocka is undertaking to create: TV is perceived along with its effects on others. Audiences embody contexts for the significance of mediated events – the signal impacts flesh. Furthermore, this contextualization of media by the presence of audiences is underscored and made active as the bar-room audience tune in to 'Radio Bravo' to help themselves understand the meaning of the interruption of television flow which occurs when Marcos disappears from the screen. This is a moment of reflexivity in the film which scripts an active role for the audience as users and makers of media, not passive receivers. Not only are audience members characters in the diegesis, they utilize media to question other media. The underground radio station announces 'a confirmed report that Rebel troops have taken over all government television stations'. The seizing of the means of communication meant the imminent fall of Marcos. However, as Brocka will emphasize, the cry which rises, 'We will be free!', is to be disappointed. The terms of power may have changed in the shift from dictatorship to what might loosely be called the rule of multinational capital (strategically misnamed 'democracy'), however, oppression remains and in certain respects escalates – both because of and as the mediation of the masses.

What is important to remember here is that EDSA was a media revolution. Taking over the streets, by taking over the radio and the television airways during the EDSA revolt, allowed for the surfacing of a communal disaffection as well as the deployment of communal force. What was at first only imagined was broadcast into being as individuals saw themselves as mediators of historical transformation. Although a media revolution was historically unprecedented, the large armatures of mediation can and do redeploy the liberatory energies of the masses to conservative ends. The fact that media could be seized and utilized to bring people into the streets at once shows the extraordinary power of the people, and stands as the exception that proves the rule: as Guy Debord writes, 'the spectacle is the diplomatic presentation of hierarchical society to itself'. Spectacular social programming is ordinarily orchestrated by an élite to organize people in such a way that their activities become sources of profit for that élite.

After showing footage from the EDSA revolt, the film follows the release of Jimmy, introduces Trixie and then moves forward two years to November 1988. In solidarity with the struggle against the oppression which persists under the Aquino administration, *Orapronobis* attacks gaps in mass media feed that are less obviously elisions than was the dead air which followed the final Marcos broadcast. But the elisions in mass media coverage are there, and they are historically no less significant, even if they are more difficult to see. Indeed, their invisibility in many ways makes them historically more significant than Marcos's departure, because it is due in part to these invisible gaps (that is, the unreported, the unknown, the marginal) in media flow that many of the conditions initiated and intensified by US imperialism and martial law persist. The continuous flow of images and sound from TV creates the illusion of a composite picture, but what actually occurs is a kind of fragmentation which isolates events and removes a more organic interrelatedness. It is for this reason that Brocka bases the key events of the film around a composite of highly mediated popular events in order to put them into a different array and reveal their inner logic. The assassination of Father Jeff, the presence of Radio Bravo, the formation of vigilante groups after EDSA, to give but a few examples, allude to well-known events taken up by mass media, events which must be put in a relation alternative to that suppressed by capitalist televisual organization.

To establish certain continuities which position martial law as a preface to the present, Brocka cuts from the EDSA period forward in time to Cory Aquino's presidency but *back* to Kumander Kontra, this time stopping a group of men who are walking home from a basketball game. In his capacity as leader of a paramilitary right-wing vigilante band during the Aquino regime, Kontra and his men accuse the villagers of aiding rebels, demand the villagers' identification cards, scatter the terrified group with a shot and then shoot the fleeing villagers in their backs in a field by the road.

Directly from the murders, the camera cuts from the countryside and moves us slowly through the domestic space of Jimmy and Trixie, past Trixie lying pregnant on the couch watching a talk show called *Forum*, and straight into the televisual (televised) space of the show. Viscerally, the camera movement is slow and 'natural' by cinematic standards. However, our gaze, which just witnessed the vicious and cold-blooded murder of nine unarmed men, is now welded to a televisual gaze in which public officials and human rights activists politely dis-cuss two issues which remarkably still haunt the liberated (liberalized) Philip-pines: salvaging and political prisoners. Brocka's camera is not content with this contrast and moves right through the screen onto the soundstage of *Forum* and then into the studio and editing suite, where one can see the image being recorded on several monitors. The overall effect is one of extreme conceptual dissonance which troubles the fact that the camera movement and editing feels so seamless. The debate on atrocities is no longer simply more noise amidst television's infinite accumulate of noise, it is the public manifestation of the terror we have just witnessed, a manifestation which is carefully modulated at every stage of its production.

Without rehearsing all the details of the plot, allow me to suggest that *Orapro-nobis* restores the human tissue to television's soundbites by suturing the viewer's televised gaze to a seeing that occurs beyond the policed spaces of television. The arrogant governors who on talk shows excuse the vigilante groups, the senators who tell eye-witnesses to atrocities not to judge all vigilantes based on a single case, the pandering hosts who seem to be there only to make sure that nothing is said that might impel viewers away from the TV and into the streets are all taken to task with the showing of the effects of their public 'positions' on the lives of the film's people, its characters.

The people whose lives the film takes up register the subjective experience and therefore the invisible meanings and unreported effects of the deceitful clichés uttered by the inheritors of privileges consolidated under martial law. At the same time, the few televised words of human rights activist Sister Marie (Ginnie Sobrino) and later of Jimmy are seen as organic elements of lives which extend beyond the screen. Their commitments and their struggles, their protests and denunciations are not safely contained by the soundbites to which the TV format reduces them, but resound in the larger social space which *Orapronobis* intends to invoke. Images created by television's fetishistic 'zoom in' on a 'scoop' (that which is scooped out of the flesh of lived relations) are given a new amplitude by the film's representations of lived realities beyond the screen.

TV appears on Brocka's screen so often in *Orapronobis* that, by the final injunction to armed struggle, viewers cannot help but be struck by the radical notion of the presence of an invisible world existing in excess of television's view-topia. Armed struggle becomes one of the media by which this excess is represented. Despite TV's claim to cover everything ('Give us twenty minutes, we'll give you the world'), Brocka shows capitalist television as a decontextual-izing force capable of liquidating the meanings of human struggles by convert-ing them into isolated spectacles. In cutting from the life world to the televised world with the regularity with which most directors cut from the restaurant to the bedroom – the very mode by which television itself inserts itself into quotidian experience – Brocka insists upon a re-evaluation of the televisual transmission of power. He passes televisual space through cinematic space, recutting its images to the measure of a people's history.

And yet despite the critique of television created by passing the viewer's gaze through it and through spaces beyond it, Brocka knows that television, like cinema, is also a medium of struggle, a space to be fought for. The struggle for the invisible of television (what exceeds its representations) and against the invisible that is television (visual modalities of social regulation) is waged both by contextualizing TV and by occupying it. When Malou's husband is kidnapped by the vigilantes who are in cahoots with a governor and the police, she goes on television to appeal for the return of her husband. For the viewer of *Orapronobis*, Malou's appeal for the return of her disappeared husband is exceedingly poignant, even if it is an appeal that might easily be lost on a garden-variety channel surfer trained by too much TV-watching not to envi-sion the social connections which accompany abstracted images. Even though we know almost nothing about these two peripheral characters, we see that Malou and her husband are part of the human fabric of history. They struggle for a more democratic society and are the latest quasi-arbitrary victims in a systematic and life-shattering war on the people's complex and enduring struggle for the right to live with dignity.

So when Commander Kontra shouts 'Long live democracy' and 'Investigate communist atrocities' during a rally, or is honoured on television as an outstanding citizen by the International Movement of Democracy, the viewer is in a position to decode the televisual perversion of the term democracy – she understands what kind of democracy is being celebrated: the kind that is only nominally 'democracy' but is, in fact, brutal inequality. Kontra's rhetorical tactic is not just particular to him but is widespread in the televised world; like others of his ilk, he labours for a society in which people are denied the right to express themselves by any means necessary. He calls such a society, one that gratifies an ego premised upon the violation of others, a democratic one. The hollowness and outright deceit of the word 'democracy' in the mouth of Kontra provides viewers with a conceptual weapon against political charlatans. Brocka helps us to debunk those liars who pretend that they have achieved democracy for the nation merely by pronouncing its name. Furthermore, he shows that those who operate in such a manner are enemies of the people.

Brocka's analysis of the role of media in political oppression in the post-martial law era is in part an effort to create a kind of television literacy capable of deciphering the coded appearance of a screened reality. The destruction of the 'integrity' of the televisual image does not result in white noise or static, but meaning. The bald intentionality of the corporate-produced and controlled images, their concerted effort to preserve the status quo and the dominant hierarchy, is broken out of the images' pretence to objectivity or mere entertainment. Consequently, the exploration of the struggle over television is necessarily an exploration of the possibilities of alternative media for the formation of empathy and the creation of connections among seemingly isolated people and events. The music sung after the murders in Sta. Filomena, the powerful testimony of the lone survivor of Kontra's killing spree (who, wounded and taken for dead, had his ear cut off when the vigilantes took trophies from their corpses), the photographs made by still cameras which go off everywhere, all testify to the experience of struggle. In doing so they propose a community that while disappeared from the screen space of mass media has the capacity to engage it. Music, the testimonial, the photograph, cinema and armed struggle are all media with which to re-inflect the dominant in the active construction of an empowered community, and it is with these counter-hegemonic mediations that *Orapronobis* allies itself. What is required is the co-ordination of all of these (voice, song, image, war, etc.), since these are precisely the fronts on which domination is secured.

In its thoroughgoing way, *Orapronobis* shows how the terms of its struggle are mediated even in the play of children as they pretend to kill one another, and in the words and feelings of the central characters as they debate the consequences of their political commitments in their most intimate moments. The film explores the total saturation of subjective possibility by the terms of the social. By passing the viewer's perception through the disparate sensual elements of a broken world, Brocka insists that we become aware of a common ground of exploitation, and with it, a common struggle to make sense of dissipated events. In short, our sight passes through the sight of people who in various ways do not accept the meanings that are given to them, and who, instead, endeavour to challenge the meanings broadcast by dominant society. In a social (and cinematic) sense the people, through thought and action, strive to become authors, directors of meaning. As viewers of Brocka's film, we might participate in that endeavour: Jimmy is freed from jail by Trixie, a media liaison officer, but that liberation is incomplete. It is through Jimmy's deep connections with others, connections which in complicated ways extend well beyond the middle-class nuclear family, that he is driven to join the movement.

THE WORK OF ART IN THE AGE OF
TRANSNATIONAL REPRODUCIBILITY

'[T]he means by which *Orapronobis* elicits audience alertness is not so much representational as technical. It would be valid, though somewhat pedantic, to say that montage is actually the main actor in the movie.'[2] Joel David follows up this keen insight, noting both the 'successful conversion of symbols of personal comfort (religion, politics, even escapist cinema) into objects of social menace', and the editing, 'which facilitates transitions and make[s] narrative commentaries in the process (as in the use of the religious-icon insert in the final rape scene) [and] progress[es] beyond film language to imaginative storytelling'. David's points here, though quite astute, have been extracted by this writer from a highly aestheticizing language, a language cathected to 'Cinema' as an art form and concerned primarily with 'the future of cinema'. If montage is the main actor in the film, and the film achieves a poetic stature which David sees as imaginative storytelling, what are the social conditions of possibility that allow a world in fragments to achieve such expressive power? Although David's sharp critical comments stand, they are in danger of being lost in the precious supplications of the aesthete. Brocka's rejoinder to such an attitude, that is, one which puts cinema, or any art, first, is worth quoting here:

> The only way one can elevate local cinema from its present *bakya* status to an artistically acceptable level is to introduce gradual changes until one succeeds in creating one's desired audience . . . The sincere Filipino film-maker should get over his hang-up about making the Great Filipino Film; he should, instead, think seriously about developing the Great Filipino Audience.[3]

Brocka's words testify to the recursive commitment of his filmmaking. What he calls the filmmaker's 'responsibility to the audience' is an effort to address what Renato Constantino called 'The Miseducation of the Filipino'. If, as Constantino wrote, 'The most effective means of subjugating a people is to capture their minds',[4] Brocka's creed implies that the liberation of a people is achieved through the freeing of their minds. It must be immediately added here that the freeing of the mind is in no sense abstract or transhistorical. As with the condition of the sublime sketched by Ronaldo Tolentino, there is no transcendental realm of purity for freedom. Freeing is always in the concrete – a loosening of the grip of structures of oppression. There is, in Brocka, more than a taste of this kind of event, an indignation and an understanding, which demand a different world.

In showing capitalized mass media as a force of unfreedom with zones for potential struggle, Brocka's reading of Philippine society in *Orapronobis* invokes the dialectical principle of the unity of opposites. When David names montage as the main actor in the film, what he is perceiving is the organizing force of the mind of the director (with scriptwriters, editors, etc.) in creating a semiotic machine. The fragmentation and reassemblage of sensibility by mass media is *the mode of the dominant*. The cutting and suturing of the life-world by media, by terrorist tactics, by economic exploitation, by the torturer's implements, etc. is the very mode of domination. Brocka's use of the same modality against the dominant results in a renewal of an imagination which is held under siege. In calling for justice for Esper, for Jimmy, for their son and for the other victims of right-wing terror, viewers themselves posit a new social order with a different collective basis which must be evolved from what exists. The audience's subjective contribution to the making of history is bent to the work of freeing.

Thus, the most important question one might ask of a film is what can it do for its audience, that is, what can it help its audience to do? The director's job is to direct the creative power of the audience. The director's responsibility is to help the audience learn to free itself, that is, to cultivate among audience members practices of freedom. Brocka codifies and makes conceptually available actually existing forms of struggle in order to amplify a vector of force directed against the expropriative and violent practices of dominant (capitalist) society and its media. The film is a vehicle, a means, not an end, a medium. It is a social machine among other social machines that makes possible the application of a new order of subjective force (labour-power) in the world.[5] There are several corollaries here, the first being that if one considers the quality of contemporary filmic production to be degraded, that is only because of the degradation of the audience. This, of course, is a purely negative critical approach. In addition to shearing off the reactionary elements of a film and of filmmaking, the progressive critic, whether writer, filmmaker or audience interlocutor, must foreground and intensify the progressive dimensions which might be found in any film form. For no revolution can make pure negation its basis; it must, in Paul Gilroy's phrase, affirm while it protests.[6]

It is for this reason that Brocka's films appeal to *the dignity that has not yet been taken from his audience*. The audience's sense of outrage at the conditions portrayed in Brocka's cinema is dependent upon its construction of its own integrity – in the present and into the future. Our passional investments, our indignation, our belief in a higher justice which we might collectively achieve in history is the spiritual dimension of a materialist vision. Even if our integrity is compromised in daily life, even if everything intimates that we live in the totalitarianism of late capital, the collective outrage articulated by and through the films of Lino Brocka enjoins audiences to become the makers of a more dignified mode of life. Although for some it might be tempting to dismiss Brocka's films as failures because they have not brought about the social changes they imply, it is far better to see them, along with the EDSA revolution, not as a disappointment, but as a promise that is ours to keep – part of a history of struggle which is activated as its continuities and implications are invoked. If the nation-state is posited by the IMF as a template for capitalist domination through the management of social mediations, alternative media must unleash the communitarian potential which exceeds this model of organization and control.

The Critical Practice and Dialectics of Third Cinema

MICHAEL WAYNE

Third Cinema is a concept in need of theoretical development in the face of its underdevelopment; a concept in need of clarification in the face of confusion and misunderstanding; a concept in need of defence in the face of contesting theories and politics. The term Third Cinema designates a body of theory and filmmaking practice committed to political and cultural emancipation. Although it has precursors, particularly in the Soviet cinema of the 1920s, it emerged in the decade after and was influenced by the 1959 Cuban Revolution. From the beginning, Third Cinema, like revolutionary praxis generally, sought to integrate theory and practice – key filmmakers, particularly but not exclusively the Latin Americans, also wrote manifestoes and considered theoretical reflections on the cultural and political implications of filmmaking. Glauber Rocha spoke of a cinema desperate for social and cultural justice (a cinema of hunger).[1] Espinosa rejected the technical and aesthetic criteria of dominant cinema, advocating instead an 'imperfect cinema'.[2] But it was Getino and Solanas who coined the term Third Cinema in their theoretical reflections on their ground-breaking documentary, *The Hour of the Furnaces.*[3]

However, although theory was always a key component of Third Cinema, as a body of theoretical work, it remains significantly underdeveloped in terms of its grasp of First Cinema and Second Cinema. Understandably, the main concern, not only in the 1960s/early 1970s, but in the 'second wave' of interest in Third Cinema during the 1980s,[4] has been to develop theory in a way that is immediately and directly relevant to Third Cinema filmmaking. First and Second Cinema was sketched by Getino and Solanas as, respectively, dominant commercial cinema and art cinema.[5] And that has remained pretty much that, within Third Cinema theory. There are four reasons why this is no longer satisfactory.

1. We need more nuanced and complex accounts of First and Second Cinema in order to rescue Third Cinema from the common conflation that is made

between Third Cinema and Third World cinema. Third Cinema is *not* to be restricted to the so-called Third World. First, Second and Third Cinemas do not designate geographical areas, but institutional structures/working practices, associated aesthetic strategies and their attendant cultural politics. Thus, if we understand First and Second Cinema in more complexity, we will be more ready to understand that we can have First and Second Cinema in the Third World and Third Cinema in the First World.

2. Since First, Second and Third Cinemas denote institutional or working practices and a set of aesthetic strategies, it follows that all three cinemas take up their own distinctive *positionings* in relation to a shared referent: i.e. the historical, social world around them. Thus, each cinema also has relations of dialogue, interchange and transformation between them as each works over and on the same cultural/political material (e.g. anti-colonial struggle), but pulls and shapes that material into different, often radically different, meanings and possibilities. From the beginning, Third Cinema was understood, by Birri, for example, as a dialectical transformation of First and Second Cinema, not a simple rejection of them.[6] But we cannot understand this dialectical transformation – what Third Cinema is/could be, what it has to offer that the other cinemas do not, why it is so urgently needed and the complex relations of interchange and difference between First, Second and Third Cinema – if we have only a rudimentary grasp of Cinemas One and Two.

3. Extending Third Cinema into areas of First and Second Cinema should also be seen as a counter-hegemonic move aimed at challenging the dominant intellectual paradigms within film studies, particularly Lacanian psychoanalysis and postmodernism, including the latter's attempt to advocate a liberal multiculturalism or hybridity at the expense of understanding the material divisions that can exist irrespective of cultural exchanges, or how the struggle for resources which have been made scarce due to the social relations of production unleashes the fundamentalist cultural politics (nationalism and ethnic tribalism) against which advocacy of liberal hybridity is a mere straw in the wind. A Third Cinema analysis of cinemas One, Two and Three helps lay the basis for a genuinely socialist, indeed Marxist, engagement with the subject and broadens the concerns of film studies beyond the rather narrow middle-class constituency which currently limits it.

4. Finally, developing the theory of Third Cinema may be seen as something of a 'holding operation' in the dark times of neo-liberalism's hegemony. Revolutionary conjunctures are the womb from which Third Cinema emerges, and while Third Cinema can be made in conditions which are temporally or spatially distant from revolutionary conjunctures (examples of Third Cinema are still being made today), inspiration, political tradition and memory are the umbilical cord which nourishes Third Cinema in a time of reaction and barbarism. When the time comes, as it surely must (the very survival of the human race depends on it), for new revolutionary upheavals, then any interim developments in the theory of Third Cinema may make a small contribution to subsequent practical interventions.

If we can find a single film which straddles First, Second and Third Cinemas, while nevertheless operating largely within the gravitational pull of First and Second Cinema, then we are in a better position to understand the complex cultural interactions designated by these numerical categories, as well as the theoretical and political issues at stake in making distinctions between these cinemas. Gillo Pontecorvo's 1966 film, *The Battle of Algiers*, will serve as one such text. As an Italian communist and anti-fascist, Pontecorvo had fought against Italian fascism and the subsequent German occupation of Italy during World War II. *The Battle of Algiers* was made in Algeria with the blessing and help of the Algerian government in 1965, three years after independence had been won from France. So clearly the film was made in conditions which allowed it proximity to the social, historical and cultural specificities of the Algerian people, while the film's key cultural worker, the director, had some first-hand knowledge and experience of the kind of guerrilla warfare which the Algerian National Liberation Front (FLN) deployed. Although Stam and Spence describe *The Battle of Algiers* as a 'Third World' film,[7] the key creative positions in the production of the film were occupied by Italians. Pontecorvo also co-wrote the script with Franco Solinas and collaborated with Ennio Morricone on the music track. It makes more sense, then, to locate *The Battle of Algiers* as a European film about the Third World. This does *not*, of course, determine its location within our three categories of cinema. Conversely, if the film were more authentically Algerian, it would not automatically qualify as Third Cinema. Locating *The Battle of Algiers* geographically as European does however give us some *indication* of the cultural influences on the film. From the perspective of Third Cinema, the task of the filmmaker is to be adequately cognisant of the politics of those cultural influences and be ready, if necessary, to rework them.

THE BATTLE OF ALGIERS: THE CRITICAL RECEPTION

The critical reception of the film has always in fact been mixed. At the time of its release, it won a number of prestigious awards on the international film festival circuit, but it was also criticized by writers and filmmakers on the left for being too similar to dominant cinema and not sufficiently reworking the language of the medium. Peter Sainsbury, for example, complained that the film mobilized the thriller format in its depiction of a 'suspenseful battle of tactics between hunters and hunted, action and counter action', which blocked exploration of the political complexities and processes of the Algerian revolution.[8] As we shall see, this critique is made with some justification. Nevertheless, one can also sympathize with Pontecorvo when he rejects what he calls the bourgeois 'rich kids' who, in advocating radical avant-garde aesthetic strategies, dismiss his film (and it is a great film in many ways) as hopelessly compromised by its attachment to dramatic action, narrative, character identification and so on. From this avant-garde position, articulated for example by the French journal *Cahiers du Cinéma*, Pontecorvo's film exists wholly 'within the system'.

Pontecorvo's critics wanted filmmakers to engage much more radically with questions of form, with the language of cinema, its aesthetic strategies, its signifying practices and interrogate the politics of those formal operations.[9] These are all perfectly legitimate and indeed urgent questions, and a vital component of Third Cinema. However, the persistent failure of the western avant-garde is its tendency to move from a self-conscious exploration of form for the purpose of 'social intelligibility',[10] to a celebration of form for its own sake (formalism). In the latter position, the politics of form (if politics remains a question at all) eclipses the 'content' of a cultural artefact, while aesthetic matters generally are severed from the political, social and economic circumstances in which the cultural artefact circulates. The tension between a necessary attention to form and the dangerous lure of formalism can be traced back to Trotsky's debate with the Russian avant-garde in the 1920s, and it drove much radical film theory and practice in the 1970s into something of an élitist cul-de-sac.[11]

The great advantage of Third Cinema is that while it is politically oppositional to dominant cinema (and Second Cinema), at the level of form and language, it does not seek to re-invent cinema from scratch (it is too interested in history for that); nor does it adopt a position of pure opposition on the question of form (it is too interested in communication for that); instead, its relation to First and Second Cinema is dialectical: i.e. it seeks to *transform* rather than simply reject these cinemas; it seeks to bring out their stifled potentialities, those aspects of the social world they repress or only obliquely acknowledge; Third Cinema seeks to detach what is positive, life-affirming and critical from Cinemas One and Two and give them a more expanded, socially connected articulation.

Pontecorvo's response to his critics correctly identified two blindspots within formalism. First, he argued that 'the system', capitalism, is contradictory, something which is evident to any cultural theory and practice which has not withdrawn from a wider world of political and social conflict:

> I believe that a producer will make a political film, even if it is against his class sense, as long as he thinks he can make money with it. I think he would even make a film which shows that his father is a thief and his mother a whore if he is sure to make money. So it depends on the situation at the moment . . .[12]

Here, Pontecorvo identifies a contradiction between the short-term interests of capitalism (to make money) and its long-term interests (not to produce ideas that may challenge its legitimacy).[13] This contradiction opens an important institutional and cultural space 'within the system' for progressive filmmaking such as Pontecorvo's, and even closer to dominant cinema, films like Costa Gavras's *Missing* (1981) and John Boorman's *The Emerald Forest* (1985). However, Pontecorvo's point notwithstanding, it is still legitimate to ask what the limits of such films are; what meanings can they not articulate? What ambitions can they not countenance? It is a crucial component of Third Cinema to expand our political and cultural horizons, to imagine alternatives to what is and refuse to accept what is as coterminous with what can be. This expansion of our horizons is as much about what cinema can and cannot do as it is about calling for change in the wider social world. So, while there are contradictions within capitalism, while there is some latitude for progressive cultural workers, we must not block up our capacity to imagine radically different cinemas and visions of radically different social and political relations. In this sense, Third Cinema is a utopian cinema, anticipating radical change, harbouring its potential in the present and remembering where it has flowered in the past.

Pontecorvo's second argument in defence of his film also has its merits, but again, there are caveats which have to be entered. Pontecorvo points out that for those people actively involved in revolutionary politics (the Cubans, the Black Panthers, etc.), the film has been received more positively. Pontecorvo's claims for his film are modest, it may not be 'a great help but a help' to such groups involved in struggles against racism and imperialism. Certainly, Pontecorvo is right to point to the role of the audience, that they are social beings located in particular times and places, potentially very active in engaging with the cinematic text. It is precisely this question of the role of the audience and the nature of their engagement with the text which is central to Third Cinema. Indeed, Third Cinema has appropriated the theme of the active spectator from the avant-garde. As Espinosa noted in an early Third Cinema manifesto:

> There's a widespread tendency in modern art to make the spectator participate ever more fully. If he participates to a greater and greater degree, where will the process end up? Isn't the logical outcome – or shouldn't it in fact be – that he will cease being a spectator altogether? This simultaneously represents a tendency towards collectivism and toward individualism. Once we admit the possibility of universal participation, aren't we also admitting the individual creative potential which we all have?[14]

The transformation which Third Cinema effects on the modern art/active spectator relationship is to relocate them both back into the broader social struggles from which they have been severed, so that the active spectator is no longer engaged in a purely aesthetic activity. It is this broader social context which Pontecorvo is addressing.

Nevertheless, if we are interested in the *relationship* between text and audience, we must still ask what the text contributes to the production of meaning. And here, *The Battle of Algiers* may be found wanting. Veronica Horwell opens her review of the film after another re-release with these words: 'I know an Army officer who screened a video of *The Battle of Algiers* to his lads in Northern Ireland almost as a training film; I've been told his opposite numbers did the same.'[15] If the British officer could show the film to his rank and file without apparently worrying that they may as a result start to question why they happen to be an occupying force in another country, then that could, from a Third Cinema perspective, indicate an unhelpful ambiguity or loss of analytical power. However, it is precisely the fact that the film could be shown to both sides in the conflict which many critics would take to be a sign of the film's greatest strength. The *Monthly Film Bulletin* describes the film's 'extraordinary fair-mindedness',[16] while *Time Out* praised the film's 'scrupulous balance.'[17]

This appeal to objectivity is a theme within the critical reception of Second Cinema and is symptomatic of this cinema's base in the middle class. The claim to see 'both sides' corresponds remarkably closely to their social position, caught as they are between capital and labour. The *Time Out* review of Mira Nair's *Salaam Bombay!* (1988), about children begging on the streets of the Indian city, notes that 'the film brings the lives of all its characters into a common embrace, never pointing a finger of blame but constantly emphasising the difficulties and dangers that surround young and old alike'.[18] Heaven help us that a film should actually identify those responsible for such poverty! Third Cinema, however, would want to point the finger, it would want, in Espinosa's words, to 'show the process which generates the problems'.[19] But to do that requires taking a position, making a commitment. Thus, Third Cinema has an entirely different epistemological foundation to Second Cinema and the critical discourse which frames and interprets such films. For the latter, knowledge about the world is generated at a higher level by *not* unequivocally committing to a position/cause. Lurking behind the critics' valorization of 'balance', 'objectivity', 'distance' and other such terms lies an old distinction between art and politics or art and propaganda. Third Cinema deconstructs this binary position because it is characterized by unequivocal commitment to a position or cause but does not see itself as 'propaganda'. Commitment to a cause, even unequivocal commitment, is not the same as suspending your critical faculties; it is not the same as dogma. Espinosa again:

> A new poetics for the cinema will, above all, be a 'partisan' and 'committed' poetics, a 'committed' art, a consciously and resolutely 'committed' cinema – that is to say, an 'imperfect' cinema. An 'impartial' or 'uncommitted' one, as a complete aesthetic activity, will only be possible when it is the people who make art.[20]

Espinosa is saying that in an ideal world, art would be considered completely autonomously from social interests. Actually, this seems questionable (or at the very least, it requires projection forward into an almost unimaginably transformed future), but it is anyway hypothetical. The key point is that we do not live in an ideal world and so art cannot be divorced from the conflictual social interests which are at play.

With the decline of the political avant-garde in the West, the critical reception of *The Battle of Algiers* has become rather uncritical. Re-released in 1997, Derek Malcolm could describe it as 'the best depiction of a struggle for independence ever made'.[21] It must be comforting for the liberal intelligentsia to know that while they are part of a European culture which imposed the most ruthless forms of exploitation on millions of people around the world, it is a culture which can nevertheless produce the best film about the struggles of just some of those millions to liberate themselves from European colonial rule.

Except, of course, *The Battle of Algiers* is not the best depiction ever and only Eurocentric arrogance, coupled with ignorance of other cinemas, could suggest that it is. And yet even Edward Said, who should know better, having written at length on how the West has framed and constructed the rest of the world, claimed in a *Rear Window* television programme on Pontecorvo that the film was 'unmatched' in its depiction of an anti-colonial struggle. To assess properly the place of *The Battle of Algiers* in the history of radical film requires some 'critical commitment' at the level of critical discourse: that is to say, acknowledging, at one and the same time, that many of the film's compelling qualities, such as its version of 'realism', are also precisely the sign of its truncated analytical and cognitive power.

THE BATTLE OF ALGIERS: FIRST, SECOND AND THIRD CINEMA

So let us turn to a more detailed analysis of *The Battle of Algiers* in order to delineate how it occupies a contradictory political and aesthetic space. It is a compromised textual formation, never quite managing to transform its First and Second Cinema elements and influences fully into the service of Third Cinema, even though it has one foot in the latter category. We are now in a position to identify four key markers which distinguish Third Cinema and through which I want to discuss *The Battle of Algiers*. They are: historicity, politicization, critical commitment, and cultural specificity.

Historicity

Third Cinema seeks to develop the means for grasping history as process, change, contradiction and conflict: in short, the dialectics of history. History is the great explainer: why we are where we are and who we are. Willemen quotes Benjamin, who saw as his task the need to develop 'the image-creating medium within us to see dimensionally, stereoscopically, into the depths of the historical shade'.[22] In *The Battle of Algiers*, it is precisely the historical shading which has been erased from the *mise-en-scène*, from the characters and the narrative generally.

At the film's conclusion, after the French paratroopers have eliminated the last FLN cell, a soldier says that 'We've lived in peace with these people for 130 years, there's no reason why we cannot do so again.' The historical record shows that this statement, unchallenged within the film, is demonstrably untrue. The French first invaded Algeria in 1830. Towards the end of the nineteenth century they began to implement settler colonization, taking over vast tracts of agricultural land and orienting exports to suit the needs of French capitalism. For more than 130 years, the Algerians sporadically organized resistance to French control only to see that resistance brutally crushed. In 1945, celebrations of the Allied victory turned into demonstrations for Algerian independence. The French slaughtered an estimated 45,000 at Setif alone.[23] The film, however, does not have the historical memory to recall even this date and event. Instead, it charts the first years of military conflict between the FLN and the French military (1954–7). How much better it would have been, a student of mine once suggested, if the film had started with the celebrations of 1945 before cutting to 1954. The massacre at Setif would not even have to be alluded to (if French sensibilities are that important): the contradiction between the liberation of France from Nazi domination in the name of democracy and freedom and the continued domination of the colonies would still be sharply revealed. Such sensitivity to the contradictions between European Enlightenment traditions and the grubby material imperatives of European capitalism is the central historical image of a film like Ousmane Sembene's *Camp de Thiaroye* (1987).[24]

It is not that the film offers no articulation of historicity. Take, for example, the scene of Ali-la-Pointe's arrest in his initial incarnation as a street hustler. Here, the soundtrack adopts an asynchronic relationship with the image track. As he is led away, a French voice reads out his details (date of birth, the fact that he is illiterate) and his record as a petty criminal stretching back to juvenile correctional institutions. The voice inhabits the space-time of the latest court through which the just arrested Ali is to pass. At a formal level, it is a wonderfully economic strategy, providing a logical transition to the next scene of Ali in prison, while also briefly sketching in Ali's back story, where we glimpse what life is like for the ill-educated and poor Algerians under French colonial rule. The problem is that this is all too rare a moment in revealing the historical determinations on the present.

Politicization

For Third Cinema, one of the key areas of concern which needs to be explored is the process whereby people who have been oppressed and exploited become conscious of that condition and determine to do something about it. For Birri, a revolutionary cinema is one which, above all, seeks to awaken a politicized consciousness in the spectator.[25] Since there is no automatic radical response to the experience of being told in countless ways that you are inferior – and, indeed, the most likely outcome is not revolutionary consciousness, but a secret and deep-seated self-loathing – one of the key challenges which *The Battle of Algiers* fails to offer an adequately complex engagement with is how Ali, a petty criminal and illiterate, is transformed into a fighter for national liberation. Whereas *Camp de Thiaroye* devotes the entire film to charting the process whereby African soldiers fighting for France and its colonies during World War II come to revolt against their masters, *The Battle of Algiers* deals with this vital question with incredible compression and ellipsis. Ali's conversion to the cause takes place in prison after his arrest. Ali is being held in a cell with other prisoners, but we do not see him engaging in dialogue with them. Then comes the key moment: Ali's political baptism. An FLN prisoner is being led through the prison to his execution. He shouts 'Long Live Algeria' and the call is taken up by other prisoners in their cells. We cut back to Ali, who now seems suddenly energized: a revelation has struck him. He leaps to the window overlooking the outside courtyard where the condemned man is now being led to the guillotine. The film cuts to several shots of the prison walls and cell windows (but we see no individuals); we hear the guillotine come down and immediately cut to a zoom close-up on Ali's watching face. This experience is almost like a religious epiphany. Ali sees a vision (of a brave man dying for a cause) and is converted. This is underlined by the ellipsis which now omits the rest of his time in prison: the next scene takes place five months later as Ali is getting his first instructions from the FLN. This is a highly individualized presentation of the process of politicization. There is no suggestion of any interaction with political activists, no learning, no asking questions, just instant revelation.

The way in which the process of politicization is elided is also reproduced in the film's coda. With the destruction of the FLN in 1957, the film jumps to 1960, when mass demonstrations broke out in Algiers against colonial rule. But our point of entry into the beginning of the uprising is from the uncomprehending French journalists whose voice-overs tell us how unexpected this surge of protest is; how mysterious after a period of calm. The spectator is positioned on the outside of the revolution, looking in from the point of view of the bewildered Europeans.

Critical Commitment

We have already seen that the film was valorized by liberal critics for its fairness to both sides. The film's aspiration towards objectivity has its roots in Pontecorvo's own national (Second) cinema: the Italian neo-realist movement of the late 1940s and early 1950s. Stylistically, *The Battle of Algiers* is firmly rooted in a 1960s reportage: hand-held camera, grainy black-and-white stock, zoom lens, long lenses; while at the level of narrative, the flashback structure would have been too elaborate for the neo-realists, who preferred simple, linear stories, unobtrusive editing and camera work. However, the *goal* of neo-realism, to reveal the world with minimal authorial comment, does manifest itself in the film's low-key commitment. It is precisely this low-key quality which liberal critics appear to be praising, because, in fact, most recognize that the film is not 'objective' but basically sympathetic to the Algerian cause. So, there is 'commitment' on the part of the film (and Pontecorvo denies being 'impartial' on the question of independence)[26] but it is just not very overt. The problem is that this low-key commitment is also a sign of a lack in the film's analytical and critical power.

This can be illustrated via Stam and Spence's discussion of the film. They praised the way the film subverts the typical focalization of First Cinema. They note how the trope of encirclement in the Western genre, where the spectator is located inside the 'besieged wagon train or fort', helps suture the spectator 'into a colonialist perspective', looking down the barrel of a gun and watching the American Indian fall from his horse as another settler's bullet finds its mark.[27]

By contrast, *The Battle of Algiers* inverts this spectator identification, locating the viewer with the 'colonised who are encircled and menaced and with whom we identify'.[28] So the language of First Cinema (Stam and Spence eschew these terms) has undergone some reworking; but if it has been filled with a new content, the form and the modes of spectator engagement which they activate have not been sufficiently reworked. Stam and Spence themselves make the point, although without drawing out the implications. Discussing the scene where the Algerian women, dressed as Europeans, plant bombs in the European district, Stam and Spence note how spectator positioning 'makes us want the women to complete their task, not necessarily out of political sympathy but through the mechanisms of cinematic identification'.[29] This, then, is a spectatorship which is not being asked to be conscious of the politics of identification; it is an identification made largely at the level of the emotions. And yet one of the key aims of Third Cinema is to seek to bring the cognitive and intellectual powers of the spectator into play. As Willemen reminds us, 'the culture industry has become extremely adept at orchestrating emotionality while deliberately atrophying the desire for understanding . . .'.[30] There is something of a Second Cinema reworking of the war film/thriller genre in *The Battle of Algiers*. The relentless emphasis on the military/tactical struggle strips away any room for character development, idiosyncrasies, romance or moments of personal intimacy which First Cinema would be tempted to write in. The war dominates the lives of the characters so totally, nothing else can come into the field of representation. Unfortunately, the focus on the military/tactical struggle to the exclusion of all else also blocks the film off from engaging, at least with any complexity, in the politics of revolutionary struggle.

The Cuban film by Sarah Gomez, *One Way or Another* (1977), would be a good example of a text which takes up a position within its sociohistorical context of critical commitment. There is never any doubt that the film is committed to the aims and ideals of the Cuban Revolution, while at the same time, it takes up a critical stance insofar as the film explores the *persistence* of class and gender conflicts within Cuba. It is this mode of intervention which means that the film is neither cheerleading propaganda nor disinterested objective observer. To return to *The Battle of Algiers*, the key figure articulating the Algerian/African politics of revolutionary struggle was Frantz Fanon.

Fanon was born in 1925 in Martinique, which had been a French colony since the seventeenth century. He was educated in Paris, where he studied medicine and became a psychiatrist. It was here that Fanon started to realize that even though he had been through the French educational system and had proved his intellectual worth, he would never be accepted as an equal. He felt that he had been wearing a white mask concealing his black skin. His book, *Black Skin, White Mask*, was published when he was just 27 years old. In response to metropolitan racism, Fanon requested a post in the colonies and was assigned to a hospital in Algeria in 1954. It was a momentous year, as Fanon was to later record:

The Battle of Algiers (1965), courtesy: BFI.

The great victory of the Vietnamese people at Dien Bien Phu is no longer, strictly speaking, a Vietnamese victory. Since July 1954, the question which the colonised peoples have asked themselves has been, 'What must be done to bring about another Dien Bien Phu?'[31]

Having lost North Vietnam, the French were determined not to lose Algeria. As the war there intensified, Fanon's clinic swelled with patients, both French and Algerian. The evident link between mental health and social context led Fanon to conclude that in order to cure patients, society had to change. He resigned from the clinic and joined the FLN. His book, *The Wretched of the Earth*, was published in 1961, the same year he died of leukaemia.

The Battle of Algiers has clearly been influenced by *some* of Fanon's political philosophy, but, I would suggest, only that which could be most easily integrated into the language of First and Second Cinema, thus excluding some of Fanon's more acute and radical ideas. The key Fanonian motif in the film is the all-pervasive role of violence within the colonial set-up. Fanon scandalized the European intelligentsia by reminding them that violence is built into the colonial process whereby one country expropriates the resources of another and subordinates its people. Inevitably, Fanon argued, only violence on the part of the native will end the violence of colonialism. It was this 'logic' which

Pontecorvo has said he wanted to get inside of and explore. There is a very Fanonian moment early on in the film. Ali is being chased by the police just before his arrest. He is tripped up by a French youth. Instead of trying to escape, Ali gets up and head-butts the smiling young man. In that moment, Ali passes through a psychological barrier and demonstrates that he is a fighter. As Fanon puts it: 'At the level of individuals, violence is a cleansing force. It frees the native from his inferiority complex and from his despair and inaction; it makes him fearless and restores his self-respect.'[32] There are other Fanonian motifs, such as the image of the colonialized city, divided into 'two zones' of 'reciprocal exclusivity', a 'world cut in two . . . inhabited by two different species'.[33] Thus, we see the camera pan across the European district – rich, affluent, wide streets with modern cars – and then onto the Algerian casbah – old, poor, its buildings crumbling, its streets narrow and squalid.

Then there is the figure of Ali himself, who corresponds to the lumpenprole-tariat, the people who have nothing, no stake within the colonial system, who are most likely to be at the forefront of the liberation struggle.[34] Faith in people to transform themselves and their lives is a prerequisite for any revolutionary. But it can be a thin line between faith and romanticism. Fanon's singling out of the 'pimps', the hooligans, the unemployed and the petty criminals as heroes of the struggle can be described as romantic because it is their outsider status, their marginality to the social order, which is seen as guaranteeing their authentic revolutionary capacity. It is a romanticism which the film itself shares. While the Algerian people as a collective force are evident within the film, this mass protagonist is counterbalanced by the centrality of Ali. The film begins in 1957: his is the last FLN cell to be destroyed by the French military. A flashback then takes us to 1954 and to Ali as a street hustler. At the end of the film, we arrive back at Ali's imminent destruction. Along the way, we have seen Ali's com-mander, Djafar, give himself up rather than die a pointless death. Ali's scene, however, brings out the Algerian people onto the rooftops, watching and wait-ing for the moment when his little hideaway is blown to pieces. The problem with focalizing much (although not all) of the story through Ali, coupled with the presentation of his conversion to the cause and the excessive focus on the military/tactical battle, is that he becomes simply the 'hardman' familiar from First Cinema: that is a thoroughly depoliticized fighter. We never learn what Ali's political convictions were/are and how they have changed or not in the course of the struggle.

The more radical elements in Fanon's political philosophy are to be found not in his writings on violence, or his lionization of the peasantry or the lumpen-proletariat, but in his broader critique of the social order. In particular, he is clear-eyed about the class differences within the liberation struggle. Exploita-tion, he suggested, 'can wear a black face, or an Arab one'.[35] He constantly warned about the necessity for the liberation leaders, overwhelmingly middle class, to communicate lucidly with the people and not in a professionalized discourse designed to prove that the 'masses have to be managed from above'.[36] For Fanon, the difficult task of developing a relationship between the revolutionary party and the people, so that the latter becomes a fully involved participant in the transformation of society, is of crucial importance. Fanon's concern with educating and politicizing the people is linked to his warnings concerning what happens after liberation has been achieved: 'We must repeat, it is absolutely necessary to oppose vigorously and definitively the birth of a national bourgeoisie and a privileged caste.'[37]

Yet *The Battle of Algiers* does not register the significance of class difference within the liberation struggle. The FLN is presented as a homogeneous unity. The historical significance of these components of Fanon's thought was unfortunately confirmed when a 1965 putsch in Algeria put in place a corrupt military junta. Today, in the wake of the disappointments of a post-apartheid South Africa, Fanon's concern about how the masses are shut out of power by the élites continues to resonate.

Another key issue in the political struggle which the film avoids altogether is that of gender. One of the film's most powerful sequences shows the Algerian women, disguised as Europeans, planting bombs in two cafés and the airport. The role of women in revolutionary struggles, involving themselves in activities, military and political, which customs and traditions around the world have usually reserved exclusively for men, always raises the most profound gender questions. It is inconceivable that the FLN's willingness to use women in the struggle would not have generated, within an Islamic culture, both resistance to

The Battle of Algiers (1965), courtesy: BFI.

and new ideas about female equality. Again, the film fails to register these seismic shifts in gender roles. It has been argued by Ranjana Khanna, in *Third Text*, that Third Cinema is incapable of engaging with gender politics in a way which calls into question male domination.[38] Her methodology though is flawed. She uses *The Battle of Algiers* as an example of the limitations of Third Cinema on the issue of gender. But as we have seen, not only is the film not sufficiently representative of Third Cinema to stand in for it as a whole, it does not belong primarily in that cinematic category at all. Part of Khanna's problem is that she misconceives what constitues Second Cinema. While correctly identifying it as a cinema which seeks to engage with the national realities marginalized by the dominant media, she wrongly suggests that Second Cinema 'uses conventional cinematic techniques'.[39] Now, this is rather vague, since all techniques use conventions – but in fact Khanna is referring to the dominant cinematic techniques of First Cinema. But historically, Second Cinema (as an art cinema) has developed alternative forms of expression to First Cinema. Khanna's example of a Second Cinema film reveals her misconception. She suggests Attenborough's *Gandhi* (1982), presumably because it is about India, when clearly it is primarily (although not exclusively) a First Cinema bio-pic with little rootedness in the national culture it represents. A better example of Indian Second Cinema might be *Bandit Queen* (Shekhar Kapur, 1994). However, the example of *Gandhi* functions strategically in her argument (because there is evidently a difference in kind between *Gandhi* and *The Battle of Algiers*) to help (mis)locate Pontecorvo's film in the Third Cinema category, when the difference between the two films is primarily the difference between First and Second Cinema.

Cultural Specificity

Essentially, the above categories have been calling for a cinema grounded in the sociohistorical processes which it seeks to represent. But a grounding in the cultural dynamics of the milieu deserves a special category, because cinema is part of culture and its greatest contribution can be in the realm of culture.

Third Cinema is characterized by its intimacy and familiarity with culture – both in the specific sense of cultural production (e.g. song, dance, theatre, rituals, cinema, literature) and in the broader sense of the word (the nuances of everyday living). Further, Third Cinema explores how culture is a site of political struggle. History has shown that one of the first things which colonialism and imperialism attempt to control, in parallel with economic resources, is culture, where values and beliefs and identities are forged and reforged. Yet Third Cinema is not a parochial defence of native or indigenous culture: its attention to class differences and its internationalism help guard against that. Fanon warned against the uncritical celebration of the native's culture as much as he warned against the uncritical assimilation of the culture of the colonialists.[40] Here, Third Cinema anticipates and touches borders with postcolonial theory and its master-concept of hybridity. Except postcolonial theory is exactly that, a theory, generated largely within academia, a discourse which largely disavows its class roots, since class is virtually absent from its critical vocabulary. Third Cinema, by contrast, is a theory and a practice; as the latter, it has involved intellectuals in concrete political struggles where their lives and liberty have often been at risk. And Third Cinema, as theory and practice has demonstrated, has a remarkable self-reflexivity about its own class roots, interrogating the intellectual's position *vis-à-vis* both the culture of the imperial metropolis and the masses below them.

The Battle of Algiers displays a considerable understanding around the importance of culture as one front – and an important front – in the wider political struggle for national liberation. Stam and Spence discuss how the European disguise which the Algerian women adopt to pass bombs through the checkpoints turns the colonizers' implicit 'us and them' racism to the native's advantage.[41] Elsewhere, we see the FLN perform a secret Islamic wedding service while also adapting and shortening it so as to reduce the risks of detection. When at a checkpoint, a child commandeers a French loudspeaker and urges the Algerians to 'have no fear', the women respond with their distinctive Arab cry. Yet the scene which shows French paratroopers torturing Algerians is cast overwhelmingly in the terms of European sound and imagery. On the image track, the Algerians are tied up, arms outstretched, or hanging upside down on a cross-like structure, heads turned to one side; and on the soundtrack, classical European music with church organs. Together, these signifiers of the crucifixion and the Christian motif of suffering, so culturally remote from the story material, de-historicize a specific struggle in time and space, turning a story from the anti-colonial liberation movements into a timeless tragedy, a universal story, a comment on the human condition and other such depoliticizing aesthetic concepts.

Post Theory

Introduction

JORELLA ANDREWS

We are supposed to be in a stage of transition from modernity to postmodern times. Colonial notions and outlooks are giving way to postcolonial ways of thinking and doing. The essays in this section present significant, albeit differently articulated, critiques of the so-called postcolonial and postmodern modes of thought. We begin with Ihab Hassan's juxtaposition of the severity of the human conditions that postmodern and postcolonial scholarship is supposed to address with what he regards as the paucity of its intellectual, linguistic, moral and spiritual resources for doing so. Despite the heterogeneity of postcolonial studies, he claims, thinkers 'tend to share certain traits, which they also share with writers in cultural studies: a political attitude, a moral stance, a kind of vocabulary'. He refers in the first instance to a proclivity for reductive and formulaic political posturings ('often quasi-Marxist, crypto-Marxist, neo-Marxist, post-Marxist'). He writes, too, of an apparent concern among theorists to follow the latest intellectual fashions, rather than search, grapple, for nuanced and effective means of unpicking problems and posing solutions – operations which must occur, *inter alia*, creatively and sensitively, at the level of language. After presenting an overview of broad concerns with respect to the discipline itself, Hassan challenges certain of the most common assumptions inherent to it. His first step is to set out the complexities and dissimulations of imperialism/colonialism (as the primary focus of postcolonial critical analysis), whether expressed in militaristic, economic or cultural terms. As he does so, he enumerates the one-sided and historically unsupported evaluations of imperialism that have shaped debate, and argues for an orientation towards this matter in which 'the relation of history to morality [is] theorized in realistic, not simply idealistic or bombastic terms'. There is an urgent need for the elaboration of open and self-critical frameworks from which to argue for the global distribution of equity and equality. 'Root out the colonial complex', he writes, 'from the mind, the heart, the gut, and learn to look at the world with level gaze.' There is a need to develop what he calls 'a politics of personal responsibility'. The essay concludes, bravely, with what he calls 'a plea for spirit', a repudiation, in other words, of the ultra-materialist nature of most contemporary attempts at solving human problems, this again, in part an inheritance of Marxist worldviews.

 We move on to an onslaught on Homi Bhabha's *The Location of Culture* by Benita Parry. If Hassan's criticisms of postcolonial critical practice focused on its over-dependence upon certain Marxist-inspired political and materialist orientations, Parry's criticism of Bhabha's position revolves around what she considers to be its anti-realist, 'textualist' stance, its prioritization of semiotic process, so that 'the generation of meaning [is] located in the enunciative act, and not in the substance of the narrated event'. A key concern for Parry is Bhabha's reliance upon poststructural (Derridean) notions of deferral and *différance* which, she claims, dispense with the crucial notion of conflict, and of having the moral resources to take a stand against certain *lived* states of affair. 'By subsuming the social to textual representation,' she writes, 'Bhabha represents colonialism as transactional rather than conflictual.' And again: 'Integral to Bhabha's revisionist work on colonialism is a concern to effect the "break-up of a binary sense of political antagonism", thereby displacing the received perception of dichotomies in conflict with the "in-between" space of negotiation.' One could argue that while Bhabha's evaluations do indeed appear to ignore what so many have experienced as the violently oppositional and coercive nature of colonial rule, this weakness in his work may primarily be of emphasis. For rather than present his position as an important and nuanced supplement to generally oppositional *anti*-colonialist approaches, he presents his postcolonialism as corrective of it. It would also seem relevant to acknowledge that a key methodological aspect of Bhabha's project is surely to find ways of breaking with the limited and repressive structures of thought inherited, via colonialism, primarily from Enlightenment thought (and incorporated into the anti-colonialist position) – to discover other intellectual foundations upon which to build. Having said this, however, his espousal of positions regarded as 'in-between' binary structures of opposition, and his promotion of hybridity as a particular marker of this mode of locatedness, may themselves ultimately be read as also framed by (and thus structurally indebted to) the same unproductive binarisms. Parry's critical exploration of Bhabha's work includes an analysis of his notion of hybridity and also examines his treatment of agency. It concludes with a useful comparison of his position with the work of other thinkers working in the field such as Said, Jameson, Mercer, Hall, Gilroy and Araeen.

Denis Ekpo explores the contemporary demise of what he calls an 'anti-West, anti-imperialist tradition of Afrocentric discourse' – or, to put it differently, the reasons for the West's continued imperviousness to the various accusations that have been directed towards it from various sources concerning the immorality, indeed criminality, of its past and present dealings with Africa. He sees postmodernism as ultimately producing precisely those conditions which effectively preclude the much-needed and meaningful debate between Africa and the West. Thus, while postmodernity has been generally (and correctly) characterized as deconstructing the systems of domination associated with modernity and the master-narratives of value and truth invented and universalized for the benefit of modernist expansionism, it is presented here as an effective *ally*, finally, of the western practices of imperialism and neo-imperialism it purports to expose and subvert. A key aspect of Ekpo's argument is that while the African radical thinker 'conditioned by his mission-school training to take very seriously the idea of a moral world order . . . unsuspectingly casts his critique of Europe in the metaphors of Europe's humanistic, moral idealism', the European or western intellectual climate is one in which, in the meantime, such value systems have been overtly abandoned as irrelevant. Within this amoral frame of reference, the Afrocentric arguments fail utterly to register. The moral indifference of the contemporary western mindset is located by Ekpo in postmodernity's indebtedness (principally through Michel Foucault and François Lyotard) to a Nietzschean prioritization of a profoundly amoral 'will to power as a kind of "biocultural principle"' as the crucial (in)former of individual and collective human action: 'the doctrine of the will to power,' he writes, 'reveals that in all her historical experiences, Europe has always acted necessarily, i.e. in accordance with the basic drives that give meaning to her world, and with which she achieves growth and strength . . .'. In such a context, accusations – and admissions – of guilt are meaningless. What is required now is the discovery of a critical language capable of engaging with (and hopefully challenging) the *realities* of the western (neo)imperialist mindset rather than its pretences, one capable of initiating real debate.

Possible ways to move forward can be discovered in Gerardo Mosquera's contribution. Mosquera's text is principally a critique of Eurocentrism, with particular focus on the assumptions that continue to misrepresent and marginalize non-western art practices. He lists, among others, the Eurocentric myth of universal value in art, and the Eurocentric accusations of derivativeness/ inauthenticity that are directed at non-western practices that engage with and contribute to the development of contemporary culture. He also identifies certain postmodern modes of thought as contributing to the marginalization of non-western practices – specifically, he sees postmodernity's emphasis upon alterity as productive not only of usefully heterogeneous/relativistic cultural perspectives but also of an exoticizing impulse that is ultimately isolating and segregationist.

For Mosquera, a proper critical response to Eurocentrism must resist the kinds of prejudices, assumptions and accusations just described. He writes, for instance, that 'the struggle against Eurocentrism should not burden art with a myth of authenticity . . .'. Rather, the postcolonial challenge is to make traditions work in a new epoch: 'The problem is not preserving [traditions] but vigorously adapting them,' he contends. 'The question is how we may also *make* contemporary art from our own values, sensitivities and interests.' He refers in this regard to an approach that is 'mostly mixed, relational, appropriative – anyway, "inauthentic", and therefore more adequate to face today's reality'. Importantly, it is from this properly reciprocal, intercultural mode of exchange that new critical responses, new strategies and understandings will emerge. Indeed, an anti-Eurocentrism is already being systematized that is not merely another western intellectual export, as is the case with the Afrocentric anti-West discourse described by Ekpo, but is derived from polyvalent non-western positions. From this position, too, a pluralistic revision of western culture can arise. As Mosquera puts it: 'Intercultural involvement consists not only of accepting the Other in an attempt to understand him or her and to enrich myself with his or her diversity. It also implies that the Other does the same with me, problematizing my self-awareness.'

Queries for Postcolonial Studies

IHAB HASSAN

It's in every paper, on CNN and on Murdoch's compromised satellite news: the condition of our world, in one place or another, is dire. And that is the condition postcolonial studies are meant, however partially, seriously to address. Do they not merit, then, our unillusioned scrutiny? I can only make a start, sketching a line of interrogations, mindful of my recent experience as visiting professor at the University of Mohamed V in Rabat, Morocco, mindful as well of my own Egyptian, colonial background.

AN OVERVIEW

Certainly, the field of postcolonial studies is not a unified field – witness the diverse essays in a mammoth collection like *The Postcolonial Studies Reader.*[1] But writers in it tend to share certain traits, which they also share with writers in cultural studies: a political attitude, a moral stance, a kind of vocabulary. Still, though my own assumptions differ from theirs – I hold liberally independent and literary values – I will endeavour to put my questions in a larger, collegial frame.

My first question concerns the partisanships that now rule the humanities: *how can postcolonial studies recover moral authority, beyond self-serving biases and the proto-cols of indignation?* They can hardly do so, I think, as long as their absolute horizon remains political, a horizon to which all issues are referred. An author, a work, an idea must be adjudicated, *a priori*, as left or right, and if the latter, dismissed by fiat on simple nomination. It becomes irrelevant to invoke any other criteria of truth, usefulness, interest, goodness or beauty. The political imperative – often quasi-Marxist, crypto-Marxist, neo-Marxist, post-Marxist – pre-empts the field. One wonders: *can there be no other theory, no eclectic body of ideas, no new vocabulary, to bring contemporary realities into sharper focus?*

It is not only postcolonial intellectuals, of course, who posture with ideology. Deep in the unconscious of the academic humanities there is a story, and it goes something like this, 'Once upon a time, a long, dark time ago, there was a tribe of writers in the American South, terribly misnamed the New Critics. They paid inordinate attention to the forms of literary works, and to special devices like irony and paradox. For an unconscionable time, they dominated the reading scene. But when the 1960s finally arrived, thank God, the New Critics were exposed for their literary exclusiveness and political conservatism. The air was cleared, and adventurous young critics began to turn to Continental Europe for inspiration: to Existentialism and Phenomenology, to the Philosophy of Consciousness and Reception Theory, to Critical Philosophy, to Structuralism. These critics gestured in the right direction, but they had to wait for the advent of poststructuralism to discover the full possibilities of their deconstructive art. Deconstruction, alas, soon became tedious, hollow, almost nihilistic. Feminist, ethnic, postcolonial and cultural studies came to the rescue, saving deconstruction from its innate sterility, and enriching their own sociopolitical "agenda" – yes, that's the word – with all kinds of subtle demystifications and demythifications. It may be safely said that with the current prevalence of cultural studies, in their varied forms, criticism has reached its apogee. It only remains for us to stand our ground against sundry humanists, reactionaries, counter-revolutionaries and proto-fascists still skulking in the corridors of academe.'

Parody, you cry, caricature. Caricatures have a disconcerting habit of coming to life in academe, especially in American academe. But let that pass: the point is that a self-congratulatory myth of progress informs criticism in the era of cultural wars. Progress? Culture is a wrinkled palimpsest, and the arrow of time moves like a swallow, if not a boomerang. As Thomas Kuhn has argued, the sciences and the humanities develop with disparate logics. There are no Ptolemaists or Nostradamists in reputable science departments; there are, however, Platonists, Aristotelians, Thomists, Kantians, Hegelians, Marxists, Nietzscheans, Freudians, Heideggerians, Lacanians . . . in reputable departments of the humanities. This is not to say that the paradigms of science are 'better'; it is only to say that they respond to different criteria of confirmation and disconfirmation. The paradigms of the humanities – Kuhn would say 'schools' – respond to fashion, true, but also to genuine needs for social change. This last is admirable, though it signals no epistemological progress. The opinions of certain influential humanists – no insult to them meant by the name – receive no sanction from a logic of inexorable ascent in our ideas about human reality.

What, you may wonder, is the relevance of all this to postcolonial studies? I counter thus: *Is it not a matter of self-criticism, of awareness that we are not always the last, best fruit of time, a matter of resisting the tendency of all systems to privilege themselves with regard to other systems?* (How easy it has become, for instance, to tar someone with the brush of 'Orientalism', though the brush is dipped only in hot air.) *Is it not also an issue of tact and precision in language?*

Indeed, the language of postcolonial studies warrants our concern. So much of it seems turbid, swollen, like the Nile or the Ganges – without their fertility. So much seems derivative, automatic in diction, untrue to its own motive, giving the impression of ventriloquism. I do not expect to find, beyond thoughtful clarity, verve, freshness, concinnity in every critic. But is it not legitimate to ask: *can a field like postcolonial studies generate distinctive languages of its own, original yet various, attuned both to local knowledges and universal hopes? Must the discourse continue to serve, in the words of Tom Flanagan, as a 'kind of safehouse where theorists with tin ears can give solace to one another'?*[2] Predictably, poets, novelists, playwrights have proven more deft than critics in this regard – witness the contributions of Wole Soyinka, Naguib Mahfouz, Octavio Paz, Nadine Gordimer, Derek Walcott and Toni Morrison to a recent issue of *The Georgia Review.*[3]

Predictably, also, the emphasis on politics is strongest in postcolonial societies themselves, where the imperatives of change, sustained by persistent poverty, disease, corruption – that is, by exploitation from within even more than from without – devalue complexity, independence, self-criticism. In that context, western thought becomes 'dogmatized' – or else rejected out of hand. In Morocco, for instance, as in other Muslim nations, an assertive Islamism – assertive but *in no way terrorist* – has emerged as an alternative to 'the other', as a Moroccan professor once put it to me, meaning communism. The Koranic devotion once accorded to Marxist texts has returned to the Koran itself. I find nothing dismaying in this: after all, Islam has sponsored no gulags; no iron curtains; no DDRs in which child spied on parent, spouse on spouse, friend on friend; no Maoist Cultural Revolution; no Albanian absolutism or Cambodian killing fields. Still, one may respectfully wonder: how can a return to medieval Arab culture be effected in the twenty-first century? Personally, I know no historical instance of cultural atavism, cancelling eight hundred years of change.

Something else is needed, needed from ourselves as from our academic disciplines, to confront our moment. I must move on, therefore, to raise particular issues, hoping for candour if not final illumination.

IMPERIALISM, HISTORY AND MORALITY

Imperialism or colonialism – for my purpose, these terms are interchangeable – is, of course, a constitutive principle of postcolonial criticism. It is an aversive term, but also a principle of historical explanation, socio-economic analysis, moral judgement, personal pathos and corrective political behaviour. What is imperialism? I will not presume to answer that question systematically; I only wish to meditate on it briefly in a historical and moral perspective.

Most often, imperialism entailed military conquest. In that sense, Ancient Egypt, Assyria, Persia, China, India, Greece, Carthage, Rome, Byzantium, the Aztecs, the Incas, the Arabs – or have you forgotten how you and I came by our names? – the Khmer, the Tartars, the Ottomans, the Ashantis, the Zulus, Portugal, Spain, England, France, Holland, Denmark, Sweden, Austria, Russia, Germany, Belgium, Italy, Japan, and, yes, the United States – I have probably left out scores of empires – have all been imperialist at some time or other. This is neither to condone nor to condemn imperialism, only to remark on its history. It seems as if a basic, amoral, historical energy has always expressed itself in the forms of domination. Whether such energy will continue to express itself in that manner is moot. Probably, economic and cultural imperialism will become, has already become, more typical.

What then does it mean to condone or not to condone imperialism? What does it mean to moralize history? True, in this instant of global communications, public opinion has emerged as a redoubtable force no superpower dares to ignore. But public opinion has also served to intensify the secrecy and mendacity of nations, the venality and manipulativeness of media and, in a truly vicious circle, the apathy and cynicism of electorates where these obtain. Indeed, the more righteous a nation seems (the United States), the more hypocritical it must be, since the requirements of national interest and individual probity rarely coincide. Propaganda, disingenuousness, outright deceit: are they not the instruments of a power which appropriates morality without becoming itself moral, only publicly moralistic?

Since Machiavelli, it has been recognized that nation-states have no firm moral principles, only compelling national interests which they labour to disguise as principles. I repeat as a challenge to postcolonial studies: *how to moralize history?* By the force of exhortation, by the power of reflection (education), by political action and moral example? Quite possibly – witness the changes effected by the anti-war, the feminist, the civil rights and the ecological movements; witness the changes in the western canon that cultural and postcolonial studies themselves have effected. Still, I have yet to feel the impact of postcolonial studies on Coca-Cola, Mercedes Benz, Mitsubishi or the IMF. The question stands: *where in postcolonial studies is the relation of history to morality theorized in realistic, not simply idealistic or bombastic, terms?* Or is it sufficient to adopt Edward Said's dictum, that the role of the intellectual is 'to speak the truth to power'?[4]

Whose truth would that be, and whose morality, and who might enforce it? Hindu, Judaic, Buddhist, Shinto, Confucian, Christian or Islamic morality? The universalist morality of the Enlightenment, so often reviled in postcolonial studies? The morality of western democracies, so often accused of imposing it on others? Or is it perhaps the morality of the Prime Minister of Malaysia, who believes that western values are western values, but 'eastern values are universal values'? And is the United Nations, the United States, the European Community or some extraterrestrial agency supposed to enforce that morality?

The Malaysian Prime Minister is not singularly erratic; western intellectuals often fall into the same trap. They constantly inveigh against universalism and laud difference; but they also invoke some abstract, incoherent morality when they criticize western imperialism or eastern despotism. *Is it too indiscreet then to enquire: what moral principle underwrites the insistent judgements of postcolonial studies? In whose or what name are all the denunciations made?* Said, at least, like a few others, knows where he stands: 'Universality means taking a risk in order to go beyond the easy certainties provided us by our background, language, nationality, which so often shield us from the reality of others,' he writes. 'It also means looking for and trying to uphold a single standard for human behavior when it comes to such matters as foreign and social policy.'[5]

Imperialism once entailed military conquest – not by the West alone. Occasionally, it still calls on military power, though more often, in the age of the Internet, CNN and multinational capitalism, it expresses itself, as I have noted, in more seductive economic and cultural forms. A word about these forms.

I confess to ignorance about the insidious procedures of international capitalism. But I recall a Moroccan writer who once blurted out to me: 'America has too much power, economic power, in the world.' I responded spontaneously: 'What is the alternative?' The woman stared at me with stunned indignation. Later, I thought: 'What does she really expect? A return to the Cold War? Or does she want Americans to reduce their productivity, lower their standard of living, liquidate Microsoft and bequeath Pepsi to the Kingdom of Morocco?' Of course, what she expected was an improvement in the conditions of her own country, and a reduction in global exploitation. But how was that kind of parity to be achieved, parity between the United States and Morocco, between Switzerland and Mali, Sweden and Bhutan? *Aren't there cultural traits that enabled the Industrial Revolution in the first place, as David S. Landes has argued?*[6]

Perhaps works like Robert D. Kaplan's *The Ends of the Earth* can also prove pertinent here. Kaplan concludes:

> But if the past is any guide, in too many places there will be a time lag between extreme social deterioration and strategies which might have prevented it. The long-range future may be bright, but the next few decades will be tumultuous. Keep in mind that the collapse of just a few small countries scattered around the globe has overwhelmed policy makers in the West. Were a major regional power to dissolve somewhere, we would have no answers . . . To escape the world is folly – we tried that before each world war. As AIDS shows, Africa's climate and poverty beget disease that finds its way to the wealthiest suburbs. We are the world and the world is us.[7]

This bears, I think, on postcolonial studies. *For shouldn't one of their goals, beyond the obligatory rhetoric of packaged rectitude, be to convince policy-makers in the West to act upon the inequities of history in their own interest?*

Concerning cultural imperialism, I can speak more confidently: I am an example of it, and do not suppose that my life in Egypt would have been infinitely richer there than it is now in the United States. More, I advocate cultural 'impurity'; that is, the complex process of cultural indebtedness, of adaptation, co-optation, appropriation, assimilation – let us simply say translation – as well as refusal. T.S. Eliot, a writer quoted infrequently in cultural studies, made the point half a century ago:

> I have suggested that the national culture which isolates itself voluntarily, or the national culture which is cut off from others by circumstances which it cannot control, suffers from this isolation. Also, that the country which

receives culture from abroad, without having anything to give in return, and the country which aims to impose its culture on another, without accepting anything in return, will both suffer from this lack of reciprocity.[8]

Eliot, of course, had European cultures foremost in mind. But the idea of cultural exchange or translation (*translatio*: trope, metaphor, transport, carrying across) remains suspect in postcolonial studies because nationalism holds it in disdain. *Is it not time, then, for postcolonial studies to reflect seriously on cultural translation: the uses, banes, benefits, procedures, goals of cultural interactions in the age of the Net?* Current anthropological work does reflect on such issues, as do some Moroccan thinkers, like Abdelaziz Benabdallah, in his voluminous studies of the Arabic language and Islamic civilization, and Mahdi Elmandjra, writing on cultural decolonization.[9] But ancient resentments still grip the subject. (Once, after a lecture on literary modernism, a Moroccan student raised his hand to ask: 'I want to know how to damn Modernism'; I replied: 'Say "Damn Modernism"'', while eyeing his steel Rolex look-alike watch.) And in the West, a corrective to imperial arrogance and 'Orientalist' discourse – oh, *some* of those 'Orientalist' clichés were true and others were oddly skewed by the astigmatism of nineteenth-century ethnology – has resulted in rampant, often comical, relativism.

SEVEN ASSUMPTIONS

Intellectuals may and should speak the truth to power, but power seems unable to maintain itself in truth, and the discrepancy must be recognized. Lack of this hard recognition makes for a certain lightness, a certain piety, in postcolonial studies. The latter, in conforming to a standard model, a kind of cast-iron dye, also shares further unexamined assumptions. I want to query seven of these.

1. 'Race is key to colonization.' Not always. Race was irrelevant for the Arabs in Africa and Asia, for the English in Ireland, the Swedes in Finland, the Danes in Norway, the Russians in the Ukraine, the Japanese in Okinawa . . . The drive to domination may be basic, but the motives of colonization are diverse. *Shouldn't a more supple apprehension of colonial impulses inform their study?*
2. 'The wealth of European nations derived from their colonies abroad.' Not invariably. Some of the most affluent nations have had no colonies for the greater part of this century: Switzerland, Sweden, Germany, Canada . . . Moreover, some dispossessed empires have continued to prosper: Britain, France, Belgium, the Netherlands, Japan, the United States . . . Then again, some former colonies have done very well – Singapore, Taiwan, South Korea, Malaysia (the current Asian monetary crisis notwithstanding) – while other former colonies have continued to do very poorly – the list is too long. *Must we not rethink the relation between wealth and colonialism, not only in the epoch of*

multinational capitalism and multicultural nationalism but also retrospectively, retroactively?

3. 'Violence and oppression occur mainly along a vertical axis, between colonizer and colonized, centres and margins.' Violence and even oppression also occur along a horizontal axis – witness the horrors in Africa, Asia, the Middle East, the Balkans; witness the work of the Australian artist, George Gittoes, drawing on first-hand experiences in Nicaragua, Somalia, Rwanda, Cambodia, Lebanon, the Philippines, the Spanish Sahara and Ulster.[10] Milder versions of these conflicts occur as well between factions and minorities in western societies. *Are all geopolitical miseries, then, attributable to imperialism? How can we understand historical violence, without recourse to sentimental ideologies or the gloomy doctrine of Original Sin?*

4. 'Difference liberates, sameness oppresses.' Really? Otherness, as we nowadays like to say, is indeed embedded in our grammars (I/you; us/them), in our psyches, in our genetic and immune codes. But an accent on *le différend* – radically incommensurate orders of discourse, as Lyotard put it[11] – is dubious. It can discourage mutual obligation, cripple empathy, defeat transcultural judgements, leaving only raw power to resolve human conflicts. It can lead to hostility, exclusiveness, less respect for others than solidarity with ourselves – the 'narcissism of minor differences',[12] as Michael Ignatieff put it, taking his cue from Freud. Thus, the discourse of difference, a rhetoric of self-empowerment really, becomes counterproductive; for cohesion may be achieved within diversity. Still, the intractable question remains: *how and when, pragmatically, to honour differences, ignore them, negotiate them?*

5. 'We are all culturally constructed, socially produced.' (This assumption oddly contradicts the assumption of difference, since constructionism cannot explain differences within the same class, gender, race and even family.) The truth is that we are not only 'constructed', we also construct back, we interact. Furthermore, we are, most of us, mysteriously self-created, and chance and genes have been known to affect human destinies. *How necessary, then, is the alibi of constructionism – like grace? like predestination? – to the purpose of postcolonial studies? Is not its solace condescending and spurious?*

6. 'There are no universals.' Indeed, there are no absolute universals, neither in nature nor in history; such universals live only as mental or formal abstractions. In practice, however, many principles serve as working generalizations or soft universals. I do not mean only biological facts like death, hunger or sexual reproduction. I also mean, empirically, some transcultural practices like languages, rituals, taboos, spirits, social organizations of marriage, hierarchy and status. These, we know, vary immensely according to time, place and tribe. Yet as human practices, they pervade the earth. *Can postcolonial studies qualify, discriminate, contextualize the idea of universals, give it texture and nuance, instead of rejecting it outright?*

7. 'Materialist philosophies best suit postcolonial studies.' Why? Philosophical materialism and idealism seem to me equally incoherent, incomplete. The former – *pace* Lucretius – cannot explain creation, the latter cannot relate it to

our facts; the former ignores mind, the latter must ultimately ignore matter. And neither can connect with the other except through an imaginary, Cartesian 'gland'. Pragmatically, I ignore the dualism, as did William James. And I observe how spiritual forces, like Hinduism, Judaism and Islam, play a decisive role in postcolonial societies. *Must the postcolonial critic consider these spiritual phenomena as opium for the people, mass delusions, archaic beliefs that the historical process will outgrow? Does materialism skew the analysis of critics who have no capacity for the willing suspension of their own disbeliefs?*

Having argued insistently for greater subtlety and nuance – these may be the form truth takes in our professions – argued against reductionism in postcolonial studies, I hesitate to attribute all lapses to a single, dread cause. Yet I must repeat here an earlier query: has the influence of Marxist doctrines, working through Foucault and other poststructuralists, gone too far afield? I am particularly mindful of the question in countries like Morocco, where intellectuals must continually juggle three conformities: Nationalism, Marxism, Islamism, in their new and diverse guises.

THE POSTCOLONIAL CONDITION

The postcolonial condition is not a happy condition. One wishes it could conform, in hybrid abundance and eclectic choice, with the image Jason Epstein projects of an American supermarket:

A dozen kinds of lettuce and other greens; piles of fennel and rhubarb; fresh herbs, including basil, coriander, thyme, rosemary, tarragon, lemon grass and mint; displays of salsify, burdock, and celeriac; taro and plantains; tofu and chiles of many kinds, Japanese daikon and several Chinese cabbages; tomatoes all year round, from Israel and, in cans marked San Marazano, indicating the highest quality, from Italy; and bell peppers in many colors from Holland – this abundance and endlessly more can be had in many cities and towns where a generation ago there was little besides iceberg lettuce and boxed tomatoes and TV dinners.[13]

Inevitably, someone will remark that the image is itself neocolonialist. Still, the world is more open, contingent and interactive than determinist theories allow. And at bottom, the postcolonial condition is one that *we all* – not just developing nations – inhabit.

More than half a century ago, Martin Heidegger dolefully predicted the 'complete Europeanization [he did not say "Americanization"] of the earth and man', an infection, he claimed, that 'attacks at the source everything that is of an essential nature'.[14] But Heidegger was impercipient in local as in geopolitics. What has come about is neither the totalization he predicted, nor the fragmentation resulting from 'the obsolescence of the metanarrative apparatus of delegitimation' that Lyotard presaged in *The Postmodern Condition*,[15] but a world turned into an immense warehouse of residues, innovations, simulacra and cargo cults, plundered or preserved, used or misused, by unequal powers.

Thus, though 'the West' may seem paramount, it is neither integral – I need only advert to the habitual negations of France – nor omnipotent. As an American living in the United States, I can testify that my compatriots feel far from omnipotent, though some, America-firsters no doubt, may preach supremacy and isolationism in the same breath. Far more representative is Clifford Geertz's view, which finds surprising approval outside the academy, that we need to see 'ourselves amongst others, as a local example of the forms human life has locally taken, a case among cases, a world among worlds'.[16] A case among cases, yes, but not all cases are equal, not by the longest shot.

In this interesting, conflictual, postcolonial condition, we are still learning to live; in this gallimaufry, potpourri or salmagundi of traditions and values, we are still trying to 'think globally and act locally', as the former president of Sony used to say. *In that condition, what can philosophical pragmatism or complexity theory, for instance, contribute to postcolonial studies? What is to be done?*

WHAT IS TO BE DONE?

I pose the question with much self-irony, mindful of Dostoyevsky's answer to Nikolai Chernyshevski's *What Is to Be Done?* The Man from Underground is still very much with us, alive and sick as ever. Consider this anecdote (from the chapter entitled 'The Narcissism of Minor Differences') in Michael Ignatieff's *The Warrior's Honor*, about the author's visit to Mirkovci, a village divided by the recent Serbo-Croatian wars:

> On the bunk next to me, leaning against the wall, wearing combat fatigues, is a compact and dapper middle-aged man with bright, wily eyes and a thick, stylish mustache. With a certain false naiveté, I venture the thought that I can't tell Serbs and Croats apart. 'What makes you think you're so different?'
>
> He looks scornful and takes a cigarette pack out of his khaki jacket. 'See this? These are Serbian cigarettes. Over there', he says, gesturing out the window, 'they smoke Croatian cigarettes.'
>
> 'But they're both cigarettes, right?'
>
> 'Foreigners don't understand anything.'
>
> He shrugs and resumes cleaning his Zastovo machine pistol.
>
> But the question I've asked bothers him, so a couple of minutes later he tosses the weapon on the bunk between us and says, 'Look, here's how it is. Those Croats, they think they're better than us. They want to be the gentlemen. Think they're fancy Europeans. I'll tell you something. We're all just Balkan shit.'[17]

I have not read much in postcolonial readers that can illuminate this event. But I know something about the colonial complex, in Cairo, in Rabat, in Mirkovci where I have never been, and I know nationalism. Both are insatiable. It is an amazing, an awesome thing, the spite and sorrow of it: to see the universe, year in and year out, through the slit of a particular wound, be it the wound of class or gender or race or imperial domination. It is a deep malady and sinister disease, mixing anger with self-contempt – no, not real self-criticism – leaving us in a state of perpetual prickliness, exquisitely on the *qui vive*, ready to take umbrage if a shadow but cross our path. What is to be done? Root it out, root out the colonial complex from the mind, the heart, the gut, and learn to look at the world with level gaze.

There is more. In Leila Abouzeid's fine, if a touch naive, novel, *The Year of the Elephant*, a novel about the independence years in Morocco, there is a crucial line: 'Hopelessness leads to carelessness.'[18] Yes, yes, I thought, but carelessness also breeds misery. Every small act of omission or remission, of sloth or self-indulgence, is an invitation to colonialism, colonialism of an insidious kind. Every burned-out bulb, littered beach, rusty knife, broken hinge, grimy cup, unfinished job, missed rendezvous, flouted traffic light and, especially, corrupt official is an invitation to colonialism. Poverty is no excuse, neither for corruption in high places nor civic indifference on the street.

There is more still. Why whinge continually about cultural imperialism, like the British and American public who lament the tabloids ceaselessly while lapping up their lurid stories? Why not, as I have said, adopt and appropriate as well as refuse? Above all, why not counter-create: that is, through our own creations, our own adaptations and refusals, make the modern culture we need? The Japanese, we know, have done so since the Meiji period, and in two or three generations have transformed their country from a medieval to a postmodern society – the most archaic, supertechnological society on earth, some snide wit may remark.

'All this is very nice, very quaint,' certain intellectuals will sneer. 'But it's all *personal*. Where's the *politics*?' Well, as Averroes (Ibn Rushd) says to Sultan El Mansur in Youssef Chahine's marvellous film, *Le Destin* (1997), try sometimes the 'politics of conscience', the politics of trust and responsibility; my house, my street, my life might change more visibly than any change the 'revolution of the proletariat' ever achieved.

I do not say that the politics of personal responsibility will suffice; some larger, some communal if not collective, concern is also required. Hence, of course, the resurgence of Islam in certain parts of the world. But I do say that postcolonial critics have, with notable exceptions like Frantz Fanon, tended to ignore the constitutive powers of the self. *Is it not time, then, to reinsert the self into history as well as history into the self?* Islam may do so, and it may act as an Archimedean point to lift societies out of their misery, an Islam of decency, tolerance, and spiritual honour – an Islam, above all, respectful of the full potentialities of women. But what might work in one time or place might not work in another, and, in any case, the whole postcolonial world is not subsumed by Islam.

What, then, is to be done?

A PLEA FOR SPIRIT

Shockingly, I want to plead for spirit. Why shockingly? Because, as I have already said, the materialist hypothesis prevails among western intellectuals. Because academics, as I have remarked elsewhere, 'deprecate . . . [spirit] intellectually, socially, politically, associating it with rappings at a seance, incense in darkened rooms, susurrations of New Age beatitude, if not machinations of cryptofascists'.[19] Because in hypercapitalist nations, like the United States, the Market is implicitly believed to resolve all moral as well as political or economic issues.

We need not endorse Samuel P. Huntington's thesis about the 'clash of civilizations' to realize that societies do not live by bread alone.[20] Yet we continue to assume that sending food and medicine, economists and engineers, sending soldiers, above all, sending money with strings attached long enough to entangle the earth can remedy any situation in the hinterlands of history. Relief, whatever its form, can be critical and can be humane – but it will not suffice. What should we send that man with his Serbian cigarettes and Zastovo machine pistol? A pack of Marlboros? An Apple computer? A more powerful, made-in-America, automatic gun? Not even a Gideon Bible would help.

I do recognize that spirit can be enormously problematic: the most malevolent wars have been waged, still are waged, in the name of one god or another. But I also recognize that the 'will to believe', as William James called it, is fundamental to humankind. My approach to spirit, then, accords with James: like him, I am willing 'to count the humblest and most personal experiences', 'count mystical experiences if they have practical consequences' and would 'take a God who lives in the very dirt of private fact – if that should seem a likely place to find him'.[21]

Spirit does not exhaust itself in theological doctrines and religious orthodoxies. It reveals itself in a vast range of immaterial facts: in common intuitions and quotidian beliefs; in sentiments like love, values like loyalty; in the sense of beauty, awe, ecstasy, the sublime; in the enigmas of the creative process in science and art; in visionary and mystical experiences – above all, perhaps, in intimations, if not of immortality, of a larger reality in the cosmos, beyond our grasp. All these 'immaterial facts' – what else should I call them, since they continue to elude researchers of the outrageous human brain? – constitute the radical impulse both to realize and to transcend one's humanity. *Is it not short-sighted, then, for postcolonial studies to ignore the radical imperatives of the human spirit?*

Spirit, however, has practical consequences, as any player on home turf or warrior in a *jihad* must know. Can spirit be put to use in our fractious, postcolonial world? Here I must be ginger on pain of self-deception. We know that conflicts can be resolved, or at least abated, by discovering shared interests – that's politics, diplomacy. Can divergent cultures also converge where their spiritual concerns meet? Such concerns can be religious or philosophical or artistic; they can even be athletic, as in the ancient or modern Olympics. A step further: is it not likely that by understanding the spiritual dimensions in our own lives we can better understand, better translate, other lives? A step beyond: is it not possible that by transcending both ourselves and our cultures we can project ourselves into other selves and other cultures, and so evolve into a spiritual multiculturalism, or rather, spiritual interculturalism? And another step beyond that: can a spiritual sense of the cosmic miracle we all share prepare us to accept our (common/uncommon) destiny on this frail planet, floating among immemorial galaxies?

Here I must stop, though I find nothing absurd in such lines of tentative speculation. And here, too, I must come to a conclusion.

Queries are odd, grammatical structures. They express curiosity; and, yes, they express a measure of scepticism, if not outright challenge. But queries also answer themselves, because the form of every question whispers its own retort. At bottom, however, queries are invocations of concord – or, if this sounds too grand, invitations to converse.

It is in that spirit that I have offered my queries. Sometimes, it may seem that I was engaging straw men in my dialogue; but that is only because I declined to engage a particular author or text, taking the dominant model of postcolonial studies as my interlocutor. Perhaps no such model exists. That would be cause for celebration. For I know history to be full of cunning surprise, and I know that we are all, in this postcolonial world, children of the fecundity of the unexpected, in cosmic, in biological, in cultural evolution.

Signs of Our Times
Discussion of Homi Bhabha's *The Location of Culture*

BENITA PARRY

The collection of essays, *The Location of Culture*, written over the last decade and already in circulation, is a strong articulation of the linguistic turn in cultural studies, distinguished by Homi Bhabha's recourse to Lacanian theories and hence foregrounding the instabilities of enunciation. The book appears at a time when there are signs of a concerted challenge to critical modes that are predicated on the autonomy of signifying processes and privilege the means of representation as the progenitor of meaning. One symptom of this move away from a practice which has been ascendant for some years, although never uncontested, is the growth of interest in Pierre Bourdieu's work on cultural production, where the textual idealism of transferring the Saussurean language

model to social and literary analyses is repudiated.[1] Another is Christopher
Norris's censure of 'facile textualist thought' which 'contrives to block the
appeal to any kind of real-world knowledge or experience', a criticism made on
ethical as well as cognitive grounds by one who has been a prominent exponent
of deconstruction.[2] There is also reason to anticipate a more widespread and
closer attention to Marxist/*Marxisant* theories of culture and history, since, as
any competent clairvoyant could foretell, Derrida's recent lectures and writings
on Marx[3] will in time persuade susceptible epigoni to defer their preparations
for the burial of an explanatory system they had declared moribund, sometimes
without observing the protocols of scrupulous examination.

As regards Bhabha's stipulations of what constitutes '*the* colonial condition'
and '*the* postcolonial experience/perspective/critique' (emphasis added to suggest a totalizing tendency which Bhabha would ordinarily eschew), these have
been disputed in discussions which follow other theoretical procedures and are
producing different objects of knowledge from the same archival material.[4]
Thus, when Bhabha buoyantly claims that 'a shift within contemporary critical
traditions of postcolonial writing'[5] is heralded by the methodologies which he
and like-minded critics have devised, this prediction of a new and unassailable
hegemony, whose pre-eminence could already be in the past tense, depends on
disregarding alternatives to the methods he espouses – and indeed it is noticeable that while Bhabha militantly combats a putative 'left orthodoxy', he gives
scant attention to the often searching questions that have been asked of his
work.[6]

This then is an appropriate moment to venture an assessment of a confident,
ambitious and influential theoretical programme seeking to examine the
translation of western discourses from the disjunctive and displacing sites of
'postcolonial' perspectives which, Bhabha maintains, provide a form of writing
cultural difference that is inimical to binary boundaries, and effect the relocation of western modernity.[7] Such an undertaking appears to have affinities
with Edward Said's 'contrapuntal' readings of the colonial archives which, in
mapping the overlapping territories and intertwined histories of metropolis and
colony, and noting the mixtures of cultures and identities on a global scale
consolidated by imperialism, restore to the history of modernism 'the massive
infusions of non-European cultures into the metropolitan heartland'.[8] It also
resembles Paul Gilroy's contention that the doubleness of the black experiences
in the West constitutes the counterculture of modernity.[9]

Bhabha's work, however, preoccupied as it is with the generation of meaning
within textual forms and functions, is situated within other theoretical spaces
and manifests an agenda and trajectory that sets it apart from the writings of
those theorists such as Frantz Fanon, Ranajit Guha, Edward Said and Fredric
Jameson, whom he generously attempts to enlist as allies in his own project. The
substance of this assignment, which is signalled by Bhabha's well-known 'taste
for in-between states and moments of hybridity',[10] and exceeds a concern to
make known a postcolonial condition of displacement and diaspora, or to nar-
rate a postcolonial transgression of boundaries, is amply evident in his usage of

paradoxical and open-ended words: ambivalent, borderline, boundary, contingent, dispersal, disjunction, dissemination, discontinuity, hybridity, in-between, incommensurable, indeterminate, interstitial, liminal, marginal, negotiation, transitional, translational and uncertain. This preference for terms which condense the free play of difference, or the elements of undecidability within any system of communication, registers Bhabha's affiliation with a critical practice which undertakes to reveal how the instability of textual meaning is produced/ undermined as permutations on a chain of signification. It also denotes an adherence to Michel Foucault's recommendation that difference be freed from an oppositional and negative system, to operate as 'thought without contradiction, without dialectics, without negation'[11] – bringing to mind Jameson's remark that at stake in such moves 'is the rolling back of Hegel and Marx by way of a conceptual discrediting of contradiction and dialectical opposition'.[12]

The implications of rewriting a historical project of invasion, expropriation and exploitation in the indeterminate and always deferred terms Bhabha proposes and implements are immense, and for me immensely troubling, since his elaborations dispense with the notion of conflict – a concept which certainly does infer antagonism, but contra Bhabha, does not posit a simplistically unitary and closed structure to the adversarial forces. But before I embark on the discussion of Bhabha's work, a word of self-exculpation is necessary: the matter of his impacted style is not one on which I will dwell, other than to observe that an enchantment with troping, punning and riddling all too often sends the signifier into free-fall, rendering arbitrary the link between word and signified. To mean what you say is not the same as to say what you mean, and because for this reader Bhabha's prose presents the hazard of inadvertent misconstruction, I have taken the precaution of illustrating my gloss with extensive citations from his writing.[13]

Given the difficulty of exegeses weighed down by the specialized terminology of linguistic and psychoanalytic theory, its density thickened by improbable juxtapositions and innumerable, fleeting allusions to the comments of critics, thinkers and writers, it may seem remarkable that Bhabha's writing has been so readily and widely redeployed by others working in cognate areas. The extent of his influence suggests the power of Bhabha's rethinking culture 'as an uneven, incomplete production of meaning and value',[14] his insights into the hierarchy retained by the liberal ethic of multiculturalism, his attention to the differential historicities of races, nations and peoples, his innovative work on the inflections of colonialism within western thought and his contributions to opening up the categories of identity, culture and nation to their heterogeneity. However, it is also apparent that when critics cite his key concepts in order to authorize their own propositions, they do so without necessarily indicating a grasp of, or interest in, the problematics within which Bhabha is writing. I will therefore attempt to discuss his work as generated by multiple determinations in the form of both theoretical modes and social location. In doing so I must declare that while appreciative of the ground Bhabha has broken in asking new questions of old problems, I am uneasy about his disposal of the language model to explain colonialism's past social processes and contemporary 'postcolonial' situations; and what I will be proposing is that Bhabha's many fecund insights into cultural processes are paradoxically denatured by the theoretical modes which inform his work.

In Bhabha's usage 'postcolonialism' does not indicate 'sequentiality', its gestures to a 'beyond' denoting a disjunctive relationship with that anterior condition by which it is indelibly marked, and which enables a critique displacing the language and precepts of both colonialist and anti-colonialist writing. As is now well known, the problems with the connotations of 'postcolonialism' are legion: Anne McClintock contends that its *singularity* 'effects a re-centering of global history around the single rubric of European time . . . reduces the cultures of peoples beyond colonialism to *prepositional* time . . . [and] signals a reluctance to surrender the privilege of seeing the world in terms of a singular and ahistorical abstraction'. Drawing attention to its 'depoliticising implications', Ella Shohat has observed that by alluding to colonialism as 'a matter of the past', the term shuts out 'colonialism's economic, political and cultural deformative traces in the present'. For Laura Chrisman, who observes its metropolitan coinage, ' "postcolonial" . . . occludes or erases the overtly political dynamics contained in the term "anti-colonial" ', allowing or implying 'the interchangeability of material . . . with aesthetic and interpretative processes', and liberating those practitioners naming themselves postcolonial 'from the messy business of political alignment and definition'.[15]

Other severe criticisms have been made by Masao Miyoshi and Arif Dirlik, who see in its deployment a licence for ignoring the contemporary actuality of global politics within a capitalist world-system. Miyoshi views its use as a device to conceal the operation of a continuing and even more active colonialism by transnational corporatism: 'Ours . . . is not an age of *post*colonialism but of intensified colonialism, even though it is under an unfamiliar guise',[16] while for Dirlik, the world 'mystifies both politically and methodologically a situation that represents not the abolition but the reconfiguration of earlier forms of domination'.[17] Furthermore, Dirlik maintains, those forms of postcolonial criticism which repudiate all master-narratives and disclaim foundational historical writing must also reject capitalism as a determinant category and with it the capitalist constitution of the world, thus occluding the changing structural position within this system of the 'Third World' – which he insists is not an essentialist but a relational category. As against Gyan Prakash, who contends that we cannot thematize colonial history in terms of development of capitalism, since this would entail accepting the homogenization of the contemporary world by capitalism,[18] Dirlik argues that while no stark dichotomy of economic and social form between First and Third Worlds can now be asserted,[19] the globalism of capitalism effects the *uneven* insertion of heterogeneous and discrepant histories and *differential* economic formations into a world-system.[20]

The implications of the above strictures are far-reaching for a project such as Bhabha's which privileges postcoloniality not only as the position from which to deconstruct colonialism's legitimizing strategies but also as the location of contemporary globalized intellectual and cultural discourses. As if heedful that 'a postcolonial critique', in welcoming the arrival of a 'transnational' culture, could seem to ignore the worldwide material conditions of division and exploitation inhibiting its realization, Bhabha notes the 'conflictual, contradictory locutions of those cultural practices and products that follow the "unequal development" of the tracks of international or multinational capital'.[21] Moreover, when observing that postcoloniality 'is a salutary reminder of the persistent "neo-colonial" relations within the "new" world order and the multi-national division of labour', and claiming that 'such a perspective enables the authentication of histories of exploitation and the evolution of strategies of resistance',[22] Bhabha alludes to a concern with the material conditions, institutions and practices of colonialism and the neocolonial which is not pursued in his efforts to derive social explanation from the 'activity of articulation as embodied in the language metaphor'.

Bhabha's agenda is starkly evident in his rewriting 'radical maroonage', or the guerrilla wars waged by runaway slaves against their erstwhile masters.[23] Here, a practice involving tactics and manoeuvres designed and conducted by subjects-as-agents on contested territory, repeated and embellished in folk memory as cherished stories of downtrodden ancestors moved to resistance, and rewritten by contemporary critics recuperating signs of enacted disobedience, is translated into a set of discursive moves: 'From this liminal, minority position where, as Foucault would say, the relations of discourse are of the nature of warfare, the force of the people of an Afro-American nation emerges in the extended metaphor of maroonage. For "warriors" read writers or even "signs".'[24] As I read, Bhabha's revision, an endlessly reworked narrative, which renders the experiential realities of slave resistance intelligible, is overwhelmed by the nominalism of the language metaphor; and in the interests of establishing the autarchy of the signifier the narrated event is existentially diminished.

This is not to question the linguistic turn in all its possible registers, and it is now surely impossible to conceive of cultural or historical analyses working within a realist paradigm that do not address the tropological ruses and effects of their archival sources, are unaware that systems of meanings are animated and borne by signs, metaphors and narratives, or are indifferent to the constitutive role of these in articulating social relationships. In its 'weak' form, which does not of course imply weak theory, this disposal of the language model actively reads texts against the grain, alert to silences, gaps, disjunctions, aporia. Recognizing that all language is figurative, such commentaries are thus attentive to the rhetorical strategies and effects of enunciations, which, in the process of naturalizing prevailing precepts and categories in order to create their objects of knowledge, displace meaning and escape or exceed self-conscious intentionality, thus marking the disjunction between programme and performance, between aspiration and experience. Among the many instances of this mode as it addresses colonialism, Bhabha's deconstructions of the fissures and ruptures in colonial texts are exercises of great subtlety, seeming to share with other studies a recognition of the *instrumentality* of colonialism's utterances.[25]

Because Bhabha has written powerfully about 'hybrid' cultural articulations when glossing the novels, poetry and films of postcolonial writers and artists, critics have readily interpreted his use of this notion as denoting culture's multiple and incongruous accents, cross-cultural inventions and transnationality – that is, as descriptive of subject positions and social conditions traversed by heterogeneous cultural inflections. Yet an examination of Bhabha's argument belies an easy identification of his concept with what was posited long ago by Caribbean and Latin American writers and intellectuals as creolization, *métissage* or *mestizaje*. It is also distinct from both Paul Gilroy's insistence on the inescapable intermixture of ideas and forms in neologistic transitional cultures, and Stuart Hall's account of the disjunctive, displaced and unstable postcolonial identities constituted in representation but which relate to real sets of histories. (I will return to Bhabha's place on the spectrum of concepts around identity within black British theory.)

Although wholly familiar with the innovative idioms deployed by such multiply located subjects, Bhabha's concern is with the production of hybridity through the *process* of a colonial and postcolonial relocating and re-inscribing, or the translating and transvaluing of cultural difference 'in the Third Space of enunciation', where it is reiterated differently from its prior context:

> Hybridity is the revaluation of the assumption of colonial identity through the repetition of identity effects. It displays the necessary deformation and displacement and domination . . . For the colonial hybrid is the articulation of the ambivalent space where the rite of power is enacted on the site of desire, making its objects at once disciplinary and disseminatory.[26]

> The hybrid object . . . retains the actual semblance of the authoritative symbol but revalues its presence by resisting it as the signifier of *Entstellung* – *after the intervention of difference* . . . the theoretical recognition of the split-space of enunciation may open the way to conceptualizing an *inter*national culture, based not on exoticism of multiculturalism, or the diversity of cultures, but on the inscription of culture's *hybridity*.[27]

As I read it, Bhabha's 'hybridity' is a twin-term for the 'catachrestic reinscription' of 'cultural difference' in the disjunctive postcolonial discursive space – that is, it is descriptive of the textual processes and effects held to constitute social forms and conditions, and not of those forms and conditions as articulated in social practices. For when contesting 'the consensual, ethnocentric notion of the pluralistic existence of cultural diversity',[28] with 'the ambivalent process of splitting and hybridity that marks the identification with culture's difference'[29] Bhabha postulates cultural difference as a discursive product and an analytic strategy:

> Cultural difference . . . is not the acquisition or accumulation of additional cultural knowledge; it is the momentous, if momentary extinction of the recognizable object of culture in the disturbed artifice of its signification, at the edge of experience.[30]

> Cultural difference must not be understood as the free play of polarities and pluralities in the homogeneous empty time of the national community . . . The analytic of cultural difference intervenes to transform the scenario of articulation . . . The aim of cultural difference is to re-articulate the sum of knowledge from the perspective of the signifying position of the minority that resists totalization . . . producing other spaces of subaltern signification.[31]

This shift from the concept as a context-dependent category deployed to legitimate discriminatory practices, or as a counter-device of political affirmation, subdues the charge immanent in 'difference' as a marker of social inequalities and a sign of resistance to oppression. In Norris's telling phrase when discussing a 'nominalist (or textualist) stance which denies any possible grounds of appeal in the realities of oppression as *known and experienced* by members of the relevant class, community or interest group', what is ignored is 'the stubborn *facticity* of . . . difference . . . the manifold differences – the real and material (not just 'discursive') differences of interest'.[32]

It is such differences that engender political and ethical collectivities;[33] for while it is now well known that our class subjectivities are crossed and modulated by various and competing identifications, the structural relations of capitalism-as-transcontinental-imperialism continue to provoke situations which demand that plurally constituted and positioned subjects, with multiple associations, different proclivities and diverse enthusiasms, mobilize around class conceived either as a socio-economic category or as a community engaged in struggle. This very notion of solidarity is resisted by Bhabha, whose reply to the question he rhetorically poses, 'Do we need to rethink the terms in which we conceive of community, citizenship, nationality, and the ethics of social affiliation?'[34] must be, given his premises, to posit difference, incommensurability and dispersal as rendering traditional constructions of communality unsatisfactory and unsafe: 'Can such split subjects and differentiated social movements, which display ambivalent and divided forms of identification, be represented in a collective will that distinctively echoes Gramsci's enlightened inheritance and its rationalism?'.[35] Implicit in Bhabha's critique of identitarianism and his valorizing of difference is a recommendation of coalition politics and rainbow alliances, but one which foregoes the necessary examination of their operations, hazards, consequences and failures.[36]

To question the deployment of 'difference' as a counter to the negatively perceived 'totalization' is not to deny the fecundity of a notion which insists on subjectivity as polymorphous, community as heterogeneous, social formations as mutable and culture as vagrant. It is to recognize that 'difference' has been diverted by a postmodernist criticism as a theoretical ruse to establish a neutral, ideology-free zone from which the social dissension and political contest inscribed in the antagonist pairing of colonizer/colonized have been expelled. A policy statement defining difference in terms of bland variations on a placid continuum, unhinged from the planned inequalities of actually existing social regimes and political struggles, can be found in the writing of the film director and critic, Trinh T. Minh-ha:

> I have often been asked about what viewers call the lack of conflicts in my films . . . Conflicts in western contexts often serve to define identities. My suggestion to the 'lack' is: let difference replace conflict. Difference as understood in many feminist and non-western contexts, difference as foregrounded in my film work, is not opposition to sameness, nor synonymous with separateness.[37]

Here, 'difference' is used to deny both class contest and anti-imperialism in the thought or practice of 'non-western' histories and societies, while also eliminating the incompatible agendas and goals at work within 'feminist contexts'. Norris has observed how poststructuralism 'operates on an abstract, quasi-systemic model of "opposition" and "difference" whereby those terms are deprived of all specific historical or experiential content, and treated, in effect, as linguistic artefacts or products of discursive definition',[38] insisting that '*difference* can only be a fashionable buzzword . . . so long as it is conceived in ideal abstraction from the contexts of real-world experience or the lived actualities of class or gender oppression'[39] – to which can be added 'colonialist and imperialist domination'.

In the pages of *Third Text*, which pointedly identifies itself as providing 'Third World Perspectives on Contemporary Art and Culture', many and competing understandings of cultural identity have been posited over the years. Among these, Rasheed Araeen, who urges the necessity 'of recognizing the critical and historical roles of autonomous individuals from non-European cultures', proposes 'cultural identity' as 'both fiction and necessity', finding that it gives 'a cutting edge to question and interrogate many of the assumptions of Western culture by which it claims its superiority and supremacy'; while Geeta Kapur has dissented from a postmodernism that 'seems to accommodate otherness as never before in the history of capitalist culture', but does so 'through a process of such infinite differentiation that all questions of identity are destroyed . . . along with the normative function of culture'.[40] It is apparent then that the empowering effects of a placed identity have not been relinquished by the critical community. What is more, there are those who have advised that the cost of the 'hybridization', attendant on colonialism and accenting the postcolonial, should not remain uncounted. In glossing Edward Brathwaite's definition of creolization 'as one's adaptation to a new environment through the loss of parts of oneself and the gain of parts of the Other', Manthia Diawara – who cautions that the question of hybridity 'as *the* correct way of being Black in the West has enabling elements as well as uncanny moments' – has observed: 'one must be aware of the fact that in fusing Whiteness with the seductiveness of hybrid-ization, one is sacrificing not only a part of Blackness, but certain Black people'.[41]

These 'certain Black people' are too often forgotten in the euphoria of cele-brating the postcolonial. It is true that Bhabha does eloquently specify 'the demography of the new internationalism' in terms of 'the history of postcolo-nial migration, the narratives of cultural and political diaspora, the major social displacements of peasant and aboriginal communities, the poetics of exile, the grim prose of political and economic refugees'.[42] This configuration acknow-ledges that '[T]he transnational dimension of cultural transformation – migration, diaspora, displacement, relocation – makes the process of cultural translation a complex form of signification.'[43] Yet his vista emerges as narrower than the above comments promise; for while this does encompass diverse 'narra-tives where double-lives are led in the postcolonial world, with its journeys of migration and its dwellings of the diasporic',[44] what is foregrounded by Bhabha, in prose that can be translucent but is sometimes purple,[45] is 'the poetics of relocation and reinscription'[46] known by the cosmopolitan artist, writer, intel-lectual, professional, financier and entrepreneur in the metropolis, rather than the 'grim prose' of low-waged workers in western capitals, and contract labour-ers in the Gulf states or other centres of capitalist growth within the Third World. Moreover, the claim that '[T]he contingent and the liminal become the times and the spaces for the historical representation of the subjects of cultural difference in a postcolonial criticism',[47] emphasizes the 'affective experience of social marginality' – which by intimating the circulation of emotion and desire, registers the experience as one of unmitigated enhancement. Indeed, assertions about the 'unhomely' as paradigmatic of postcolonial social and cultural dis-placement, or 'the liminality of migrant experience', 'the migrant culture of the in-between' and the 'indeterminacy of diasporic identity'[48] now constitute the near-consensual opinion: consider Bruce Robbins's commendation of Bhabha's essay 'DissemiNation' as providing 'a portrait of trans-national hybridity as an increasingly unavoidable condition of emotional and intellectual life'.[49]

It is, I would suggest, a configuration in urgent need of unpacking. In repre-senting the productive tensions of its own situation as normative and desirable, the privileged postcolonial is prone to denigrate affiliations to class, ethnicity and emergent nation-state which continue to fashion the self-understanding and energize the resistances of exploited populations in the hinterlands of late imperialism, as well as of immigrant labourers living on the outskirts of one or other metropolis. The stance of the élite thus further severs their modes of cognition from those of communities which, while themselves also inhabiting cultural spaces that are multiply inflected and impure, do not share in the free-wheeling pleasures of commuting between cultures available to the privileged postcolonial.

Such different situations are starkly noted in the inventory compiled by Neil Lazarus:

In Mozambique, Nigeria, Korea and El Salvador, the question of the nation-state has never before seemed so pressing or so central. In Brazil, Jamaica, Ghana and Malaysia, the concepts of 'diversity', 'mobility' and 'communication' are of practical significance only to foreign élites and indigenous comprador classes.[50]

In a related register, Masao Miyoshi, who has voiced concern that the new cultural configurations of transnational corporate capitalism threaten the survival of local cultures, is acerbic about those critics who rejoice at the imagined camaraderie of an amalgamated world culture. Remarking that ' "[M]ulticulturalism" is a luxury largely irrelevant to those who live under the most wretched conditions', Miyoshi moves from the preoccupation in cultural studies with 'recognizing different subject-positions from different regions and diverse backgrounds', to urging the need for a project that will address political and economic inequalities as differences that must be erased.[51] With this he turns the discussion in the direction of political economy and international class politics, towards which Bhabha's writings, enclosed as they are in a theoretical mode that subdues the continuing exploitation of the Third World and the growing disparities of resources and opportunities within the First, can do no more than gesture.

Although Bhabha situates himself within French critical theory, his translations of an expatriate postcolonial location have been deeply inflected by the particular modulations of the theoretical discussion conducted within Britain. The presence of Marxism as a strand in British intellectual and academic life, together with socialism's established place on the political spectrum and the existence of a small but important tradition of anti-colonialism[52] – and to both of which colonials living in the metropolis contributed – may have prompted Bhabha to associate his writing with 'the materialist mode', and offer his work as an effort both 'to enhance understanding of political struggle',[53] and to 'historicize the event of the dehistoricized'.[54] Perhaps more significantly, the course of his work displays affinities with the particular trajectory of British poststructuralism, which in drawing on French critical theory redeployed both psychoanalytic writing and Marxism-via-Althusser. Francis Mulhern has suggested that

> [S]emiotics, developing through a critical ingathering of modern scientific initiatives in poetics and linguistics – formalist, structuralist and other – offered concepts and taxonomies that bore the promise of a post-aesthetic, materialist analysis of textual forms and functions. Psychoanalysis appeared not merely as a potent analogy but as a decisive contributor to the understanding of subjectivity. Marxism furnished terms of historical understanding and defined the politics of text and subject.[55]

During the 1970s, according to Antony Easthope, the film journal *Screen* – to which Bhabha later contributed – 'set out to theorise "the encounter of

Marxism and psychoanalysis on the terrain of semiotics" ', the commitment to materialism manifested in the thesis that 'the semiological determination of film was realised in its specific materiality and that this presented itself at the level of the signifier'. For Easthope, the 'intervention of post-structuralism in cultural studies' was exemplified in *Language and Materialism: Developments in Semiology and the Theory of the Subject* (1977), which its authors, Rosalind Coward and John Ellis, offered as performing the meeting of psychoanalysis with Marxism, and which proposed that 'the subject is an effect constituted in the process of the unconscious, of discourse and of the relatively autonomous practices of the social formation'.[56] Even if Bhabha's implementation of materialist methods could be considered as at least eccentric, it is, I think, apparent that the traces of a putative materialism in his work conform to the forms devised by British poststructuralism.

The subsequent elaboration of Bhabha's work is further accented by the British version of post-Marxism devised during the 1980s. In Bhabha's valorizations of decentring, dispersal and dissemination, although spoken in his own inimitable voice, echoes can be heard of *New Times* celebrating the effects of post-Fordist productive modes in 'flexibility, diversity, differentiation, mobility, communication, decentralization and internationalization'. (Curiously, the thinking of *Marxism Today* closely followed a base/superstructure model, unproblematically deriving perceived shifts in consciousness and ideology from changes in the mode of production.) These processes, as Neil Lazarus points out in 'Doubting the new world order', were hailed as rendering the old conceptual paradigms, political identities and political strategies obsolete, and heralding the arrival of 'culturalism' – a move tracked in a scathing essay by A. Sivanandan, where he attacked the dissociation of the economic and political from the cultural, and lambasted those intellectuals who located the political struggle in the discursive.[57]

An intellectual environment in which Marxism circulated as an important current, a trend which was subsequently, and perhaps temporarily, diverted by the denigrations of 'post-Marxism', provides Bhabha with targets who, without being named, are casually assembled as a 'left orthodoxy'. By attaching disqualifying clauses that render suspect the concepts of alternative explanatory categories, Bhabha represents his unspecified antagonists as Manichaean dualists, identitarian mystifiers, diverse pedlars of class, people, nation and gender as unified and uniform sets, and dialectical materialists bent on defusing energizing disjunctions through sublation. 'Monolithic category' is joined to 'community', 'essentialist identities' to 'communal', and 'homogenized' to 'national culture'; 'a simplistic sense of intentionality' characterizes notions of 'collective agency'; 'polarities' are 'primordial'; leftist forms of writing history are 'historicist', 'transcendent and teleological'; 'holistic form' deforms 'social explanation'.

Bhabha has produced some powerful work opening up the categories of culture and nation to reveal their inner differentiations and disjunctions, and his case surely does not require that he traduce those who insist on the political and experiential uses of constructing insurgent identities around notions of communalities, and of retaining class as a primary conceptual category.[58] Indeed, his polemic against 'the left' is marred by a levity only available to that generation who arrived at post-Marxism without ever having occupied the anterior position, and superseded 'anti-imperialism-in-itself'[59] without participating in the struggles which this stance animated:

> Political positions are not simply identifiable as progressive or reactionary, bourgeois or radical, prior to the act of *critique engagée*, or outside the terms and conditions of their discursive address. It is in this sense that the historical moment of political action must be thought of as part of the history of the form of its writing.[60]

Instead of 'identikit political idealism' demanding that critical discourse produce 'a pure ideology of analysis whereby the prior principle is simply augmented . . . its identity as socialist or materialist . . . consistently confirmed in each oppositional stage of the argument', Bhabha is concerned to stress the fully historical and discursive *différance* between them; instead of 'a primordial and previsionary division of right or left, progressive or reactionary', Bhabha argues for a 'language of critique . . . which . . . overcomes the given grounds of opposition and opens up a space of translation'[61] – thus returning us to his abhorrence of concepts of conflict and his under-theorized notions of a ubiquitous middle ground and coalition.

Bhabha's theories mark his distance from a black British legacy that is still manifest in the continuing significance of *Race and Class* as a forum for discussions in the Marxist mode. In his chapter on 'C.L.R. James and the Black Radical Tradition', Cedric Robinson[62] places James among a community of expatriate intellectuals from the British Empire who as internationalists participated in the communist and labour politics of the metropolis and who, as Tim Brennan notes, were subsequently written out of the history of the British left by the British New Left.[63] It was in Britain, too, that many of the programmes for the anti-colonial struggle were devised, as well as it being the place from which countless students from all corners of the then empire returned to their native lands as doctors, lawyers and teachers, and as Marxists of one or other denomination who participated in the liberation struggles of their communities. That *this* vibrant narrative of transnational intellectual exchange is now being forgotten in the annals of postcoloniality can only impoverish its revisionist chronicles.

There are numerous critics who have long urged as a moral imperative that theory engage in the struggle against the arrogance of capitalism's international power; and if instead of citing their compelling arguments, I choose Derrida's words on 'the foreign debt', it is because these articulate the calculated absence in the utterances of so many of his followers:

> With this name or with this emblematic figure, it is a matter of *interest* and first of all of the interest of capital in general, an interest that, in the order of the

world today, namely the worldwide market, holds a mass of humanity under its yoke and in a new form of slavery . . . Now, these problems of the foreign debt – and everything that is metonymized by this concept – will not be treated without at least the spirit of the Marxist critique, the critique of the market, of the multiple logics of capital.[64]

Derrida's disparagement of those who evangelize in the name of the ideal of liberal democracy is made on the firm grounds of specifying actually existing conditions, and may disturb the convictions of those who reprove the error of representing facts as transparent and outside the form of their writing: 'never have violence, inequality, exclusion, famine, and thus economic oppression affected as many human beings in the history of the Earth and of humanity'. His reluctance to celebrate '"the end of ideologies" and the end of the great emancipatory discourses' will make the postmodern scorn for metanarratives appear as yesterday's argot, and could even persuade some critics that it is fitting to associate their work with the still unfinished global emancipatory project. Above all, Derrida's appeal to the principle of hope animating political action in the interest of constructing a different future must surely reveal the poverty of theories which, by refusing a Marxist eschatology, turn and turn in the gyre of the present:

> Now, if there is a spirit of Marxism which I will never be ready to renounce, it is not only the critical idea or the questioning stance . . . It is rather a certain emancipatory and *messianic* affirmation, a certain experience of the promise that one can try to liberate from any dogmatics and even from any metaphysico-religious determination, from any *messianism*. And a promise must promise to be kept, that is, not to remain 'spiritual' or 'abstract', but to produce events, new effective forms of action, practice, organization.[65]

The Failure of Postmodernity
How Africa Misunderstood the West

DENIS EKPO

The anti-West, anti-imperialist tradition of Afrocentric discourse appears to have either collapsed or undergone a drastic de-radicalization. So sudden has been the eclipse or total exit from the Afrocentric horizon of the radical, fire-spitting anti-West intellectual/agitator, whether of the left or of the right, that many may not hesitate to look for an explanation in the most momentous event of the decade, namely, the end of Soviet-legitimated planetary communism and the emergence of a post-Cold War era. No doubt, many radical anti-imperialist Afrocentrics did indeed feel, soon after the disappearance of the communist demiurge, so orphaned and so disinherited that they either retired into oblivion or slowly and surreptitiously converted. But then not all radical critics of the West sourced their codes or their grants from the Kremlin. Indeed, the tradition of conservative anti-westernism represented by Afrocentrics like Cheik Anta Diop and Chinweizu, among others, has been probably more influential than Marxist-based motifs in shaping contemporary African perception of the West. The truth appears to be that even this conservative (i.e. non-Marxian) strand of African anti-imperialism has also recently lost its radicality if not its voice. It may therefore not be entirely implausible to ascribe the waning of African anti-West discourse to the fall of the Berlin Wall. However, while that event undoubtedly brought about an international paradigm shift that necessarily affected the fate of anti-imperialism in Africa and elsewhere, it would appear on closer examination that even if the Berlin Wall had not fallen, Afrocentric critique of the West would still have suffered its present fate, namely, it would still have remained a largely ineffectual posturing, a discourse bereft of performative force, a failed attempt to get a hearing from the West. Here, we are speculating that Afrocentric critique of the West seems to have never really hit its target: the mind of what can be called the 'essential West'.

I will reappraise, in the light of current knowledge especially on the structure of western imperial thinking, the grounds and claims of the whole project of Africa's radical critique of the West in order to suggest that its failure, i.e. its lack of performative force on its target, is not accidental or purely political, but stems mostly from our basic misunderstanding of the imperial mind, notably, the mute foundations of its historical rationality, the cultural/civilizational drives and impulses that impel its world-historical actions in the imperial and post-imperial eras. Today, new insights into the workings of Europe's modernist/historical rationality have become available thanks to the latest shift in western thinking and sensibility generally referred to as postmodernism. However, here, our understanding of postmodernism has been narrowed to mean a mode of thinking or a set of gestures that seeks drastically to deconstruct, or unmask, western reason/power practices most appropriately at a time when Europe, having virtually completed its world-historical mission and ensured for itself a permanent immunity against reprisals, can afford the coquetry or cynical luxury of drastic self-unmaskings and confessional openness. But aside from this penchant for self-demystificatory bluntness, one very significant feature of the postmodernist turn is the revival of interest in Nietzsche, seen, most interestingly, as the proto-postmodernist. Among modern European thinkers, Nietzsche stands out (along with Sade perhaps) as the one who set aside the seduction and comfort of the Enlightenment self-understanding of Europe in order to prosecute a more naturalistic theory of its modernist society, civilization and history. His critique of Europe's modernist project was therefore like an explosive that discharged amid the scaffoldings of Europe's world, leaving behind nothing but the nature-like instincts and impulses that drive it. The successors to Nietzsche such as Lyotard and Foucault have, in postmodernity, actualized this Nietzschean cultural deconstructionism mostly by putting it in the vocabulary of the age. I hope to combine both the insights of Nietzsche, the proto-postmodernist, with the vocabularies of Lyotard or Foucault, the practising postmodernists, to try to tackle the cultural/civilisational backdrop to Europe's imperviousness to the 'sins' imputed to it by Afrocentric anti-imperialists. The current revival of the civilizational/cultural angle to the 'West versus the Rest' debate provides an appropriate context for this cultural study into the constituting conditions of western world-historical thinking.

As we know, the immediate task before the African postcolonial thinker was to carry out a comprehensive critique of colonial culture and European imperialism. Two currents of African thought contended for the execution of this task: (1) Revolutionary/Marxist anti-imperialism inaugurated by Nkrumah and continued thereafter by a myriad of leftist intellectuals; (2) neo-conservative, Afrocentric anti-West radicalism pioneered by Cheik Anta Diop's *Nations nègres et culture*, but actualized and popularized by Chinweizu through such works as *The West and the Rest of Us, Towards a Decolonization of African Literature*, etc.[1] Though the first current at certain moments of Africa's postcolonial history exerted some degree of influence in shaping perceptions of and relationship with the West, it is actually the second, the neo-conservative Afrocentric strand, that seems to have put in place the paradigmatic idiom and codes of the Africa versus the West self-understanding of the cultural-cum-political thought of contemporary Africa. It is therefore on this current of African anti-imperialism that I shall focus our critical attention. However, whether of the left or of the right, the verdict of Africa's postcolonial reinterpretation of European colonialism/imperialism was unmitigatedly the same: namely, Europe is guilty of underdeveloping Africa and bears responsibility for Africa's past and present woes. The task before the Afrocentric thinker therefore was not only to work to show 'how Europe underdeveloped Africa'[2] but, more crucially, to convince Europe of her historical guilt against and responsibility towards Africa. Accordingly, contemporary Afrocentric counter-West discourse has come to be, in many respects, synonymous with perpetual accusation of the West, the search for historical guilt and moral responsibility, the denunciation of western duplicity, hypocrisy and cynical amoralism. The current clamour for reparations seems to be the logical culmination of the Afrocentric's relentless trials and convictions of the West.

One most notable example of this accusatory, conspiratorial apprehension of Europe's intervention in Africa is Chinweizu's book *The West and the Rest of Us*. Forcefully polemical and comprehensive in scope, the book is often cited as a summation of Africa's historical, moral and political grievances against Europe. The author considers it to be 'a critical investigation into the purposes and styles of western imperialist expansion during the past five hundred years, and, within the context of that expansion, into the man-made causes of Africa's backwardness'.[3] At the end of that investigation, his findings are overwhelming and his verdict unmitigated. For 500 years, the West has conspired systematically to dehumanize Africa, first by enslaving its people, then colonizing them and finally reducing them to the present half-life condition of perpetual underdevelopment, poverty and instability. Today, the West's world power systems – the monetary system, world trade, loans policy, foreign aid, etc. – are carefully designed traps aimed at keeping Africa perpetually at the West's feet. Based on this, Chinweizu declares a near total war against the West and launches a campaign of a second, postcolonial emancipation from it.

Judged strictly on its own Afrocentric terms, Chinweizu's case against Europe looks weighty. So many other but less aggressive Afrocentrics condemn Europe in no less unmitigated terms. There is, however, the trouble that the enemy, i.e. the essential West, might not even be aware of the Afrocentric's case against it, let alone take its verdict into account. To the best of my knowledge, Europe has yet to take any moral or policy stand commanded by the nature and magnitude of the crimes imputed to it (e.g. paying reparation, offering a public apology and perhaps undertaking to be better behaved in the future). For an insight into one possible explanation for Europe's indifference *vis-à-vis* the charges against it, let's listen to what Nietzsche, via the postmodernists, has to tell us about the ways of the essential West.

In seeking to divest Europe's modernity of its self-gratifying Enlightenment claims and postures, Nietzsche isolated a non-Enlightenment impulse, the will to power as a kind of 'biocultural' principle; the foundational, subjectless, overdetermining mover of men and the world. 'The world is will to power and nothing else beside.'[4] Today, the Nietzschean power theory has been reactualized by Foucault through his 'genealogical criticism', a mode of thinking which seeks to uncover the power practices, i.e. the practices of domination which men, societies or institutions try to conceal through different masks and 'technologies of power'. In Foucault's genealogical practices, Europe's higher ideals such as truth, morality or knowledge come off as mere modalities of power (i.e. technique of domination) either as masks or instruments. This is hardly surprising given that to him power is foundational and invincible: 'The only thing that lasts is power, which appears with ever new masks in the change of anonymous processes of overpowering.'[5] Above all, power is the meaning of the countless events that appear to drive history:

> An 'event' . . . is not a decision, a treaty, a reign or a battle, but the reversal of a relationship of forces, the usurpation of power, the appropriation of a vocabulary turned against those who had once used it, a feeble domination that poisons itself as it grows lax, the entry of a masked other.[6]

One outcome of this Nietzschean–Foucault power theory is the opening up of fresh insights into the workings of the mind of the essential West. By 'essential

West' I mean the West whose essence is indistinguishable from her idea of a distinct world-historical destiny, actualizing itself in endless but specific world-domination drives and activities. Given that the will to power can be considered as a major or even foundational self-representation of this essential Europe in modernity, the question is not whether it is true or false, adequate or inadequate. On the contrary, coming out as it is from right inside the western mind itself, the power theory should be taken at face value: that is the way the West, or at any rate, the essential West, views itself. On that score, the power metaphor might prove a particularly useful handle on the West, especially in its relationship with the Rest. So the question now is, how does this Europe's will to power operate in world-history? How has it impinged on Africa? In other words, given the Nietzschean power hypothesis, how can one explain certain forms of European historical actions like the slave trade, colonialism, neocolonialism etc., *vis-à-vis* those in Africa who suffered from them or continue to suffer from them?

The consensus among most Afrocentric intellectuals is that these acts – slavery, imperialism, etc. – were unjust acts of violence, a thievery without parallel, a deliberate negation of the human dignity of the African. Chinweizu calls them 'the assault by the West on the Rest of Us' and speaks of the 'holocaust of slavery, the trauma of invasion and conquest, the humiliation and complexes of occupation . . . a systematic and continuing impoverishment'.[7] For Marcien Towa, imperial domination is 'a crime of "bèse-humanité" and must be considered as absolute evil'.[8] Beneath these highly emotive terms is, of course, the unmistakable assumption that these acts were/are morally wrong, unjust and bad. In other words, by being imperialistic, Europe was/is deliberately and wickedly conspiring to negate our being and trample upon our dignity as Africans. This itself presupposes another assumption, namely that Europe had/has the choice not to engage in such acts. Not surprisingly, of all the criticisms levelled against Europe one of the most widely believed is that the West is a cynical pack of imperialist demons who know the good but still pursue the bad and the wrong.

Now, assuming that these acts were immoral and unjust, with regard to which order, which system of justice are they so? Who feels that these actions were trauma, a holocaust and a humiliation and why? The Afrocentric totalized moral judgement on European imperialism is valid but only in regard to a world moral order existing either as a cosmic principle or a human institution. As a human institution, a world moral order presupposes a consensus of nations concerning certain principles of behaviour and above all the unconditionally binding force of such principles on the whole of humanity. On the basis of such an order, it will then be meaningful in respect of certain acts committed by one people against another, one race against another etc., to talk of just and unjust, moral or immoral. However in the nineteenth century when Europe conquered Africa and up until the middle of the twentieth century when she colonized and exploited it, nothing resembling such an order existed. The UN, a postwar creation and the nearest approximation to such a concept, cannot in strict terms be said to embody a moral order for the reason that it operates mostly as one more power instrument of the big, mostly western, nations. Second, its decisions have very little or no binding force on anyone. Similarly, the existence of a world moral order as a cosmic force has never been proven. Indeed, according to Nietzsche, a world moral order in this latter sense was merely the invention of Christianity as part of a grand use of their slave revolt against the morality of the masters. But the real world in which men live, work, conquer others and make history is, according to Nietzsche, 'will to power and nothing else besides'. In other words, the world of history floats above and beyond the moral order narrative. Life in this world operates 'essentially, that is in its basic functions through injury, assault, exploitation, destruction and simply cannot be thought of at all without this character'.[9] To Nietzsche, calling any of these life functions just or unjust, moral or immoral in themselves will therefore be quite senseless given that 'it is part of the concept of the living that it must grow – that it must extend its power and consequently incorporate alien forces'.[10]

Product of the 'mute foundations' of western reason, the doctrine of the will to power reveals that in all her historical experiences, Europe has always acted necessarily, i.e. in accordance with the basic drives that give meaning to her world, and with which she achieves growth and strength and which defines the most favourable conditions for her preservation and continuous growth. Consequently, at specific periods of her history, the slave trade, colonialism, imperialism, neocolonialism, etc., became not accidental adventures, not chance games, not errors but fatalities of her will to power, i.e. her will to expansion, growth and influence. Europe's historical essence, her reason in history, is captured in her endless drive to increase her power by overcoming or seeking to overcome the rest of the world. Essential Europe is therefore nothing but the will to world-power. Above all, she is nothing but precisely her world-power activities. Therefore, considered from the point of view of the will to power, as a mute foundation of western reason in modern history, Europe's world-historical actions, notably colonialism, imperialism, etc. are merely actualizations of Europe's essence, i.e. self-definition, in history – these are acts without which Europe as we know it today would not be Europe. Consequently, these acts, strictly speaking (on Europe's terms) lie outside the reach of any moral discourse – they are beyond good and evil, above blame and praise.

But if this is so, from whence come the near-obsessive ideas of guilt and responsibility, injustice and immorality that have become indissociable from the Afrocentric interpretation of the West's past and present encounters with Africa? Why didn't we look at colonialism strictly as an encounter with a stronger power (i.e. a different will to power) whom we had to fight because it wanted to assimilate us for its growth?

Paradoxically, the impetus and justification for a moralized reaction to Europe's intervention in Africa came originally not from Africa but from Europe itself. European Christianity taught (perhaps unwittingly) the mission-school educated Afrocentrics to interpret history in terms of a God-ordained world moral order that rigorously discriminates between good and evil, the guilty and the innocent, victims and executioners, etc. These reconditioned native minds were to turn this Christian/European moral-religious framework against colonialism (i.e. against Europe itself) by viewing colonial conquest as a grave violation of the divine order of the world; in other words, as a horrid crime against God and man.

Christian Europe therefore furnished the ground, the prototype and the vocabulary of the deeply ingrained moral idealism of the Afrocentric's inter-pretation of European imperialism. In other words, such ideas as guilt, responsibility, crime, victim, etc., which until today constitute the overt or hid-den infrastructure of the anti-West discourse of many Afrocentrics, derived originally not from the native's reaction to Europe's intervention in Africa, but from the Christian, moral breeding of the Afrocentrics. Evidence abounds that original native reaction to colonial conquest was virtually devoid of any European moral-religious idiosyncrasies.[11]

However, whatever the origin of Africa's moralization on European world-power deeds, Nietzsche's power theory, it appears, had already underlined its efficacy in the historical arena. His fable of the lamb and the eagle graphically illustrates this. According to this fable, the eagle that devours a lamb acts in accordance with its essence as a bird of prey and not from a malicious will or intent to destroy the lamb: 'Realizing that the wolf is going to devour it, the lamb cannot be aware that this negation of its person has an affirmative nature. The lamb perceives only the negative consequences for itself.'[12] As Nietzsche points out, this reaction from the lamb is perfectly normal and understandable except for the inference from it, i.e. demanding that the eagle should behave like the lamb:

> That lambs dislike great birds of prey does not seem strange: only it gives no ground for reproaching these birds of prey for bearing off little lambs. And if the lambs say among themselves 'these birds of prey are evil, and whoever is least like a bird of prey, but rather its opposite, a lamb, would he not be good?' There is no reason to find fault with this institution of an ideal except perhaps that the birds of prey might view it a little ironically and say 'we don't dislike them all, these good little lambs, we even love them: nothing is more tasty than a tender little lamb'.[13]

As we can see from the above passage, there is nothing wrong with the lamb wanting the eagle to behave like itself (the lamb), for it is in the power logic of lambness to conserve itself and seek more power, just as it is in that of eagleness. The only problem with this position is that with regard to the power rationality of the eagle, it might be depressingly inefficacious.

When we translate this fable into the logic of Afrocentric critique of the West, we discover that it is by getting stuck to the logic of the lamb and refusing or being unable to examine the logic of the eagle that our Afrocentrics find unmitigated ground for conspiracy, guilt, responsibility or reparation theories. From such a position, the West comes out without attenuating circumstances and eternally as an evil pack of predators bent on devouring the gentle and innocent lambs of Africa.

However, from the Nietzschean power theory perspective, one can say that this kind of thinking is as it should be except for one thing, namely, any theories that seek to reproach Europe for being just that (i.e. a predator) or that pass sentences of guilt and responsibility on it must first have to demonstrate that Europe had the choice not to engage in these predatory deeds. Conversely, such a theory must also show that Africa's pacifist, moralistic posture is also a matter of choice.

It would seem that such demonstrations are possible, according to Nietzsche, only if one is a victim of the tricks of language or of morality, especially the Christian story of free will. For under the spell of grammar or the illusion of popular morality, one can reproach the West for its immoral eagle's deeds and praise ourselves for having acted so morally, i.e. for being lambs. However, such thinking has very little efficacy, since:

> To demand of strength that it should not express itself as strength, that it should not be a desire to overcome; a desire to throw down, a desire to become master, a thirst for enemies and resistance and triumphs is just as absurd as to demand of weakness that it should express itself as strength.[14]

In other words, it is to demand that Europe, which was possessed of a superior technological, material and psychological strength, should not have acted as strong and superior at a particular point in time. That is, in the nineteenth century, it had the choice not to colonize us, as in the present day it could have refrained from neocolonizing us. But to think so is, according to Nietzsche's power theory, to be held captive by language or morality. Language separates action into subject and act, agent and activity, and morality separates strength from expressions of strength, 'as if there were a neutral substratum behind the strong man, which was free to express strength or not to do so.'[15] But to him, 'there is no such substratum; there is no being behind doing, effecting, becoming; the doer is merely a fiction added to the deed – the deed is everything'. In other words, essence, existence and activity are indissolubly the same. According to Nietzsche, it is this linguistic confusion and perhaps also the Christian story of free will that

> vengefulness and hatred exploit for their own ends by believing that the strong man is free to be weak and the bird of prey to be a lamb. For this they gain the right to make the bird of prey accountable for being a bird of prey.[16]

Thus, as the theory goes, Europe had no choice not to be imperialistic at a particular time – in fact at all times – just as we had no choice not to fight colonialism at a particular period. To be imperialistic or anti-imperialistic are fatalities of historical becoming: 'Aggressive and defensive egoisms are not matters of choice, to say nothing of free-will, but the fatality of life itself.'[17] That

Europe now practises peace and the brotherhood of planetary democracy does not indicate that she has renounced imperialism or that she has abandoned her world-power mission and will. She has merely set about the same mission, in a new setting, with different, perhaps more subtle weapons. In a post-imperial world, Europe's will to world-power has to form itself out of new materials, seek new detours, new cunnings. It is as if, having concluded its world-conquering mission, Europe now finds itself in the position of an unemployed or retired conqueror who now craves peace and quiet probably so that he can enjoy the fruits of his conquests. But peace and quiet can only prevail if the rest of the world adopts the ways of the West. A democratized planet means a planet tailored to the West's will to world leadership and subtle domination.

Conversely, Africa's pacifist, moralistic posture is no proof of our being morally better or of our lack of will to power, but is, according to this theory, merely dictated by our weakness, i.e. by our impotent will to power. That we did not set out to conquer Europe in revenge is not a matter of choice or of our higher moral standpoint. We had no choice in the matter. Our weakness, our material inferiority, dictates our 'moral', forgiving posture.[18]

What this power theory of European imperialism and neocolonialism seems to do is remove the ground beneath the feet of Afrocentric activist moralism – guilt-hunting, searching for reparations, etc. – by showing that Africa's 'lamb morality' and Europe's 'predatory eagleness' are essentially the same, namely, actualizations of wills to power. The difference between the lamb's will to power and the eagle's is a difference only of degree (of power), not of essence or substance. In other words, because Africa lacks strength, the will to power of the Afrocentric is turned inward and drawn into becoming reactive. On a Nietzschean account, all the Afrocentric diatribe of a Cheik Anta Diop, or the impassioned anti-West declamations of a Chinweizu would be no more than the expression of this impotent, reactive will to power.

Now, whether we approve or not of this power theory of European history does not appear to matter, for it is apparently pre-programmed in a seemingly bio-cultural or civilizational way, not to seek approval, i.e. to ignore non-approval. However, in spite of its apparently over-weening cynicism, this theory seems to have this advantage over most other interpretations. It can provide an answer to the question, why has Europe, despite the endless flow of accusations, denunciation and lamentations from Africa, never at any moment regretted or deplored its past and present deeds in Africa? Why has it not, in reaction to our ceaseless litany of woes and jeremiads, felt a mighty sting of conscience, an irrepressible feeling of guilt, a thousand-fold shudder and shock such that it will not rest until it has tendered a world-historical apology to Africa and to humanity? From the perspective of a Nietzschean power theory, the reason seems to be very simple indeed: there is absolutely nothing to regret, nothing to apologize for. According to Nietzsche, there is simply no room for such depressive feelings like regret or repentance in the psyche of the real operators of European world-historical actions. How do these regard their past deeds? Nietzsche gave us a clue through his study of the ways of the Greek aristocratic conquerors to whom the modern-day technocrats of Europe's world-power are civilizational heirs. At best, says Nietzsche, they might express some wonder if the event in retrospect appears strange: 'Here something has unexpectedly gone wrong.' But they will not say, 'I ought not to have done that.'[19] In other words, they look back to their past adventures and world-conquering mission with that stout-hearted fatalism and free conscience with which, according to Nietzsche, strong peoples and proud nations have always digested and assimilated their past. This would suggest that only weaklings are left to mourn dejectedly and eternally over their own or other people's alleged 'mis-deeds'.

Consequently, based on this Nietzschean gloss, one can say that it is not to the real operators of western world-historical action that our Afrocentrics should go with their 'grand narratives' of guilt, responsibility and reparation, for, like the state-forming, artist-conquerors of old, of whom they are heirs:

> They do not know what guilt, responsibility or consideration are, these born organizers; they exemplify that terrible artist's egoism that has the look of bronze and knows itself justified to all eternity in its works, like a mother in her child.[20]

Here, Nietzsche's unmasking bluntness becomes significant, appearing to shed more light on what today is often staged as Europe's self-criticisms, i.e. the denunciations, by some Europeans, of certain past or present activities of Europe in Africa. Do these amount to a recognition of guilt or are they merely sublimations of Europe's internal problems? We notice first of all that no such criticisms or self-criticisms ever emanate from the real operators, the hardly visible technocratic élite (those charged to plot and execute Europe's world-power destiny). But suppose any such self-critical gesture emanates from the political class, it certainly does not amount to a recognition of guilt or responsibility; it is most likely a political rhetoric motivated simply by world-power systemic imperatives: the need to pacify complainers so as to ensure a conducive environment for the optimal functioning of Europe's world-power systems. It is the same pacification imperative that seems to govern the politics of development aids and grants. Similarly, if one day Europe decides to accede to the Afrocentric demands for reparation, it will most likely do so in response to the selfsame world-power systemic imperatives. It will be one more example of the thousand-fold craftiness of Europe's post-imperial power practices. To be sure, there is no shortage of western Africanists, intellectuals or activists who indulge in severe critique of Europe's imperialism in Africa, or who even participate in certain forms of anti-West struggles on the Continent. However, many of such blasé intellectuals are bereft of any real power and as such their gestures may not amount to much. But granted that these gestures are well meaning, it would seem to us that any 'penitential Africanism' coming from a European intellectual should be seen not really as a penance for European imperialism, but most probably as a sublimated response to the internal politics of the present post-material, postmodern disgust in Europe. In any case, given the imperialistic over-determination of the essentials of modern European history and of the modern European identity, any postcolonial tears shed by a European, even with the best will in the world, could really only amount to crocodile tears.

But whether as crocodile tears or as hypocritical masks, Europe's present post-imperial gestures may not survive the unmasking torch of a Nietzschean deconstruction. For behind these little masks of goodness and post-imperial decency lurks the same implacable will to power sublimated into the will to dominate through cunning and subterfuge, etc.

Now, what Nietzsche said in such ornate terms, and with so much pathos, about the ways of the essential West has been put in an infinitely more blunt and terse language appropriate to the tempo of our age. Postmodernism is the name for this highly desublimated Nietzschean. Thus, when Lyotard announces that postmodernism means the abolition of master-narratives,[21] what he most likely means to say is that all the self-deceptive masks behind which Europe hid to execute her will to world-power have been deliberately thrown off and that people can now have a de-bewitched peep at the inner workings of Europe's power constructions. A visit to Lyotard's 'deconstruction sites' of western power in postmodernity will most certainly enable us to further shed light on how Africa, and a few other Third World peoples, continue to misunderstand the West.

Based on Lyotard's account of postmodernism, Africa's misunderstanding of Europe can be explained in terms of a 'mixing of tongues'. For the African radical critic of Europe, a mixing of tongues takes the following form. The African radical thinker criticizes the West; denounces its imperialist stranglehold on Africa, its violent and unjust exploitation of its peoples and resources. But to articulate these denunciations, he has recourse to concepts, notions and ideals drawn from Europe's humanistic discourse of legitimation. Such ideas include emancipation, truth, good and bad, right and wrong, etc. Conditioned by his mission-school training to take very seriously the idea of a moral world order, he unsuspectingly casts his critique of Europe in the metaphors of Europe's humanistic, moral idealism. But unknown to the Afrocentric critic, western rationality had undergone a major self-mutation; Europe had undertaken a paradigm shift in her discourse of legitimation. She had abandoned the per-spective of mind, the tradition of thought from which humanistic idealism meant anything other than a museum of grand fanciful stories, i.e. in Lyotard's idiom, 'master-narratives'. It had returned to a Nietzschean 'innocence of becoming', having like Nietzsche himself 'banished and extinguished the con-cepts of guilt and punishment from the world'.[22] More specifically, among the elements of this radical shift in Europe's self-understanding in the postmodern era, Schürmann has listed the following: (1) abolishing the primacy of teleology in action; (2) abolishing the primacy of responsibility in the legitimation of action; (3) disinterest in the future of mankind.[23]

Indeed, instrumentalist, western rationality, since the nineteenth century, had ceased to legitimate and self-legitimate by recourse to humanistic master-narratives like Truth, Justice, etc. Rather, it had become the discourse of modern power, i.e. according to Lyotard, the discourse of legitimation by success, efficiency and performativity. Hegel was diagnosing this paradigm shift in the nineteenth century when he declared 'what is effective is rational' and 'the conquerors are right for they embody the progress of humanity'. Nietzsche admitted with glee this casting away of humanistic moral idealism out of his epoch: 'If anything can reconcile us to our age, it is the great amount of immorality it can permit itself without thinking any the worse of itself.'[24] Meanwhile, only from the perspective of legitimation by master-narrative could Europe's actions – colonialism, capitalist explanation, and so on – be seen to be wrong, unjust or evil. But if, since the nineteenth century, in the imperialist era, legitimation by grand narratives had lost its force, or had simply disappeared, then a critique of colonialism in the past or neocolonialism in the present carried out in the perspective of grand narratives (truth, wrong and right) not only ceases to be pertinent but misses its mark. This much, Lyotard's postmodern de-legitimations seem to have made abundantly clear. Furthermore, his diagnosis has revealed that advanced western industrial societies are ruled by the imperative of a systems rationality whereby legitimation and pertinence are achieved solely by the criteria of success, performativity and efficiency of systems. My contention is that this state of affairs – the systemic logic of legitimation by efficiency, power and success – was already in operation, had already been reached in the days of imperialism. The imperial capitalist economic system which to many was the prime mover was already operating according to a systemic rationality. According to Lyotard, in a context of technocratic rationality, power (measured in terms of performativity, efficiency and success), by increasing one's capacity to administer proofs, increases the capacity for being right.[25] This is a direct replication of the colonial conquerors' maxim: Whatever happens, we've got the maxim-gun and they have not.

Consequently, the question of Europe's actions in Africa has never been an ethical one: the question was not whether it was right or wrong, just or unjust, to colonize or exploit; it has been a technocratic power problem. Can it be done, how and to what power effects? To reproach the West with immorality or injustice therefore, on this account, amounts to mixing mutually exclusive tongues: grand narratives and the technocratic discourse of power and systems.

The Marco Polo Syndrome

GERARDO MOSQUERA

The second Habana Biennial, in 1986, included an installation by the Cuban artist Flavio Garciandía entitled *El síndrome de Marco Polo*. Various ambiguous images depicted the adventures of a popular character from the comics – a captain in the wars of independence in the nineteenth century and a symbol of Cubanness – during and after a trip to China. The work, drawing on forms of orientalist kitsch, humorously questioned the problems of intercultural communication. The character, like Marco Polo, was a pioneer in the experience of understanding the Other, but his chances of bridging two cultures were lost through the suspicion provoked from both sides, especially from his.

We had to wait until the end of the millennium to discover that we were suffering from the Marco Polo Syndrome. What is monstrous about this syndrome is that it perceives whatever is different as the carrier of life-threatening viruses rather than nutritional elements. And although it does not scare us as much as another prevalent syndrome, it has brought a lot of death to culture. Only now has an understanding of cultural pluralism and the usefulness of dialogue begun to spread to such an extent that the intercultural problematic has become a major issue.

The possibility of a more diversified consciousness has been opened up, while the question of ethnicity and nationality fills the new maps with many colours. Dominant Eurocentrism – the main symptom of the disease – is undergoing a critical treatment increasingly more effective in its power of persuasion. All these mutations have targeted art, presenting it with urgent and very complicated problems. Only some of them will be touched upon here.

The notion of Eurocentrism is very recent. In anthropology we find an acknowledgement of ethnocentrism in the eighteenth century,[1] and a consolidation of the idea of cultural relativism by Boas before the end of the nineteenth century. But, until recently, this idea had not significantly infiltrated the studies and interpretations of art and literature, centred as they were in the criteria of values linked to the myth of the 'universal'. The discourses called postmodern, with their interest in alterity, have gradually introduced a more relativist attitude to the scene. A new consciousness of ethnicity is taking shape as a result of several contemporary processes, among them decolonization, the greater space gained by the Third World in the international arena, the influence of ethnic groups from the margins in the great northern cities, the increase of information and improved facilities in travel and communication. Postmodernism itself, as Geeta Kapur suggests, could be regarded as a consequence and not as a description of a 'realigned universe' through the praxis of societies previously completely marginalized.[2]

Eurocentrism is different from ethnocentrism. It refers not only to the ethnocentrism exercised by a specific culture but also to the often forgotten fact that the worldwide hegemony of that culture has imposed its ethnocentrism as a universal value, and has persuaded us of it for a long time.[3]

Here, we leave the rather aseptic field of cultural relativism to come up against social problems and issues of power. The fact is that, from the Industrial Revolution, the global expansion of capitalism began to involve the whole world in an economic process which had Europe as its centre, and which, from then on, determined the course of the planet. Western metaculture established itself through colonization, domination and even the need to articulate it in order to confront the new situation within itself. Even so, Amílcar Cabral went as far as to say that imperialist domination 'was not only a negative reality', and that 'it gave new worlds to the world'.[4] Modernity, full of good intentions, contributed not a little to this planetary cultural revolution, although Adorno, Horkheimer and Huyssen have connected its negative aspect with imperialism.[5]

Ethnocentrism always suggests the naive vanity of a villager who, as José Martí said, assumes that 'the whole world is his village', believing everything originated there even if it were imposed on him through conquest. Eurocentrism is the only ethnocentrism universalized through actual worldwide domination by a metaculture, and based on a traumatic transformation of the world through economic, social and political processes centred in one small part of it. As a result, many elements of this metaculture cease to be 'ethnic' and become internationalized as intrinsic components of a world shaped by western development. But if these components are irrefutable, so should be the need to end the lack of focus, limitation, boredom and injustice of planning the world like a one-way street.

The very fact of the rise of the idea of Eurocentrism demonstrates an awareness of the monocultural trap in which we have all found ourselves prisoners. I say 'all', because Eurocentrism affects not only non-western cultures but the West itself, given the widespread impoverishment of perspective inherent to any monism. The tragedy is that the notion of Eurocentrism is also *made in the West*, even though, as Desiderio Navarro has pointed out, it is starting to take shape, especially in Eastern Europe,[6] at those peripheries exposed to closer contact with non-western countries.[7] Colonialism brought about a split whereby non-western countries took on board the problems of their own cultures in the sphere of traditions isolated from the contemporary scene, at the same time as they adopted those of the West, without making a connection capable of transforming both of them to the benefit of their own interests and values in the existing global situation.[8] This has started to change. Roughly, three moments can be summarized. First, the cultures that we currently call traditional were 'arrested' by western expansion, which carried forward, according to its point of view, the great centrifugal development of art and science from the eighteenth century, generalizing it as 'universal'. Second, the realization by one faction of thought in the western world of the absurdity of this situation. 'Not a single Ibn in the index to *Literary Theory*!' René Etiemble eloquently exclaimed, thereby disqualifying the classical work of Wellek and Warren.[9] Third, anti-Eurocentrism from non-western positions has begun to be systematized.

This does not mean a return to a past prior to western globalization, but the construction of a contemporary culture – one capable of acting in today's reality – from a plurality of perspectives. This development is a matter of some urgency, since we are running the risk that the West, apart from anything else, may also give the Third World a philosophy of intercultural exchange and a critique of Eurocentrism. Such an autocritique, despite its good intentions and its indisputable value, would perpetuate the distortion produced by its single perspective and existing circuits of power.

Postmodern interest in the Other has opened some space in the 'high art' circuits for vernacular and non-western cultures. But it has introduced a new thirst for exoticism, the carrier of either a passive or a second-class Eurocentrism which, instead of universalizing its paradigms, conditions certain cultural productions from the periphery according to paradigms that are expected of it for consumption by the centres. Many artists, critics and Latin American curators seem to be quite willing to become 'othered' for the West.

The problematic of Eurocentrism and the relations among different cultures is particularly complex in the contemporary visual arts, where the Marco Polo Syndrome embodies a double-edged sword. Art, in today's conception of a self-sufficient activity based on aesthetics, is also a product of western culture exported to others. Its full definition is also very recent, no older than the end of the eighteenth century. The aesthetic tradition of other cultures, like that of the West in other periods, was a different kind of production, determined by religious, representational and commemorative functions, and so on. Today's art in these cultures is not the result of an evolution of traditional aesthetics: its very concept was received from the West through colonialism.

This generates contradictions and brings the evils of dependency on and mimicry of the centres. But it forms part of the postcolonial challenge, because our cultures should not lock themselves in isolating traditions if they want to take part in today's dynamic and offer solutions to their own problems. Instead, what should be done is to make traditions work within the new epoch. The problem is not preserving them but vigorously adapting them. The question is how we may also *make* contemporary art from our own values, sensitivities and interests. The de-Eurocentralization in art is not about returning to purity, but about adopting postcolonial 'impurity' through which we might free ourselves and express our own thought.

A paradigmatic case of these complexities can be seen in the Cuban artist José Bedia. White and blue-eyed, this artist of popular origin practises the *palo monte*, an Afro-Cuban religious and cultural complex of Kongo origin. A graduate and ex-professor of the Instituto Superior de Arte de La Habana, Bedia is a sophisticated, well-informed western artist with a wide range of resources at his command. But his conceptually oriented work, in its content rather than in its language, is mostly based on the cosmology of the Kongo still alive in Cuba, a result of his interest in a contemporary reflection on the problems of the human being derived from the Kongo's interpretation of the world. His work intelligently takes advantage of openings, resources and sensitivities from current art of the centres, to confront us with a different vision. This syncretism also occurs in his technique, effortlessly integrating technological, natural and cultural elements, drawing and photography, ritual and mass-cultural objects, all within the sobriety of an analytic discourse. He also appropriates 'primitive' techniques, but not in order to reproduce their programmes: he creates elements with them that articulate his personal discourse and iconography. Bedia is making western culture from non-western sources, and therefore transforming it towards a de-Europeanization of contemporary culture. But, simultaneously, we could say that he is making postmodern Kongo culture. Besides which, he opens himself up to so-called 'primitive' cultures in what he has called a voluntary transculturalization in reverse: from his 'high art' education to a 'primitive' one.[10] Although this is an intellectual process, it is also interiorized in the artist, given the mestizo character of his own cultural background.

The Marco Polo Syndrome is a complex disease that often disguises its symptoms. The struggle against Eurocentrism should not burden art with a myth of authenticity which, paradoxically, may add to the discrimination that Third World visual art suffers on the international circuits. This myth precludes its appreciation as a living response to contradictions and postcolonial hybridities, and demands instead an 'originality' defined according to tradition and old cultures corresponding to a situation long since passed. More plausible is to analyse how current art in a given country or region satisfies the aesthetic, cultural, social and communicative demands of the community from and for which it is made. Its response is mostly mixed, relational, appropriative – anyway, 'inauthentic', and therefore more adequate to face today's reality.

One of the great Eurocentric prejudices in the critique and history of art is its complete undervaluing of this production as 'derivative' of the West. Third World artists are constantly asked to display their identity, to be *fantastic*, to look like no one else or to look like Frida . . . The relatively high prices achieved by Latin American art at the great auctions have been assigned to painters who satisfy the expectations of a more or less stereotyped Latin-Americanicity, able to fulfil the new demand for exoticism at the centres. As a consequence, Rivera is valued well above Orozco, Remedios Varo more than Torres García, and Botero considerably more than Reverón.[11] In other cases, all contemporary practice is discredited as spurious. Witness the opinion of an eminent Africanist: 'Authentic African art is that produced by a traditional artist for traditional purposes and according to traditional forms.'[12]

In this view, Africa is tradition not the present. An anti-Eurocentrism like this freezes all African cultures, relegating them to a museum, without understanding that they are living organisms which need to respond actively to the reality of their time. If we have to fight relentlessly against colonialism, which castrates much contemporary art from the Third World, we should not do it through nostalgia for the mask and the pyramid.

Extreme relativism constitutes another danger. It is said that a village may be ignorant of what happens in the neighbouring village, but knows what happens in New York. Anyone who has ever travelled through Africa knows that it is often easier to go from one country to the next via Europe. One of the worst problems of the southern hemisphere is its lack of internal integration and horizontal communication, in contrast with its vertical – and subaltern – connection with the North. The cultures of the South, so diverse, confront common problems derived from the postcolonial situation, and this has determined structural similarities in the mosaic. 'Speaking about the Third World and wrapping up in the same package Colombia, India and Turkey'[13] is as rhetorical as ignoring what unites, or might unite them, in their confrontation with hegemonic power, even if it is just poverty.[14] These cultures urgently need to know and think of each other, to exchange experiences, to embark on common projects. A radical conception of relativism should not exacerbate their isolation, separating them from our efforts to approach the Other and learn from him or her (even about things we don't like, as Venturi would say). If postmodernity places otherness in the foreground, it does so through a process of infinite differentiation which eliminates even the necessity of choice.[15] The strategy of the dominated moves towards integration through what unites them, and activates their difference 'in the face of international postmodern dominance'.[16] The South-South 'Robinsonism' benefits only the centres by entrenching North-South verticalism. If the translation of one culture into another in all its nuances is impossible, this should not preclude their capacity for mutual closeness, enrichment and solidarity. Jorge Luis Borges said that Quixote is still winning battles against his translators.[17]

The myth of universal value in art, and the establishment of a hierarchy of works based in their 'universality', is one of the heritages of Eurocentrism that continues to survive, despite our becoming less naive with respect to the 'universal', which has so frequently been a disguise for the 'western'. But this should not disable our reception of artwork beyond the culture which made it; even if that response is 'incorrect'[18] it may still generate new meanings. Art is very linked to cultural specificity, but possesses a polysemic ambiguity, open to very diverse readings. We live in 'a great time of hybrids', as a Mexican rock star sang,[19] which offers an unconventional challenge by reinterpreting instead of rejecting dependency on the great circuits. In contemporary experience, contextualization, recycling, appropriation and re-semanticization gain more and more power as a consequence of increased interaction among cultures.

The critique of Eurocentrism forms part of a new awareness towards the ethnic, the consolidation of which would sense, for the first time, the possibility of a global dialogue among cultures, capable of facilitating a cure for the syndrome. However, in the visual arts, little progress has been made in this direction. Contemporary, non-traditional production from the South finds few outlets. Excluded from the great centres and supposedly international circuits,

its presence in exhibitions like ' "Primitivism" in Twentieth-Century Art' or 'Magiciens de la terre' is insignificant, despite the fact that it could have contributed a lot more, especially by deepening and problematizing their perspectives.[20] The 'contemporary artistic scene' is a very centralized system of *apartheid*.[21] More than being Eurocentric, it is Manhattan-centric. But, I insist, the barrier is not just South-North due to centre-periphery relations of power, but South-South, as a consequence of a postcolonial deformation.

Despite its deformed structure, the dictates from the centre and the imposition of their arrogant judgements of art, the diversification of artistic circuits clashes with the difficulties of intercultural evaluation already pointed out. Critics, curators and historians have a great responsibility in this sense. To paraphrase Harold Rosenberg, we should realize that the way towards an intercultural evaluation of the work of art is not just a question of seeing, but also of listening. Careful account should be taken of how an artwork functions in its context, what values are recognized there, what sensibility it satisfies, what perspectives it opens, what it contributes . . . Only after such thorough understanding would we recognize the messages of interest that art can communicate to the viewers addressed by the exhibitions, and how it can contribute towards a general enrichment. Given that it has been demonstrated that the role of the viewer is fundamental in art and literature, this does not mean that one only sees from one's self and one's own circumstance, but also that reception is active and therefore capable of expanding.

The fundamental problem for exhibitions and texts with an intercultural meaning is communication. On the one hand to inform and contextualize; and on the other to orientate towards what interests new receivers. As mediators they must accept compromise, but need to make an effort to avoid centrisms and clichéd expectations. It is easy to say it, but in practice we are far from possessing exemplary solutions.

Apart from polyfocal, multi-ethnic decentralization, one last problem is that the dismantling of Eurocentrism demands an equally pluralistic revision of western culture. When Robert Farris Thompson assigned Fu-Kiau Bunseki, a traditional Kongo expert, to comment on the 'Africanist' painting of Picasso,[22] he was not simply making a gesture of deconstructing in reverse the appropriation of African sculpture by modernism, and making eloquent the ingenuity of his concerns with universality. He was also opening up a pluralistic methodological perspective. Not only in the sense of an erudite explanation of traditional Africa through others inspired by it. Bunseki's analyses deepen our appreciation of those works, and even of a western point of view. Cubism revolutionized the visual culture of the West by appropriating formal resources from Africa. But these forms were not free-floating; they were designed to support specific meanings which, on a more general level, can also function within the coded system of Picasso's paintings. Those forms belong to a cosmic vision whose perceptual foundations continue to be present in the new vision by which the Cubists transformed western painting, even without their acknowledging the functions and meanings of their African models.

Intercultural involvement consists not only of accepting the Other in an attempt to understand him or her and to enrich myself with his or her diversity. It also implies that the Other does the same with me, problematizing my self-awareness. The cure for the Marco Polo Syndrome entails overcoming centrisms with enlightenment from a myriad of different sources.

Globalization

Introduction

JULIAN STALLABRASS

The very term 'globalization' has been the subject of intense debate. Does it describe anything coherent enough to warrant a single description, or is the portmanteau of changes that are grouped under the word misleading? Or, if some of its elements are agreed upon, does 'globalization' describe anything novel? Is the nation-state truly in decline or is this simply a misdescription of a much older force in a new guise – the dominance of some nations over others? Has global trade a truly unprecedented role within the world economy, or was the Belle Epoque in this sense more globalized than the twenty-first century?

Rustom Bharucha, in his essay on the Asian museum, reminds us what an uneven process globalization can be. There are dangers, to be sure, in the establishing of 'new' Asian museums, in how they present their exhibits, what audiences they set out to foster and how their agendas are guided by those who fund them. There are also perils in what they hide, including a history of looting, and of cultural identities moulded, at least in part, by colonial and local overlords. These dangers centre upon identity: for whom and to whom do such museums speak, who do they represent, and how? New Asian museums may also be expected to fit into the gigantic spectacle that is capitalist culture, just as most contemporary art, in its museums and biennales, does with such ease. Yet in India, museums can also be found that have been completely untouched by such modernizing forces: their roofs leak, their labels remain in Latin and their audiences are unmolested by marketing but also uncared for. The two are poles apart, and it is unclear which is to be preferred.

Given such fundamental contestation over descriptions of globalization (and these may in part be determined by the place from which one sees it), it is unsurprising that two essays in this section dwell upon the difficulties of naming and representation.

For Zygmunt Bauman, introducing a debate on the notion of 'obscene powers' (carried in *Third Text*, No. 51, Summer 2000), the relevance of such a discussion cannot simply be explained by the perception that violence, the illegitimate exercise of coercion, is on the increase, but is rather to do with the increasing difficulty of saying for sure whether some act of coercion is legitimate or not. This is partly a result of the fast-changing roles of nation-states and supra-national powers. As Bauman points out, it was not long ago that Milošević and the NATO bombers of Yugoslavia could have appeared in the opposite guises of, respectively, villain and hero that they recently took on. Of course, there were many people for whom they did. That Milošević ends up before a war crimes tribunal, while Bush (Senior) and Clinton do not, is hardly a clear-cut matter, though naturally it would be foolish to believe that such processes are set in train by justice alone.

John Byrne, in discussing the activities and closing down of a TV station transmitting to Kurdish people, and thus putting out a message addressed to a state that does not yet exist, questions issues of representation on a most basic level. He uses Adorno's remarks about the naming of a crime, 'genocide', to highlight both the utility and the brutality of such naming. Do we now have, as Adorno predicted, debates about whether particular crimes qualify for the category, and are those debates influenced by national interest? Rwanda, in which the term was at first shied away from so that intervention could be avoided, gives the reply. Byrne recommends only that we be aware of the limits of our position, and guard against any hasty imposition of our categories of understanding over that which we cannot know. In elaborating this position, he uses a particular, postmodern reading of both Walter Benjamin and Slavoj Žižek that sidesteps the Marxist politics of both authors. While it is unclear for Byrne what form resistance to globalization should take, or even whether it should, others in this section take a more robust stance.

George Ritzer, while acknowledging the power and usefulness of the postmodern critique, supports a fully modernist social theory, one capable of stripping away the fantastic illusions of capitalist mass culture to reveal its administered and utilitarian workings. In contrast to Baudrillard's idea of obscenity (as discussed in Bauman's essay), a condition of too much visibility in which nothing is concealed, indeed a pulsing, buzzing flux of impressions that owes something to Bergson (though it is produced not by innocence but by overexposure to consumer society), for Ritzer the highly visible obscures much that must remain hidden. Casinos, theme parks and malls conceal their instrumental character behind diverting displays, and humanize themselves with cuddly, animated emblems. Of this analysis, we may ask: for whom do these effects remain hidden? Disney fantasy looks very different from inside a giant Mickey Mouse head. For those on the wrong end of the economic processes of globalization, the system may appear all instrumental ruthlessness, while its spectacle is both present and as remote as the gods.

For Žižek, too, examining the bombing of Yugoslavia, the global political order clearly hides its character, this time behind the oppositions it establishes. Milošević was a fascist leader who enjoyed much popular support among Serbians, standing against a neo-liberal power structure that was intent on making the world safe for the Multilateral Agreement on Investment. To support one over the other is to play along with the concealment of their secret complicity: that Milošević, like Saddam Hussein, Manuel Noriega, the Taliban (one could go on), was a creature of the global powers before he became their enemy, and that he exploited the fundamentalist religious and regional reactions formed by globalization itself. The solution, says Žižek, can only be trans-national opposition to the system as a whole.

Such opposition, previously building slowly, has come to global prominence,

first in Seattle in 1999, and since in every place where the political and economic administrators of the global order have met. While Žižek's message was
broadcast by radio, and Byrne dealt with television, it is the Internet that has
been an important tool for this new oppositional politics, allowing the rapid
dissemination of information and remote organization. There is something that
unites those who run the global neo-liberal economy and those who oppose it:
the existence of such a phenomenon, and the global consciousness it produces.
Their struggle takes place over a global ideal, one founded upon free trade,
transnational corporations and the existing forms of liberal democracy; the
other on equality, the protection of the environment and the extension of
democracy. Here, finally, is an opposition that does oppose.

Scene and Obscene

ZYGMUNT BAUMAN

Jock Young and other writers of the 'critical criminology school' pointed out
many years ago that the grounds for public alarm about rising crime are difficult, nay impossible, to verify objectively. Statistics of crime committed or
crime detected won't help: one would never know for sure what they record –
the growing numbers of policemen, of hired and voluntary police informers or
of criminals and their activities; perhaps they reflect none of the three, but our
new sensitivity to the elusive, unknown and unknowable threats, lurking in dark
and impenetrable corners and ready to lash out at any moment and without
rhyme and reason, as is the habit of criminals – those eponymical breakers of
routine and desecrators of order.

Following the critical criminologists' hint, I wonder what the widespread
impression of powers being 'obscene' and growing more obscene by the day
may signal. The term 'obscene' does not help to clear one's mind; its reference-
frame is neither avocado- nor coconut-like, managing instead to be simultaneously soft in the centre and mushy at the edges. The *Oxford English Dictionary*
explains the 'obscene' as 'offensive to modesty and decency', 'to the senses or
the mind', and, for that reason, 'abominable, disgusting, filthy'. Those definitions bristle with references to affections and thoroughly subjective *Erlebnisse*,
starting with 'modesty' and 'decency', notoriously controversial qualities,
through 'disgusting', obviously a matter of taste, and ending with 'filthy', which
as Mary Douglas taught us is always a side-effect of notoriously diverse and
changing visions of order (if Bertrand Russell suggested that obscenity is what

'happens to shock some elderly and ignorant magistrate', Lord Longford accused the whole of the British press of 'trembling on the brink of obscenity').

When it appears in the sociologists' writings, 'obscenity' does not beckon (or at least this is what the writers try to avoid) to the established usages recorded by the compilers of dictionaries. In its sociological usages, 'obscenity' claims an idiosyncratic meaning, with which the term has been invested by Jean Baudrillard. That meaning, though, does not help either when it comes to the unpacking of the 'obscene power' idea.

In conversation with Guy Bellavance,[1] Baudrillard defined the 'obscene' as 'the loss of scene'. Scene, another sample of Baudrillardesque idiomatics, is 'the very possibility of creating a space where things transform themselves, to play in another way, and not at all in their objective determination'. The scene, one is invited to conclude, is a space of freedom from convention and a space one can take a distance from in order to put oneself outside the realm of rules and determinations rather than be overwhelmed, swept over, incapacitated or drowned. With the eruption of obscenity, 'the possibility of inventing an enchanted space . . . and the possibility of playing on that distance are lost'. Obscenity means 'total promiscuity of things', a dense crowd inside which nothing can be seen at a distance, examined and contemplated; no place to breathe freely and take a longer breath, pause and ponder, see what is what and what one could do to make it into something else. Baudrillard is the late twentieth-century Rabelais, or Rabelais with a taste for theorizing; Baudrillard's 'obscenity' is the name given to a gargantuan world complete with a thesis that it is a world in which we, the herd of greedy, bewildered and frightened Pantagruels face constant confusion in the pursuit of life's pleasures.

Baudrillard signals a fateful passage in that collection of our biographies which is called current history: a passage from scene to obscene. There was a scene once, there is none now. Something has happened 'out there', in the world in which we move, having no other world left to move around. But two years before talking to Bellavance, Baudrillard chose to describe that brave new world of ours as 'simulacral',[2] that is, of a condition in which the distinction between reality and its simulation can no longer be drawn, when the question 'what is real' and 'what is not' cannot be asked and, if asked, would find no convincing answer. Simulacrum is not a simulation; it does not mean feigning or pretending, an act which cannot but be an oblique tribute to the unsullied majesty of reality; it is rather akin to a psychosomatic disease, in which the pains of the victim are quite genuine and so cast in doubt the very difference between 'illness' and 'health'. It is not that reality is chased away by simulacra; it is rather that there is no way to know, let alone to know for sure, what is real and how much one thing is more real than another. I would suggest that this is exactly what hides behind the present-day talk of the 'obscenity' of power.

Power has always been a two-edged sword, a bewildering mixture of enabling and disabling capacity and a name for the differential and differentiating distribution of these two capacities. That distribution cannot but be hotly contested, and that contest is what we call 'power struggle' – a tug-of-war aimed at another redistribution of the 'enabling' and 'disabling' impacts of powers-that-be. Power struggles tend to be waged in the form of legitimacy wars. 'Having power' means being able to have one's way whether or not the other side is happy about it and however dearly it might like to slow down or arrest one's progress; it implies therefore a degree of coercion, an application of force – the other side needs to be *forced* into obedience. If that forcing into obedience is legitimate, force feels no more like coercion, let alone violence, and the obedience to command can be safely expected, while resistance to command becomes an exception.

One can calculate the degree of force needed to achieve the desired effect of obedience only if coercion is accepted as legitimate; the primary way of rendering force inoperative is the rejection of its legitimacy – first voiced by the objects of coercion but sooner or later sapping the power-holder's resolve. Coercion whose legitimacy has been questioned, dented or denied is reclassified as violence. The principal aim of the 'legitimacy battles' is not the winning of war, but making the waging of war irrelevant to the legitimacy of the powers-that-be by rendering it unlikely that it will be initiated by their challengers. That situation is reached when coerciveness of power has been successfully institutionalized; when it is no more noticed by its objects; when it is inseparable from the daily, habitualized routine and lived through as a part and parcel of 'things as they are'. The 'scene of power' is where mystery plays and morality tales are repeatedly staged and *Bildungsromane* recited, rehearsing for public consumption the unshakeable and eternal truths of the human condition. All other manifestations of force are then unambiguously 'out of scene', obscene – and it is crystal clear to everyone involved what is what.

In every case of well-established and stable distribution of enabling/disabling capacities of power, a clear line is drawn to separate the 'legitimate coercion' from violence. I suggest that what the term 'obscenity of power' is trying to grasp is the present-day tenuousness and haziness of that line. Or perhaps it would be more to the point to talk about the once widely respected and securely guarded frontiers turning into frontlines, sites of guerrilla warfare and targets of stubborn and continuous, blatant or clandestine trespassing.

I propose that the rise of the 'obscene' forms of power does not necessarily signal a rise in the volume of 'illegitimate coercion', that is, of violence. Power becomes obscene when it is not clear whether the coercion applied is legitimate and the question of its legitimacy is thrown open, turning into a standing invitation to 'battle tests'.

In his insightful analysis of the 'literary field', Pierre Bourdieu ridiculed the 'positivist' literary studies that try to take stock of the immanent and 'objective' qualities of literature which, in their view, would allow the establishment equally 'objectively' of what is and what is not a 'work of literature', or who is and who is not a 'writer'. Against such hopes and intentions, Bourdieu pointed out that 'one of the major stakes in the struggles conducted inside the literary or artistic field is the definition of the field's boundaries' – that is, of the aggregate of people 'with the legitimate right to participate in the struggle'. The stake in question is the 'definition of legitimate practice', and ultimately the right to articulate the 'authoritative', that is *binding*, definitions.[3] I suggest that this analysis, though dealing with literary or artistic struggles, could be easily raised to a higher level of generality and so made directly relevant to our topic: everything that has been said by Bourdieu about the dynamics of the literary field concerns the attributes which that field owns in its capacity as a specimen of the wider class of 'social fields'. *All* social fields, however distinct and specific the subject of their defining/classifying action may be and whatever their tools and products, are sedimentations of past power struggles and are 'kept in shape' by ongoing power struggles. The essence of all power is the right to *define with authority*, and the major stake of power struggle is the appropriation or retention of the right to define and, no less importantly, of the right to invalidate and ignore the definitions coming from the adversary camp. As Edward Said noted in the aftermath of the eruption of violence in Kosovo:

> The International Tribunal which designated Milošević as war criminal lost its credibility if, following the same criteria, it refrained from inculpation of Clinton and Blair, Madeleine Albright, Sandy Berger, General Clark and all those who violated, simultaneously, all forms of decency and the laws of war. In comparison with what Clinton has done to Iraq, Milošević is almost an amateur.[4]

We can safely assume that the naivety of these remarks was deliberate. Surely, Edward Said, a most perceptive analyst of the fads and foibles of our civilization, must have known that the criteria followed by the International Tribunal were not those of the measurable degree of cruelty and the volume of human suffering which that cruelty caused (let alone criteria as ethereal and elusive as 'decency'), but those of the *right to be cruel*; and that, consequently, the criteria applied by the Tribunal to Milošević and Clinton were, indeed, the same. It is by these criteria that the first could be declared a criminal and the other allowed to bask in the glory of bringing him to his knees. It is conceivable that some years ago, when the principle of state territorial sovereignty had not yet crumbled under the unremitting pressure of globalization, 'the same' criteria would have prompted the aquittal of Milošević and a charge of aggression – the eponymically illegitimate violence – raised against NATO forces.

In all order-building and order-maintenance endeavours, legitimacy is, by necessity, the prime stake of the game and the most hotly contested concept. The fight is conducted around the borderline dividing the proper (that is, unpunishable) from the improper (that is, punishable) coercion and enforcement. The 'war against violence' is waged in the name of the monopoly of coercion. The 'elimination of violence', the declared objective of such war, is visualized as the state in which that monopoly is no more contested, let alone compromised. The 'non-violence' presented as the attribute of civilized life does not mean the absence of coercion, but only the absence of *unauthorized* – illegitimate – coercion; or, more precisely, the de-legitimation of all applications of force except for those that carry official approval and are therefore represented as instances of the defence of law and order. These are the prime reasons for which the war against violence as such is unwinnable, and a 'non-violent' social order is for all practical purposes a contradiction in terms.

Our modern civilization had listed 'elimination of violence' as one of the principal items of its order-building agenda. Taking the project of modernity on its word and remaining oblivious to the agenda which the choice of words was meant to hide (or make more palatable if unconcealed), numerous scholars have theorized modern civilization as an arrangement bent on the 'softening' of human intercourse and cohabitation and on the steady elimination of the coercive methods of promoting order. So far, such theorists have been sorely disappointed in their attempts to document convincing progress, though with each change of the setting and the rules of the ongoing power game they celebrated in advance the breakthrough bound to follow shortly.

The trouble with the game a-changing is that while continuously refreshing the fading promises of better chances for the future it cannot but repeatedly re-evaluate the past: what had been recorded in its time as a triumph of civilized order tends to be some time later rewritten as the history of wicked, cruel and disreputable violence – as has been the fate of the 'pacification' of 'violent tribesmen' of India, of the taming of Indian 'savages' in America and the extermination of aboriginal 'savages' in Australia or Newfoundland. Just how vulnerable and transient are the borders between violence and 'civilizing progress' is shown vividly by the notorious troubles haunting American history textbooks – denounced, censured, vilified and one by one withdrawn from circulation as 'politically incorrect', that is jarring with somebody's idea of the legitimacy of gun-wielding by respective adversaries.

To cut the long argument short: it is impossible to say with any degree of objectivity whether modern history is a story of growing or diminishing, rising or receding violence – as it is quite impossible to find the way of measuring 'objectively' the overall volume of coercion and violence. The treatment of the applications of force as 'violent acts' is much too inconstant and erratic to allow uncritical acceptance of stochastic series, however diligently they have been collated and however laboriously the facts they convey have been researched. All estimates of historical tendencies of violence are plagued with endemically short life expectancy; they are bound to be as contentious and contested as the legitimacy of coercion and the classification of coercion as violence that depends on such legitimacy.

The substance of order-building and order-protection is, principally, the exemption of a large assortment of coercive measures from the opprobrium reserved for violence (for instance, bombing of Serbs as distinct from bombing by Serbs). Since the objective of the exercise is the redistribution of legitimacy, the guardianship of order is as much a struggle to eliminate violence (that is, *the illegitimate* coercion) as it is an effort to *legitimize* 'useful and necessary' violence. Condemnation of force and compulsion can be only selective; more often than not it tends as well to be disputed. And so the perception of endemic, 'ordinary' and 'normal' coercion as 'violence' varies together with the degree of legitimacy of social order. If the order's claim to legitimacy is shaky and poorly grounded, much of the force deployed in the service of order would be conceived as violence; and conversely, challenge to the order's legitimacy consists in the questioning and leads to the condemnation of its enforcement as a case of violence. To deny the right to use force equals the refusal to grant legitimacy to the extant powers – refusal associated as a rule with a competitive power-bid. In times of transition, much of the coercion endemic in the daily 'orderly' life of society surfaces in public consciousness as violence.

Ours are such times of transition – and a transition no less profound and comprehensive as that which went down in history as the birth of modern society and whose saturation with violence has been now, retrospectively, widely recognized. No wonder that the impression of 'living in violent times' and the conviction that the volume and cruelty of violence is rising are so widespread; the perception of a large and growing number of power-wielding cases as 'obscene' is another wording for that common perception. When the old institutional scaffoldings of daily routine are falling apart, few if any 'musts' once taken to be a 'part of life', unpleasant and irritating yet bound to be lived with and suffered in silence, seem as obvious and look as inevitable as before. Suffering is recast from implacable fate to wicked malpractices, and suffering meekly and placidly saps self-esteem and shifts resolutely out of fashion.

When securely institutionalized, coercion melts into the background of daily life on which eyes rarely focus. It is unnoticed, and so 'invisible'. And the more routine, repetitive and monotonous the coercion is, the lesser is its chance of drawing attention. It is only when the routine is broken or comes under intense pressure that the coercion which used to sustain it all along comes into view. This is also the moment when in the eyes of its targets the routine spectacle of power looks 'obscene': coercion acquires all the trappings of violence – of an unwarranted, unjustified and inexcusable use of force, a vile and vicious assault against 'human rights', personal integrity and sovereignty.

This is, however, but one part of the story. The impression of a rising frequency with which people nowadays resort to a use of force, which in the absence of institutionalized frameworks can be only classified as violence, has its grounds and cannot be dismissed as a *trompe-l'oeil* and blamed on the cognitive confusion natural at times of transition.

'Ours are times of transition' means: the old structures are falling apart or dismantled, while no alternative structures of equal institutional hold are about to be put in their place. It is as if the moulds in which human relationships had been poured to acquire shape have now been thrown, themselves, into a melting pot. Deprived of such moulds, all patterns of relationships become as suspicious as they are uncertain and vulnerable, amenable to challenge and provoking renegotiation. It is not just that the actual human relations, as all human attributes in the era of modernity, require an effort to fit them into a pattern; the present-day problem is that the *patterns themselves* are no more 'given'. The moulding of patterns has itself turned into a task, and this task is to be performed under the conditions haunted by the absence of any 'normative regulation' and clear-cut criteria of successful accomplishment. *We are all playing these days a curious game, a game in which the game's rules and purposes are themselves major stakes.*

Since the effort of pattern-making has no pre-established finishing line and since there are no ready-made designs by which one could monitor and guide the progress of the enterprise, let alone measure its success, the effort can proceed only through a series of trials and errors. Pattern-making consists nowadays in a process of *continuous experimentation*. But an initial supposition, which experiments in their original sense were meant to be testing, tends to be vague or altogether absent; the purpose of experimentation is itself the topic of experiment.

The trials and errors by which the pattern-making proceeds take as a rule the form of a 'reconnaissance through battle'. In military practice, the term refers to the engaging of the enemy forces in a skirmish, whose purpose is to reveal what the resources and strategic ideas of the other side are, what are its defensive or offensive capacities, and so what sort of response to one's own gambits could be expected; or, conversely, to find out how secure one can reasonably presume one's own position to be. Attempts to reconnoitre all these things through a brief yet intense military engagement are sometimes undertaken when the strategic plan has been completed and signed and what remains is to test just how realistic the prospects of its success are. But it happens as well that the 'reconnaissance through battle' is initiated before any aim has been thought of – in order to find out how wide the range of feasible options is. No plans have been worked out as yet; what targets will be set for action depends instead on the results of preliminary combat and the conclusions one may derive from them about the strength and the resolve of resistance and the obstacles one is likely to encounter when trying to overcome it.

Since old patterns seem no more obligatory and their holding power feels less than overwhelming and awe-and-obedience-inspiring, while no new patterns bidding for universal consent and permanent institutional entrenchment (let alone the likelihood of obtaining either of them) are in sight, more and more conditions are experienced as *fluid, under-defined and contentious*, and so calling for constant vigilance and constant wearing of battle fatigues. Ours is an increasingly embattled society; a society in which violence, accusations of violent intentions and expectations of violent acts turn into major vehicles of individual and group self-assertion. The ancient principle *si vis pacem, para bellum* seems topical as never before – from the top to the bottom of the social system, whether at the global, local or domestic level.

The suspicion of violence is itself an ample source of anxiety: as the problem of legitimacy stays permanently unsolved and debatable, no demand likely to arise from the circumstances of sharing space, home or life is free from the charge of overt or hidden violence. No wonder that the ambient fear of violence prompts a strategy of disengagement, of territorial separation made safe by the modern equivalents of moats, turrets and drawbridges (like neighbourhood watch, gated condominia, closed TV circuits and security or vigilante patrols) – but also by the replacement of a 'till death us do part' type of commitment with 'trial marriages' and flexible households whose fragility and non-committal character is protected by the annulment-on-demand clause.

The currently rising volume of 'family' and 'neighbourhood' violence calls for a two-stage explanation. First, due to the perceived weakness of the once all-powerful, self-evident and unquestioned patterns of relationships, much of the coercion entailed in their daily reproduction has been stripped of its past legiti-macy. It is no more taken for granted nor viewed as irresistible, and so tends to be reclassified as violence. Second, the new fluidity and flexibility of relation-ships released from patterned constraints prompts a widespread use of the 'reconnaissance by battle' stratagems: the strength, the resourcefulness and resilience of the sides are put to a daily 'trial of force', in order to find out how far one's own territory could be expanded and how much one may flex one's muscle without fear of counterattack, or how much of one's nagging and push-ing the other side is likely to bear meekly before it 'gets its act together' and responds in kind. This is the case of the use-of-force-in-search-of-legitimacy; and for the time being, as long as the sought-after legitimacy has not been won and securely fenced off, the 'trial by force' is by definition an act of violence. If new patterns do not emerge and the terms of armistice need to be reinforced or renegotiated daily, the coercion which normally underlies all cases of 'peaceful cohabitation' may don the garb of violence for a long time to come. There is a long and tortuous way from the exilic lands of obscenity back to the scene.

The newly named varieties of family and neighbourhood violence – marital rape, child abuse, sexual harassment at work, stalking, prowling – illustrate the ongoing 'reclassification' processes. The conducts which all such catchwords that generate panic and outrage try to grasp are hardly new. They have been around for a very long time, but either used to be treated as 'natural' and suffered in silence like other unwelcome, yet unavoidable nuisances of life, or stayed unnoticed, like so many other features of 'normality'. Quite often, under the names of marital loyalty, parent-child intimacy or the arts of courtship, they were praised and keenly cultivated alongside other similarly indispensable con-ditions of the orderly world (so-called 'socialization' consists, after all, in inducing the individuals to do willingly what according to the rules of their society they must do). The new names refer not so much to the new phenomena they pretend to denote, as to the new refusal to put up with them as placidly, as hands down, as before. *The new names, we may say, are the question marks replacing full stops.* The phenomena they name are now called to justify themselves or apolo-gize, their legitimacy is refuted, their institutional foundations shaky and no more exuding an air of authority, solidity and permanence; and illegitimate coercion, as we remember, is violence, while the spectacle not billed as part of the stage repertoire is obscene. The recalcitrant and out-of-(established) order are prime candidates for demonization – the 'Fatal Attraction'-style demoniza-tion of women, the 'underclass'-style demonization of the poor or the current panic around the sexual appetites and murderous instincts of children.

The institutionalized patterns crumble and disintegrate at all levels of social organization with similar consequences: at all levels, ever more types of inter-action are reclassified to the category of violence, while acts of violence of the 'reconnaissance by battle' kind become a permanent feature of the continuous de- and reconstruction of power hierarchies. Two levels, though, deserve par-ticularly close attention: one, occupied until recently by state and nation merged into one, and another, up to this point poorly institutionalized, until recently virtually a 'no-man's land' but keenly colonized now by the emerging 'global', or in Alberto Melucci's vocabulary, 'planetary', system.

The construction of modern nation-states was a story of violence perpetrated by the relatively few resourceful and successful ethnicities upon the multitude of inchoate or inept, lesser and hapless ones – the 'would be' but 'never to be' nations or nations permanently 'in waiting'. Histories of battles are written by their victors, and so the suppression and physical or cultural extermination of the defeated minorities, never given the chance to write their own histories, came to be recorded and retold as the edifying and uplifting story of progress or civilizing process: of a gradual yet relentless pacification of daily life and purify-ing human interaction from violence. When surveyed with the benefit of hind-sight, that purification looks rather as the successful elimination of *unauthorized* coercion and the institutionalization ('naturalization') of the *authoritative* coercion embroidered in the tissue of human bonds. Later repaintings of the picture notwithstanding, the matter of violence was for many decades confined to the problem of antisocial, criminal margins. With the stormy beginnings of the nation-states conveniently forgotten, a clear and no more disputed line could be drawn between the coercion dressed as 'defence of law and order' and the 'naked' and 'savage', but scattered and dispersed, violence, easy to locate and isolate.

This is no more the case, though. With the sovereignty of nation-states con-tinually eroded by globalizing pressures, and the threshold requirements for the bids of self-determination radically lowered, the power-assisted, compulsory assimilation and incorporation of ethnic minorities and the annihilation of their separate identities (the updated version of Claude Lévi-Strauss's ethnological category of *anthropophagic* strategy – the prime technique of order-building deployed by nation-states of the past) is no more available; the sporadic attempts to deploy it now tend to be spectacularly ineffective. Accordingly, the deployment of an alternative strategy (a present-day rendition of Lévi-Strauss's *anthropoemic* strategy) – that of disengagement, mutual separation, eviction and deportation – is a temptation difficult to resist. The other who is no more assimilable needs to be destroyed or deported beyond the boundary of com-munity, which can only rely upon the uniform similarity of its members when it comes to the imposition and the defence of the patterns of cohabitation. For the newly emerging states, the policy of compulsory assimilation and the suppres-sion of local traditions, memories, customs and dialects is no more a feasible or viable option. We have entered the era in which ethnic cleansing, an overtly violent exercise, turns into the principal expedient of nation-building strategy.

Ambitions and demands once occupying the centre stage have turned obscene.

Inside the nation-state, the top rungs of the power ladder, once basking in the light of divine anointment and quasi-divine mission, are now enveloped in the thick cloud of corruption and do not look superhuman at all.

'Corruption at the top' is not, of course, a novelty. Its ubiquitous presence was, since time immemorial, one of the least doubted truths of the popular wisdom. When Thomas Mathiesen wrote 'that the penal system strikes at the "bottom" rather then at the "top" of society',[5] he merely, by his own admission, recorded the criminologists' belated effort to 'catch up' with the wisdom of the folklore. But once the truth of popular apprehensions is admitted, it also becomes clear that 'corruption at the top' is a phenomenon seldom ever displayed at the centre stage and more often than not played out 'behind the scene'; a prime candidate, in other words, for the charge of obscenity.

Why this should be the case has been amply explained by the sociologists of law and practices of punishment. Several causes have been repeatedly discussed.

The first among them are the selective intentions of the lawgivers, concerned with the preservation of a certain specific kind of order. The actions most likely to be committed by the people for whom that order has no room – by the underdog now renamed as the 'underclass' – stand the best chance of appearing in the criminal code. Robbing whole nations of their resources is, on the other hand, called 'promotion of free trade'; robbing whole families and communities of livelihood and the sole way of life they had been trained to pursue is called 'downsizing', 'outsourcing', 'flexibility' or just 'rationalization'. Neither of the two has been so far listed among the criminal and punishable deeds.

Second, as all police units dedicated to 'serious crime' would have repeatedly found out, the illegal acts committed at the 'top' are exceedingly difficult to disentangle from the dense network of daily and 'ordinary' company dealings. In the activity which openly pursues personal gain at other people's expense, the borderline between the moves allowed and disallowed is necessarily poorly defined and always contentious – nothing to compare with the comforting unambiguity of the act of trespassing, safe-breaking or forcing a lock. No wonder that, as Mathiesen finds out, the prisons 'are above all filled by people from the lower strata of the working class who have committed theft and other "traditional" crimes'.[6]

Poorly defined, the crimes 'at the top' are in addition exceedingly difficult to detect. They are perpetrated inside a close circle of people united by mutual complicity, loyalty to the organization and *esprit de corps*, people who usually take effective measures to close the ranks and to spy out, silence or eliminate the potential whistle-blowers. The detection of 'crimes at the top' requires a level of legal and financial sophistication not available to the non-players and so remains virtually beyond the ken of outsiders, particularly of the lay and untrained outsiders. To make the whole thing even more confusing, such crimes have no 'body', no physical substance: they 'exist' in the ethereal, imaginary space of pure abstraction. They are, literally, *invisible* – it takes an imagination on a par with the ingenuity of their perpetrators to spy out a substance in the elusive form. Guided by intuition and common sense, the public may well suspect that theft played its part in the history of fortunes, and goes on playing it in the creation of new ones – but to point one's finger to it remains a notoriously daunting task. Only in rare and extreme cases do 'corporate crimes' come to court and into public view. Embezzlers and tax cheaters have an infinitely greater opportunity for an out-of-court settlement than do pickpockets or burglars. With the 'top' becoming ever more global, perched at nebulous heights for the grounded agencies of law and order, one more factor yet complicates the matter: the agents of local orders are only too aware of the superiority of global powers and so would consider it a success if they get as far as a behind-the-scene deal.

Furthermore, as far as 'the crimes at the top' are concerned, the vigilance of the public is at best erratic and sporadic, at worst non-existent. It takes a truly spectacular fraud, but above all a fraud with a 'human touch', where the victims, for instance pensioners or small savers, can be personally named, or when the damage can be personalized, as in the case of a poisoned water supply or nicotine addiction, to arouse public attention and keep it aroused for longer than a day or two (and even then it takes, in addition, all the imaginative and persuasive gifts of a small, or not that small, army of popular press journalists). In most cases, though, what is going on during the trials of high-level fraudsters defies the intellectual abilities of the ordinary newspaper readers, and anyway is abominably short of the drama which makes the trials of simple thieves and murderers such a fascinating spectacle.

All this is not news. That legitimacy of acts is a coveted privilege, and that the award or denial of legitimacy is one of the principal tools in the construction and maintenance of social hierarchy would hardly surprise a trained sociologist. This means, though, that under ordinary circumstances, 'white collar crime' or 'corrupt company practices' (concepts whose very appearance in public discourse makes one wonder just how 'ordinary' the circumstances are) are relatively immune to the charge of 'obscenity'. That they tend to be nowadays so charged is a testimony of anything but an 'ordinary' condition: it implies instead a situation when the legitimacy of actions is once more a matter of bargaining, trial and error and reconnaissance-through-battle.

Such a situation could be only expected, given the new global scale on which the big players of company games operate. The global space is poorly marked and mapped, the traffic lights are few and far between and the roads are made in the course of riding them, only for the tracks to be rubbed off again once passed. During most of modern history, 'no-man's land' was an abomination and a battle-call to invade, conquer, establish garrisons and outposts, and colonize; but the exterritorial space in which the global élite moves these days remains a 'no-man's land' which no one thus far has made a convincing bid to take under their wing and administer. It looks to the wide-eyed globetrotters just as the old American frontier appeared to the 'Westward-ho' pioneers: as the land of new beginnings and infinite opportunities in which everything goes and pistols can be drawn quickly from the holsters; a fairy-tale country where every-thing can happen, anything can be abandoned and tried again, and very few, if any, points are of no return. Everything that is done here may be baptized obscene, but then there is no established stage in sight against which to measure the extent of its obscenity. Unbridling of hands prompts great temptations; it also augurs great dangers.

When facing the guardians of order grounded in the physical space which underpins the exterritorial cyberspace, the global élite enjoys tremendous advantage. Orders are local, while the élite and the free-market game it plays are translocal. If the wardens of a local order get too inquisitive, obtrusive, pernickety and otherwise obnoxious, there is always the possibility of appealing to the as-yet-uncodified, and for that reason open to free invention, prerequisites of the wider, poorly explored (global) space in an effort to change the local concepts of order and the local rules of the game. And, of course, there is the possibility to run away if things get too hot for comfort locally; 'globality' of the élite means mobility, and mobility means the ability to escape and evade. There are always places where local orders do not clash with the global market usages, or where the local guardians of order are glad and willing to look the other way in case a clash does happen. Commitments are short term, undertakings are until further notice, and so rules are best embraced for the duration of the next step and abandoned when no more useful.

All power corrupts, said Lord Acton, and absolute power corrupts absolutely. We may add that the global powers corrupt globally. Or, the globally 'deregu-lated', and for that reason obscene, power corrupts obscenely.

The 'New Asian Museum' in the Age of Globalization

RUSTOM BHARUCHA

In this paper I will raise a series of questions on global cultural politics, out of which – and against which – the desire and modalities of the 'new Asian museum' can be problematized.[1] I will begin by questioning the very category of 'the new Asian museum': How exactly is 'Asia' being invoked here? Which Asia do we have in mind – South Asia, Southeast Asia or East Asia? If Asia is not being reduced to an ahistorical cultural essence or to a mere geographical expanse, then how exactly is it being conceived? To what extent are the upholders of the 'new Asian museum' aware of the economic disparities that divide Asia, perhaps more so than in any other continent? Do these disparities matter in First World cultural contexts where it is possible to metaphorize 'Asia'? To what extent does this 'Asia' continue to be part of a residual Orient that refuses to die even as it is in the process of being deconstructed? How does one negotiate the hierarchies of cultural hegemony that operate within Asia? And to what extent do they matter in determining the criteria and standards upheld in the curatorial policies of the 'new Asian museum'?

From the politics of my own location, I would acknowledge that while we have a vibrant cultural discourse in India on a plethora of identities – regional identity, caste identity, communal identity, national identity – there is almost no inscription of an 'Asian' identity in the emergent field of Indian cultural studies. It is not that Asia doesn't matter, or that we don't feel part of it; it is simply not our priority.[2] This is not the case in countries like Malaysia and Singapore where the discourse around 'Asian values', for instance, has been upheld for a long time in political and intellectual circles, despite the recent discrediting of these dubious 'values' through their now-acknowledged associations with cronyism, authoritarianism, pseudo-Confucianism, paternalism and corruption.[3]

Significantly, even while 'Asian values' get discredited, they are being replaced, if not reinforced, by a new affirmation of the 'Asian Renaissance'[4] – a renaissance that is being manufactured not only by the agencies of the state in Singapore and Malaysia but, tacitly, by a great many intellectuals, architects and cultural practitioners as well, who are riding piggy-back on its rhetoric. Simultaneously, in the field of intercultural theatre practice, we are witnessing the projection of an 'inter-Asian' aesthetic, which is gaining a new clout through the substantial funding received for exclusively Asian work provided by the Japan Foundation Asia Center and the ubiquitous Ford Foundation. Out of these funding initiatives are emerging new infrastructures of exchange centred for the most part in Singapore, Hong Kong and Tokyo – the metropolitan centres of an increasingly consolidated 'East Asian' configuration in which the 'other Asias' would seem to be on the margins.

From a South Asian perspective, I would acknowledge that the opportunity to work in Asia with other Asian colleagues offers a positive alternative in reversing the predominantly East–West trajectories of earlier modes of intercultural exchange. But a more critical perspective on these developments would reveal that, yet again, the funding is being controlled and framed precisely in those centres of global capital where a critique of global capitalism is politically unacceptable by the cultural agencies of the state. More problematically, the values of the market would seem to be thoroughly integrated within the ethos of corporate yuppie-dom in which Asian (and more specifically, ASEAN) artists are increasingly implicated.

The 'Asia', therefore, that is being celebrated in recent inter-Asian collaboration has less to do with the propagation of democracy through people's movements or emergent struggles in civil society, than with the creation of spectacles and events in which 'Asia' becomes a new manifestation of cultural capital itself.[5] The very diverse resources of Asian cultures, particularly in the ritualistic, folk and traditional sectors of performance, supplemented by a spectrum of visual traditions, contribute to the lure of this capital. With appropriate adaptation, these resources can be ingeniously re-invented in the form of new narratives, contributing lucratively to the global cultural industry and the spate of mega art shows, biennales, triennales and blockbusters.

In presenting this synoptic view on some of the cultural developments being manufactured in the name of 'Asia', my point is simply to emphasize that the 'new Asian museum' cannot be separated from its larger implications in global culture. The museum offers a particularly embattled site to study the tensions between the global and the local, the intercultural and the multicultural, 'Asia' in Asia and the 'Asia' supported by the increasingly privileged hegemonies of the diaspora. Since I cannot claim to be a critical insider to the intensely charged contradictions of the 'local' Canadian art scene – I was a witness to its extremely articulate and strategic positioning at the symposium in Vancouver[6] – I will continue for the rest of this essay to focus on the larger global implications of the 'new Asian museum', drawing on my own discomfort with museums in general, specifically within my cultural context in India.

'THE OLD ASIAN MUSEUM': AN INDIAN PREDICAMENT

We have already questioned the inscription of 'Asia' within the construction of the 'new Asian museum'. Hopefully, in clarifying the *raison d'être* of this museum, we will not fall back on any attempt to authenticate 'Asia' in the diaspora by drawing on the legacies of 'old Asian museums', which are, for the most part, colonial relics, if not bureaucratic nightmares. Certainly, this would seem to be an accurate description for museums in India, where, arguably, the very idea of the museum remains somewhat alien to millions of people in the absence of a vibrant museum culture.

Tellingly, even as intellectual production in India on postcolonial theory, subaltern history and popular culture has been internationalized in recent years, museum studies in India (particularly in the contemporary domain of public culture) remains woefully neglected. Even the most basic facts and data relating to collections and subsidies are not available for public scrutiny. Annual reports are not published. Despite their almost total absence of transparency and accountability, museums get away with their improprieties. In this context, would it be false to assume that they don't really matter to intellectuals in India or to the public at large? Quite unlike the enormously popular cinema halls, theatres, football stadiums, parks, amusement centres, *melas* (fairs), all-night musical soirees and book exhibitions, museums cannot be said to contribute with any resonance to the cultures of 'time-pass' in contemporary India. Museums are boring, and most of all, they don't make sense.

Clearly, this is not the view shared by Arjun Appadurai and Carol Breckenridge, in their influential essay 'Museums are good to think: heritage on view in India',[7] wherein they subsume their empirically thin perspective on Indian museums within a transnational framework of public culture. In this overly valorized theoretical terrain, it is not the actual state of Indian museums that matters but their 'inter-ocular' possibilities of spatialization through their alleged linkages with travel, tourism, pilgrimages, leisure, the mass media, department stores, exhibition-cum-sales and ethnic national festivals, among other manifestations of public culture in India.

Without denying the mobilizing power of these cultural phenomena, one needs to question how exactly they impact on the phenomenon of the museum itself. Take department stores, for instance, which are an extremely new up-market phenomenon that are to be found almost exclusively in more prosperous metropolitan cities like Bangalore – how can this consumerist site, arguably a 'glocal' phenomenon, be related to the economic desuetude of Indian museums, which survive for the most part on meagre state subsidies? Can they be assumed to share the same public sphere, regardless of their divergent accessibilities to communities discriminated on the basis of class and education? So seemingly rapturous is Appadurai and Breckenridge's apparent faith in the democratization of public culture that they highlight Indian museums as repositories of 'informal learning'. While this is a dubious compliment for a country with widespread illiteracy, it would be worth reflecting on if the authors could analyse visual literacy within an actual study of museum reception in India. This does not materialize, because such a comprehensive study does not exist for the contemporary state of museums in India. It does beg the question, however, whether the construct of 'informal learning' remains at the level of theoretical desire, rather than actual fact.

Tellingly, even while acknowledging the colonial heritage of Indian museums and the lingering premodern modes of perception internalized by the Indian public, Appadurai and Breckenridge fail to confront the disjunction that exists between this 'heritage' and its postcolonial residue. At one level, this can be ascribed to their 'non-dialectics of seeing' (to reverse Susan Buck-Morss's valuable category), which prevents them, despite their own recommendation, from intersecting the reception theory informing 'the *contexts* of current museum viewing [in India]' with an 'analysis of the colonial modes of knowledge and classification', pertaining to the *texts* contained in the museums.[8] Instead of acknowledging the extraordinarily intricate back-and-forth temporalities of seeing Indian artefacts, both within and beyond the boundaries of the museum, the authors settle for an evolutionary perspective of cultural spectacle, whereby 'older Indian modes of seeing and viewing are being gradually transformed and spectacularised'.[9] Once again, the globalizing process of capital is being assumed unequivocally without being interrogated within the disparate economic contexts of India, where one would need to take into account the 'de-spectacularizing' tendencies of urban cultures in India, facing the breakdown of basic civic amenities and public services.

Museums in India, I would argue, are merely symptomatic of the larger indifference on the part of the government – and the public – towards the maintenance of cultural institutions. No longer can they be affectionately evoked with colonial nostalgia as '*Ajaib Khana*' (translated by Kipling as 'Wonder House'), or as '*Jadu Ghar*' (Magic House), which is how the Indian Museum instituted in 1814 in my home city of Calcutta has been memorialized. There is nothing 'magical' about this museum today – if it continues to attract crowds of people on a daily basis, it should be kept in mind that drawing an audience almost anywhere in India with its population of one billion people does not pose a challenge. At the risk of sounding élitist, I would urge some discrimination between a 'crowd' and a 'public', drawing on the very fine emphasis made by Appadurai and Breckenridge themselves that, 'In India, museums need not worry so much about finding their publics as about making them.'[10]

Sadly, in the absence of any real confrontation of this difference between 'finding' and 'making', they land up *assuming* a public, which could be the most problematic factor in the thinking of Indian museums today. As Tapati Guha-Thakurta has demonstrated convincingly in what remains one of the very few scholarly assessments of 'the museumised relic'[11] in India, 'the public' has almost always remained an 'illusory entity' in the discourse around Indian museums; the disjunction between its 'actuality' and its 'absence' has never been fully confronted. Playing into deeply entrenched colonial prejudices by which 'appropriate' and 'inappropriate' subjects are implicitly differentiated, the nebulous notion of the public is fractured further through the 'vast gap' that exists between modes of 'seeing' and 'knowing'. The Indian museum remains caught between an obligatory need to generate 'mass recreation' through visual stimuli and the advocacy of 'specialized knowledge' perpetuated through an unconsciously grotesque parody of orientalism. To this day the *Jadu Ghar* of Calcutta displays inscrutable handwritten Latin inscriptions attached to thousands of indistinguishable rocks, stones and fossils. There's a time-warp in this colonial spectacle that could be the subject of a postmodern fiction were it not so depressingly evocative of the ruins of a (post)colonial present.

With the rise of the Indian bureaucrat masquerading as a museum director, 'specialized knowledge' has given way to an anachronistic adherence to the 'living traditions' of 'ancient India', now almost fossilized beyond recognition. As for extending the popularity of museums, the failure has been even more abysmal in the absence of new interactive technologies, or the most basic user-friendly conveniences and attractions – a tea-room or a gift shop, for instance, would be hard to find within the precincts of any Indian museum. Unable to do its job, the bureaucracy has 'fumbled, floundered, turned increasingly inwards.'[12] Insular rather than introspective, it has 'failed', as Guha-Thakurta has put it candidly, within the parameters of its own national preoccupations to disseminate knowledge to its citizens. At the heart of the failure remains the unresolved 'problem of the public', which refuses to be homogenized within 'a natural community of citizen-viewers', but which has yet to be 'pitched centrally within the particular trajectories of . . . modernity and democracy [in contemporary India]'.[13]

In the context of this predicament, the attempts on the part of diasporic global intellectuals like Appadurai and Breckenridge to subsume the Indian museum within the larger dynamics of public culture are somewhat misleading. Today, it is not simply a matter of whether '[Indian] museums are good to think'. *How* do we think about them when their very survival is at stake? Excluding the 'islands' of success like the Crafts Museum, sequestered in the arid wasteland of Pragati Maidan in New Delhi, or the even more exclusive Calico Museum in Ahmedabad, most of the museums that exist in India today do not function as museums: they have no shows, no exhibitions, no publications, almost no media representation whatsoever; their exhibits are layered in dust; the rooms are not always lit; there is almost no security; and the buildings themselves are often in a state of disrepair (on my last trip to Bharat Bhavan in Bhopal, designed by the internationally acclaimed Charles Correa, the roof was leaking in the gallery itself).

Under these circumstances, are museums good to *think*? What needs to be *done* about them? How can they be dismantled – and re-invented – to contribute more substantially to the public culture in India itself? While this question lies beyond the boundaries of this particular essay, which is concerned with the hypothesis of the 'new Asian museum', it precipitates the discussion that follows on how to deal with the 'Indian past' (and pasts elsewhere) through the principle of erasure, which I would now like to submit to critical scrutiny.

THE POLITICS OF ERASURE

Risking an amateur reflection on what could be described as a deeply internalized common sense, I would argue: If museums are repositories of the past, they risk being redundant in countries like India, where the past is alive in any number of unprecedented ways. Mutating, hybridizing and becoming juxtaposed with modern and postmodern incursions in our public sphere, the past is less a repository of seemingly eternal resources than a dynamic, even interruptive, element in the shaping of new narratives. The 'premodern' can catalyse conflicting modernities, as indeed, the 'folk' can defy the nomenclature of 'folklore' by assuming, if not asserting, a contemporary significance.

The 'Indian past', I would argue, challenges the very grammatology of the Euro-American museum structure (and its non-western derivations), which continues to rely on the periodization, classification and categorization of its artefacts. Indeed, the ironies deepen as one encounters this 'past' in specially designed crafts museums, which inevitably ethnicize cultural difference, and thereby reduce the folk to the cottage industries. What is worse is the live participation of traditional craftsmen and artisans, who are made to demonstrate their skills 'informally' within the precincts of the museum. Such dehumanizing instances of manufactured 'contemporary relevance' merely enhance the divisions between the 'real' folk and their urban clientele, while appearing to ameliorate the conditions of the rural poor.

The 'new Asian museum', it seems to me, will need to dismantle this projection of a factitious 'past' by exploring new imaginaries, in which multiple times – indeed, multiple pasts – can be staggered rather than juxtaposed through discrete combinations. New principles of visualizing 'Asia' could also be explored by drawing on the ecological principles that are embedded in traditional forms – principles relating to erasure, renewal and impermanence, as can be discerned in the rich gamut of ritual and cultural practices like *kolams* (traditional floor-drawings). Here, the entire point of the artwork lies in the *erasure* of the floor-drawing after it has been completed, following hours of meticulous work. In such practices, which have a continuing significance in the cultures of everyday life, the resistance to conservation and commodification provides a useful provocation in structuring new ways of 'visualizing' Asian pasts.

Let me deepen the provocation further: How does one translate the principle of erasure embedded in premodern practices by intersecting it with, say, postmodern Derridean readings of erasure? Here I am not just thinking of the possibility of creating 'biodegradable' installations, which could play with the possibilities of self-destruction. I would like to push the provocation even further: To what extent can the principle of erasure challenge the very ethos and structure of the museum itself? Can a museum erase itself?

Clearly, the seemingly anarchist subtext of this question needs some unpacking. A few qualifications would be in order: While articulating the possibilities of erasure, I am aware that it can be essentialized as a primary principle on the basis of which the 'integrity' of an art practice can be guaranteed. There is also a suggestion in my earlier comments that erasures are endowed with a premodern sanctity and that there may be no other options for the existing practitioners of premodern cultural practice than to hold on to the 'authenticity' of their ritual processes. By pre-empting such possibilities of misunderstanding, I must necessarily elaborate on the sources inspiring my understanding of 'erasure'.

Apart from the practice of *kolam*-drawing, I have in mind the traditional clay modelling of Hindu deities like Durga, Kali and Lakshmi during the Pujas (religious festivals) in Calcutta. These exquisite figures of the goddess are meticulously designed and shaped by the traditional artisans of Kumartuli, following which they are transported to roadside *pandals* (pavilions) on the streets of Calcutta, where they are worshipped with celebratory fervour and the active involvement of entire neighbourhoods of people. Indeed, it would be hard to think of a more 'public' form of worship almost anywhere else in the world. Following the three-to-five day worship of the goddess, the deities are transported once again on open trucks to the Hooghly River, where they are unceremoniously tossed into its muddy waters. This immersion of the goddess can be read as another kind of erasure, where the very 'object' of the 'art' produced by the Kumartuli artisans is ultimately cast into the waters, leaving no trace beyond its accessories.

To complicate the narrative, it is significant to note that the Kumartuli artisans are now re-inventing their skills for other purposes. During the lean season of the year, when they are out of business, they have taken to sculpting contemporary figures relating to vignettes from everyday life. Street scenes incorporating life-size naturalistic clay models depicting vendors and pedestrians, juxtaposed with the interiors of shops, vehicles and implements, were prominently featured in their first public exhibition in Calcutta (April–May 2000). Here, within the precincts of a makeshift 'art gallery' in Kumartuli itself, it was clear that the artisans wanted to be recognized *as artists*, not least because they wanted to display and sell their 'artworks', which necessarily had to be permanent.

At this point, there are at least two hypothetical interventions that could be made by the representatives of the 'new Asian museum'. One possibility would be to extend the visibility of the new artworks of the Kumartuli artisans through diasporic representations in global art forums. Given the growing interest among alternative, multicultural curators in featuring subaltern art from Third World countries, the possibility of transporting 'Kumartuli Art' to western art centres does not seem to be unduly bleak. Offbeat, yet 'neotraditional', the Kumartuli Art show could attract public attention on the lines of Satish Sharma's rich collection of snapshots from the roadside photographic studios of Indian cities and small towns – highly choreographed and fantasized images, with working-class men and small-town families posing alongside luridly painted film stars, gods, luxury goods, sports cars, fountains, the Himalayas and the Taj Mahal, among other icons of 'Street Dreams' (the catchy icon which provided the curatorial framework for Sharma's collection in its tour through numerous towns in Britain).

I will let pass for the moment the risks involved in exoticizing the 'real' through the blow-ups of anonymous snapshots and the close-ups of 'significant' details guaranteed to titillate the insatiable First World voyeuristic interest in *desi* (indigenous)/brown sexualities.[14] What I would emphasize instead is that it is one kind of challenge to transport the subaltern art of the Third World into the 'new Asian museum'; it is quite another matter for metropolitan artists affiliated to this museum to engage creatively and critically with those principles embedded in premodern practices that challenge the very norms of commodification embedded in the structure of the museum itself.

At least two possible caveats could be raised at this point. One relates to the implicit separation between 'them' (the Kumartuli artisans) and 'us' (the cosmopolitan interlocutors of the 'new Asian museum'). Such a separation would seem to deny a 'cosmopolitical'[15] status to the artisans themselves, apart from undermining the metropolitan possibilities of negotiating the 'premodern'. Neither of these positions, I should qualify, is absolute; indeed, both are capable of being implicated in each other's scenarios with the appropriate mediations and dialogue.

The second caveat is more pertinent to the immediate challenge presented to the 'new Asian museum' by local Asian-Canadian artists questioning the global hegemony of 'Asia': Why should minorities think of erasing their artworks when their very identities have been so ruthlessly marginalized by the art establishment over the years? Why not claim the most prestigious museum space in order to 'display' one's work with all the trappings of social and artistic recognition?

To this response, I would qualify that erasure, as a creative principle, need not deny either the significance of an artwork or the recognition of an artist. In erasing our work, we do not necessarily erase ourselves. Besides, even as erasures are materialized in practice, they inevitably leave traces, if not faint signatures. Second, I would add that there are many different kinds of erasure that are open to being *imagined* within the specific materials and constructions of different modes of art practice. The principle of erasure needs to push the boundaries of the imagination, not lend itself to being neutralized in the process. Finally, I would add that when I posit the erasure of the museum, I don't mean it literally – in other words, I am not saying that museums shouldn't exist, even though metaphorically that would seem to be my intent. Metaphors are not meant to be taken literally; they are valuable not so much in indicating *what* to think, but *how* to think. It is in this context that I would suggest that the metaphor of erasure should be constantly translated – and re-translated – within the mutations of specific practices.

AGAINST MUSEUMIZATION

In problematizing my own reflections on erasure, I have focused primarily on the transforming roles of the artist/artisan and the work of art produced. But the larger question remains the erasure of the museum itself as a structure, *as an institution*. Moving beyond the safe hypothesis of a 'museum without walls', we need to confront the basic power relations that sustain 'new Asian museums' in an age of globalization. If there is an agenda hidden in the possibility of erasing museums, it is surely tied up with a critique of capital whose stability in the museum context is ensured through the investment in a building (more extravagantly termed 'the site') and a permanent art collection – the primary 'assets' of a museum, which invariably determine its structure, public relations and marketing profile.

This brings us to the crucial issue of money: Who's paying for the 'new Asian museum'? How will it sustain itself financially? Is the initial capital investment likely to come from private foundations, the State or donations made by rich Asian families, who are a new force to reckon with in the propagation of global culture? To what extent is the 'long-distance absentee national feeling' of these families, to borrow Benedict Anderson's construction, a stimulus in reterritorializing the 'imagined communities' of their erstwhile homelands within their new locations? How does this 'feeling' get translated politically not only within multicultural scenarios but in relation to the endorsement of communal and fundamentalist movements 'back home'? To what extent can rich Asian families – the potential sponsors of the 'new Asian museum' – be regarded as adequate spokespersons for their own communities? And indeed, how do they relate to one another *across* communities?

One is calling attention here to the inter-Asian tensions that exist in almost all diasporic immigrant contexts. How can the 'new Asian museum' assuage these tensions rather than highlight them through the prioritization of one 'Asia' over another? If, for example, the chief donor of the museum happens to be an arts foundation based in Hong Kong, with its clearly stated prioritization of contemporary Chinese art, then how is this representation likely to exclude (or marginalize) contemporary artworks from other Asian nations? And what is the likely fallout of this seeming equation of 'Asia' with 'China' (the new superpower of our times) in the reception to the museum across non-Chinese Asian communities?

If we suspend the problematic of 'Asia' in the 'new Asian museum' by accentuating its 'newness', then what makes it 'new'? Simply the addition of a new body of work from Asian countries that can compete with 'the best in the West' – is this 'new Asia' not another exoticization of the contemporary? How else can the 'new' be problematized? Perhaps we can begin by deconstructing the colonial and imperial legacies of 'old museums', which remain disturbingly uncontested in actual practice, despite the increasing evidence of the loot which is synonymous with the display of Asian artefacts and artworks in almost all the leading museums in Europe and the Americas. There is also the increasingly shady mediation of auction houses, which have succeeded in 'laundering' loot, at times by selling it back to their rightful owners. So how does the 'new Asian museum' position itself in relation to this history of loot? Here, there can be no coyness through the elision of responsibility: 'The loot is not of our times, so what can we do about it? How can we be held responsible for the peripheral activities of colonial agencies? It's all in the past anyway. And besides, that past is our global multicultural present.' Is 'contemporary Asian art' then a new camouflage for the diffidence in dealing with loot? Or is it a compensation for the wrong doings of the past? If this seems unduly cynical, we should keep in mind the devious and hypocritical strategies by which loot can be – and, indeed, has been – transformed into intellectual property. Loot can also be legitimized on multicultural grounds: First, you loot a country of its treasures, you display what appeals to you on the walls of your most established museums, you bury the rest in the warehouses, and then, when the time is ripe for a bit of museum expansion, the buried treasures can be exhumed for the edification of Asian immigrants in order to reconnect them to their lost cultural heritages. Such multicultural logic is vicious in its self-righteous duplicities and should no longer be endorsed through silence, indifference or, worse still, a resurgence of lapsed patriotism for one's country of origin.

The 'new Asian museum', it seems to me, could benefit from radicalizing its agenda beyond the display of artworks from Asia. Here, it would be useful to reinscribe the tensions between the 'civil' and 'political' dimensions of society in order to enhance the oppositional potentiality to the new institutionalization of culture in our times. While museums are traditionally located within the domain of civil society, they are increasingly more insulated from the emergent cultures of struggle in political society, cutting across nations, languages and constituencies, which are succeeding in bringing together unprecedented alliances of activists, environmentalists and cultural workers, who are substantially redefining the very grounds of intercultural meeting, dialogue and practice.

At the start of the new millennium, it would be useful to widen the boundaries of civil society beyond the contestatory claims of its acknowledged participants; we need to recognize the challenge posed to the bastions of 'high culture' in civil society, notably museums, by the new incursions and configurations of public culture in national and global forums. Museums need to confront the insularity of their implicit 'non-trespassing' zones, which have in effect denied vast sections of the population, particularly from the minority and immigrant sectors, not merely access to the museum, but the right to interrogate its assumed privileges and reading of history.

It is my plea that instead of shutting ourselves up in the box – whether it is the 'black box' of theatre, or the ultra-white, air-conditioned, dust-free box of the museum – that we should open ourselves to those seemingly disruptive energies 'beyond the box' that can enable us to forge new links between the public and the private, the civil and the political. Only then will it be possible to 'twist' the box, if not to collapse its sides altogether, thereby preventing the 'new Asian museum' from becoming yet another front for the promotion of the contemporary Asian market. What we need is not a new museumization of museums, but a new socialization of its radical possibilities.

Cybersublime
Representing the Unrepresentable in Digital Art and Politics

JOHN BYRNE

On Thursday, 3 September 1998, the Mediated Nations Panel of the Ninth International Symposium of Electronic Arts (ISEA98) was joined via a live link by the Kurdish satellite station Med TV. For one hour, a special broadcast of the regular programme *Zaningeha Med* (University Med)[1] took the form of a discussion programme focusing on the impact of technology on cultural identity. Using phone-in, fax and e-mail interactivity, guests in Med TV's Belgian studios (who included the programme's producer and host Joe Cooper, Gilane Tawadros, Director of inIVA, Mustafa Rasid, specialist in Kurdish folklore and computer engineering and the artist Simon Tegala) were joined, via phone, by Professor Amir Hassanpour of the Department of Near and Middle Eastern

Civilization at the University of Toronto, and by Dee Dee Halleck and José Carlos Mariátegui, who phoned in questions from the panel session in Liverpool, UK. According to the October 1998 edition of Med TV's *Sterka Med* newsletter:[2]

> The unique nature of the event meant that the broadcasting agency of a stateless nation was participating in a section of an international conference. For Hikmet Tabak, then Director of Med TV, the venture showed 'how Med TV is involving itself in the academic debates on the interaction between technology and culture'. As we enter the millennium, according to Tabak, Med TV provides 'a wonderful example of how the satellite technology of the modern world, so often seen as an implement to abolish cultural differences, can also be a tool to preserve them'.[3]

During the post-broadcast debate in Liverpool, a member of the audience raised the question of what he perceived to be the programme's poor production standards. What, he asked, was the point of a minority Kurdish broadcasting agency imitating the kinds of programmes made by the BBC? Surely, part of the issue for such broadcasting agencies was to find their own way of producing programmes, one which would represent, more clearly, the station's own specificity. This, to a greater or lesser degree, was a fair point to make and engendered some lively debate among the audience who stayed to watch the show. However, as it transpired some time later, there were other less medium-specific reasons for the 'quality' of the programme. To put it simply, due to newsworthy developments which were happening in Turkish Kurdistan, Med TV's journalistic responsibilities to a Kurdish diaspora across the footprint of Hotbird 4 (Europe, the Middle East, North Africa and large parts of the former Soviet Union) came before the broadcast of a minority arts and cultural programme in English. In a paradoxical way, our questioner was probably more accurate than he could have imagined.

Some months later, while browsing through the Documenta X catalogue, *Politics–Poetics*,[4] I came by chance across two articles by Jean-François Lyotard on the Algerian crisis. Intrigued by the appearance of these texts, I consulted the introduction to *Documenta X: Short Guide*. The introduction informed me that

> In the age of globalization and of the sometimes violent social, economic, and cultural transformations it entails, contemporary artistic practices, condemned for their supposed meaninglessness or 'nullity' by the likes of Jean Baudrillard, are in fact a vital source of imaginary and symbolic representations whose diversity is irreducible to the (near) total economic domination of the real.[5]

What struck me here was a certain set of assumptions; the 'likes' of Baudrillard, the 'age of globalization' and the presumption of radical social and cultural transformation. However much I may sympathize with a utopian political role and function for art (whatever that may be), such assumptions, like the question levelled at Med TV's production standards, are obviously questions of representation themselves. Questions of representation at the level of assumption, at the level of common sense, at the level of reality.

Intriguingly enough, the two articles embedded in the Documenta X catalogue are, like Lyotard's later writings on the sublime and the differend,[6] about a western inability to represent. In both essays, taken from 'The social content of the Algerian struggle' and 'Algerian contradictions exposed' (originally published in 1958 and 1959 respectively), Lyotard questioned both the legitimacy and the possibility for the French left wing to account for the complexity and diversity of the Algerian crisis. More specifically he took, as his core critical concern, the inability of the French left wing to account for the complexity and diversity of the Algerian crisis without the paradoxical imposition of inadequate, misrepresentative and colonialist terms.[7]

In the light of this, what follows is, from my partial and western perspective, an attempt to re-map some of the co-ordinates which have haunted the perennial problematic of representation and the production of identities and subjectivities in the western tradition. More specifically, I would like to readdress the general relationship between art and politics as they have mutated in and between the cultural shift from analogue to digital forms of production, reproduction and exchange. Finally, I would like to take the opportunity to begin to make sense of, and to offer a way of reading, the use of technology that was Med TV.

For Martin Heidegger, the modern age was demarcated by its ability to conceive of itself in terms of its own world picture. Modernity also signalled the move from art to aesthetics which, for Heidegger, also meant that the artwork became the mere object of subjective experience and, consequently, an expression of human life. Here, Heidegger was referring to the development of the meaning of the terms 'art' and 'aesthetics' which took place in western philosophy of the eighteenth century. The European eighteenth century also established classificatory systems of knowledge, and the now common distinction between the empirical accuracy of science and the subjective and incalculable domain of taste. For Heidegger, this modern distinction has its roots in the earlier establishment of Cartesian ratiocination as the basis for all forms of empirical scientific mapping. It is only with the development of modernity, as that period which can imagine itself as a world picture, that truth becomes determined by scientific certainty and that certainty itself comes to be located in the subject which measures.

In the light of this, the realm of the aesthetic, from Kant onward, becomes key to defending the concept of individual subjectivity from its own imminent collapse into processes of scientific representation. In other words, if a Cartesian subject, whose presence to itself is predicated upon the exteriority and otherness of that which it measures and represents, regresses, via a solipsistic and narcissistic twist, into the ultimate subject of its own operations of mapping, then how can this subject guarantee, any longer, the truth of its own objectivity? It is at this philosophical juncture that art, the aesthetic and the sublime (in the Kantian sense of an experience which lies beyond our means of representation but, however, requires us to try) begin to function as the palpable borders of a reductive positivism which, if it were to encroach any further on such matters, would simultaneously deny its own possibility of meaning.

Heidegger wanted to trace back the roots of this impasse – the separation of idealism and materialism in the respective philosophical programmes of Plato and Aristotle – in order to think through the ontological nature of Being in a way that is not made possible by either school of thought. He did this by conceiving of both metaphysical idealism and scientific technologism as a 'forgetting' of being – a forgetting which has led to the alienation of modern man from himself within a barbaric, consumerist society. The irreducibility of the authentic work of art marked, for Heidegger, the resistance of Being itself to the representative and reproductive machinations of Cartesian self-identification.[8] So the thinker and the poet became, for him, those through whom Being represents itself or is spoken – a condition of responsibility which is opposed to the invasive discourses of a predatory science.

The work of art then comes to signal, for both Walter Benjamin and Heidegger, resistance to a form of reproduction. The artwork promises, in this denial, the possibility of another, yet unimagined form of communicability, one which would destroy the 'tradition' of a reproducibility or mapping which is, of necessity, predicated on the supplementary *a priori* exile of bourgeois subjectivity. That subjectivity that remains secure only in so far as it lacks identity with that which it must produce. In short, the resistance of the authentic work of art is a truly destructive and revolutionary cry for the collapsing of high and low culture into a radically new form of reproducibility and communicability which would finally readmit a truly permeable subjectivity into the discursive matrix of its own identity.

But this radical cry from the 1930s, this utopian resistance of the work of art in the modern age of industrialized analogue production, reproduction and exchange is dispersed, all too quickly, across the complex network of choices and refusals which characterize the cultural shift to the Post. In the period since 1945, the ideological function of representation, in the form of an emancipatory digital dream which needs no referent, begins to mutate into a nightmare of third order simulation which is haunted, in advance, by the ghost of a subjectivity which it cannot afford to kill. Under such conditions, how would one begin to reconcile the relationship between art and politics in the digital age?

In order to identify more clearly some of the problematics inherent in such a broad, complex and fundamental question, I would like to return briefly to the catalogue to Documenta X. More specifically, I would like to quote the final paragraph of rationale/disclaimer which is to be found on the inside of the book's dust jacket: 'This book is necessarily incomplete, and necessarily biased by the subjectivity of those who contributed to it. Even more, it is internally fissured by the attitudes of utopian or critical intransigence which characterise the relations of art to the real.'[9] This is not to say that I don't find the catalogue either good or interesting. On the contrary, I find it both. What I am trying to point to is a set of contradictory conditions whereby 'intransigence', either utopian or critical, is used to characterize *relations* of art to the real. In doing so, the relative separation of art and life is critically maintained. However, the difference may now be that, rather than occupying a privileged position in cultural discourse, it is an antinomy which has simply become one among others.

> While others worry about the media destroying national identity, MED-TV is proving that the opposite can be the case, even in the worst of circumstances. It is a remarkable unifying force, bringing together – perhaps in itself creating – a nation.[10]

As stated at the beginning of this article, Med TV was a minority-language satellite TV station which had its main office based in London's Regent Street and its major production studios in Belgium. Privately owned and funded by the Kurdish Foundation Trust (an organization that funds educative and relief projects in the Kurdish community around the world) and private investors, under the strict guidelines of the UK's Independent Television Commission (ITC), Med TV was a unique international enterprise, a shoestring operation relying heavily on volunteers but broadcasting across Europe, the Middle East and North Africa. Med TV brought Kurdish broadcasting to the scattered Kurdish nation.

In the 1930s, Britain and France created a set of borders which divide Kurdistan into four, splitting Turkish Kurds from Kurds in Iran, Iraq and Syria. Limiting the use of the Kurdish languages has been part of the policy of those governments which oppress the Kurds. On the 30 March 1995, Med TV began to broadcast the images of singers from the Yerevan radio, whom many Kurds had heard but never seen. Prior to this date, Yerevan radio was the only regular broadcasting that Kurds had been able to hear in their own tongue. Transmitted from Armenia in the days of Soviet control, the station mainly transmitted news of Cold War politics but it also broadcast Kurdish traditional music. Although Med TV had called neither a press conference, nor issued any press release, on the first day of its broadcast, according to former director Hikmet Tabak, 'by word of mouth Kurds were waiting in front of their TV in anticipation'.[11]

As the sole existing Kurdish language broadcaster, its objective was the promotion of Kurdish language and culture. As such, Med TV sought to provide a familiar broadcast diet of news, entertainment and cultural programming to a dispossessed Kurdish diaspora. For Tabak, some of the issues that were raised by Med TV highlighted the problems of a region which is still struggling to define its relationship to western powers and the technology of the West. Satellite technology, for him, allowed Kurds to re-examine their past in a way they never thought possible. As Dr Amir Hassanpour of the University of Toronto has commented, 'Med TV has created an audiovisual culture, through satellite technology, that has crossed borders and created a national, or rather, a trans-national audience'.[12]

Med TV's objectives were neither to circumscribe nor to contain an identity that was geographically reducible to a nation or state: sovereignty has been denied historically to the Kurdish peoples. Instead, Estella Schmid, co-ordinator of the Kurdistan Solidarity Committee, said in a 1999 press interview, 'we didn't have a homeland but we had a Kurdish nation on the airwaves'.[13] In this sense, at least, Med TV functioned as the inversion of Baudrillard's map of hyperreality. For Baudrillard, the territory of the real has faded away, leaving us, as a society, mourning the loss of a referent which had once anchored our knowledge and saved us from being washed into a sea of meaningless spectacle. Med TV's function, on the contrary, was to produce just those political iden-tities, and weave those referents across the airwaves, whose reality was denied to them by external forces. How can one begin, even speculatively, to represent this complex project which, by defying the technological collapse of identity into endless digital indifference, itself defies reduction to the colonial imposition of an abstract term or political predicate. And how, in the digital age, can one begin to approach terms such as 'identity' and 'referent' without equally run-ning the risk of a politically conservative return to repressive modernist para-digms? In order to begin this undertaking, I want to examine some writings of Jean-François Lyotard, concerning the sublime, the avant-garde and the post-modern condition, to test their critical and political legitimacy in accounting for the presentable, the unpresentable and the political in the digital age.

Writing in 'Answering the question: what is postmodernism?'[14] Lyotard attempts to address directly the problematic of sustaining 'the severe re-examination which postmodernity imposes on the thought of the Enlighten-ment',[15] while simultaneously avoiding the familiar collapse of postmodern diversity into the fragmentation of eclecticism. He does this by conceiving postmodernity as a form of resistance. Principally, this resistance was to be applied to any type of neo-conservative manoeuvre which sought to dismiss the technical radicalism of modernity and to reimpose an ideological link between language and an external referent. However, Lyotard also sought to transcend re-appropriations of modernism, such as those found in Habermas, whereby the 'gap' between cognitive, ethical, political and aesthetic discourses could be bridged by a new kind of experience, or aesthetics, capable of opening up the way to a unified experience. In order to do this, Lyotard, like Benjamin, began by reassessing what he saw as the pivotal impact of reproductive technologies on the means of representation in the nineteenth and twentieth centuries. Equally, like the author of the 1936 essay, 'The work of art in the age of mechanical reproduction', Lyotard saw no critical value residing in the revolutionary nature of the technologies themselves, but only in the challenge they raised to the regulatory discourse of representational realism:

Industrial photography and cinema will be superior to painting and the novel whenever the objective is to stabilize the referent, to arrange it according to a point of view which endows it with a recognizable meaning, to reproduce the syntax and vocabulary which enable the addressee to decipher images quickly, and so to arrive easily at the consciousness of his own identity as well as the approval he thereby receives from others – since the structures of images and sequences constitute a communication code among all of them.[16]

This argument enables Lyotard, if somewhat oversimplistically, to identify consensus as the enemy of avant-garde radicalism and to place realism as a tool in the repressive hands of totalitarian party politics. Here, any attack on experimentation is, when undertaken in the name of the party, inherently reactionary. Likewise, any aesthetic judgements made under such conditions of general consensus would be formal judgements, in the Kantian sense, according to which the only decision to be made would be whether or not a particular work conforms to an accepted standard of beauty. However, for Lyotard, when the power is no longer the totalitarian party but capital, the transavantgardism and eclecticism of such critics as Achille Bonito Oliva and Charles Jencks become the solution. Here, art begins to imitate the fragmentary nature of its patron's tastes and, in the period of 'anything goes', art becomes assessed by profit. For Lyotard, such realism accommodates all needs and art itself becomes threatened not only by cultural policy but by the whims of the market.

In the same way, for Lyotard, science under capitalism is equally culturally constrained. Science does not match up to its ideological gloss of freedom and innovation, but produces objects and initiatives whose function is measured solely in terms of improved performance. Therefore, scientific developments within capitalism merely convey the rule which supports their own possibility – the rule that there is no reality (once again) unless testified to as a consensus between parties. Such consensus, necessary for the propagation of science, technology, art and capital as 'performance' is, for Lyotard, a flight from the questioning of Enlightenment modernity which made scientific innovation a possibility in the first instance. For Lyotard, 'Modernity, in whatever age it appears, cannot exist without a shattering of belief and without discovery of the "lack of reality" of reality, together with the invention of other realities'.[17] This 'lack of reality', we are told, is close to the Kantian sublime and present in the negativity of the avant-garde.

For Meaghan Morris,[18] there are obvious critical, theoretical and political drawbacks to a postmodern re-institution of a term more frequently associated with Kant and Burke. Not the least of these is that Lyotard, in denouncing the 'wanton yet dreary limbo of our times', could himself be accused of initiating a '(revived) Methodist revival'. How else, asks Morris, could we initially receive Lyotard's position as being anything other than 'both fundamentalist, and Pro-testant'.[19] However, Morris resists simply circumscribing the sublime as a set of contemporary art discourses in Lyotard's name. Instead, she sets about a critical re-examination of the political potential of the sublime itself as a discourse on historical experience to which Lyotard has contributed. In doing so, Morris is able to readdress Lyotard's use of the sublime in the broader context of his philosophical work.

Initially, Morris likens Lyotard's use of the 'sublime' as 'lack of reality' and the invention of new realities to the role and function of a paralogism in science or philosophy. Paralogism is a formal trope in philosophy, 'the unexpected move in a politics of opinion', 'the traditional imperative to break with tradition'. Morris argues that Lyotard distinguishes the figure of 'true paralogism' as 'a "move" of formal fallacy made to enable further thought and thus a displacement in the pragmatics of knowledge, from "innovation" understood as a requirement of a given system to improve its efficiency'.[20] By appropriating for postmodernism a gesture classically associated with the avant-garde, Lyotard has, for Morris, achieved two key critical aims. First, the traditional role and function of the avant-garde becomes secured even at a time of 'post' rhetorics which predicate themselves on an escape from such modernist traditions. Second, and more crucially, Lyotard conserves the possibility of rejecting the academicization of art which will, henceforth, be called modernism. This is achieved by Lyotard's insistence that the sublime avant-garde act, as a moment of historical rupture, is the recurring moment of postmodernism. At this moment, that which has come before can be understood with the certainty of a consensus and, as such, becomes consigned to the modern historical past. The advantage of this, for Morris, is that it undermines the persistent normative opposition made between *modernism* as a problematic of self-reference, purism, ontological preoccupation and concern with media specificity, and *postmodernism* (avant-gardism) as an insistence on problems of reference. The disadvantage of this, for Morris, is that it runs the risk of turning the avant-garde gesture into a 'rough equivalent of the Human Condition for the age of incredulity' and turning 'the whole matter of "Postmodernism" into an elaborate joke'.[21]

In the face of such ontological and humanistic difficulties, Morris turns to Lyotard's earlier and more developed writings on the unpresentable, the indeterminate and the inexpressible, concerned more with issues of reference and the strategic definitions of reality than with inspiration, self-expression or the ineffable. Morris specifies the Lyotard of *The Differend* as prepared to defend the reality of the Holocaust in the face of revisionist historians like Robert Faurisson, who claim that it did not take place. However, Morris does not view this as a political and historical retreat to common sense in Lyotard's work. Instead, Morris argues that, for Lyotard 'the annihilation named Auschwitz now requires a formal transformation of what counts as history and as reality, and in our understanding of reference and the function of the proper name'.[22] It is now those historians who argue that the Holocaust never happened who have pushed common-sense notions of reality and evidence to an extreme. Rather than argue that annihilation included the annihilation of evidence, they argue that if there is now no evidence it is because it didn't happen. As Morris points out, this is an argument which may confuse anyone who associates reality-values with the left, and formalism with explicit or implicit conservatism.

It is at this point, for Lyotard, that the differend itself becomes one of the names of incommensurability. If no common ground can be found in a dispute between two or more parties, and the imposition of a final ruling may wrong one of the parties by the application of inappropriate criteria, then victimization is the result. From this basic premise, as Morris points out, Lyotard rapidly expands the scope of the differend by subjecting it to constant enquiry. The differend becomes constitutive of victimization if a victim (like those of the Holocaust) has not only been wronged but has also been deprived of the means to prove it. The differend becomes the lack of ability to prove that a wrong ever took place because the terms of what counts as proof have been changed, withdrawn or are simply deemed inapplicable to a particular situation. The differend becomes that which cannot be presented, that which cannot be expressed, that which hovers in the spaces between legitimized discourses and carries with it the imperative to have it said. It becomes, for Lyotard, the imperative for historians to break the rules of their cognitive regimes and to listen to that which cannot be presented within their own reality.

On 23 April 1999, the ITC, Britain's regulatory body for television and radio, formally served Med TV a final notice revoking its licence to broadcast. The statute was to come into effect twenty-eight days later and, until then, the service was to remain suspended. Med TV's licence had originally been suspended on 22 March 1999, under Section 45A of the 1990 Broadcasting Act, following four broadcasts which allegedly included inflammatory statements encouraging 'acts of violence in Turkey and elsewhere'. According to the ITC, these broadcasts were 'likely to encourage or incite crime or lead to disorder'[23] counter to the 1990 and 1996 Broadcasting Acts. According to the diplomatic editor of the *Guardian* newspaper, the closure of Med TV followed repeated accusations by the Turkish government that Med TV supported the Kurdish Workers Party or PKK, whose leader, Abdulha Ocalan, was seized in Kenya earlier in the year and returned to Turkey to stand trial for treason.[24] Other reasons for the station's closure widely reported in the UK media included the suggestion of a conflict of interest: Sir Robin Biggam, Chairman of the ITC, is also a board member of British Aerospace, who have extensive contracts with Turkey.[25] Moreover, Turkey was to be an important NATO ally in the renewed conflict in the Balkans during the same period. However, judging the political, social and economic legitimacy of Med TV's closure is not at all the point here. To deal in such broad terms as 'Turkey', 'PKK' and 'treason' – the necessary language game of political journalism – is exactly to fall into the trap, outlined by Lyotard in his articles on Algeria, of enforcing abstract representations on a diffuse and complex situation which defies the imposition of external consensus.

Med TV was a unique set of communicative possibilities. It provided an identity to a diasporan, stateless nation. This identity was not fixed, but was the shifting and developing result of a dynamic and ongoing debate held through the airwaves and across the traditionally mapped inscriptions of national borders. It would be simple enough to describe this activity as sublime, on the grounds that its scale and complexity defies the limited powers of description of any one commentator, but that would be colonialism in the name of the avant-garde. Rather, I want to suggest that in ensuing debates surrounding Med TV and any other communicative initiatives – be they political, artistic or both – we need not only to assess the measurable outcomes of audience figures and political influence but also to analyse the necessity of constantly renegotiating the borders between terms like sublimity and representation. Equally, we must also remain alert to the voice of the differend (or however we choose to describe it): to the cultural, ideological and political gap where Med TV, and the voice of the overlooked and dispossessed, can sometimes be heard most clearly in their struggle to have something said. Finally, we must also be constantly and critically vigilant when giving substance, in any language of representation, to the unpresentable and the unspeakable in the futures we wish to build.

Theodor Adorno pointed to this when, in his original manuscript for *Minima Moralia*, he speculated on the conception and function of the term genocide. For Adorno the unspeakable, when named and codified in the International Declaration of Human Rights, 'was made, for the sake of protest, commensurable'.[26] Adorno contemplated what would happen if the United Nations were to debate the subject of whether or not a new atrocity should come under the heading of genocide. Would such a decision imply that member states should intervene on behalf of the international community? If so, would such an intervention be against their own interests? If this were the case, would a debate ensue and, as a result of the difficulty of applying the term genocide in practice, would the term be removed from the statutes altogether? Soon afterwards, Adorno speculated, there would be 'inside page headlines in journalese: East Turkestan genocide programme nears completion'.[27]

Against the Double Blackmail

SLAVOJ ŽIŽEK

The following pages contain Slavoj Žižek's original text for the exhibition 'Against the Double Blackmail' at the Cubitt Gallery, London, 7–28 May 1999. The English text was sent via e-mail to the gallery where it was enlarged to A1 size, installed and broadcast from a radio transmitter set up by the North American artist Gregory Green.

Electronic media have formed a vital part of the cultural landscape of the Balkan conflict, and such tactical media have now become important to the ways in which network artists understand the relationship between art and politics. Žižek's participation, and the use of radio, recalls the use of Net radio technologies during the siege of

Sarajevo and more recently the closure of Radio B92 by the Serbian authorities. In both cases, some art organizations and galleries have provided resources and public spaces for an inquiry into the meanings of democracy in contemporary arts, media and culture. The interventionist aesthetic of tactical media *breaks down Anglo-Saxon cultural boundaries between the academic and the journalistic, the political and the creative; its unfinished prose the signifier of its urgency. A new media art: technology in the service of political passion.*

The winner in the contest for the greatest blunder of 1998 was a Latin-American patriotic terrorist who sent a letter bomb to a US consulate in order to protest against the American interference in the local politics. As a conscientious citizen, he wrote on the envelope his return address; however, he did not put enough stamps on it, so that the post returned the letter to him. Forgetting what he put in it, he opened it and blew himself to death – a perfect example of how, ultimately, a letter always arrives at its destination. And is not something quite similar happening to the Slobodan Milošević regime with the recent NATO bombing? For years, Milošević was sending letter bombs to his neighbours, from the Albanians to Croatia and Bosnia, keeping himself out of the conflict while igniting fire all around Serbia – finally, his last letter returned to him. Let us hope that the result of the NATO intervention will be that Milošević will be proclaimed the political blunderer of the year.

And there is a kind of poetic justice in the fact that the West finally intervened apropos of Kosovo – let us not forget that it was there that it all began, with the ascension to power of Milošević: this ascension was legitimized by the promise to amend the underprivileged situation of Serbia within the Yugoslav federation, especially with regard to the Albanian 'separatism'. Albanians were Milošević's first target; afterwards, he shifted his wrath onto other Yugoslav republics (Slovenia, Croatia, Bosnia), until, finally, the focus of the conflict returned to Kosovo – as in a closed loop of destiny, the arrow returned to the one who lanced it by way of setting free the spectre of ethnic passions. This is the key point worth remembering: Yugoslavia did not start to disintegrate when the Slovene 'secession' triggered the domino-effect (first Croatia, then Bosnia, Macedonia . . .); it was already at the moment of Milošević's constitutional reforms in 1987, depriving Kosovo and Vojvodina of their limited autonomy, that the fragile balance on which Yugoslavia rested was irretrievably disturbed. From that moment onwards, Yugoslavia continued to live only because it didn't yet notice it was already dead – it was like the proverbial cat in the cartoons walking over the precipice, floating in the air, and falling down only when it becomes aware that it has no ground under its feet. From Milošević's seizure of power in Serbia onwards, the only actual chance for Yugoslavia to survive was to reinvent its formula: either Yugoslavia under Serb domination or some form of radical decentralization, from a loose confederacy to the full sovereignty of its units.

It is thus easy to praise the NATO bombing of Yugoslavia as the first case of an intervention, not into the confused situation of a civil war, but into a country with full sovereign power. Is it not comforting to see the NATO forces intervene not for any specific economico-strategic interests, but simply because a country is cruelly violating the elementary human rights of an ethnic group? Is not this the only hope in our global era – to see some internationally acknowledged force as a guarantee that all countries will respect a certain minimum of ethical (and, hopefully, also health, social, ecological) standards? However, the situation is more complex, and this complexity is indicated already in the way NATO justifies its intervention: the violation of human rights is always accompanied by the vague but ominous reference to 'strategic interests'. The story of NATO as the enforcer of the respect for human rights is thus only one of the two coherent stories that can be told about the recent bombings of Yugoslavia, and the problem is that each story has its own rationale. The second story concerns the other side of the much-praised new global ethical politics in which one is allowed to violate the state sovereignty on behalf of the violation of human rights. The first glimpse into this other side is provided by the way western media selectively elevate some local 'warlord' or dictator into the embodiment of Evil: Sadam Hussein, Milošević, up to the unfortunate (now forgotten) Aidid in Somalia – at every point, it is or was 'the community of civilized nations against . . .'. And on what criteria does this selection rely? Why Albanians in Serbia and not also Palestinians in Israel, Kurds in Turkey, etc. etc.? Here, of course, we enter the shady world of international capital and its strategic interests.

According to the 'Project CENSORED', the top censored story of 1998 was that of a half-secret international agreement in working, called MAI (the Multilateral Agreement on Investment). The primary goal of MAI will be to protect the foreign interests of multinational companies. The agreement will basically undermine the sovereignty of nations by assigning power to the corporations almost equal to those of the countries in which these corporations are located. Governments will no longer be able to treat their domestic firms more favourably than foreign firms. Furthermore, countries that do not relax their environmental, land-use and health and labour standards to meet the demands of foreign firms may be accused of acting illegally. Corporations will be able to sue sovereign states if they impose too severe ecological or other standards – under NAFTA (which is the main model for MAI), Ethyl Corporation is already suing Canada for banning the use of its gasoline additive MMT. The greatest threat is, of course, to the developing nations, which will be pressured into depleting their natural resources for commercial exploitation. Renato Ruggerio, Director of the World Trade Organization, the sponsor of MAI, is already hailing this project, elaborated and discussed in a clandestine manner, with almost no public discussion and media attention, as the 'constitution for a new global economy'. And, in the same way in which, already for Marx, market relations provided the true foundation for the notion of individual freedoms and rights, *this* is also the obverse of the much-praised new global morality celebrated even by some neo-liberal philosophers as signalling the beginning of the new era in which the international community will establish and enforce some minimal code preventing sovereign states from engaging in crimes against humanity even within their own territory. And the recent catastrophic economic situation in Russia, far from being the heritage of old socialist mismanagement, is a direct result of this global capitalist logic embodied in MAI.

This other story also has its ominous military side. The ultimate lesson of the last American military interventions, from the Operation Desert Fox against Iraq to the bombing of Yugoslavia, is that they signal a new era in military history – battles in which the attacking force operates under the constraint that it can sustain no casualties. When the first stealth fighter fell down in Serbia, the emphasis of the American media was that there were no casualties – the pilot was SAVED! (This concept of 'war without casualties' was elaborated by General Colin Powell.) And was not the counterpoint to it the almost surreal way CNN reported on the war: not only was it presented as a TV event, but the Iraqis themselves seemed to treat it this way – during the day, Baghdad was a 'normal' city, with people going about their normal business, as if war and bombardment was an irreal, nightmarish spectre that occurred only during the night and did not take place in effective reality.

Let us recall what went on in the final American assault on the Iraqi lines during the Gulf War: no photos, no reports, just rumours that tanks with bulldozer-like shields in front of them rolled over Iraqi trenches, simply burying thousands of troops in earth and sand. What went on was allegedly considered too cruel in its sheer mechanical efficiency, too different from the standard notion of a heroic face-to-face combat, that images would perturb public opinion too much, and a total censorship black-out was strictly imposed. Here we have the two aspects joined together: the new notion of war as a purely technological event, taking place behind radar and computer screens, with no casualties, *and* the extreme physical cruelty too unbearable for the gaze of the media – not the crippled children and raped women, victims of caricaturized local ethnic 'fundamentalist warlords', but thousands of nameless soldiers, victims of nameless, efficient technological warfare. When Jean Baudrillard made the claim that the Gulf War did not take place, this statement could also be read in the sense that such traumatic pictures that stand for the Real of this war were totally censured . . .

How, then, are we to think these two stories together, without sacrificing the truth of each of them? What we have here is a political example of the famous drawing in which we recognize the contours either of a rabbit head or of a goose head, depending on our mental focus. If we look at the situation in a certain way, we see the international community enforcing minimal human rights standards on a nationalist neo-communist leader engaged in ethnic cleansing, ready to ruin his own nation just to retain power. If we shift the focus, we see NATO, the armed hand of the new capitalist global order, defending the strategic interests of the capital in the guise of a disgusting travesty, posing as a disinterested enforcer of human rights, attacking a sovereign country which, in spite of the problematic nature of its regime, nonetheless acts as an obstacle to the unbridled assertion of the New World Order.

However, what if one should reject this double blackmail (if you are against NATO strikes, you are for Milošević's proto-fascist regime of ethnic cleansing; and if you are against Milošević, you support the global capitalist New World Order)? What if this very opposition between enlightened international intervention against ethnic fundamentalists and the heroic last pockets of resistance against the New World Order is a false one? What if phenomena like the Milošević regime are not the opposite of the New World Order, but rather its *symptom*, the place at which the hidden *truth* of the New World Order emerges? Recently, one of the American negotiators said that Milošević is not only part of the problem, but rather *the* problem itself. However, was this not clear *from the very beginning*? Why, then, the interminable procrastination of the western powers, playing for years into Milošević's hands, acknowledging him as a key factor of stability in the region, misreading clear cases of Serb aggression as civil or even tribal warfare, initially putting the blame on those who immediately saw what Milošević stands for and, for that reason, desperately wanted to escape his grasp (see James Baker's public endorsement of a 'limited military intervention' against Slovene secession), supporting the last Yugoslav Prime Minister Ante Marković, whose programme was, in an incredible case of political blindness, seriously considered as the last chance for a democratic market-oriented unified Yugoslavia, etc. etc.? When the West fights Milošević, it is *not* fighting its enemy, one of the last points of resistance against the liberal-democratic New World Order; it is rather fighting its own creature, a monster that grew as the result of the compromises and inconsistencies of the western politics itself. (And, incidentally, it is the same with Iraq: its strong position is also the result of the American strategy of containing Iran.) In the last decade, the West followed a Hamlet-like procrastination towards the Balkans, and the present bombardment has effectively all the signs of Hamlet's final murderous outburst in which a lot of people unnecessarily die (not only the King, his true target, but also his mother, Laertes, Hamlet himself . . .) because Hamlet acted too late, when the proper moment was already missed.

So the West, in the present intervention, which displays all the signs of a violent outburst of impotent aggressivity without a clear political goal, is now paying the price for the years of entertaining illusions that one can make a deal with Milošević: with the recent hesitations about the ground intervention in Kosovo, the Serbian regime is, under the pretext of war, launching the final assault on Kosovo and purging it of most of the Albanians, cynically accepting bombardments as the price to be paid. When the western powers repeat all the time that they are not fighting the Serb people, but only their corrupted leaders, they rely on the (typically liberal) wrong premise that Serbs are victims of their evil leadership personified in Milošević, manipulated by him. The painful fact is that the Serb aggressive nationalism enjoys the support of the large majority of the population – no, Serbs are not passive victims of nationalist manipulation, they are not Americans in disguise, just waiting to be delivered from the nationalist spell. On the other hand, this misperception is accompanied by the apparently contradictory notion according to which Balkan people are living in the past, fighting again and again old battles, perceiving the recent situation through old myths . . .

One is tempted to say that these two clichés should be precisely *turned around*: not only are people not 'good', since they let themselves be manipulated with obscene pleasure; there are also no 'old myths' which we need to study if we are really to understand the complex situation, just the *present* outburst of racist nationalism which, according to its needs, opportunistically resuscitates old myths. To paraphrase the old Clintonian motto: no, it's not the old myths and ethnic hatreds, it's the *political power struggle*, stupid!

So, on the one hand, we have the obscenities of the Serb state propaganda: they regularly refer to Clinton not as 'the American president', but as 'The American Führer'; two of the transparents on their state-organized anti-NATO demonstrations were 'Clinton, come here and be our Monica!' (i.e. suck our . . .), and 'Monica, did you also suck out his brain?' This is where the NATO planners got it wrong, caught in their schemes of strategic reasoning, unable to forecast that the Serb reaction to bombardment will be a recourse to a collective Bakhtinian carnivalization of the social life . . .

And the western counterpoint to this obscenity is the more and more openly racist tone of its reporting: when the three American soldiers were taken prisoners, CNN dedicated the first ten minutes of the news to their predicament (although everyone knew that *nothing* will happen to them!), and only then reported on the tens of thousands of refugees, burned villages and Priština turning into a ghost town. Where is the so-much-praised Serb 'democratic opposition' to protest *this* horror taking place in their own backyard, not only the – till now, at least – bombardments with relatively very low casualties?

The atmosphere in Belgrade is, at least for the time being, carnivalesque in a faked way – when they are not in shelters, people dance to rock or ethnic music on the streets, under the motto 'With music against bombs!', playing the role of the defying heroes (since they know that NATO does not really bomb civilian targets). Although it may fascinate some confused pseudo-leftists, this obscene carnivalization of the social life is effectively the other, public, face of ethnic cleansing: while in Belgrade people defiantly dance on the streets, 300 kilometres to the south, a genocide of African proportions is taking place.

It is interesting to watch in the last days the Serb satellite state TV which targets foreign public: no reports on atrocities in Kosovo, refugees are mentioned only as people fleeing the NATO bombing; the overall idea is that Serbia, the island of peace, the only place in ex-Yugoslavia that was not touched by the war raging all around it, is attacked by the NATO madmen destroying bridges and hospitals . . . So when, in the night-time, crowds are camping out on the Belgrade bridges, participating in pop and ethnic music concerts held there in a defiantly festive mood, offering their bodies as the live shield to prevent the bridges from being bombed, the answer to this faked pathetic gesture should be a very simple one: why don't you go to Kosovo and hold a rock carnival in the Albanian parts of Priština?

In the recent struggle of the so-called 'democratic opposition' in Serbia against the Milošević regime, the truly touchy topic is the stance towards Kosovo: as to this topic, the large majority of the 'democratic opposition' unconditionally endorses Milošević's anti-Albanian nationalist agenda, even accusing him of making compromises with the West and 'betraying' Serb national interests in Kosovo. In the course of the student demonstrations against Milošević's Socialist Party falsification of the election results in the winter of 1996, the western media, who closely followed the events and praised the revived democratic spirit in Serbia, rarely mentioned the fact that one of the regular slogans of the demonstrators against the special police forces was 'Instead of kicking us, go to Kosovo and kick out the Albanians!' In today's Serbia, the absolute *sine qua non* of an authentic political act would thus be to unconditionally reject the ideological topos of the 'Albanian threat to Serbia'.

In the last years, Serb propaganda is promoting the identification of Serbia as the second Israel, with Serbs as the chosen nation, and Kosovo as their West Bank where they fight, in the guise of 'Albanian terrorists', their own *intifada*. They went as far as repeating the old Israeli complaint against the Arabs: 'We will pardon you for what you did to us, but we will never pardon you for forcing us to do to *you* the horrible things we had to do in order to defend ourselves!' The hilariously mocking Serb apology for shooting down the stealth bomber was: 'Sorry, we didn't know you are invisible!' One is tempted to say that the answer to Serb complaints about the 'irrational barbaric bombing' of their country should be: 'Sorry, we didn't know you are a chosen nation!'

One thing is for sure: the NATO bombardment of Yugoslavia will change the global geopolitical co-ordinates. The unwritten pact of peaceful coexistence (the respect of each state's full sovereignty, i.e. non-interference in internal affairs, even in the case of the grave violation of human rights) is over. However, the very first act of the new global police force usurping the right to punish sovereign states for their wrongdoings already signals its end, its own undermining, since it immediately became clear that this universality of human rights as its legitimization is false, i.e. that the attacks on selective targets protect particular interests. The NATO bombardments of Yugoslavia also signal the end of any serious role for the UN and Security Council: it is NATO under US guidance that effectively pulls the strings. Furthermore, the silent pact with Russia that held till now is broken: in the terms of this pact, Russia was publicly treated as a superpower, allowed to maintain the appearance of being one, on condition that it did not effectively act as one. Now Russia's humiliation is open, any pretence of dignity is unmasked: Russia can only openly resist or openly comply with western pressure. The further logical result of this new situation will be, of course, the renewed rise of anti-western resistance from Eastern Europe to the Third World, with the sad consequence that criminal figures like Milošević will be elevated into the model fighters against the New World Order.

So the lesson is that the alternative between the New World Order and the neo-racist nationalists opposing it is a false one: these are the two sides of the same coin – the New World Order itself breeds the monstrosities that it fights. Which is why the protests against bombing from the reformed communist parties all around Europe, inclusive of PDS, are totally misdirected: these false protesters against the NATO bombardment of Serbia are like the caricaturized pseudo-leftists who oppose the trial against a drug dealer, claiming that his crime is the result of the social pathology of the capitalist system. The way to fight the capitalist New World Order is not by supporting local proto-fascist resistances to it, but to focus on the only serious question today: how to build *transnational* political movements and institutions strong enough to seriously constrain the unlimited rule of the capital, and to render visible and politically relevant the fact that the local fundamentalist resistances against the New World Order, from Milošević to Le Pen and the extreme right in Europe, are part of it?

Obscene from Any Angle

GEORGE RITZER

Over the last decade I have been thinking and writing about processes – McDonaldization, consumerism; and entities – fast-food restaurants, credit cards and the new means of consumption that can be seen as 'obscene powers'. From a modern perspective, all can be viewed as part of increasing external (especially corporate) control over our lives, especially as consumers, and as posing threats to 'social justice, human rights and democratic decision-making'. Of course, such a set of judgements implies that analysts are operating with an 'Archimedean point' that allows them to judge certain social phenomena 'obscene' in the sense that they are perceived as threats to foundational notions of what is social justice, what rights humans should possess and what counts as democratic decision-making. It is tempting to get into the difficulties, even impossibilities, of making such judgements in the age of the pre-eminence of postmodern perspectives, but that is already a road well travelled in the literature on postmodern social theory. Thus, instead of debating that issue at length at the beginning of this essay, I simply will operate, at least at first, as a modernist and discuss the degree to which the phenomena of concern here are 'obscene powers' in the sense described above. I will leave postmodern social theory, or at least one perspective derived from it, to the second section. Although I will offer some thoughts on the reconciliation of the two views, there is, as we will see, an apparent contradiction here between modern obscenity traceable to the invisibility of a wide range of problems and postmodern obscenity tied to hypervisibility.

When one casts aside postmodern doubts and equivocations, one is

immediately confronted with the problem of being overwhelmed by the obscenities associated with these processes and entities. There are so many that it is
difficult to decide which to discuss and in what order to discuss them. I will
manage to select a few and to present them in some sort of order, but before I do
I feel compelled to point out that these entities and processes are not without
their redeeming qualities. The vast majority of the 'haves' within advanced
societies eagerly embrace processes like McDonaldization and consumerism
and are anxious to eat in fast-food restaurants, utilize credit cards to their upper
limits and to shop and spend their leisure time in such new means of consumption as shopping malls, mega-malls, theme parks and cruise ships. The great
preponderance of 'have nots' within those societies would dearly love to change
places with the haves and to be more involved in these processes, to spend more
time in the new means of consumption and to have access to more credit cards
with higher credit limits. Similar desires characterize many of those in less
'advanced' societies who up to now have had little access to and experience with
these obscene powers. After all, even the seemingly ubiquitous McDonald's has
'only' managed, at last count, to make its way into 115 of the world's nations. In
short, most of those connected with these processes and entities are quite
content with them, and those with little or no involvement crave to be more
implicated in them.

Furthermore, these obscene powers have many redeeming qualities. To mention just a few – McDonaldization not only standardizes goods and services, but
serves to elevate the quality of one or both in some parts of the world;[1] consumerism serves to increase demand and lower price thereby bringing a wide
array of goods and services to an ever-increasing number of people; fast-food
restaurants bring a kind of McDonaldized diversity to parts of the world that
had heretofore been more monocultural as far as various kinds of foods are
concerned; credit cards are a boon to those consumers who pay their credit card
bills in full each month ('convenience users') and thereby get a month of 'free'
credit; and the new means of consumption offer large numbers of people spectacular settings which they can consume, and in which they can consume a wide
range of goods and services. In spite of the near-universal acceptance of these
entities and processes, and their many desirable aspects, I will focus in the first
section of this essay on what are, from a modern perspective, some of their most
obscene characteristics.

A MODERN VIEW: INVISIBLE WORLDS, INVISIBLE OBSCENITIES

From a modern point of view which emphasizes the need to get at the truth
hidden behind appearances, invisibility is central to the obscenity of the processes and entities of interest here. Many of their most 'obscene' qualities are
barely visible, even invisible, and thus it becomes necessary to reveal at least
some of those obscenities. It is the very lack of visibility of the workings of these
processes, to say nothing of the problems associated with them, that helps to

make them obscene. In fact, it is just those aspects of these processes and entities that are invisible that are likely to have the most negative impact on people. A discussion of this invisibility is not only important in itself, but it would also go a long way toward allowing us to ameliorate some of the greatest obscenities associated with them.

The spread of McDonald's and fast-food restaurants is obvious to all, but far less visible is the degree to which innumerable phenomena throughout the world have been McDonaldized.[2] (McDonaldization is defined as the process by which the principles that lie at the base of the fast-food restaurant – efficiency, predictability, calculability and control through the replacement of human with non-human technology – characterize more and more sectors of society and an increasing number of parts of the world.) McDonald's restaurants are themselves by design very obvious, as is the proliferation of those outlets as well as the similar spread of other American chains of fast-food restaurants. Far less visible, and perhaps even invisible, is the degree to which other social structures and settings are adopting and adapting these principles; the degree to which they are becoming McDonaldized. For example, the media are becoming increasingly McDonaldized as reflected in the success of *USA Today* ('McPaper') in the newspaper business and CNN Headline News on television. Then there is the *McDonaldization* of the university and the rise of what has been labelled by several scholars, 'McUniversity'.[3] The medical profession has experienced McDonaldization as reflected in the rise of hospital chains and the development of local, drive-in, no-appointment-necessary McDoctors. Within medicine, birth and death have been McDonaldized, as reflected in advanced technologies that allow us to choose the characteristics of our offspring ('designer babies') and to keep people alive almost indefinitely. While most of us are aware that the media, the university, medicine and many settings have changed, few see it as part of a wide-ranging process of McDonaldization. If we cannot connect these developments, how can we see that the problems associated with each are part of a broader process and a larger set of problems? Furthermore, the invisibility of the process makes it all-but-impossible to develop any sort of co-ordinated strategy for dealing with them.

Similarly invisible is the spread of McDonaldization to other cultures. Again, the incursion of McDonald's and other, largely American, chains into other societies is abundantly obvious, but what is not at all clear is the development of indigenous chains that emulate McDonald's and are based on the principles of McDonaldization. Examples abound including Juicy Burger in Beirut, with J.B. the clown standing in for Ronald McDonald, and the chain Russkoye Bistro in Russia, which is consciously modelled after McDonald's and regards it like an older brother. The most famous restaurant in Beijing – Quanjude Roast Duck Restaurant – sent its management staff to McDonald's in 1993 and then introduced its own 'roast duck fast food' in early 1994. In a sense, it is the largely invisible incursion of the principles of McDonaldization into local institutions that is a far greater threat to indigenous cultures than the spread of McDonald's itself (and other American fast-food restaurants) to other nations. After all,

McDonald's is, by design, highly visible and this is especially the case outside the United States. This visibility is reflected in the fact that McDonald's often becomes the target of protests, such as those that occurred in recent years in Yugoslavia over NATO bombing, and in France over US tariffs on French cheese. However, when local institutions McDonaldize, the process and its roots in the American chain become invisible to the indigenous population and ultimately to those who work in and even run those settings. It is far harder to see, let alone oppose, McDonaldization when it worms its way into local settings than when it takes the form of the importation of a McDonald's or Pizza Hut restaurant.

Yet, there is sense that even McDonald's becomes a part of local culture and, as a result, its role in a larger international process becomes invisible to the local population. For example, there are so many McDonald's restaurants in Japan, they have by now been around so long, and they have adapted in so many ways to Japanese culture, that many Japanese, especially children, now see McDonald's as a Japanese chain. Thus, when a Japanese boy scout arrived in Chicago on a tour he was surprised to find a McDonald's there; he thought McDonald's existed only in Japan and was a Japanese institution.[4] Such an infiltration into local culture makes it very difficult to see that the process, as well as the problems associated with it, are international in scope. However, it is still the incursion of the principles of McDonaldization into local settings that poses the greatest threat to local communities, largely because in that instance the process becomes so much more invisible.

Given the various ways in which McDonaldization has grown invisible, what are some of the major obscenities, or what I call irrationalities of rationality, associated with that process? We can start with homogenization, since if the process itself is invisible, then the degree to which it is homogenizing not only American culture but also culture around the world would also be invisible. McDonaldization involves a set of four basic principles and to the degree that those principles are applied more or less uniformly across areas of the United States or nations of the world, it is an homogenizing process. The appearance of McDonald's in every major nation in the world, and the application of those basic principles to indigenous restaurants and restaurant chains, makes for a great deal of uniformity in the ways in which people around the world eat as well as engage in other activities that have been similarly McDonaldized. While there are certainly many local adaptations, the basic principles are applied universally. To the degree that McDonaldization is invisible, the trend toward homogeneity is similarly imperceptible.

Another problem associated with McDonaldization is disenchantment. Pre-modern, non-rational settings tend to be more enchanted than their contemporary counterparts. A major factor in the progressive disenchantment of these settings, as Max Weber demonstrated long ago, is the process of rationalization, or what I have termed more contemporaneously McDonaldization, utilizing a different paradigm (the fast-food restaurant) than that used by Weber (the bureaucracy). While some McDonaldized settings make their lack of enchantment abundantly obvious – the basic structure of fast-food restaurants and 'warehouse' supermarkets and hardware stores come to mind – most seek to conceal the absence of enchantment behind a veil of simulated enchantment. Thus, while fast-food restaurants are bare, highly functional structures, they seek through various tie-ins to associate themselves with enchanted worlds. Particularly notable here is the relationship between McDonald's and Disney, especially the fact that McDonald's actively promotes, and thereby associates itself with, the 'magical world of Disney'. Such associations are designed to obscure the absence of enchantment in eating in a fast-food restaurant, especially from children who are so important to those restaurants both as consumers and as agents luring parents and other adults into these settings.

To take one more major irrationality, McDonaldized settings are highly dehumanized settings in which to eat (and in which to work in 'McJobs'). Yet, these settings strive to put on a human face in order to obscure the dehumanization that lies at their core. Thus, Wendy's has its founder, the avuncular Dave Thomas, serve as a major figure in most, if not all, of its TV ads. Kentucky Fried Chicken used to do the same thing with its founder, Colonel Sanders, but since he is long dead, it must be satisfied with a cartoon version of the 'Colonel'. While his face is somewhat obscured by greasepaint, the smiling and endlessly friendly Ronald McDonald plays this role for McDonald's. To take one other McDonaldized (or as Alan Bryman has argued, 'Disneyized')[5] setting, Disney World is a highly rationalized theme park which seeks to hide that fact behind the benign and friendly image of the long-dead Walt Disney himself, as well as the super-friendly (albeit scripted) actions of park employees, in and out of costume.

The list of obscenities associated with McDonaldization, but obscured by McDonaldized systems, could be greatly extended – environmental destruction hidden behind public relations campaigns and some reforms (often coerced by external forces), danger to people's health obscured by claims about the nutritional value of fast food and the token offering of more nutritional foods, lack of a hospitable environment hidden behind advertisements that seem to communicate a sense of community among those who dine in fast-food restaurants (in fact, fast-food restaurants are so inhospitable that a large proportion of diners use the drive-throughs and take their meals with them, perhaps eating them in their cars parked in the adjacent parking lot or while driving on to their next McDonaldized activity), and so on. Such hidden obscenities are very familiar to modernists, who often take as their task the tearing away of veils in order to reveal the irrationalities that lie just below the surface.

It should come as little surprise to anyone that we are just completing a decade in the United States (and other developed nations) of unprecedented economic growth fuelled by, and fuelling, rampant consumerism; hyperconsumerism. While this is hardly hidden from general view, many aspects of consumerism (some of which will be touched on below in discussions of specific aspects of our consumer society) are less visible, including, for example, the degree to which sectors we do not usually associate with consumerism have come to be affected (infected) by it. For example, while we do not usually think of college students (and their parents) as consumers of educational services, that is exactly what they are and there is evidence that they are coming to think of themselves increasingly as such. Similarly, hospital patients and those who use a wide range of other medical services are similarly thinking of themselves as consumers of medical sites and services. Changes like these mean that consumerism is leeching its way out of its well-known commercial domains and coming to affect increasing aspects of society. Thus, consumerism involves far more than shopping at the mall or at an e-tailer; it involves obtaining goods and services at universities, hospitals, as well as museums, athletic stadia and churches and synagogues. Largely hidden from view is the fact that consumerism has come to affect an ever-increasing number of structures and institutions. The result is that being a student is frequently no longer about getting a good education but getting a 'good deal'; going to the hospital may involve assessing the quality of the rooms and the food being served more than the skills of the medical staff; going to a ball game is often more about buying souvenirs and shopping in the various concession stands than it is about watching the game; and being involved in religion is sometimes more about participating in clubs, socials, trips and spectacular, albeit peripheral, events than it is about the 'religious experience'.

Similar obscenities, as well as efforts to conceal them, are associated with the other entities and processes of concern in this essay. Credit cards are presented by the banks and credit card companies as the consumer's helper.[6] Short of cash, as most consumers are, people are urged to charge their purchases. Consumers can have what they want now and the only cost to them will be a 'modest' interest charge each month until the balance is paid. The credit card is presented as merely a 'tool' that is firmly under the control of the consumer.

While such claims have a significant element of truth, what they obscure is that a large number of people, perhaps a third of all credit card users, who 'revolve' their accounts rather than pay them in full (as 'convenience' users do), end up being controlled by their credit cards, or more accurately by the credit card companies. Many find themselves in perpetual debt to the credit card companies and that 'modest' interest rate (often a usurious 18 per cent) turns into a crushing debt when it is multiplied month after month, and credit card after credit card (since many people have multiple credit cards). Large numbers of people have several cards, and often in college and increasingly before, because the credit card companies function, albeit silently, as 'pushers' seeking, because of the great profitability of the credit card business, to get credit cards into as many hands as possible. The credit card companies do not want this known; for obvious reasons they do not want to be put in the same category as drug dealers.

While perpetual indebtedness is the major problem associated with credit cards, and the major fact that the companies seek to hide, there are other important and hidden problems associated with credit cards. For example, the huge data banks compiled and controlled by the credit card companies and the credit bureaus (to which the credit card companies supply information and upon which they rely for judgements on creditworthiness) constitute an enormous danger to the privacy of millions of people. The nature of this threat in general, and more particularly of the ease with which others can find out very personal things about people's backgrounds, spending habits and consumption patterns, is obviously hidden from public view. Another example is the issue of fraud. While the credit card companies are quite public about the frauds committed against them, they are silent about their own fraudulent activities that include excessive rates and fees as well as exploitive billing practices, including the way grace periods are handled for those who revolve their accounts (they pay interest from the day a charge is made rather than after the grace period expires as is the case for 'convenience users') and the offers of 'payment holidays' even though interest accrues during those 'holidays'. It is also the case that credit cards can be seen as part of the process of McDonaldization. Credit cards have McDonaldized credit by making it more efficient to obtain it (often all one needs to do is sign one's name to get a pre-approved card; on-line, credit cards can be obtained in seconds by providing only a few bits of information), by making consumption more predictable in allowing people to consume even when they have no available funds, by emphasizing quantitative factors like credit limits and minimum payments, and by being a non-human technology that is part of a huge technological system that controls people rather than being controlled by them. Of course, as a McDonaldized system, credit cards spawn a series of irrationalities (some of which were discussed above) that, like the fundamentally McDonaldized nature of the system, are hidden from consumers.

Then there are the 'new' (post-World War II) 'means of consumption', which include the previously discussed fast-food restaurants (as well as credit cards, but they facilitate the use of the means of consumption rather than being such means themselves), fully enclosed shopping malls, mega-malls (e.g. the Mall of America), cyber-malls and e-tailers, superstores (e.g. Staples, Toy 'Я' Us), 'eatertainment' (e.g. Hard Rock Café), theme parks (especially Disney World), cruise lines, Las Vegas-style casino hotels, and so on.[7] One of the things that all of the new means of consumption have in common is the use of spectacle in order to attract customers and to hide the fact that their simulated forms of enchantment obscure the disenchanted, rationalized systems that lie at their core. The need to conceal this underlying reality is shared with all other McDonaldized systems.

However, what I would like to focus on in discussing the new means of consumption is the hidden mechanisms that they employ in order to control people and to get them to consume more and to spend more money. For example, Disney World is a carefully constructed and planned environment designed to give people the impression that they are making a series of free choices when, in fact, they are being tightly controlled and led to make many of the choices they do. For example, Walt Disney believed in what he called 'wienies', visible and appealing sights like a mountain or a castle, that lead visitors to move toward them and thereby in the direction the Disney organizers wished them to move. Similarly, the visitor to Disney World is forced to enter and leave through what is essentially a shopping mall: Main Street. The visitor is led to shop, almost unconsciously, on both entry and exit from the park. Alternatively, the existence of the mall at the entrance is there to remind visitors that they can consume when they leave without having to cart around parcels with them throughout their visit to the park. Of course, this conceals a deeper reality, which is that Disney World is all about consumption – of the experience, of the food and goods sold on the grounds, and most importantly of the whole panoply of Disney goods and services sold in the company's stores, clubs and cruise line, as well as in independent movie theatres, video stores and toy stores around the world. In other words, what is concealed at Disney World is the consumerism that is its essence and that also lies at the heart of all of the new means of consumption.

There is a whole hidden world of such control in all the new means of consumption and this is made clear by Paco Underhill, a consultant to many of them, in his book, *Why We Buy: The Science of Shopping*.[8] Take the following example, in which a vice president of a national chain of young women's clothing stores (one of the new means of consumption) seeks to control the presentation of T-shirts so that something that costs them $3 can be sold for $37:

'We buy them in Sri Lanka for $3 each,' she began. 'Then we bring them over here and sew in washing instructions, which are in French and English. Notice that we don't say the shirts are made in France. But you can infer that if you like. Then we merchandise the hell out of them – we fold them just right on a tasteful tabletop display, and on the wall we hang a huge, gorgeous photograph of a beautiful woman in an exotic locale wearing a shirt. We shoot it so it looks like a million bucks. Then we call it an Expedition T-Shirt, and sell it for $37. And we sell a lot of them, too.'[9]

Underhill describes this as a 'depressing', but 'valuable' lesson.[10] A number of steps are described here to deceive consumers and lead them to purchase a product at an unconscionable mark-up. Needless to say, retailers do not want their subterfuges known to consumers, and they certainly do not want consumers to know how much of a mark-up is involved in the pricing of goods like these T-shirts.

Interestingly, a parallel kind of deception is involved in Underhill's book. Underhill sees himself as doing a 'science of shopping' and he sells his research and advisory services to various organizations, especially retailers. He provides them with data and with recommendations about how to attract more consumers and how to get them to consume more. For example, he shows that people are limited in what they can buy if they only have use of their hands. Thus, he recommends the widespread deployment of baskets and speaks highly of the chain Old Navy where customers are offered a handsome bag on entry that allows them to load up on items. Not missing a trick, Old Navy cashiers even ask at checkout whether consumers also want to purchase the bag! The tools that he offers to retailers to heighten consumption are hidden beneath a rhetoric that emphasizes that his researchers are only tracking what customers do and recommending that retailers give them what they want. More extremely, Underhill has the audacity to present his organization as 'providing a form of consumer advocacy'.[11] Perhaps he regards getting people to pay $37 for a $3 item an example of consumer advocacy. The reality that Underhill is offering retailers methods to heighten consumerism and increase profits is made less visible, while a more humble (and deceptive) role of merely providing consumers with what they want and serving as an advocate for them is the most visible aspect of the book.

A POSTMODERN VIEW: A VISIBLE WORLD, VISIBLE OBSCENITIES

A starkly different view on the obscenity of the processes and entities of concern here is derivable from Jean Baudrillard's ideas on the scene and the obscene.[12] Baudrillard argues that the contemporary world has grown obscene because things that were at one time invisible (and therefore a 'scene') have grown increasingly visible. What makes something a scene is some degree of mystery, of enchantment, and that is only possible when at least some aspects are hidden from view. The problem with the contemporary world from this perspective is that the kinds of processes and structures of concern here have been made increasingly visible and thereby they have lost their ability to enchant us. Baudrillard's paradigm for this is pornography. His point is that concealing parts of the body is more likely to be enchanting and even sexually arousing than simply confronting the viewer with a naked body or specific body parts. The partially covered, or even fully clothed, body would be more of a scene, whereas the naked body, especially displayed to satisfy prurient interests, is obscene.

In what ways are the entities and processes of interest here obscene in this sense of the term? Let's start with the fast-food restaurant. Most have an open 'kitchen' in which everything that goes on is visible to consumers waiting in line to place or receive their orders. Clearly, there is little mystery involved in what goes into the preparation of fast food. This stands in stark contrast to the traditional restaurant where food preparation is done out of the view of the consumer. Then, there is the fact that customers do much of the work (on an unpaid basis, by the way) – carrying their own food to the table, making their own salads, filling their own soda cups, bussing their own debris, and so on. There is clearly no mystery involved when customers perform such tasks on their own (except, perhaps, to the proprietors, who might wonder why customers do it).

The spread of fast-food restaurants, and more generally of McDonaldization, often takes highly visible forms. Originally, McDonald's restaurants sported huge golden arches that loudly announced their arrival and presence as well as signs that crassly kept track of how many millions, then billions, of hamburgers they sold. Forced to mute structures and signs in recent years, the opening of a new McDonald's, especially in an area or country that heretofore lacked one, is often marked by a major publicity campaign. Then there is the enormous amount of money spent by McDonald's on advertising, especially on television. The advertisements and the arches (albeit in a muted form) seem to be everywhere one turns. Much the same could be said about other McDonaldizing systems. Visible structures, active publicity campaigns and a ubiquitous presence on TV and other media define virtually all of them.

Credit cards also have a high profile, as reflected in the innumerable offers one receives in the mail, the signs on the door of virtually every retailer and the highly visible advertisements and advertising campaigns. Also highly visible is the fact that when we are in a consumption setting, virtually everyone around us is paying by credit card. Thus, a consumer is now likely to feel self-conscious about paying with cash at a department store. Almost everyone uses a card and the employees often make it plain that they prefer payment by credit card.

Since spectacle defines the new means of consumption, and spectacles must be visible in order to be, well, spectacles, visibility defines the new means of consumption. Las Vegas in general, and its most important casino-hotels, are among the most visible aspects of our consumer society. There are the advertisements, of course, but there is also the free media coverage frequently given to the city and its casinos. The openings of recent casino-hotels like New York, New York, Bellagio, Venetian and Paris are big news. More importantly, visibility is the name of the game in Las Vegas. The hotels compete with one another to see which one can attain the greatest visibility. Lights, water displays, sea battles and the like are used in an effort to make one casino-hotel stand out from the other. More generally, the Las Vegas strip is one of the most visible places in the world – its lights can undoubtedly be seen from high in the stratosphere. Inside the casino-hotels, the most visible aspect is the casino. There is no effort to hide it; indeed, it is usually right in one's face when one enters the hotel lobby. And most visible within the casino are its biggest and most reliable money-makers – the slot machines. And, they are ringing, whistling, lighting and displaying how much can be won on a particular machine. There is no subtlety here; no effort to seduce the gambler into playing the slots. Rather, gamblers are beaten over the head with and by them.

Similar points could be made about Disney World and cruise ships. Disney World has succeeded in making itself extraordinarily visible throughout much of the world. Indeed, like Las Vegas, it has become a 'destination' for large numbers of the world's tourists. Few people are unaware of Disney World and what it has to offer. The advertisements, especially those featuring the winners of major sporting events announcing at the conclusion of a game or match 'we're going to Disney World', have served to embed Disney World in people's consciousness. The Disney cable network can be seen as one long advertisement for the various Disney enterprises, including Disney World. The big draw is the well-known and quite spectacular attractions at the park. People go to see those attractions. In fact, given the long lines at many attractions, they spend far more time looking at them than participating in them. Of course, there is much that is unseen, or 'behind the scenes' at Disney World, but people are led to gaze on what is visible. Similarly, what distinguishes the modern cruise ship is its enormous size and thus it is abundantly visible not only to passengers but also to those who see the ships as they pass from port to port.

Thus, in various ways, a case can be made that what characterizes these entities and processes is their great visibility. Furthermore, it could be argued that that is about all there is to them; there is nothing, at least as far as the visitor/customer is concerned, below the surface. From the postmodern perspective, the superficial and most visible aspects exhaust what these entities and processes have to offer. There is nothing more to them than meets the eye. As a result, from a Baudrillardian perspective, the absence of a scene, of hidden elements, means that these entities and processes lack the ability to seduce. Thus, they are disenchanted domains and it is that lack of any mystery that gets to the essence of their problematic character, at least to the postmodernist. There are no deeper problems, of the type discussed in the preceding section, to be uncovered by the debunking modernist sociologist.

RECONCILING MODERN AND POSTMODERN OBSCENITIES

Can both of these perspectives be true ('truth', of course, is an issue anathema to postmodernists)? Are the phenomena discussed throughout this essay obscene both because they are highly invisible *and* highly visible? Or, are these alternative perspectives to be bought into depending on whether one adopts a modern or a postmodern perspective?

One way of reconciling these two perspectives is to argue, undoubtedly from a modernist perspective, that a high degree of visibility exists to distract the consumer from the hidden problems and prospects. Distracted or enthralled by the visible, the consumer is less likely to think about the invisible irrationalities that lie hidden below the surface. Thus, one obscenity allows the other to exist. Of course, it would seem that postmodernists would have none of this. There are no underlying, hidden realities to postmodernists; all we have are the superficial surface appearances. However, on this issue, as on so many others, we must be wary of discussing postmodern social theory in global terms. In fact, there *are* postmodernists who think in just this way and one example is Paul Virilio, who argues that 'new apperceptual techniques essentially tended *to cover what was invisible to the naked eye with the mask of the visible*' (Virilio's emphasis).[13]

While I find postmodern social theory in general, and especially Baudrillardian theory, extremely useful, I do not find it particularly helpful in this case (Virilio is one exception). I would agree that hypervisibility is an issue, even a concern, in the contemporary world, but it just does not strike me as nearly as important as the kind of underlying problems of concern to the modernist. Of course, that may well be due to the fact that I approach these issues as a modernist schooled in postmodern ideas and not as a postmodern social theorist. Thus, to relate this to the work of Zygmunt Bauman,[14] I am doing a sociology of postmodernity rather than a postmodern sociology. While I have great respect for the latter as a source of new and refreshing ideas, I find it far more useful to disengage those ideas from their roots in postmodern social theory and to use them in modern analyses of issues of the day.

Of course, I am mindful, following Bauman and others, that there are grave dangers associated with modernism in general and modern social theory in particular. In fact, much of my recent work involves, as should be clear above, a critical analysis of the deeper problems associated with modern processes – McDonaldization, consumerism and structures – fast-food restaurants, credit cards and the new means of consumption. However, what I do seem to be guilty of, again following Bauman, is of being a legislator seeking to dictate the appropriate interpretation of these structures and processes and the problems associated with them. Fearful of that, allow me to reinterpret what I am saying here as an effort to serve as an interpreter offering a sociological interpretation of these phenomena to an audience with varying backgrounds, some of whom are unfamiliar with a sociological view. Thus, what I offer is not an 'answer', but rather one perspective among many possible perspectives on the objects and processes discussed here. I do not think this will assuage my postmodern critics, but it at least puts this analysis in its proper, humble position and dissociates me from a long line of modernists who, often quite disastrously, thought they best understood a problem and had the optimum solution to that problem.

THE OBSCENE CONSUMER

Much of the above has focused on the obscenities associated with sites of consumption, those things that facilitate their use, and processes associated with them. However, there is far more to consumption including the consumer, the goods and services consumed, as well as the process of consumption. Unable to cover all of these issues here, I would like to close with a few thoughts on the consumer from the perspective of the obscene.

Zygmunt Bauman has correctly argued that along with the transition from the predominance of production to that of consumption, concern in post-modern society has shifted from the problematic producer to the problematic consumer. He labels the latter 'flawed consumers', or those who are 'unable to respond to the enticements of the consumer market because they lack the required resources'; the resources needed 'to be seduced by the infinite possibil-ity and constant renewal promoted by the consumer market, of rejoicing in the chance of putting on and taking off identities, of spending one's life in the never-ending chase after ever more intense sensations and even more exhilarating experience'.[15]

In the terms of this essay, Bauman is arguing that flawed consumers are

obscene from the perspective of postmodern society because they do not have
the resources to participate adequately in the consumer society. In other words,
they do not consume enough. However, I do not think that Bauman has taken
this argument far enough. It is not only that flawed consumers do not consume
enough, but when they do consume, and in a consumer society virtually everyone consumes, they consume the 'wrong' things, things that pose serious threats
to those deeply involved in, or who profit from, consumption. I would argue that
we need to specify further the 'flaws' of the 'flawed consumer' and it would be
more accurate to identify the problematic type as the 'dangerous consumer'.

Part of the reason that this group is dangerous is that, following Bauman,
they simply do not consume enough. The danger there is that escalating consumerism requires that nearly everyone consume at ever-increasing levels. The
absence of a high and escalating level of consumption poses a threat to those
who profit from and have a vested interest in a robust economy driven by
consumerism. However, the threats posed by the 'dangerous consumer' go
beyond merely not consuming enough; the dangerous consumer consumes the
wrong things. For example, because they lack adequate resources, such people
consume a variety of public and welfare services that are a drain on the economy. Because they lack the resources, but share the goals of a consumer society,
they are more likely to engage in criminal activities and thereby to 'consume'
the services of the police, the courts and the prisons, thus further draining the
economy of resources. Further, when they consume in a more conventional
sense, they are more likely to consume the 'wrong' things, things that are apt to
be perceived as 'wrong' by the winners in our 'winner takes all' consumer
society. For example, they are more likely to consume the 'wrong' drugs. Rather
than champagne or even cocaine, they are likely to consume heroin, crack and
the like. The latter are more likely to be seen as dangerous drugs leading to more
threatening behaviours. Minimally, they are the drugs that are more likely to be
criminalized and absorb the interest of the criminal justice system. Dangerous
consumers are more likely to consume guns, or at least those guns that are likely
to be used in crimes against property and the relatively well-to-do people who
own that property. Thus, dangerous consumers are so designated because *both*
what they do, and what they do not, consumerism poses a threat to consumer
society. Bauman's 'flawed consumers', those unable to participate adequately in
consumption, are too limited and too passive to pose a real threat to consumer
society. Dangerous consumers, both by their relative inactivity and by their
activity, pose a much more active and serious threat to consumer society. Of
course, Bauman recognizes this in discussing the fact that the flawed consumers
are those who tend to be ghettoized and criminalized.

It is important to recognize that even those who are threats to consumer
society are themselves consumers. No one is able to escape the imperatives of
the consumer society, even those who are seen as threatening it. The fact that
they are consumers, and aspire to be bigger and better consumers of conventional goods and services, indicates that ultimately 'dangerous' consumers
pose no real threat to consumer society. They are already playing the game and

if they were to obtain more resources through illegal means, they would proceed to be more active, more mainstream consumers. This complements Bauman's argument that because consumption is inherently individualizing, it is therefore far less likely to produce a revolutionary class than production, which is a collective enterprise and thereby apt to produce collective opposition in the form of a revolutionary social class.

Thus, just as there are obscene sites of consumption, and processes implicated in those sites, there are also obscene consumers – those who threaten the raucous consumer party going on all around us at the dawn of the new millennium. Of course, they are obscene from the modern optic of what Bauman calls (and practises) the (modern) sociology of postmodernism. From the perspective of Baudrillardian postmodern sociology we would need to identify another type of obscene consumer – almost certainly one whose practice of consumption and display of consumer goods is hypervisible. Interestingly, the obscene consumer from this perspective sounds strikingly like Veblen's modernist conspicuous consumer. But, however we identify the obscene consumer, it is clear that the notion of the obscene applies as well to the consumer as it does to the other concerns in this essay.

Nevertheless, it is difficult to see the consumer in the same light as the processes and entities of concern highlighted earlier in this essay. That is, the latter are far greater obscenities, especially from a modern point of view, than the 'obscene' consumer. To point the finger at the consumer is in modern terms to 'blame the victim' for obscenities that are far more traceable to processes like McDonaldization and consumerism and entities like fast-food restaurants, credit cards and the new means of consumption. It is in these arenas that the real obscenities lie and it is there that both modernists and postmodernists should focus their attention.

Epilogue

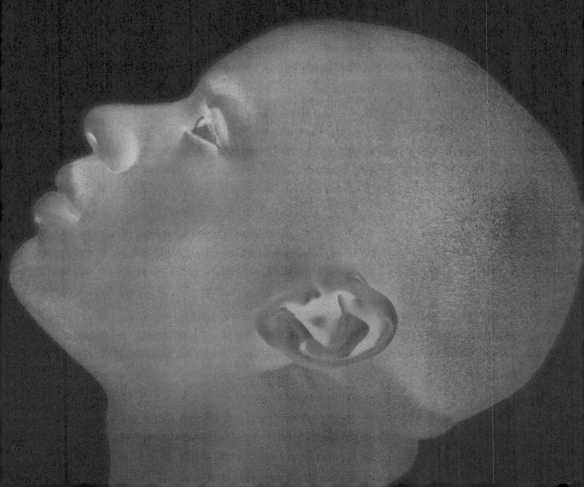

A New Beginning
Beyond Postcolonial Cultural Theory and Identity Politics

RASHEED ARAEEN

Art journals are often the products of their times, representing what goes on around them – such as the art magazine *Frieze*, which represents young British artists (yBa) whose success was guaranteed by a corporate interest. But the story of *Third Text* is not only different but unusual; it positioned itself against what makes an art journal successful in the contemporary art scene. It came into being not as part of an emerging cultural phenomenon or art movement, to represent and give it legitimation, but to explore, expose and analyse what has been excluded and repressed by institutional power.

The 1980s saw two contradictory and opposing developments. On the one hand, a debate which questioned the institutional policies and attitudes towards the artists who were not white, and accused the system of institutional racism. On the other, the emergence of multiculturalism supported and promoted by the establishment which began to overshadow the issues the debate had raised.

The main issue was not just the exclusion of the artists from the art scene, but the ignorance and suppression of the whole history of their contribution to the mainstream developments. This issue also had an international dimension: many Third World critics and art historians also questioned the way the history of modern art has been perceived and written, including only white artists from Europe and North America.

Third Text took the position that the prevailing situation was not merely the result of human neglect or an oversight on the part of those who were involved in writing art history. It represented the very ideology of the art institution. We were encouraged in this respect by the work being done in postcolonial critical theory, particularly the writing of Edward Said.

This issue was however dismissed by the establishment – which also included those who were promoting multiculturalism – with its usual arrogance and complacency. This prevented any debate taking place within the mainstream discourse. It therefore became essential for us to take up a critical position in order to explore and debate this issue.

It was with this position that in the autumn of 1987, *Third Text* came out with its first issue, outlining its specific aims and objectives. Its first editorial, entitled 'Why Third Text?', concluded:

> Third Text represents a historical shift away from the centre of the dominant culture to its periphery in order to consider the centre critically. This does not imply a fixed distance. The movement can be repeated or reversed as long as

a critical relationship is maintained. In view of the crises of western corporate culture, it appears necessary to develop a constructive international
communication beyond the intellectual paralysis which has characterised
much of western critical discourse in the 80s.

The crises of western culture were caused, in our view, by the inability of the
system to come to terms with its colonial past and recognize the reality of
the postcolonial world and its aspiration and struggle for human equality,
creating intellectual paralysis in its discourse; this paralysis was particularly
evident in art-history scholarship, which was still riddled with Eurocentric and
racialist assumptions.

It was a formidable stance – to position ourselves against the might of the
dominant culture. But, at the same time, we were aware of the difficult task
ahead. We did not think that the journal would last beyond a few issues. But we
have survived.

Twelve years and fifty issues on, we have managed to build up a network of
like-minded contributors from all over the world as well as a small but important
global readership which aspires and is committed to the radical change we want
and have been struggling for. In other words, we managed to establish a global
platform for what we consider to be a continuing struggle against colonial
structures. This time, it was not for the liberation of a particular land or country
but against continuing western cultural domination. This domination does not
necessarily manifest itself in suppressing other cultures, or artistic forms of
other cultures, but in denying other cultures or peoples from other cultures their
subject positions in modernism.

However, *Third Text*'s mere survival cannot and should not be considered an
achievement in itself. What we need now is not a celebration – since the task is
not over – but first to look back and examine critically what exactly we have
achieved and what have been our shortcomings or failures. What exactly we
meant when we said that we wanted to create 'a historical shift away from the
centre'? Did we succeed in this respect? Did we manage to demonstrate analyti-
cally the crisis of western culture? Did we go 'beyond the intellectual paralysis . . .
of western critical discourse' and offer something which would free us from this
paralysis?

We also claimed that we wanted to represent the Third World and its artistic
and cultural achievements. But what were and are these achievements? Are
these the achievements now being celebrated institutionally in the West?

These questions are fundamental not only in the scrutinizing and evaluation
of what we have so far done but also in determining the direction we should
now take. It is not enough to enumerate what we have achieved; to move
forward and justify *Third Text*'s continuity, it would be more important to look at
what has prevented us from achieving our full objectives.

Of course, we faced many difficulties, both internal and external. It was not
easy to run an art journal of a professional standard without sufficient financial
support and experienced staff, particularly when we had to start from scratch

and without an already defined constituency. It was particularly difficult when we wanted to keep a distance from, and stay in opposition to, the status quo of the academy. Not that we dismissed all that was being done in the academy, but it was necessary to remind ourselves of its limitations and self-serving interests.

Any shortcomings *vis-à-vis* art scholarship were compensated by other voices dealing with the problems of culture as a whole in the age of growing hegemony of global capital, legitimated by the eclecticism of neo-liberal thinking. This has helped us go beyond the limits of art and its hermetic discourse, and look at cultural practices in a discursive manner.

However, our aims of penetrating the historical body of modernism and affecting its central core remain unfulfilled. This was not unexpected. We knew that it would not be possible for us alone to change the institutional structures which protect modernism from the onslaught of those who are considered to be its others. We also realized that there would be resistance from the establishment, but we did not expect this from liberal institutions of the academy whose enlightened function we thought was a pursuit of knowledge and truth.

THE INSTITUTIONAL STRUCTURES

These structures are not the bricks and mortar of the modern museums or galleries or the academy, but their ideological underpinning formed by the ideas of modernity. In fact, the concept of modernism in art, its language and history represents a dominant structure of art institutional power in the West, a bastion of white intellectual supremacy, and this power has been maintained by the exclusion from it of non-whites.

Unlike other discourses, such as literature, modernity of art is closely linked with the philosophical ideas of subjectivity going back to when Descartes declared, 'I think, therefore I am.' This statement was not politically or ideologically as innocent as it may appear; it was made under the shadow of emerging European colonial power and its subjugation of other peoples, which then became a foundation stone of western philosophy. The ideas of subjectivity and aesthetics were then developed by Kant and Hegel, among others, and given a historical function. These were the ideas which would modernize and civilize the world, and which were meant to be carried to the world, according to the ideology of modernity, by whites only. The history of modern art therefore still reflects this function.

If modernity is constructed by and carries with it the universal spirit *à la* Hegel, what is this spirit, and why has it been imposed on the world? Does this spirit only define and construct the European subject, or can it also represent a complex body of ideas – no matter how they have been formulated – which can go beyond the initial objectives of their producers and be taken up by humanity as a whole? If we stick to the former, we continue facing the kind of human catastrophes and tragedies that happened in the twentieth century.[1] But if we accept the latter, that is, modernity must not be confined or trapped in the

European body, then this could pose a challenge to the former and liberate humanity from the oppressive forces of the colonial past.

This challenge was in fact the cornerstone of the anti-colonial struggle: liberation from colonialism did not mean a return to precolonial structures but a redefinition of modernity, and a Third World claim to its own modernizing and progressive ideas, empowering the liberated in their journey to full freedom and self-determination.

When modernity, and with it modernism, was imposed on the colonized world, the colonized accepted it at its face value, its progressive and enlightened ideas, and equipped themselves to get rid of colonialism.[2] This process or struggle is still continuing not only at political and economical levels but also within cultures. In art this struggle took the form of challenging the prevailing concept of modernism and redefining it. It was not just a question of finding a place for oneself within modernism, but redefining the world – through a symbolic practice – which was free from Eurocentric structures.

The end of colonialism also liberated its artists from their colonial bondage, and when they began to arrive in the West about fifty years ago they wanted to test and prove, as they were no longer the colonial subjects, that they had the same freedom to express themselves as their white/European contemporaries. Being the product of western art education, which infused them with the ideas of modernism, artists from Asia, Africa and the Caribbean were now prepared to claim a central place in modernism. Their story is therefore the story of a struggle between what these artists wanted to do and what was denied to them by the dominant culture.[3] While these artists struggled to place themselves at the centre of what was then going on within modernism, they were constantly pushed out on the basis of their Otherness – which was invoked both racially and culturally.

It was our aim in *Third Text* to challenge those assumptions, formed not only by the colonial discourse in general but also by its racist views about others,[4] which constantly defined the work of artists from other cultures in terms of their Otherness. But when this challenge openly became political and ideological, and the art institution began to feel under pressure, the system started to deploy its liberal tactics to deflect and displace this challenge. This was achieved through multiculturalism, among other things, drawing in many ideas of postcolonial cultural theory which helped the institution to legitimize its neo-liberal agendas.

THE TYRANNY OF POSTCOLONIAL CULTURAL THEORY

In this section I want to show that postcolonial cultural theory, which supposedly challenges dominant assumptions, has in fact reinforced these assumptions.[5] I am concerned with those ideas which articulate the experiences of postcolonial mass migration, and which then prescribe and legitimate the art practice not only of those who are presumed to have undergone these experiences but anyone who has migrated to the West. These ideas are based on an assumption that every postcolonial migrant has suffered displacement and loss and is now exiled from his or her original culture or home.

It is true that many have suffered this displacement and loss, and there are many living in the West who feel exiled. I am not disputing this. What worries me, and what is disturbing, is that a new/postcolonial subject is being created, socially, culturally and ontologically, on the basis of this displacement and loss, with the result that this subject has been made less capable of dealing with the modern world than the white/European subject.

Edward Said's exile is a genuine exile, and his articulation of the experiences of this exile is part of the struggle of Palestinian people. What is most significant here is that Said has used these experiences to look at the system which has caused this exile, and has then developed a profoundly critical position which exposes the inhumanity of the system. When Said talks about displacement, he is not indulging in the rhetoric of loss but reveals a condition of modernity, which is both negative and positive. If modernity creates a disjunction of an individual from the whole – an exile – it also provides the individual with an insight which goes beyond one's experiences of exile. It is this transgressive insight which empowers the individual, not only to compensate the loss but also to position him or herself critically in the world. The exiled subject, therefore, does not operate from the position of a loss or as a victim but as the one who can locate him or herself in the world as a free subject and change it. Said therefore speaks not as a victim but from a position of power which he attains as a subject; he does not expect any sympathy from anyone but he puts the sympathizer on the spot so that he can critically engage him or her in a process of change.

Said's achievement in this respect is unique, and I have great respect and regard for him. What bothers me is that his articulation of the experience of his own exile has not only been universalized, through its institutional appropriation, but has become a basis from which to look at the non-white immigrant in the West. It is not necessarily Said's fault that his ideas are being misused, but the problem is that the idea of exile has become a fundamental pillar of post-colonial cultural theory; and Said is often quoted to justify facile art practices on the basis of exile. In fact, exile is no longer a loss from which one necessarily suffers, but it is now used by many to elicit sympathy, which in turn allows the ruling system to define and construct them as postcolonial Others. I do recognize Said's difficulty here: he cannot respond to this appropriation by the art institution (which includes both the art promotional institutions and the academy) because he is not concerned or sufficiently engaged in the discourse of art. One does not expect him to be engaged in every discourse, but his lack of seriousness in this regard and his apparent uncritical acceptance of whatever is being done institutionally in art today is a matter of concern. He gives an impression that there is no serious ideological struggle in art.

Homi Bhabha takes up the cue from the idea of exile and constructs his Other on the basis of displacement and loss. This Other is a hybrid. Many writers have objected to his use of the word 'hybrid', suggesting that the hybrid should be replaced with the syncretic.[6] But these writers are mistaken; they have not understood that the hybrid in Bhabha's discourse is a specific form of the syncretic whose premises are *predetermined and are fixed by racial and cultural differences*. The hybrid does not stand for a process of all cultural interchanges or intermixings and what results from them in the contemporary global world, but it is something which results only when a non-western culture enters western culture. This entry also takes place through specific carriers, artists from other cultures who must carry identity cards showing their cultural origins and must locate themselves within a specific space – an in-between space – in order to enter or encounter the dominant culture. It is assumed that the enunciation of difference – racial or cultural – is essential in empowering these artists. The result is the power of the mule which always carries the burden and the sign of its breeding.

The theory of hybridity is not based on a recognition of the reality of the historical encounter between the people of non-western cultures and western culture, and what this encounter had *historically* produced and achieved. In fact, the theory of hybridity negates this history, because without this negation this theory cannot seek legitimation from the institutions in the West. But when we look at the art produced by the so-called artists from other cultures in this century, the bogusness of this theory becomes clear.

The encounter of the 'other artists' with western culture took place not recently but much before Mr Bhabha was born. This was in fact an encounter with modernity which produced modernism in the colonized countries. This modernism suffered from all the problems of colonialism, its lack of resources and underdevelopment, but when it entered the mainstream of modernism, both in the metropolis and its so-called periphery, it transformed itself into a critical force to challenge its established premises. Bhabha always cites examples from past literature in order to validate his theory, but when it comes to art he has no example to quote, because he cannot use them without demolishing his theory. If the theory of hybridity rests on a bogus ground, how come it has been accepted by the art institutions and the academy in the West?

Stuart Hall has made a significant contribution to the understanding of popular or mass culture, and its importance in the development of a multicultural society (which is different from the neo-liberal multiculturalism). His emphasis on the importance of not sticking to one ethnicity, so that one is not *essentially* attached to one particular cultural identity, is extremely important. But, on the other hand, Hall does not dismiss or sufficiently problematize the use of one's ethnicity in the formulation or articulation of one's experiences, as part of a cultural process which can empower those who have been displaced from their cultural roots. Although he is not interested in cultural roots, he has emphasized the importance of the various *routes* different people or artists take to enter modernity. He often cites the difference between Joyce and Woolf; the former is supposed to have taken an Irish route, while the latter enters modernity with her Englishness. This may be true, particularly in literature whose structures must constitute some kind of narrative, but this does not resolve the confusion between the subject matter and the content of the work. The implication of Hall's position seems to be that the route one takes must be transparently apparent in the work; he seems also to imply that the appearance of this route is important in the understanding of the work. The problem here is not the cultural identity of one's work, but the fact that within the context of multiculturalism and its ideology the idea of culturally specific routes leads to a celebration of the Other. My criticism here is not about the route, but seeing the route as an essential content of the work.

Picasso, Mondrian and Brancusi, for example, come from different cultures. One can also say that they took different routes to modernity. But what exactly are these routes and how do they show up in their works? Were these routes determined by Spanish, Dutch and Romanian cultures respectively, or was there something else which led them on to the routes to Paris? I am not denying the influences of their cultures on their works. Their works are also different and they look different – but is this difference the result of their cultures or the different routes they took? Do we invoke their differences when we look at or evaluate their work? How do we explain the disappearance of the difference between Spanish and French cultures in one of the most important and pioneering developments of modernism early this century, Cubism, when Picasso and Braque worked together? It can be argued that there is really no difference between different cultures of Europe; they are all parts of the same whole. Their movement from one place to another was within the same culture.

Using this argument, I would like to assert that the movement of artists from Asia, Africa and the Caribbean to the West was also not between different cultures but a movement within the same culture defined and constructed by modernity. In the early twentieth century, modernism travelled from Paris to other countries of Europe, triggering off other movements in many countries (Futurism, Constructivism, Supermatism, etc.), and to the Americas, but it also moved to the colonies in Asia, Africa and the Caribbean (as well as to the countries of Latin America, which are not being considered here). When Afro-Asian artists from different parts of the world arrived in Europe, they were not carrying another culture but *a different levels of the same culture* which they had left behind.

It can also be said that Picasso, Mondrian and Brancusi, among many others, were exiled from their countries. But if they felt that they were in exile, why did they not go around beating their chests and declaring this to be the case? Because they knew that their exile was not important to the work they wanted to do. They had something *much more important* in their mind. They knew they had to be in exile, not for the sake of being in exile and celebrating it, but because it was essential for them to be at the centre of modernism in order to produce new ideas. It was essential for them to transgress not only the cultures they left behind but also their experiences of exile. We can say the same thing about the earlier generation of artists from Asia, Africa or the Caribbean.

It is in fact a fallacy to presume that migration in itself creates displacement, loss and exile. If people feel that they are in an exile, because they happened to be in a different country than their own, then there must be other reasons for them to feel like this. The first generation of Afro-Asian artists in the West did not consider themselves to be in exile, despite the fact that the new environment they encountered was not all that hospitable.

Their ambitions were no different from those of Picasso, Mondrian or Brancusi. This is something the postcolonial cultural theory does not understand or does not want to understand, because it has a different agenda. The apparent rhetoric of many postcolonial intellectuals may be against the system, and they are good at producing very complicated texts, but in reality they want to be part of the system. Careers cannot really be made by confronting the system. This is not a contradiction. After all, we all came here to be successful, and it would be silly if we threw away the opportunity to be successful. I remember a famous radical, postcolonial intellectual coming up to me after I had finished my paper in a conference and saying laughingly: 'Well, it is all right for you to make this statement, but I'm an academic. I've got to earn my living.'

Postcolonial cultural theory *per se* is not tyrannical; the tyranny is located in some of its ideas, which have very little to do with the specificity of art and have now been appropriated by institutions which use them to reinforce their colonial idea of the Other. This has helped them redefine the postcolonial subject as the new Other, but also to predetermine their role in modern society. With the result that any art activity which does not conform to or defies this new definition is looked upon as inauthentic and is suppressed.

THE POSTCOLONIAL OTHER

Many eminent thinkers have criticized multiculturalism as an attempt by neo-liberalism to contain and displace the struggle of the deprived and oppressed; Slavoj Žižek has in fact described it as a new form of racism.[7] While there is no point in repeating their arguments, what I want to do here is to disentangle multiculturalism from the idea of a culturally plural society. A culturally plural society is a society in which all its culturally different components are considered equal, not necessarily quantitatively but conceptually, so that they form a heterogeneous whole. This heterogeneous whole must then define the whole society without the notion of majority and minority cultures. In a culturally plural society all individuals must have the full right to decide how and where they want to locate themselves; and the recognition of their creative ability should not be dependent on their identification with the cultures they originated from.

This may appear to be unachievable idealism, but if we really want human equality what is the alternative? We have to start somewhere. Either we should be honest enough and give up the idea of human equality altogether – you can not have equality only for some – or we must lay a proper foundation on which we can build this equality. Multiculturalism does not provide us with this foundation. It is based on a separation of the dominant majority culture from the cultures of the minority population so that they cannot interact to create the

change necessary for all citizens in a society to be equal. If the majority dominant culture – it could also be a dominant minority culture, as was the case in
South Africa – is intransigent in maintaining its dominant identity in such a way
that its power structure is not allowed to be affected by minority cultures or their
demands for equality, then it leads the minority cultures into a subcategory or a
supplement of the dominant culture; and those who do not belong to the
dominant culture are thus contained within this subcategory. Multiculturalism
represents exactly this subcategory: it is not about the equality of all cultures but
how the dominant culture can accommodate those who have no power in such a
way so that the power of the dominant is preserved. Talking about multiculturalism, Homi Bhabha once remarked that 'we have been caught with our
pants down'. Well, what is he going to do now? Is he going to pull his pants up
and fight? I doubt it. Does he not realize that his Other can only be successful
when his pants are down?

If we examine Bhabha's ideas, which seem to have a direct influence on the
development of multiculturalism, then it becomes clear that his critique of
multiculturalism is disingenuous. Since his concept of hybridity and in-between
space has created *a separate* space, specified by the cultural differences of non-
white peoples, it has created a separation or dividing line between whites and
non-whites; the result is that while white artists can carry on with what they
always did, appropriating any culture they like and without carrying with them
any sign of their cultural identity, non-white artists must enter the dominant
culture by showing their cultural identity cards. Even when they interact with
the dominant cultural forms, and produce something new, it must display the
signs of their Otherness. We only have to look at the contemporary art scene to
see what our recognized young artists are doing. It is pathetic: most of them are
acting like juveniles, clowning and buffooning; wearing their respective colour-
ful ethnic dresses and carrying cultural identity cards, they are happily dancing
in the court of the ethnic King Multiculturalism. Having thus achieved their
recognition, and been celebrated with the Turner Prize, the hybrid children of
multiculturalism are in no mood to upset the establishment. They do not even
want to know that art has a historical responsibility, that it has a subversive
function which can only be achieved if one is able to penetrate the system and
challenge its structures. How can they achieve this function when they are held
at the door – the threshold of Bhabha's liminality – and are celebrated outside
the citadel of modernism in which the power of the system resides?

Celebration of the exotic Other today is not new. What is new is that the
Other is no longer just the culturally exotic Other. Now, we also have a politically exotic Other, who is supposed to be either exiled from, or is critical about,
his or her country of origin. This new category includes, for example, Palestinians, Iranians, Chinese, South Africans; there is also a slightly different category
of diasporic Others, which mostly includes African Americans and black Africans living abroad in various countries of the West. What is common to all of
them is either the predicament of being outside where they long to be or a
concern about the countries of their origins. In the name of a political or

critical engagement, a Palestinian artist can now articulate his or her experiences of exile; an Iranian artist living in New York can now represent the condition of Iranian women in Iran today in a highly exotic fashion; Chinese artists can make fun of what is going on in China; South African artists can show us what happened during apartheid, and so on. All these artists can now be celebrated institutionally in the West. *But the buck stops here.* Try to turn your eyes towards the ideological and institutional structures of the institutions which are now so concerned with the plight and struggle of peoples in other countries, and you will see how the doors shut in your face.

It would be foolish to deny the suffering of the exiled or those who see themselves as diasporic, or the anguish of those who are concerned with events in their own countries. But it is important to see what this predicament of others does in terms of an artistic discourse, whether it is a critical tool to disrupt the dominant system or whether it merely attracts the powerful to entice sympathy.

The predicament of others has always attracted the powerful, particularly its liberal section, because it is the way for the powerful to show their sympathy and charity towards those who are deprived and are suffering. The *victim* is important for the liberal gaze, it is the way the powerful prove their humanism, and thus deflect the critical gaze of the deprived from its source of power.

It is not that one should not express one's predicament or use the predicament of the deprived as part of one's discourse. But the artwork which at the same time fails to engage critically with the system from which it seeks recognition is simply reduced to a reified commodity for the art market. I am not just questioning the nature of these activities, but also the power of the art institutions which legitimate them. What is the basis of this legitimacy? Is it the power of the powerful, or have they a theoretical basis which recognizes the work of both white and non-white artists? How come these institutions never use the ideas which recognize the importance of radical innovations and historical shifts in art when it comes to the work of non-white artists? The ideas of the postcolonial theory and postmodernism are not only inadequate but also inappropriate in this respect.

Native collaborators have always played an important role in perpetuating colonial power and domination, and the situation today is no different. They have always occupied the in-between space, to create a buffer between the ruler and the ruled. The recent globalization of capitalist economy, still dominated and controlled by the West, has attained a new power and confidence, which is now being translated through the globalization of world cultures. This has created a new space and job opportunities for the neocolonial collaborators, and with this has emerged a group of ethnic or multicultural functionaries, in the form of writers-cum-curators from different parts of the Third World. With the rhetoric of exclusion on their tongues and an appeal to the liberal conscience of western society, these new functionaries of the system drag anyone and everyone, so long as they belong to their own ethnic or national groups, to the art market of the West. We thus have Chinese, Africans, Latin Americans, etc., promoting their Chinese (which could include Southeast Asians), African and Latin American artists respectively. As for history or ideology, they are no longer needed.

WHAT SHOULD BE DONE NOW?

A new beginning implies – if not demands – new thinking. It implies that we can no longer continue our journey as we started in the 1980s but must find a new direction. If we have achieved our aims, then we must set up a new agenda to continue the work. If, on the other hand, we have failed in our objectives, we must examine this failure and change our approach. The failure might have been due to external factors. In our naivety, we might have underestimated the institutional will and determination to resist, and its power to deploy resources from unexpected quarters to undermine our efforts.

The ground has now shifted, and what we face today is an entirely different situation. The struggle has been highjacked. With the success of the young breed of non-white artists, writers and curators, from the metropolis as well as from the Third World, legitimized with the use of postcolonial cultural theory, the system has now built a thick wall of multiculturalism around it. This success has also attracted many eminent postcolonial celebrities, who seem always happy to oblige – in contradiction to their own radical positions – and have provided an added legitimacy to, and reinforced, this situation.

It is perhaps necessary to clarify here that we are not against what the present generations of artists, writers and curators are doing; nor do we reject any form of art activity. People should be free to do whatever they want to do. Nobody should impose any prescription or precondition for human activities. What we are concerned here with are those activities whose success the system uses to camouflage its oppressive structures.

The struggle now is not just against what some 'black' artists in Britain used to call 'white institutions', but with the system which now also includes black, brown and yellow faces. It should therefore be clear that we cannot build solidarity only on the basis of race, culture, ethnicity or nation. Our new alliance should be with those who are committed to a genuine change and are prepared to enter into a dialogue with us. We are not against genuine reforms in the system, but if they do not lead to a structural change we must expose the limitations of such reforms.

The legitimacy of the institutions which are still underpinned by the colonial ideology cannot be left to the institutional power or be taken for granted. If the colonial discourse has lost its historical validity, on what basis are the institutions operating and legitimating art today?

The prevailing art education system and its resources is another important issue to which we should give serious consideration. Are these resources – both intellectual and material – appropriate and adequate for the educational needs of a multiracial society?

The question of human agency is extremely important. The agencies of white and non-white artists have been historically formulated and formed differently and oppositely by the dominant culture. Can one's individual stance now, based on self-identity, be enough to provide an agency? Is this individualism not based on the bourgeois myth of the autonomous self?

We must recognize that what in fact we face today is the most disturbing period in the history of modern art. It is in fact the end of a historical period which began after Hegel's historicization of art. Someone, somewhere has said that modernism is dead but dominant. But it is not modernism which is dead but only European modernism. It is this dead body of European modernism which has become a highly desired and precious commodity. The dominant culture is celebrating the collapse of its enlightened foundation. But this collapse has led to an art scene where nihilism, cynicism, exhibitionism, pornography and self-mockery are spreading like a poison in the body of art and destroying its critical and affirmative potential.[8] It is influencing not only the young non-white artists but also artists around the world. Artists in China today want to be more sensational than the sensation of BritArt.

It is easy to critique what the young artists, both white and black, are doing today. But what choice do they have, when their only ambition is to be successful? The only choice they have is the commodity market, for which they can only supply commodities. It is therefore important to expose the art institutions, which are funded by public money, for their dependence on and alliance with the art market, which is not in the interest of the public at large.

In order to deal with this difficult situation, we need radically new ideas, new strategies and a new discourse not only to produce art but in order to recognize and legitimize it. We should interrogate the whole history of ideas – theoretical and art historical – which has built the edifice of Eurocentric discourse. But more: we must develop an alternative radical scholarship which can penetrate and expose the true nature of these ideas and how they are camouflaged by humanism.

I have only outlined some issues, but they need to be looked at in some detail and depth. The ideas about art in philosophy are not as simple as I have presented them here, and we should persuade those who have better expertise in this area to contribute to the debate. The ideas of postcolonial critical theory also have many different aspects, and we should expect postcolonial theorists to come forward to clarify these ideas *vis-à-vis* art. What we cannot do is not accept the ideas of literary theory for the structurally different discourse of art.

For us, the Third World was an ideological position, in solidarity with the oppressed people. The artists, art writers and curators from the Third World are not the ones who are now excluded from or oppressed by the system. The oppression is now concentrated somewhere else; it is the masses of the Third World who are now bearing the brunt of the economic, political and military oppression of the globalized economy and its New World Order.

It would be naive to think art can offer a solution to this oppression; nor can we deal with the problems of economic, political and military oppressions in the pages of *Third Text*. Art as a specific formation of culture has its own structural problem, and to ignore this problem in favour of representing the oppressed would lead us into a sentimental solidarity. However, our job should not just be critiquing the prevailing system, but out of this critique we must also develop a positive vision of the future. This new vision must include the liberation of the world masses.

Clearly, *Third Text* alone cannot develop this vision. We need radically new thinkers (including postcolonial theorists and intellectuals), philosophers, visionary politicians, economists, artists and writers to set a new direction, not just for the peoples of the Third World but for the whole of humanity – a humanity that is not divided by race, colour or cultural differences.

Notes

Prologue

1. Angel Rama, *The Lettered City*, trans. John Charles Chasteen. Duke University Press, Durham, NC, 1996, p. 37.
2. Frantz Fanon, *Black Skin, White Masks*, trans. Charles Lam Markmann. Penguin, London, 1968.
3. Laura U. Marks, *The Skin of the Film: Intercultural Cinema, Embodiment, and the Senses.* Duke University Press, Durham, NC, 2000, p. 9.
4. Robert B. Reich, *The Work of Nations: Preparing Ourselves for Twenty-First-Century Capitalism.* Alfred A. Knopf, New York, 1991.
5. Saskia Sassen, *Cities in a Global Economy*, 2nd edn. Pine Forge, Thousand Oaks, CA, 2000.
6. See, in particular, Rasheed Araeen, 'Our Bauhaus, others' mudhouse', *Third Text*, No. 6, Spring 1989, pp. 3–14.
7. Etienne Balibar and Immanuel Wallerstein, *Race, Nation, Class: Ambiguous Identities*, trans. of Etienne Balibar by Chris Turner. Verso, London, 1991, p. 21.
8. Michael Hardt and Antono Negri, *Empire.* Harvard University Press, Cambridge, MA, 2000, p. 194.
9. Ziauddin Sardar, *Postmodern and the Other: The New Imperialism of Western Culture.* Pluto Press, London, 1998.
10. See, for example, Jürgen Habermas, *Moral Consciousness and Communicative Action*, trans. Christian Lenhardt and Shierry Weber Nicholson. MIT Press, Cambridge, MA, 1993.
11. Slavoj Žižek, 'Multiculturalism or the cultural logic of multinational capitalism', *New Left Review*, No. 225, September/October 1997, pp. 28–51, p. 50.
12. Arif Dirlik, 'The global in the local', in Rob Wilson and Wimal Dissanayake (eds), *Global/Local: Cultural Production and the Transnational Imaginary.* Duke University Press, Durham, NC, 1996.
13. As exemplified by, for example, 'Third World Wide Web', Special Issue, *Third Text*, No. 47, Summer 1999.

History

Introduction

1. Karl Popper, *The Poverty of Historicism.* Routledge and Kegan Paul, London, 1957.
2. Marshall G.S. Hodgson, *Rethinking World History.* Cambridge University Press, Cambridge, 1993.

3. Jean-François Lyotard, *The Postmodern Condition: A Report on Knowledge*, trans. Geoff Bennington and Brian Massumi. Manchester University Press, Manchester, 1983.

4. Sheila Rowbotham, *Hidden from History: 300 Years of Women's Oppression and the Fight Against It*. Pluto Press, London, 1973.

5. Ziauddin Sardar, Ashis Nandy and Merryl Wyn Davies, *Barbaric Others: A Manifesto on Western Racism*. Pluto Press, London, 1993; and Silvia Federici (ed.), *Enduring Western Civilization*. Praeger, Westport, CT, 1995.

Contemporary Cultural Practice

1. Fredric Jameson, 'Third world literature in the era of multinational capitalism', *Social Text*, No. 15, Fall 1986. The reply by Eijaz Ahmad, 'Jameson's rhetoric of otherness and the "National Allegory"', *Social Text*, No. 17, Fall 1987, provides for a substantial part of the argument in this essay.

2. See Nelly Richard, 'Postmodernism and the periphery', *Third Text*, No. 2, Winter 1987/8, pp. 13–24, for an excellent discussion on the subject.

The Latin American Origins of 'Alternative Modernism'

1. For the etymology of the term *modernismo*, see Max Henrique Ureña, *Breve historia del modernismo*. Siglo XXI, Mexico City, 1954, pp. 158ff. See also Juan Ramon Jiménez, *El modernismo* (1953). Aguilar, Madrid, 1962; Angel Rama, *Rubén Darío y el modernismo*. Ediciones de la Biblioteca, Caracas, 1920.

2. For a fine analysis of Darío's poetry and politics, see Jean Franco, *Modern Culture of Latin America: Society and the Artist*. Pelican, Harmondsworth, 1970; and J. Franco, *Introduction to Spanish-American Literature*. Praeger, New York, 1967, pp. 142–7. See also David E. Whisnant, 'Rubén Darío as a focal cultural figure in Nicaragua', *Latin American Research Review*, Vol. 27, No. 3, 1992, pp. 7–49; Edelberto Torres, *La dramatica vida de Rubén Darío*. Ediciones Grijalbo, Mexico City, 1966; and Charles D. Watland, *Poet-Errant: A Biography of Rubén Darío*. Philosophical Library, New York, 1965.

3. Rubén Darío, 'Cabezas: Angel Zárraga', *Mundial Magazine*, Vol. II. No. 19, November 1912, pp. 640–1. This included the reproduction of Diego Rivera's *Portrait of (Retrato de) Angel Zárraga*.

4. Ulrico Brendel, 'El salón de otoño', *Mundial Magazine*, Vol. II, No. 19, November 1912, pp. 623–4.

5. See Renato Poggioli, *Theory of the Avant-Garde* (1962), trans. Gerald Fitzgerald. Harvard University Press, Cambridge, MA, 1974; and Peter Bürger, *Theory of the Avant-Garde* (1974), trans. Michael Shaw. University of Minnesota Press, Minneapolis, 1982.

6. Rubén Darío, 'Palabras luminares', *Prosas profanas y otros poemas (1896–1901)*, reprinted in *Rubén Darío poesia*, ed. Julio Valle Castillo and Ernesto Mejía Sanchez. Editorial Nueva Nicaragua, Managua, 1994, p. 180: '*Si hay poesía en nuestra América, ella esta en las cosas viejas: en Palenke y Utatlán, en el indio legendario y el inca sensual y fino, y en el gran Moctezuma de la silla de oro. Lo demás es tuyo, demócrata Walt Whitman.*'

7. José Martí, 'Nuestra América' (1891), in *Our America*, trans. Elinor Randall and ed. Philip Foner. Monthly Review Press, New York, 1977, pp. 84–95.

8. See José Martí, *Ensayos sobre arte y literatura*, ed. Roberto Fernández Retamar. Editorial Letras Cubanas, Havana, 1979.

9. Philip Foner, Introduction, *Our America*, op. cit., p. 58.

10. Martí, op. cit., p. 88.

11. Ibid., pp. 94 and 93.

12. See Whisnant, op. cit., pp. 7–49.

13. Darío, 'A Roosevelt', in *Rubén Darío poesía*, op. cit., pp. 255–6.

14. Ibid.

15. José Enrique Rodó, *Ariel* (1900), trans. Margaret Sayers Peden. University of Texas Press, Austin, 1988. See also Roberto González Echevarría, 'The case of the speaking statue: Ariel and the magisterial rhetoric of the Latin American essay', in *The Voice of the Masters*. University of Texas Press, Austin, 1985, pp. 8–32.

16. Rubén Darío, 'El rey burgués (cuento alegre)', reprinted in *Rubén Darío: cuentos completos*, eds Ernesto Meijía Sánchez and Julio Valle-Castillo. Editorial Nueva Nicaragua, Managua, 1994, pp. 127–31.

17. Darío, 'La canción del oro', reprinted in *Cuentos completos*, op. cit., pp. 141–4.

18. Dore Ashton, public lecture on modernism at the Museum of Fine Arts, Santa Fe, New Mexico, April 1994.

19. Charles Baudelaire, 'Le Peintre de la vie moderne' (1863), reprinted in *The Painter of Modern Life and Other Essays*, trans. Jonathan Mayne. Phaidon, London, 1965, pp. 12–15.

20. Rubén Darío certainly was influenced by Baudelaire, as Jean Franco and others have pointed out. See Franco, *Introduction*, op. cit., pp. 357–63.

21. Baudelaire, op. cit., pp. 12–15.

22. Ibid.

23. See, for example, Roland Barthes, *Le Degré zero de l'écriture* (1953), trans. Annette Lavers and Colin Smith. Hill and Wang, New York, 1983, pp. 75–6.

24. Perry Anderson, 'Modernity and revolution', *New Left Review*, No. 114, 1984, pp. 97–8. See also, Marshall Berman, *All That Is Solid Melts into Air*. Simon & Schuster, New York, 1982, pp. 15–16.

25. E.P. Thompson, *The Poverty of Theory and Other Essays*. Monthly Review, London, 1978, pp. 98ff.

26. See Enric Jardí Casary, *Historia de Els Quatre Gats*. Editorial Aedos, Barcelona, 1972, p. 66. For a fine look at Picasso's relation to the café, see the catalogue essay by Marilyn McCully in: *Els Quatre Gats: Art in Barcelona Around 1900*. Princeton University Press, Princeton, 1978. For a broader look at the relation of anarchism to avant-garde art and popular culture in Barcelona, see Temma Kaplan, *Red City, Blue Period: Social Movements in Picasso's Barcelona*. University of California Press, Berkeley, 1992.

27. Cited by Olivier Debroise, *Diego de Montparnasse*. Fondo de Cultura Economica, Mexico City, 1979, p. 65.

28. See B.W. Ife and J.W. Butte, The literary heritage', in *The Spanish World: Civilization and Empire*, ed. J.H. Elliot. Harry N. Abrams, New York, 1991, pp. 212–13.

29. Kenneth Frampton, *A Critical History of Modern Architecture*. Thames and Hudson, London, 1980, pp. 64–73.

30. Ibid.

31. Antoni Gaudí, *Manuscritos, articulos, conversaciones y dibujos*, ed. Marcia Codinachs.

Consejería de Cultura del Consejo Reyional, Murcia, 1982, p. 93: 'Originalidad es volver al origen'.

32. Frampton, op. cit.
33. Ibid.
34. George R. Collins, *Antonio Gaudí*. George Braziller, New York, 1960, pp. 7, 13.
35. Walter Benjamin, 'The work of art in the age of mechanical reproduction' (1936), in *Illuminations*, trans. Harry Zohn. Schocken Books, New York, 1969.
36. Benjamin, 'Thesis VII on the philosophy of history' (1940), in *Illuminations*, op. cit., p. 256.
37. Benjamin, 'Thesis IX' in *Illuminations*, op. cit., pp. 257–8.
38. O.K. Werckmeister, 'Walter Benjamin, Paul Klee, and the angel of history', *Oppositions*, No. 25, Fall 1982, pp. 103ff.
39. Pablo Picasso, 'The picture as a sum of destructions' (1935), in *Picasso on Art*, ed. Dore Ashton. Viking Press, New York, 1972, p. 38.
40. Patricia Leighten, 'The white peril and *L'Art nègre*: Picasso, primitivism, and anti-colonialism', *The Art Bulletin*, Vol. LXXII, No. 4, December 1990, pp. 604–30. See also Kaplan, op. cit., pp. 24–8; and James Joll, *The Anarchists*. Methuen, London, 1979, pp. 207–57.
41. R. Wollheim, 'Looking at Picasso's *Demoiselles d'Avignon*', public lecture, University of New Mexico, Albuquerque, 5 March 1996.
42. Patricia Leighten, *Reordering the Universe: Picasso and Anarchism*. Princeton University Press, Princeton, 1989, pp. 13ff.
43. Gladys March, *Diego Rivera: My Life, My Art* (1960). Dover Press, New York, 1991, p. 58.
44. Thomas Crow, 'Modernism and mass culture in the visual arts', in *Pollock and After*, ed. Francis Fascina. Harper & Row, New York, 1985, p. 250.
45. This is, of course, the argument made in Clement Greenberg, 'Modernist painting' (1965), in *The New Art*, ed. Gregory Battock. Dutton, New York, 1973, pp. 66–77.
46. For a discussion of Bakhtin on this, see Craven, 'Clement Greenberg and the "triumph" of western art', *Third Text*, No. 25, Winter 1993/4, pp. 3–9.
47. Rosalind Krauss, 'In the name of Picasso', in *The Originality of the Avant-Garde and Other Modernist Myths*. MIT Press, Cambridge, MA, 1986, pp. 23–41.
48. See, for example, both Meyer Shapiro, 'The nature of abstract art' (1957) and 'Recent abstract painting' (1957), in *Modern Art: 19th and 20th Centuries*. George Braziller, New York, 1978, pp. 185–227.
49. For a survey of the 200 Cubist paintings executed by Rivera between 1913 and 1917, see *Diego Rivera: The Cubist Years*. Phoenix Art Museum, 1984, pp. 104–9.
50. Oriana Baddeley and Valerie Fraser, *Drawing the Line: Art and Cultural Identity in Contemporary Latin America*. Verso, London, 1989, p. 102.
51. Ibid.
52. André Breton, 'A great, black poet, Aimé Césaire' (1943), in *What is Surrealism?*, ed. Franklin Rosemont. Pathfinder, New York, 1978, p. 232.
53. Breton, 'Interview with Rene Belance' (1945) and 'Speech to young Haitian poets', in *What is Surrealism?*, op. cit., pp. 256, 259.
54. James Clifford, *The Predicament of Culture*. Harvard University Press, Cambridge, MA, 1988, pp. 120ff.

55. For an extended discussion of these issues, see David Craven, *The New Concept of Art and Popular Culture in Nicaragua Since the Revolution in 1979*. Edwin Mellen Press, Lewiston, 1989.

Reverse Appropriation as Nationalism in Modern African Art

1. A.D. Galloway, 'Missionary impact on Nigeria', *Nigeria Magazine*, Special issue, October 1960, p. 63.
2. Uche Okeke, 'History of modern Nigerian art', *Nigeria Magazine*, No. 128–9, 1979, p. 103.
3. Sir Edward Cust, *Reflections on West African Affairs Addressed to the Colonial Office*. Hatchard, London, 1839.
4. Quoted in Dapo Onabolu, 'Aina Onabolu', *Nigeria Magazine*, No. 79, December 1963, p. 295.
5. George Fowler in Aina Onabolu's visitors' book, Lagos, 13 August 1938.
6. Akinola Lasekan, 'Western art on African shores', unpublished manuscript, University of Nigeria, Nsukka, 1966.
7. G.A. Stevens, 'The future of African art: with special reference to problems arising in Gold Coast colony', *Africa: Journal of the International Institute of African Languages and Cultures*, Vol. III, 1930, pp. 150–60.
8. Cust, op. cit.
9. Revd Glover, Record of Sunday Service, Roman Catholic Mission, Esa Oke, Western Nigeria, 8 September 1935.
10. Much of the credit for this must go to the detailed but mostly unpublished and largely unacknowledged work of Nigerian art historian Ola Oloidi, which nevertheless has provided the documentary basis for the genealogy of modern Nigerian art. See Kojo Fosu (1986), Susan Vogel (1992), Jean Kennedy (1993).
11. In his *Gallery of Gold Coast Celebrities*, Dr I.S. Ephson writes about Attabora Kweku Enu (1742–98), an ex-slave who became a painter in Britain and worked 'in 1788 ... in the service of Cosway, the first painter to the Prince of Wales' (p. 31). Unfortunately, I have been unable to trace Enu's slave narrative, *Reflections on the Slave Trade and the Slavery of Negroes*, reportedly published in English and French, to which Ephson refers.
12. Ola Oloidi, 'Constraints on the growth and development of modern Nigerian art in the colonial period', Arts Faculty seminar, University of Nigeria, Nsukka, 1986, unpublished, p. 24.
13. Aina Onabolu, 'The lonely beginning', artist's notes, unpublished, 1922.
14. Aina Onabolu, 'My pioneering efforts', artist's private document, 27 August 1937.
15. Oloidi, op. cit., p. 29.
16. Cust, op. cit.
17. J. Holloway, 'Dear Aina', letter dated 4 October 1910, archives of the Onabolu family.
18. In a note in Onabolu's visitors' book of 21 February 1939, a certain F. Miller remarks on the significance of Onabolu's work in a time when Europeans still 'could not see how an African could excel' in an art that was considered western.
19. Writing about Onabolu in *Nigeria Magazine* (No. 79, December 1963, p. 295), his son, Dapo Onabolu, describes Onabolu as 'a man who believed in the intrinsic quality of his people as men who have identical artistic inclinations and potential

with men of other races'. Elsewhere in the same article, he notes that Onabolu saw all art, western or otherwise, as 'a human quantity which was a human legacy, and which like the motor car, the steamship, and the legacy of law, though originating in its various aspects from different but precise localities of the world, was nevertheless part of a general harvest of human thought and endeavour'.

20. L. Richards, April 3, 1919. Letter in the collection of Akinola Lasekan Estate.
21. Ibid.
22. Dapo Onabolu, op cit., p. 295.
23. In Chinua Achebe's novel, *Arrow of God*, the chief protagonist, Ezeulu, explains sending his son to join the white man thus: 'When we want to make a charm we look for the animal whose blood can match its power . . . And our fathers have told us that it may happen to an unfortunate generation that they are pushed beyond the end of things, and their back is broken and hung over a fire. When this happens they may sacrifice their own blood'. *The African Trilogy*, Pan Books, London, 1988.
24. See Susan Vogel, *Africa Explores*. New York, Museum of African Art, 1992.
25. See letter to the Education Department, Lagos, by K.C. Murray, 4 November 1937, urging that 'Mr Onabolu on whose request I have been brought be given every possible cooperation which will encourage him to train more boys in Lagos'. Papers of K.C. Murray, Archives of the National Museum, Lagos.
26. Oloidi, op. cit., p. 29.
27. Ibid., p. 114.
28. Steven Sack, *The Neglected Tradition: Towards a New History of South African Art (1930–1988)*. Johannesburg Art Gallery, 1988, p. 10.
29. Ibid., p. 10.
30. T. Couzens, *The New African: A Study of the Life and Work of H.I.E. Dhlomo*. Ravan Press, Johannesburg, 1985, p. 253.
31. Sack, op. cit., p. 11.
32. P. Savory, *Gerard Bhengu: Zulu Artist*. Howard Timmins, Cape Town, 1965, p. 10.
33. Although Sack contends that of the early artists only Mohl had any influence on South African art (see Sack, op. cit., p. 15), Sekoto's presence can be detected clearly in the work of Ephraim Ngatane, one of the most engaging artists of the late 1950s and early 1960s, who, though he studied under Sihlali and Skotnes of the Polly Street Centre, pursued a muscular style quite distinct from that of Polly Street. Ngatane died tragically young in 1971.
34. F. McEwen, 'Personal reflections', in *Contemporary Stone Carvings from Zimbabwe*. Yorkshire Sculpture Park, 1990, p. 27.
35. Ibid., p. 30.
36. M. Shepherd, in *Stone Carvings from Zimbabwe*, op. cit., p. 18.
37. Ibid., p. 19 (emphasis is mine).
38. F. McEwen, 'Return to origins', *African Arts*, Vol. 1, No. 2, Winter 1968.
39. Ibid., p. 26.
40. McEwen, 'Personal reflections', op. cit., p. 26.
41. Ibid., p. 27.
42. Ulli Beier, *Thirty Years of Oshogbo Art*. Iwalewa, Bayreuth, 1991, p. 6.
43. Ibid., p. 6.
44. Ibid.

45. Sack, op. cit., p. 12.

46. *The Natal Advertiser*, 9 June 1936, quoted in Sack, ibid., p. 12.

Displaying Authenticity *and* Progress

1. In recent years, a growing literature has appeared on the topic of colonial exhibitions, propaganda and iconography. Discussions on (the ambiguity of) the colonial sections' architecture, however, are rare: see Sylvianne Leprun, *Le Théâtre des colonies: scénographie, acteurs et discours de l'imaginaire dans les expositions 1855–1937*. Editions l'Harmattan, Paris, 1986; and Zeynep Çelik, *Displaying the Orient: Architecture of Islam at Nineteenth-Century World's Fairs*. University of California Press, Berkeley/Los Angeles/Oxford, 1992.

2. See E. Hobsbawm, *The Invention of Tradition*. Cambridge University Press, Cambridge/New York/Melbourne, 1983.

3. The economic and political goals of the 1931 Congolese section have been analysed in detail by Etienne Deschamps in 'La Participation de la Belgique à l'Exposition Coloniale Internationale de Paris/Vincennes 1931. L'affirmation d'une politique coloniale sur le scène internationale', unpublished thesis, Université Catholique de Louvain, 1994.

4. Gustave Drèze, *Le Livre d'or de l'Exposition Universelle et Internationale de 1905*, Vol. I. Imprimerie Auguste Bénard, Liège, 1905, p. 487.

5. It is significant, for instance, that Emile Bayard, apart from focusing mainly on those colonies with a monumental heritage – the built environment of *l'Afrique noire* is treated only marginally – also repeatedly tries to link impressive architectural ensembles, like the mosques of Djenné, to stages of western civilization. See Emile Bayard, *l'Art de reconnaître les styles coloniaux de la France*. Librairie Garnier, Paris, 1931, pp. 118, 125.

6. See François Béguin and Gildas Baudez, '"Arabisances": observations on French colonial architecture in North Africa between 1900 and 1950', *Lotus international*, No. 26, 1980, pp. 41–52; and François Béguin, *Arabisances: décor architectural et tracé urbain en Afrique du Nord 1830–1950*. Dunod/Bordas, Paris, 1983.

7. An asterisk indicates that the project in the indicated style was not executed. In 1897 the Congo pavilion was designed in a Beaux-Arts style, but had an Art Nouveau interior.

8. R. Cogniat, 'L'Exposition Coloniale: les palais métropolitains, les colonies étrangères, les pays sous mandats', *l'Architecture*, Vol. XLIV No. 9, 1931, p. 332. If this quote seems to point at Cogniat's sympathy for *art nègre*, the word 'instinctive' reveals that his comment stays in tune with the ethnocentrism of the contemporary colonial discourse.

9. See Jean-Claude Vigato, 'The architecture of the colonial exhibitions in France', *Daidalos*, No. 19, March 1986, p. 30; and Peter Greenhalgh, *Ephemeral Vistas: The Expositions Universelles, Great Exhibitions and World's Fairs, 1851–1939*. Manchester University Press, Manchester, 1988, pp. 71–2.

10. This quote from Louis Madeleine is taken from G. Périer, 'Le Congo Belge à Vincennes', *L'Illustration Congolaise*, No. 117, June 1931, p. 3555.

11. Vigato, op. cit., p. 26.

12. Marcel Temporal, 'De la lettre et de l'esprit de l'architecture dite "moderne" à

l'Exposition Coloniale Internationale de 1931', *l'Architecture d'Aujourd'hui*, nr. hors série 'Paris', June–July 1931, p. 151.

13. Vigato, op. cit., p. 30.
14. Lacoste's own comment on the design of the Congo pavilion is particularly revealing in this respect. See *L'Emulation*, No. 12, December 1931 (issue devoted to the 1931 Congolese section).
15. See Gaetano Minnuci, 'Notiziario tecnico: coperture a lamelle', *Architecttura e Arti Decorative*, anno X, 1931, Vol. V–VI, p. 408.
16. I am referring to what Pat Morton has described as 'hybrids', ambiguous architectural forms that 'ruptured a colonial power structure predicated on the strict segregation of things metropolitan and things colonial'. See Pat Morton, 'A study in hybridity: Madagascar and Morocco at the 1931 Colonial Exposition', *The Journal of Architectural Education*, Vol. 52, No. 2, November 1998, pp. 76–86.
17. Marcel Schmitz, 'L'Architecture coloniale', *Le Bâtiment*, August 1931, pp. 17–18 (Africa Archive, Brussels).
18. Letter from Raymond Cloquet to the Minister of Colonies, 3 January 1933 (Africa Archive, Brussels). Cloquet's critique, however, was not without bias, because in his letter he was himself applying for the commission to design the Congolese section of the 1935 Brussels World's Fair.
19. Letter from Raymond Moenaert to the Minister of Colonies, 3 November 1931 (Africa Archive, Brussels).
20. The project, ambitiously entitled 'Reconstruction géohydrographique et climatérique d'un voyage d'exploration au Congo Belge', was also announced in the colonial press. See *L'Illustration Congolaise*, No. 146, 1 November 1931, pp. 4708–15.
21. For a more extensive discussion of the Congolese section at the 1935 Brussels World's Fair, as well as a general survey of the architecture, see Johan Lagae and Jef Vervoort, *The Universal and International Exhibition in Brussels, 1935*, website, Department of Architecture and Urbanism, Ghent University, 2000. arch.rug.ac.be/expo35
22. See Gaston-Denys Périer, 'L'Enchantement congolais à l'exposition', *Revue du Touring Club de Belgique*, 15 April 1935, pp. 116–20; and the correspondence between the Commissaire Général and the Minister of Colonies (Africa Archive, Brussels).
23. These frescoes were probably painted by the contemporary Congolese artist of Bapende origin, Massalaï, who also decorated the colonial enterprises pavilion, a design by Schoentjes and Douret. Massalaï was one of the artists who at the time were promoted in the Belgian artistic milieu by Gaston-Denys Périer.
24. Bourgeois's contribution to the Brussels Congolese section blurs the image of Bourgeois as a 'master of modern architecture in Belgium', but one has to remember that Bourgeois's importance lies primarily in his activity as a critic and promoter of modernist ideology in Belgium, rather than in the quality of his architectural *œuvre*.
25. In this respect, the situation in the Belgian Congo differs from that in French, British or Italian colonies. No comprehensive analysis of colonial architecture in the Congo has been made. For a brief introduction to the topic, see Anne Van Loo, 'Page coloniale', *Paysages d'architecture*. Archives d'Architecture Moderne, Brussels, 1986, pp. 52–5.
26. See 'Congo Belge', in *Exposition Internationale des Arts et des Techniques dans la Vie Moderne, Paris 1937: Rapport Général présenté par Ed. Labbé*, Paris, 1938–40, Vol. 9, pp. 106–10. The design was by the architect Fernand Petit.

27. See Johan Lagae, 'In search of a "comme chez soi": the ideal colonial house in Congo: a survey', in Jean-Luc Vellut (ed.), *Irruptions de la modernité dans l'ancien Congo Belge c. 1900–1950.* Louvain-la-Neuve, Tervuren, 2000.

28. I am quoting a definition of the notion of 'architectural ambivalence', as suggested by Hilde Heynen and André Loeckx in their comment on Pat Morton's discussion of the Madagascar pavilion at the 1931 'Exposition Coloniale Internationale'; see 'Scenes of ambivalence: concluding remarks on architectural patterns of displacement', *The Journal of Architectural Education*, Vol. 52, No. 2, November 1998, p. 103.

29. The Congolese section in New York, designed by Victor Bourgeois and Léon Stynen under the supervision of Henry Van de Velde, was commented on in detail in *L'Illustration Congolaise*, Nos. 213 and 215, 1939, pp. 7352–3 and 7439–42. For the official ambitions of both the New York and Liège exhibition, see *L'Illustration Congolaise*, No. 214, 1939, pp. 7404–5, 7417.

30. See G. Dedoyard, 'L'Architecture à l'exposition', in *Exposition Internationale de la Technique de l'Eau, Liège 1939: Rapport Général*, pp. 75–107; and Xavier Folville, 'Le Corbusier, le Groupe Equerre et l'Exposition de l'Eau' [1939], in P. Burniat (ed.), *Le Corbusier en Belgique*. CFC-Editions, Bruxelles/Fondation LC, Paris, 1997, pp. 187–98.

31. Design note by Henri Lacoste (Africa Archive, Brussels). Further information on the Congolese section in Liège was found in the *Rapport Général*, the Lacoste files in the Archives d'Architecture Moderne, Brussels, and the personal archives of the Lacoste family.

32. 1956 marked a turning point regarding the indigenous population's claims for independence in the Belgian Congo, and many historians consider the 1958 Brussels fair as a catalyst for the Congo's struggle for independence, leading to the end of Belgian colonial rule only two years later. Yet, within most of the colonialists' minds, the idea of the Congo becoming independent in June 1960 was inconceivable as late as 1958.

33. Leprun, op. cit., p. 212.

Colonial / Postcolonial Intersections

1. Pierre Nora, 'Preface to the English-language edition', in Pierre Nora (ed.), *Realms of Memory: Rethinking the French Past.* Columbia University Press, New York, 1996, Vol. 1, p. xvii.

2. Pierre Nora, 'Between memory and history', in ibid., pp. 3, 14–15.

3. Ibid., p. 18.

4. 'Rapport au Comité du Génie, séance du 1 octobre 1831', Société Historique de l'Armée de Terre (SHAT), Génie, Alger, art. 8, section 6.

5. For a reconstruction of this area before the French interventions, see André Raymond, 'Le Centre d'Alger en 1830', *Revue de l'occident musulman et de la Meditérranée* Vol. 31, No. 1, 1981, pp. 73–81.

6. 'Song about the Taking of Algiers' (composed by Si Abd al-Qadir), quoted in Alf Andrew Heggoy, *The French Conquest of Algiers, 1830: An Algerian Oral Tradition.* Ohio University Center for International Studies, Athens, OH, 1986, p. 23.

7. 'Place d'Alger, 1831', Feuille no. 1, SHAT, Génie, Alger, art. 8, section 1, carton 2.

8. 'Rapport au Comité du Génie, séance du 11 novembre 1831', SHAT, Génie, Alger, art. 8, section 6. With this appeal, Lemercier prepared the way and predicted Napoleon III's well-known *royaume arabe* (Arab kingdom) policies developed in the 1860s. Qualifying the Arabs as 'an intelligent, proud, and warrior' race, Napoleon called for treating Arabs as compatriots and declared that Algeria was 'not a colony, but an Arab Kingdom', with himself as the emperor of the Arabs as much as he was the emperor of the French. See Benjamin Stora, *Histoire de l'Algérie coloniale (1830–1954)*. Editions La Découverte, Paris, 1991, p. 20. Napoleon's policies made a significant impact on French architecture in Algeria, specifically in the introduction of 'Arab' details into European-style buildings.

9. 'Projets pour 1833', SHAT, Génie, Alger, art. 8, section 1, carton 2.

10. 'Projets pour 1834', SHAT, Génie, Alger, art. 8, section 1, carton 3.

11. Maurice Agulhon, *Marianne into Battle: Republican Imagery and Symbolism in France, 1879–1880*, trans. Janet Lloyd. Cambridge University Press, Cambridge, 1981, p. 70. The Duc d'Orléans was Ferdinand-Philippe who died in a carriage accident in Neuilly in 1842, without ascending to the throne.

12. The al-Djadid mosque acquired an unusual feature when the French authorities placed a clock on its minaret facing the square in 1852. (See Fernand Arnaudiès, *Esquisses anecdotiques et historiques du Vieil Alger*. Editions A. Bathélemy, Avignon, 1990, p. 107). The treatment of the minaret as a clock tower reflects a blatant act of appropriation. Although a Muslim religious monument was left to stand on the main plaza, it was transformed in an act of secularization.

13. 'Song about the Taking of Algiers' quoted in Heggoy, op. cit., p. 23.

14. Arnaudiès, op. cit., p. 202. The replica is now in the Château d'Eu in Normandy; the original was transported to Neuilly after Algerian independence. See Anne-Marie Briat, Janine de la Hogue, André Appel and Marc Baroli, *Des Chemins et des hommes: la France en Algérie (1830–1962)*. Editions Harriet, Hélette, 1995, p. 175.

15. René Lespès, *Pour comprendre L'Algérie*. Heintz, Paris, 1937.

16. Jean-Jacques Jordi and Jean-Louis Planche, '1860–1930: une certaine idée de la construction de la France', in Jean-Jacques Jordi and Jean-Louis Planche (eds), *Alger 1860–1919: le modèle ambigu du triomphe colonial*. Editions Autrement, Paris, 1999, pp. 45–6.

17. Nora, 'Between memory and history', op. cit., p. 19.

18. Michel de Certeau, *The Practice of Everyday Life*, trans. Steven Rendall. University of California Press, Berkeley, 1984, p. 108.

19. I quote Terence Ranger and extend his analysis of the British colonies in Africa to the Algerian situation. See Terence Ranger, 'The invention of tradition in colonial Africa', in Eric Hobsbawm and Terence Ranger (eds), *The Invention of Tradition*. Cambridge University Press, Cambridge, 1983, p. 237. In the same volume, Bernard Cohen applies the argument to India; see 'Representing authority in Victorian India', p. 209.

20. I thank Nabila Fertani Bakli and Raja Khabcheche, students in my graduate seminar (spring 1999) at the Ecole Nationale d'Architecture et d'Urbanisme, University of Tunis, for this information.

21. De Certeau, op. cit., p. 93.

22. Théophile Gautier pointed to this ambition in a cynical tone when he described the buildings that lined the Place du Gouvernement as pretending 'to recall the architecture of the Rue de Rivoli'. See Théophile Gautier, *Voyage pittoresque en Algérie*

(1845), reprinted with an introduction and notes by Madeleine Cottin. Librairie Droz, Geneva, 1973, p. 183.

23. For a discussion of the growth of Algiers during the French period, see Zeynep Çelik, *Urban Forms and Colonial Confrontations: Algiers under French Rule*. University of California Press, Berkeley, 1997, chapter 2.

24. This point was articulated by Eugène Fromentin, who wrote 'the New Gate (Bab-el-Djedid) . . . is the one through which the Army entered in 1830'. See Arnaudiès, op. cit., p. 205.

25. Fromentin quoted in Arnaudiès, op. cit., p. 205. In 1962, Maréchal Bugeaud's statue was transported to a family property in Excideuil, Dordogne. See Briat *et al.*, op. cit., p. 48.

26. In addition to the Milk Bar, bombs were also placed in the 'Cafeteria', the 'Mauritania' building, where the Air France offices were located, and the Boulevard Admiral Pierre. There were casualties in the Milk Bar and the Cafeteria. These attacks are memorably re-created in Gillo Pontecorvo's epic film, *Battle of Algiers* (1966).

27. Priscilla Parkhurst Ferguson, *Paris as Revolution: Writing the 19th Century City*. University of California Press, Berkeley, 1994, pp. 14–15.

28. Daniel Milo, 'Street names', in *Realms of Memory*, ed. Pierre Nora, trans. Arthur Goldhammer. Columbia University Press, New York, 1997, Vol. II, pp. 365–6.

29. The volatility of such change is pointed out by Ferguson with reference to Paris. See Ferguson, op. cit., p. 197. A good example that attests to such volatility in Algiers is the aforementioned vernacular reference to the Place des Martyres as Place du Cheval.

30. Discussing the fervour that followed the French revolution, Milo qualifies the years 1792–4 as 'the great wave of debaptisings' and gives many examples from the renaming of streets in Paris and other French cities that substituted religious and royal signs with revolutionary ones. For example, Place Louis XV became Place de la Révolution, Quai Conti became Quai de l'Unité, Pont Notre-Dame became Pont de la Raison. See Milo, op. cit., p. 372. The phenomenon is similar in Algeria, but the oppositional choice is more straightforward in the examples cited above.

31. Leonard Kodjo, 'Noms des rues, noms des maîres', unpublished paper, 1987, quoted in Christopher Miller, *Theories of Africans*. University of Chicago Press, Chicago, 1990, p. 102, note 71.

32. Djamila Amrane, *Les Femmes algeriennes dans la guerre*. Plons, Paris, 1991, p. 45.

33. On French colonial postcards on Algeria, see Malek Alloula, *The Colonial Harem*, trans. Myrna Godzich and Wlad Godzich. University of Minnesota Press, Minneapolis, 1986.

34. Assia Djebar, *Femmes d'Alger dans leur appartement*. des femmes, Paris, 1979, pp. 170–8. This is a slightly modified version of the argument I presented in the epilogue of *Urban Forms*, op. cit.

35. For a comparative discussion of various versions of Picasso's *Femmes d'Alger*, see L. Steinberg, 'The Algerian women and Picasso at large', in Steinberg, *Other Criteria: Confrontations with Twentieth Century Art*. New York, Oxford University Press, 1972, pp. 125–234.

36. Djebar, op. cit., pp. 186–9. The association of Algerian women's bodies with the memory of the war is a recurring theme in Djebar's work. See, for example, the discussion by Ranjana Khanna on *La Zerda et les chants de l'oubli* (1980), a film Djebar

made with Malek Alloula on the French occupation of Algeria. *La Zerda* begins with the sentence 'La mémoire est corps de femme' ('memory is the body of women'). Ranjana Khanna, '*The Battle of Algiers* and *The Nouba of the Women of Mont Chenoua*', *Third Text*, No. 43, Summer 1998, p. 26.

37. Steinberg, op. cit., p. 130.
38. Leila Sebbar, *Les Carnets de Shérazade*. Stock, Paris, 1985, p. 152.
39. Nora, 'Between memory and history', op. cit., p. 15.

Whose Heritage?

1. Michel Foucault, *Discipline and Punish*. Tavistock, London, 1977.
2. Benedict Anderson, *Imagined Communities*. Verso, London, 1983.
3. Carol Duncan and Alan Wallach, 'The universal survey museum', *Art History*, No. 4, December 1980, p. 451.
4. Norman Davies, 'But we never stand quite alone', *Guardian*, 13 November 1999.
5. David Scott, *Re-fashioning Futures: Criticism after Post-Coloniality*. Princeton University Press, Princeton, NJ, 1999.
6. Raymond Williams, *The Long Revolution*. Pelican, Harmondsworth, 1963, pp. 66–7.
7. On this whole question, see Norman Davies, *The Isles: A History*. Macmillan, Basingstoke, 1999.
8. Raphael Samuel, *Theatres of Memory*. Routledge, London, 1997.
9. Jacques Derrida, *Margins of Philosophy*. Harvester, Brighton, 1982.
10. C.L.R. James, 'Popular art and the cultural tradition', *Third Text*, No. 10, Spring 1990, pp. 3–10.
11. Ashis Nandy, *The Intimate Enemy*. Oxford University Press, Oxford and New Delhi, 1983.
12. Salah Hassan, in *Reading the Contemporary: African Art from Theory to Market-Place*, eds Olu Oguibe and Okwui Enwezor. Institute of International Visual Arts (inIVA), London, 1999.

Representation

Introduction

1. Stuart Hall, 'Introduction', in S. Hall (ed.), *Representation: Cultural Representations and Signifying Practices*. Sage, London, 1997, p. 10.
2. Gayatri Chakravorty Spivak, 'Reading *The Satanic Verses*', *Third Text*, No. 11, Summer 1990, p. 41.
3. For a useful account of the paradoxical necessity of the local for the global, see Kevin Robins, 'Tradition and translation: national culture in its global context', in John Corner and Sylvia Harvey (eds), *Enterprise and Heritage: Crosscurrents of National Culture*. Routledge, London, 1991, p. 38.
4. Avtar Brah and Annie E. Coombes (eds), *Hybridity and its Discontents: Politics, Science, Culture*. Routledge, London, 2000; see also, Ruth Phillips, *Trading Identities: The Souvenir in Native North American Art from the Northeast, 1700–1900*. University of Washington Press, Seattle, 1999.

5. For an opposing position, see Roger Benjamin, 'Aboriginal art: exploitation or empowerment?', in Rex Butler (ed.), *What is Appropriation? An Anthology of Critical Writings on Australian Art in the '80s and '90s.* Institute of Modern Art and the Power Institute, Brisbane, 1996; see also, Fred Myers, 'Representing culture: the production of discourse(s) for Aboriginal acrylic paintings', *Cultural Anthropology*, Vol. 6, No. 3, 1991.
6. Kobena Mercer, 'Black art and the burden of representation', *Third Text*, No. 10, Spring 1990, p. 78.

Discovering the European Wild Men

1. A related reflection on this topic is my essay 'Identity and wilderness: ethnography and the history of an imaginary primitive group', *Ethnologia Europaea*, No. 21, pp. 103–23.
2. I use the Spanish edition prepared by Pedro Gálvez: *Libro de las ninfas, los silfos, los pigmeos, las salamandras y los demás espíritus* de Philipus Aureolus Theophrastus Bombastus von Hohenheim, known as Paracelsus, bilingual edition. Obelisco, Barcelona, 1983. The original German work can be read in Vol. 14, pp. 115–51, of *Samtliche Werke*, 1. *Medizinische naturwissenschaftliche und philosophische*, Karl Sudhoff edition. Munich/Berlin, 1922–33. An English translation is found in *Four Treatises of Theophrastus von Hohenheim called Paracelsus*, ed. Henry E. Sigerist. The Johns Hopkins Press, Baltimore, 1941.
3. J. Geiler von Kaysersberg, *Die Emeis*. Strasbourg, 1509–19, sermon twenty, p. 40, cited by Frank Tinland, *L'homme sauvage*. Payot, Paris, 1968, p. 44; and Richard Bernheimer, *Wildmen in the Middle Ages*. Harvard University Press, Cambridge, 1952, p. 199.
4. Paracelsus, op. cit. V:97.
5. Ibid., I:I:35.
6. Ibid., I:I:37.
7. Ibid.
8. Quoted in the entry 'Paracelsus' of the *Encyclopaedia Britannica*, 1986. In an excellent essay on Paracelsus, Alexandre Koyre observes that in fact most of his teachings consisted of folklore, to which he would add extraordinary names, invented and adapted with a puerile and naive enthusiasm. Thus, in Paracelsus, we can find references, in addition to those mentioned, of the *Evestra, Larvae, Leffas* and *Mumiae*. (See Alexandre Koyre, *Mystiques, spirituels, alchimistes*. Armand Colin, Paris, 1955, p. 48.)
9. Quoted from Thomas Bendyshe, 'The history of anthropology', in *Memoirs of the Anthropological Society of London*, Vol. I (1863–4), pp. 353–4.
10. Anthony Pagden, *The Fall of the Natural Man*. Cambridge University Press, Cambridge, 1982, p. 23.
11. See Edmundo O'Gorman, 'Sobre la naturaleza bestial del indio americano', in *Filosofía y Letras*, Vols. I and II (1941); and Juan A. Ortega y Medina, *Imagología del bueno y del mal salvaje*. Unam, Mexico, 1987, pp. 29–48. For a general study on these problems, see the excellent book by Peter Mason, *Deconstructing America: Representations of the Other*. Routledge, London, 1990.
12. Paracelsus, op. cit., I:II:31–7.

13. See note 10 by Pedro Gálvez, translator of the treaty of Paracelsus, op. cit.

14. Ibid., II:51.

15. Ibid.

16. Ibid., III:65.

17. Ibid., III:67.

18. Ibid., II:63.

19. This can be seen in Kraemer and Sprenger's *Malleus Maleficarum*, Part One, III and X; Part Two, I and VIII. I use the Spanish translation: *El martillo de las brujas*, trans. M. Jímenez Montserín. Felmar, Madrid, 1976.

20. K. Gesner, *Historia animalium*, Zurich, 1551, Vol. I, p. 979.

21. See the 1498 Spanish edition of *Viaje a tierra santa* in the facsimile reproduction of the Instituto Bibliográfico Hispánico, Madrid, 1974.

22. Gesner, op. cit., p. 970.

23. Carl von Linné and C.E. Hoppius, *Amoenitates academicae*. Erlangen, 1789, Vol. 6, p. 76.

24. Ambroise Paré, *Monstruos y prodigios*. Siruela, Madrid, 1987.

25. Ibid., XIX:64.

26. Ibid., IX:46.

27. On this subject, see Jurgis Baltrusaitis, *Aberrations: essais sur la légende des formes*. Flammarion, Paris, 1983; Jules Berger de Xivrey, *Traditions tératologiques ou recits de l'Antiquité et du moyen âge en occident sur quelques points de la fable, du merveilleux et de l'histoire naturelle* . . . Imprimerie Royale, Paris, 1836; John Block Friedman, *The Monstrous Races in Medieval Art and Thought*. Harvard University Press, Cambridge, 1981; Patrick Tort, *L'Ordre et les monstres*. Le Sycomore, Paris, 1980.

28. Quoted by Tort, op. cit., pp. 7–8.

29. Paré, op. cit., IV:29.

30. Gesner, op. cit., p. 970.

31. *De Animalibus*, II:4; see translation into French: *Histoire des animaux* (I–IV), by P. Louis. Belles-Lettres, Paris, 1964.

32. Christóbal Colón, *Textos y documentos completos*. Alianza Editorial, Madrid, 1982, p. 144.

33. Ibid., pp. 144 and 142.

34. M. de Cuneo, letter to Annari of 28 October 1495, *Raccolta colombiana*, III, Vol. 2, pp. 95–197, cited by T. Todorov, *La Conquete de l'Amérique: la question de l'autre*. Seuil, Paris, 1982, pp. 53–4.

35. See Pagden, op. cit.

36. Bartolomé de las Casas, *Opúsculos, cartas y memoriales*. Biblioteca de Autores Españoles, Madrid, Vol. 110, 1958, pp. 307–8.

37. Lewis Hanke, *Aristotle and the American Indian: Study in Race Prejudice in the Modern World*. Regnery, Chicago, 1959.

38. Ernst Cassirer, *La Philosophie des formes symboliques. 2: La Pensée mythique*. Minuit, Paris, 1972, p. 18.

39. *Phaedo*, 229 D–E.

40. Ibid., 230. For a neo-Kantian thought, see Cassirer, op. cit., p. 16. A different interpretation of this passage of *Phaedo* is found in Marcel Detienne, *La invencion de la mitologia*. Península, Barcelona, 1985, p. 106. In *Paideia* (Fondo de Cultura Económica, Mexico, 1962, p. 970n), Jaeger observes that the word *agroikos* became the most common word for lack of culture, as expressed in Aristotle (*Rhetoric*, III, 7,

1408–32, and *Nicomachean Ethics*, II, 7, 1108–26), as well as in Teophrastus (*Characters*, IV).

Cowboys and . . .

1. Wilbur F. Gordy, *Elementary History of the United States*. Charles Scribner's Sons, New York, 1930.
2. Davey Crockett, diary, 1813.
3. Tzvetan Todorov, *The Conquest of America*. Harper & Row, New York, 1984.
4. Jean Fisher, 'Jimmie Durham', in *Matoaka Ale Attakulakula Anel Guledisgo Hnihi*, exhibition catalogue. Matt's Gallery, London, 1988.
5. Jean Fisher, private letter, n.d.
6. *The New Yorker*, 21 November 1988.
7. V.S. Naipaul, *A Turn in the South*. Vintage International, New York, 1988.
8. *Confucian Analects*, Book XIII, trans. James Legge, as quoted in Morton Fried, *The Notion of Tribe*. Cummings, Menlo Park, CA, 1975.
9. Letter from Gauguin to Theo Van Gogh, 'On painting', *c*. 20 November 1989, as cited in *Gauguin: A Retrospective*, eds Marla Prather and Charles F. Stuchey. Park Lane, New York, 1989, p. 109.
10. This is the inscription over the entrance to Mexico City's Museum of Anthropology, but it is so widely quoted in Mexico that it has become almost a motto.
11. James Luna, catalogue, Centro Cultural de la Raza, San Diego, 1985.
12. Bogota, Colombia.

Ethnicity and Internationality

1. Simon Ford, 'The myth of the Young British Artist' (1996), in Duncan McCorquodale, Naomi Siderfin and Julian Stallabrass (eds), *Occupational Hazard: Critical Writing on Recent British Art*. Black Dog, London, 1998, pp. 132–41.
2. Howardena Pindell, 'Art (world) & racism', *Third Text*, Nos. 3/4, Spring–Summer 1988, pp. 157–90. Similar shifts in the UK are examined in Janice Cheddie, 'Storm damage', *make*, No. 76, June–July 1997, pp. 15–16.
3. Jean Fisher, 'The syncretic turn: cross-cultural practices in the age of multiculturalism', in Melina Kalinovska (ed.), *New Histories*. Institute of Contemporary Arts, Boston, 1996, p. 35.
4. Herman Gray, *Watching 'Race': Television and the Struggle for Blackness*. University of Minnesota Press, Minneapolis, 1995, p. 230.
5. Henry Louis Gates Jr, 'Black London', *The New Yorker*, 28 April–5 May 1998, p. 199.
6. Fisher, op. cit., p. 35.
7. Stuart Hall, 'New ethnicities', in *Black Film/British Cinema*, ICA Documents No. 7. Institute of Contemporary Art, London, 1988.
8. See my 'Art that is ethnic in inverted commas', *frieze*, No. 35, November–December 1995, and 'Inter-culturality is ordinary', in Ria Lavrijsen (ed.), *Inter-cultural Arts Education and Municipal Policy*. Royal Tropical Institute, Amsterdam, 1997.
9. Yinka Shonibare, 'Fabric, and the irony of authenticity', in Nikos Papastergiadis (ed.), *Annotations*, No. 2. inIVA, London, 1996, p. 40.

10. Kelly Jones, 'In the thick of it: David Hammons and hair culture in the 1970s', *Third Text*, No. 44, Autumn 1998, pp. 17–24.

11. See texts by Godfrey Worsdale, Lisa Corrin and Kodwo Eshun in *Chris Ofili*, exhibition catalogue, Serpentine Gallery, London, and Southampton City Art Gallery, 1998.

12. In Patricia Bickers, 'Let's get physical', *Art Monthly*, No. 202, December–January 1996–7, p. 4.

13. Iwona Blazwick, in 'Oh My God! Some notes from a conversation with Jaki Irvine and Steve McQueen', *make*, No. 74, February–March 1997, p. 7.

14. John Roberts, 'Mad for it! Philistinism, the everyday and the new British art', *Third Text*, No. 35, Summer 1996, p. 29.

15. Renée Green, 'Artist's dialogue', in Alan Read (ed.), *The Fact of Blackness: Frantz Fanon and Visual Representation*. Bay Press, Seattle, 1996, p. 146.

16. In Bickers, op. cit., p. 5.

17. Stuart Hall, 'The local and the global pt 1: globalization and ethnicity', in Anthony King (ed.), *Culture, Globalization and the World System*. State University of New York, Binghampton, 1991, p. 29. Neo-liberal wishes for a race-free future are critically dissected in Paul Gilroy, *Joined-Up Politics and Post-Colonial Melancholia*. ICA Diversity Lecture, Institute of Contemporary Arts, London, 1999.

18. Michael Bracewell, *England is Mine: Pop Life in Albion from Wilde to Goldie*. Harper-Collins, London, 1997, pp. 211, 212; Coward cited p. 222.

19. Ibid., p. 231.

20. Ibid. Tony Parsons cited p. 222.

21. In Nikos Papastergiadis, 'Global proposals: a conversation with Gilane Tawadros', in *Dialogues in Diaspora*. Rivers Oram, London, 1998, p. 136.

22. See Nikos Papastergiadis, *The Complicities of Culture: Hybridity and 'New Internationalism'*, Cornerhouse Communique No. 4. Cornerhouse Gallery, Manchester, 1994; and 'Back to basics: British art and the problems of a global frame', in Bernice Murphy (ed.), *Pichtura Britannica: Art from Britain*. Museum of Contemporary Art, Sydney, 1997, pp. 124–45.

23. Homi Bhabha, 'Beyond the pale: art in the age of multicultural translation', in Elisabeth Sussman *et al.* (eds), *1993 Biennial Exhibition*. Whitney Museum of American Art/Abrams, New York, 1993.

24. Ann Walmsley, *The Caribbean Artists Movement 1966–1972: A Literary and Cultural History*. New Beacon, London and Port of Spain, 1992.

25. Insights from 'The syncretic turn' are expanded in Jean Fisher, 'The work between us', in Okwui Enwezor (ed.), *Trade Routes: History and Geography*, catalogue to the 2nd Johannesburg Biennale, Greater Johannesburg Metropolitan Council and Prince Claus Fund, 1997.

26. Stuart Hall, 'When was the post-colonial? Thinking at the limit', in Lidia Curti and Iain Chambers (eds), *The Post-Colonial Question*. Routledge, London and New York, 1996. Relatedly, see Bruce Robbins and Pheng Cheah (eds), *Cosmopolitics: Thinking and Feeling Beyond the Nation*. University of Minnesota Press, Minneapolis, 1998.

Art as Ethnocide

1. Pierre Clastres, 'On ethnocide', *Art & Text*, No. 28, Sydney, 1988.

2. It is this kind of overview produced by art history that allows Ann Stephen and Ian

Burn to connect Albert Namitjira to present concerns and to make the tentative and highly debatable claim of his art as a form of resistance rather than assimilation. 'Traditional painter: the transfiguration of Albert Namitjira', *Age Monthly Review*, Melbourne, November, 1987.

3. Vivien Johnson, 'Our appropriation is your dispossession', *Praxis M*, No. 17, 1987, p. 5.
4. Ibid.
5. Ibid., p. 4.
6. Bernice Murphy, 'Curating contemporary Aboriginal art', *Praxis M*, No. 17, 1987, p. 23.
7. Pam Nathan and Dick Leichleitner Japanangka, *Settle Down Country Pmere Arlaltyewele*. Kibble Books/Central Australian Aboriginal Congress, Melbourne and Alice Springs, 1983.
8. Reports in the *Sydney Morning Herald*, 29 September, 3 and 4 October 1988.
9. John Mulvaney, 'A question of values: museums and cultural property', in I. McBryde (ed.) *Who Owns the Past?* Oxford University Press, Melbourne, 1985.
10. Henrietta Fourmile, 'Museums and Aborigines: a case study in contemporary scientific colonialism', *Praxis M*, No. 17, 1987, pp. 9–10.

Identity

Introduction

1. Drew Leder, *The Absent Body*. University of Chicago Press, Chicago and London, 1990, p. 1.
2. See, for instance, Thomas McEvilley, 'Opening the trap', in *Art and Otherness: Crisis in Cultural Identity*. McPherson and Company, New York, 1999. Here, he argues that involvement in practices of collecting (whether as curator or viewer) are, above all, connected to individual and/or communal attempts at *self*-definition or redefinition.

Identity: Reality or Fiction?

1. Sebastián López, 'Latjnsamerikaanse kunstenaars in Nederland' ('Latin American artists in the Netherlands'), in *Vulkaan van handen*. Centrum voor Chilense Cultuur, Amsterdam, 1987.
2. BKR: Beeldende Kunstenaarsregeling (system of [official] artists' allowances) [Van Dale].
3. H. Sermaat, 'De Kunst van het artijokken eten, evaluatie beleid kunstuitengen van allochtonen' ('The art of eating artichokes: an evaluation of the policy concerning the artistic productions of foreigners'), *Raad voor de Kunst*, Den Haag, November 1989, p. 2.
4. Lucy Lippard, *Mixed Blessings*. Pantheon Books, New York, 1990, p. 7.

Restless Hybrids

1. Gilberto Freyre, *The Masters and the Slaves*, trans. S. Putnam. Alfred A. Knopf, New York, 1946, p. xx. When referring to the general development of such a culture, Freyre does not speak of a process of hybridity, preferring the term *mestizo*, and when addressing the specific formations of the Brazilian national identity, he proposed the term 'Luso-Tropical'.
2. Max Raphael, *Proudhon, Marx, Picasso*, trans. I. Marcuse. Lawrence and Wishart, London, 1980, p. 130.
3. Don F. Miller, *The Reason of Metaphor*. Sage, New Delhi, 1992, p. 120.
4. Ashis Nandy, *The Intimate Enemy*. Oxford University Press, New Delhi, 1983, p. xv.
5. Ibid., p. 7.
6. Robert J.C. Young, *Colonial Desire: Hybridity in Theory, Culture and Race*. Routledge, London, 1995, pp. 20–2.
7. Y. Lotman, *The Universe of the Mind*, trans. A. Shukman. Tauris, London, 1991, p. 123.
8. J.M. Lotman and B.A. Uspenskij, *The Semiotics of Russian Culture*, trans. A. Shukman. Michigan Slavic Contribution, No. 11, Ann Arbor, 1984, p. xii.
9. Lotman, op. cit., p. 150.
10. Ibid.
11. Michel Serres, *Hermes*. Johns Hopkins University Press, Baltimore, 1982, p. 80.
12. Lotman, op. cit., p. 131.
13. Ibid.
14. Serres, op. cit., pp. 66–7.
15. Stuart Hall, 'Old and new identities, old and new ethnicities', in Anthony King (ed.), *Culture, Globalization and The World-System*. Macmillan, London, 1991, p. 49.
16. Ibid., p. 51.
17. Ibid., p. 35.

Film

Dancing with Words and Speaking with Forked Tongues

1. *Dances with Wolves* (1990), director Kevin Costner, Majestic Films International. Although the lead Indian characters are played by Native Americans, very few are Lakota Sioux.
2. Jimmie Durham, 'Cowboys and . . .', *Third Text*, No. 12, Autumn 1990, p. 5.
3. Governor George Gilmer, quoted in Robert Berkhofer Jr, *The White Man's Indian*. Vintage Books, New York, 1978, p. 161.
4. President George Bush, State of the Union Address, House of Representatives, 29 January 1991.
5. Max Horkheimer, *Eclipse of Reason*. Oxford University Press, New York, 1947, pp. 7–9.
6. For a comprehensive account of treaties and the federal government, see Vine Deloria Jr, *In Utmost Good Faith*. Straight Arrow Books, San Francisco, 1971.
7. Berkhofer, op. cit., p. 103.
8. Kevin Costner, interview in *The Media Show: Dances with Wolves*, Channel 4, 1990.

9. Rudy Martin, interview in *The Media Show*, 1990.

10. *The Sunday Times Magazine*, 9 February 1991.

11. Henry Nash Smith, *Virgin Land: The American West as Symbol and Myth*. Harvard University Press, Cambridge, MA, 1970.

12. *Powwow Highway*, 1988, directed by Jonathan Wacks, Handmade Films.

13. *War Party*, 1989, directed by Franc Roddam, Hemdale Independent Film. The film recounts a collaboration by the town and tribal councils to restage a local historical battle to attract tourists. But 'history repeats itself', with overtones of Wounded Knee 1973. The central protagonists are both white and native actors.

14. *Harold of Orange*, 1984, directed by Richard Weise, script by Gerald Vizenor, Film in the Cities, Minneapolis. See Fisher, 'Other cartographies', *Third Text*, No. 6, Spring 1989, p. 79.

15. References to writing permeate this frontier space, and are associated with death. The post commandant who scribbles Dunbar's orders on a scrap of paper commits suicide soon after. On finding a corpse on the way to the outpost, Dunbar's guide jokes 'folks back home are probably saying "Why don' he write?"'; but he falls victim to the Pawnee war party on his return journey.

16. Agnes Heller, *Beyond Justice*. Basil Blackwell, Oxford, England, and Cambridge, MA, 1987, p. 121.

17. Jimmie Durham, personal communication, n.d.

18. Merrill E. Gates, quoted in Berkhofer, op. cit., p. 173.

19. Horkheimer, op. cit., p. 42.

20. Ibid., p. 52.

21. In the final draft of the Declaration of Independence, 'pursuit of Happiness' replaced an earlier reference to private property.

22. 'Humanity has often wept over the fate of the aborigines of this country, and Philanthropy has been busily engaged in devising means to avert it, but its progress has never for a moment been arrested, and one by one have many powerful tribes disappeared from the earth. To follow to the land the last of his race and to tread on the graves of extinct nations excites melancholy reflections. But true philanthropy reconciles the mind to these vicissitudes, as it does to the extinction of one generation to make room for another.' President Andrew Jackson, Second Annual Message to Congress, 6 December 1830.

23. President Andrew Jackson, quoted in Michael Paul Rogin, *Father and Children: Andrew Jackson and the Subjugation of the American Indian*. Alfred A. Knopf, New York, 1975, p. 217.

24. Jonathan Bentham, one of the primary architects of utilitarianism, also invented the panoptical penitentiary. The efficiency of this system depends on its control of architectural space and light: a central surveillance machine which renders the observer invisible while maintaining the observed in a constant state of visibility.

25. Alasdair MacIntyre, *After Virtue: A Study in Moral Theory*. Duckworth & Co., London, 1985, pp. 51ff.

26. Michael Sandel, excerpts from *Liberalism and the Limits of Justice*, in *What Is Justice? Classic and Contemporary Readings*, eds. R.C. Solomon and M.C. Murphy. Oxford University Press, New York and Oxford, 1990, pp. 138, 351.

27. MacIntyre, op. cit., p. 263.

28. Edgar Heap of Birds' multiple-panel installation *Hey No Wah Maun Stun He Dun* (What Makes a Man), 1987, explores the complex individual and communal

identities of manhood in contemporary Cheyenne/Arapaho society. See Matt's Gallery publication, October/November 1988.

29. Pierre Clastres, *Society Against the State: Essays in Political Anthropology*. Zone Books, New York, 1989.

30. Fredric Jameson, 'Postmodernism, or the cultural logic of late capitalism', *New Left Review*, No. 146, 1984, pp. 53–92.

Walt Disney and the Double Victimization of Pocahontas

1. 'Virginia Born Lady' is the inscription that appears on Pocahontas's grave in St George's Church, Gravesend.

2. 'From the very beginning of this project, the filmmakers were determined to make a movie that would be both entertaining and true to history,' says Donald Ogden Stiers in the commentary on the documentary, *Pocahontas: Two Different Worlds, One True Love*, produced by the Wrightwood Company for the Walt Disney Company, 1995.

3. See Peter Mason's excellent *Deconstructing America: Representations of the Other*. Routledge, London, 1990.

4. From the documentary, *Pocahontas*, op. cit.

5. John White's drawings are in the collection of the British Museum and were first reproduced to illustrate Thomas Hariot's *A Briefe and True Report of the New Found Land of Virginia*. Frankfurt, 1590; facsimile edition, Dover Publications, New York, 1972.

6. See Malik Alloula, *The Colonial Harem*. Manchester University Press, Manchester, 1986.

7. For an extended discussion of these points, see Ziauddin Sardar, Merryl Wyn Davies and Ashis Nandy, *Barbaric Others: A Manifesto on Western Racism*. Pluto Press, London, 1993.

8. For a good discussion of this point, see Lawrence J. Korb, 'Our overstuffed armed forces', *Foreign Affairs*, Vol. 74, No. 6, November/December 1995.

9. From the Letter Patent known as the Charter of the Virginia Company, issued on 10 April 1606. Quoted in Philip L. Barbour (ed.), *The Jamestown Voyages under the First Charter 1606–1609*, 2 vols. Hakluyt Society, Cambridge, 1969, pp. 49–54.

10. Ibid.

11. From the Instructions of the London Council of the Virginia Company, quoted in Barbour, ibid.

12. Ibid., p. 111.

Directing the Real

1. I am indebted to Augustin L. Sottos' entry for *Orapronobis*, in his extraordinary filmography of Lino Brocka, for some of the information in this paragraph. This essential work for Brocka scholarship comprises the last seventy pages of *Lino Brocka, the Artist and His Times*, ed. Mario A. Hernando. Cultural Center of the Philippines, Manila, 1993.

2. Citations from Joel David, *The National Pastime: Contemporary Philippine Cinema*, intro. by Bienvenido Lumbera. Anvil, Manila, 1990, p. 188.

3. Lino Brocka, 'Philippine movies: some problems and prospects', in *Readings in Philippine Cinema*, ed. Rafael Ma Guerrero. Manila Film Center, Manila, 1983, pp. 260–1. The ethos expressed in this comment might be seen in relation to Brocka's pivotal role in the selection of Roland Joffe's *The Mission* over Andrei Tarkovsky's *The Sacrifice* for the 1986 Palme D'Or at Cannes. See Sottos, op. cit., pp. 115ff.

4. Renato Constantino, 'The miseducation of the Filipino', in *Sinaglahi: An Anthology of Philippine Literature*, ed. M.L. Santaromana. Writers Union of the Philippines, Manila, 1975, p. 14.

5. For more on the work of spectatorship as labour and on cinema as the paradigm of an emergent visual economy, see my essays, 'Cinema, capital of the twentieth century', *Postmodern Culture*, Vol. 4, No. 3 [pmc@unity.ncsu.edu], Oxford University Press, May 1994; 'The spectatorship of the proletariat', *boundary 2*, Vol. 22, No. 3, Fall 1995, pp. 171–228; 'Capital/cinema', in *Deleuze and Guattari: New Mappings in Politics/Philosophy/Culture*, eds Eleanor Kaufman and Kevin Heller. University of Minnesota Press, Minneapolis, 1998; Jonathan Beller, 'Dziga Vertor and the film of money', *boundary 2*, Vol. 26, No. 3, 1999, pp. 151–99.

6. See Paul Gilroy, 'Diaspora, utopia and the critique of capitalism', in *The Subcultures Reader*, eds Ken Gelder and Sarah Thornton. Routledge, London, 1997, pp. 340–9.

The Critical Practice and Dialectics of Third Cinema

1. Glauber Rocha, 'An esthetic of hunger', in *New Latin American Cinema: Theory, Practices, and Transcontinental Articulations*, ed. Michael T. Martin. Wayne State University Press, Detroit, 1997, pp. 59–61.

2. Julia García Espinosa, 'For an imperfect cinema', in *New Latin American Cinema*, ibid., pp. 71–82.

3. Fernando Solanas and Octavio Getino, 'Towards a Third Cinema', in *New Latin American Cinema*, ibid., pp. 33–58.

4. Telshome Gabriel, *Third Cinema in the Third World*. UMI Research Press, Ann Arbor, MI, 1982. Also see Roland B. Tolentino, '*Inangbayan*, the mother-nation, in Lino Brocka's *Bayanko, Kapit Sa Patalim* and *Orapronobis*' in *Screen* Vol. 37 No. 4, pp. 368–88.

5. Solanas and Getino, op. cit., pp. 33–4.

6. Birri, 'Cinema and underdevelopment', in *New Latin American Cinema*, op. cit., pp. 87–8.

7. Robert Stam and Louise Spence, 'Colonialism, racism and representation: an introduction', in *Movies and Methods*, Vol. II, ed. B. Nichols, University of California Press, Berkeley, 1985.

8. Peter Sainsbury, *Afterimage*, No. 3, Summer 1971, pp. 2–7.

9. Sylvia Harvey, *May 68 and Film Culture*. BFI, London, 1980, p. 62.

10. This useful phrase refers to the ambition to make the social world intelligible or explicable. It yokes the question of artistic form to cognition and knowledge. It is borrowed from Paul Willemen's excellent essay, 'The Third Cinema question: notes and reflections', in *Questions of Third Cinema*, eds Jim Pines and Paul Willemen. BFI, London, 1989.

11. Harvey, op. cit., pp. 108–10.

12. Gillo Pontecorvo, in D. Georgarkas and L. Rubenstein, *Art, Politics, Cinema: The Cineaste Interviews*. Pluto Press, London, 1981.

13. See Terry Lovell's discussion of this contradiction in *Pictures of Reality, Aesthetics, Politics and Pleasure*. BFI, London, 1983, pp. 59–61.

14. Espinosa, op. cit., p. 77.
15. Veronica Horwell, 'Mother of all battles', *Guardian 2*, 20 June 1997, p. 9.
16. Jan Dawson, *Monthly Film Bulletin*, October 1972.
17. *Time Out Film Guide*. Penguin Books, Harmondsworth, 1998, p. 60.
18. Ibid., p. 751.
19. Espinosa, op. cit., p. 8.
20. Ibid., p. 79.
21. Derek Malcolm, 'The wrench revolution', *Guardian*, 27 June 1997, p. 9.
22. Willemen, op. cit., p. 11.
23. Frantz Fanon, *The Wretched of the Earth*. Penguin Books, Harmondsworth, 1990, p. 62.
24. See Biko Agozino, 'The third debt to the third world: the politics of law and order in *Camp de Thiaroye*', *Third Text*, No. 36, Autumn 1996, pp. 3–13.
25. Birri, op. cit., p. 86.
26. Pontecorvo, op. cit.
27. Stam and Spence, op. cit., p. 641.
28. Ibid., p. 642.
29. Ibid.
30. Willemen, op. cit., p. 13.
31. Fanon, op. cit., p. 55.
32. Ibid., p. 74.
33. Ibid., p. 30.
34. Ibid., p. 103.
35. Ibid., p. 116.
36. Ibid., p. 152.
37. Ibid., p. 163.
38. Ranjana Khanna, '*The Battle of Algiers* and *The Nouba of the Women of Mont Chenoua*: from Third to Fourth Cinema', *Third Text*, No. 43, Summer 1988, pp. 13–31.
39. Ibid., p. 13.
40. Fanon, op. cit., pp. 166–99.
41. Stam and Spence, op. cit., pp. 643–4.

Post Theory

Queries for Postcolonial Studies

1. Bill Ashcroft, Gareth Griffiths and Helen Tiffin (eds), *The Postcolonial Studies Reader*. Routledge, London and New York, 1995.
2. Tom Flanagan, 'The literature of resistance', *The New York Times Book Review*, 17 March 1996, p. 6.
3. *The Georgia Review: The Nobel Laureates of Literature*, 49, 1, Spring 1995.
4. Edward W. Said, *Representations of the Intellectual: The 1993 Reith Lectures*. Pantheon, New York, 1994, p. xvi.
5. Ibid., p. xiv.
6. David S. Landes, *The Wealth and Poverty of Nations: Why Some Are So Rich and Some So Poor*. W.W. Norton, New York, 1998.
7. Robert D. Kaplan, *The Ends of the Earth: A Journey to the Dawn of the 21st Century*. Random House, New York, 1996, pp. 437–8.

8. T.S. Eliot, *Notes Towards the Definition of Culture*. Faber and Faber, London, 1948, p. 121.

9. Mahdi Elmandjra, *La Décolonisation culturelle, défi majeur du 21ème siècle*. Edition Walili, Marrakesh, 1997.

10. George Gittoes, *George Gittoes*. Craftsman House, Sydney, 1998.

11. Jean-François Lyotard, *Le Différend*. Editions de Minuit, Paris, 1983.

12. Michael Ignatieff, *The Warrior's Honor: Ethnic War and the Modern Conscience*. Henry Holt, New York, 1997.

13. Jason Epstein, 'Dishing it out', *The New Yorker*, 13 October, 1997, p. 91.

14. Martin Heidegger, *On the Way to Language*. Harper & Row, New York, 1971, p. 15.

15. Jean-François Lyotard, *The Postmodern Condition*. University of Minnesota Press, Minneapolis, 1984, p. xxiv.

16. Clifford Geertz, *Local Knowledge*. HarperCollins, New York, 1983, p. 16.

17. Ignatieff, op. cit., p. 36.

18. Leila Abouzeid, *The Year of the Elephant*. University of Texas Press, Austin, 1989, p. 23.

19. Ihab Hassan, 'The expense of spirit in postmodern times: between nihilism and belief', *The Georgia Review* 51, 1, Spring 1997, pp. 10–11.

20. Samuel Huntington, *The Clash of Civilizations*. Simon & Schuster, New York, 1996.

21. William James, *Pragmatism*. Meridian Books, New York, 1955, p. 61.

Signs of Our Times

1. See, for example, V.Y. Mudimbe, 'Reading and teaching Pierre Bourdieu', *Transition*, No. 61, 1994, pp. 144–60; Anthony Arnove, 'Pierre Bourdieu, the sociology of intellectuals, and the language of African literature', *Novel*, Vol. 26, No. 3, Spring 1993, pp. 276–95; Toril Moi, 'Appropriating Bourdieu: feminist theory and Pierre Bourdieu's sociology of culture', *New Literary History*, No. 22, 1991, pp. 1021–49; Nicholas Thomas, *Colonialism's Culture: Anthropology, Travel and Government*. Polity Press/Blackwell, Oxford, 1994.

2. Christopher Norris, *The Truth About Postmodernism*. Blackwell, Oxford, 1993.

3. For an abridged version of the lectures, see Derrida, 'Spectres of Marx', *New Left Review*, No. 205, 1994, pp. 31–58. The lectures have been compiled for English publication as *Spectres of Marx: The State of the Debt, the Work of Mourning and the New International*, trans. Peggy Kamuf. Routledge, London, 1994.

4. As examples, see Abdul Jan-Mohamed, 'The economy of Manichean allegory: the function of racial difference in colonialist literature', *Critical Inquiry*, Vol. 12, No. 1, 1985 ('"Race", Writing, and Difference'); Laura Chrisman, 'The imperial unconscious? Representations of imperial discourse', *Critical Quarterly*, Vol. 32, No. 3, 1990, pp. 38–58; Neil Lazarus, 'Disavowing decolonization: Fanon, nationalism, and the problematic of representation in current theories of colonial discourse', *Research in African Literatures*, Vol. 24, No. 4, Winter 1993, pp. 69–98; Arif Dirlik, 'The postcolonial aura: third world criticism in the age of global capitalism', *Critical Inquiry*, No. 20, Winter 1994, pp. 329–56; Masao Miyoshi, 'A borderless world? From colonialism to transnationalism and the decline of the nation-state', *Critical Inquiry*, No. 19, Summer 1993, pp. 726–51. Also the papers of Chrisman, Miyoshi and Lazarus given at the conference 'The Politics of Identity, Secular Criticism and

the Gravity of History: The Work of Edward Said', Warwick University, March 1994, Lawrence and Wishart, London, 1995.

5. Homi Bhabha, *The Location of Culture*. Routledge, London and New York, p. 241.

6. For critiques addressing Bhabha, see Lazarus, op. cit.; Ania Loomba, 'Over-worlding the "Third World"', *Oxford Literary Review*, ed. Robert Young, Vol. 13, Nos. 1–2, 1991, pp. 164–91; Loomba also cites the criticisms of Bhabha made by Suvir Kaul in 'The Indian academic and resistance to theory', p. 174. See also my 'Problems in current theories of colonial discourse', *Oxford Literary Review*, Vol. 9, Nos. 1–2, 1987, pp. 27–58; Manthia Diawara, 'The nature of mother in *Dreaming Rivers*', *Third Text* No. 13, Winter 1990/1, pp. 73–84; and Thomas, op. cit.

7. Bhabha, op. cit., p. 251.

8. Edward Said, *Culture and Imperialism*. Chatto and Windus, 1993, p. 292.

9. Paul Gilroy, *The Black Atlantic: Modernity and Double Consciousness*. Verso, London, 1993.

10. Bhabha, op. cit., p. 208.

11. Michel Foucault, 'Theatricum philosophicum', *Language, Counter-Memory, Practice*, trans. Donald F. Bouchard and Sherry Simon. Cornell University Press, Ithaca, 1977, p. 185.

12. Fredric Jameson, *Postmodernism: Or the Cultural Logic of Late Capitalism*. Verso, London, 1991, p. 344.

13. A harsher estimate of the implications to this style is offered by Arif Dirlik, who finds Bhabha to be 'a master of political mystification and theoretical obfuscation', observing that while the same tendencies are apparent in much postcolonial writing, these are rarely evident 'with the same virtuosity (and incomprehensibleness) that he brings to it' ('The postcolonial aura', op. cit., footnote 4, p. 333).

14. Bhabha, op. cit., p. 172.

15. See Anne McClintock, 'The angel of progress: pitfalls of the term "Post-Colonialism"'; Ella Shohat, 'Notes on the "Post-Colonial"', *Social Text* Vol. 31, No. 2, 1992, pp. 84–98 and 99–113; and Laura Chrisman, 'Inventing post-colonial theory: polemical observations', *Pretexts* (University of Cape Town), to appear. Shohat suggests that 'post-colonial theory' should articulate itself as 'post-anti-colonial critique', as a movement beyond a relatively binaristic, fixed and stable mapping of power relations between 'colonizer/colonized' and 'centre/periphery', pp. 105, 108. I would dispute Shohat's designation of 'Third World nationalist discourse': see my 'Resistance theory/theorizing resistance', in *Colonial Discourse/Postcolonial Theory*, eds Francis Barker, Peter Hulme and Margaret Iversen. Manchester University Press, Manchester, 1994. It is Lazarus's contention that Bhabha uses the concept of postcoloniality *against* the nationalism or nationalitarianism of liberation discourses, thereby repeating the move prevalent among radical critics, to disavow nationalism *tout court* by positioning nationalist discourses, both metropolitan and anticolonial, 'as coercive, totalizing, elitist, authoritarian, essentialist, and reactionary', and hence obscuring these 'as the open site of political and ideological contestation' ('Disavowing decolonization', op. cit., p. 70).

16. Miyoshi, op. cit., pp. 728, 750.

17. Dirlik, op. cit., p. 331.

18. Gyan Prakash, 'Writing post-orientalist histories of the Third World: perspectives from Indian historiography', *Comparative Studies in Society and History*, No. 32, 1990;

and 'Postcolonial criticism and Indian historiography', *Social Text*, No. 31/2, 1993, pp. 8–19, pp. 13 and 15.

19. See Aijaz Ahmad, *In Theory: Classes, Nations, Literatures*. Verso, London, 1992; and Michael Sprinker, 'The national question: Said, Ahmad, Jameson', *Public Culture*, Vol. 6, No. 1, Fall 1993, pp. 3–29.

20. Arif Dirlik, 'Post-socialism/flexible production: Marxism in contemporary radicalism', *Polygraph*, No. 6/7, 1993, pp. 133–69.

21. Bhabha, op. cit., p. 241.

22. Ibid., p. 6.

23. See Houston A. Baker Jr, *Modernism and the Harlem Renaissance*. University of Chicago Press, Chicago, 1987, pp. 75–9.

24. Bhabha, op. cit., p. 145.

25. See, for example, V.Y. Mudimbe's discussion of Africanist discourse, *The Invention of Africa: Gnosis, Philosophy and the Order of Knowledge*. James Currey, London, 1988; Mary Louise Pratt, *Imperial Eyes: Travel Writing and Transculturation*. Routledge, London, 1992; and Laura Chrisman, *Empire and Opposition: Literature of South Africa*, Oxford, Oxford University Press, 1995.

26. Bhabha, op. cit., p. 112.

27. Ibid., pp. 115, 38.

28. Ibid., p. 177.

29. Ibid., p. 224.

30. Ibid., p. 126.

31. Ibid., p. 162.

32. Norris, op. cit., pp. 23, 24.

33. See David Harvey, 'Class relations, social justice and the politics of difference', in *Principled Positions: Postmodernism and the Rediscovery of Value*, ed. Judith Squires. Lawrence and Wishart, London, 1993, pp. 85–120.

34. Bhabha, op. cit., p. 174.

35. Ibid., p. 29.

36. For a believer's view, see R. Radhakrishnan, 'Poststructuralist politics – towards a theory of coalition', in *Postmodernism/Jameson/Critique*, ed. Douglas Kellner. Maisonneuve Press, Washington DC, 1989.

37. Trinh T. Minh-ha, 'Not you/like you: post-colonial women and the interlocking questions of identity and difference', *Inscriptions*, No. 3/4, 1988, pp. 71–7, p. 73.

38. Norris, op. cit., p. 182.

39. Ibid., pp. 26, 24.

40. Rasheed Araeen, 'How I discovered my oriental soul in the wilderness of the West', *Third Text*, No. 18, Spring 1992, pp. 85–107, pp. 86, 101; Geeta Kapur, 'Contemporary cultural practice: some polemical categories', *Third Text*, No. 11, Summer 1990, pp. 109–17, p. 116.

41. Diawara, op. cit., p. 82.

42. Bhabha, op. cit., p. 5.

43. Ibid., p. 172.

44. Ibid., p. 213.

45. See, for example, ibid., pp. 1 and 139.

46. Ibid., p. 225.

47. Ibid., p. 179.

48. Ibid., p. 224.

49. Bruce Robbins, 'Review essay: colonial discourse: a paradigm and its discontents', *Victorian Studies*, Vol. 35, No. 2, Winter 1992, pp. 209–14, p. 212.
50. Neil Lazarus, 'Doubting the new world order: Marxism, realism, and the claims of postmodernist social theory', *Differences: A Journal of Feminist Cultural Studies*, Vol. 3, No. 3, 1991, p. 99.
51. Miyoshi, op. cit.
52. See Stephen Howe, *Anticolonialism in British Politics: the Left and the End of Empire 1918–1964*. Oxford University Press, Oxford, 1993.
53. Bhabha, op. cit., p. 208.
54. Ibid., p. 198.
55. Francis Mulhern, 'Althusser in literary studies', in *Althusser: A Critical Reader*, ed. Gregory Elliott. Blackwell, Oxford, 1994, p. 166.
56. Antony Easthope, *British Post-Structuralism Since 1968*. Routledge, London, 1988, pp. 34, 35, 72.
57. A. Sivanandan, 'All that melts into air is solid: the hokum of New Times', *Race and Class*, Vol. 31, No. 3, 1989, pp. 1–30, p. 23.
58. For a powerfully argued case on the continuing need for forms of class politics, see Harvey, op. cit.
59. Bhabha, op. cit., p. 241.
60. Ibid., p. 22.
61. Ibid., p. 25.
62. Cedric Robinson, *Black Marxism: The Making of the Black Radical Tradition*. Zed Books, London, 1983.
63. Tim Brennan, 'Black theorists and left antagonists', *The Minnesota Review*, No. 37, Fall 1991, pp. 80–113.
64. Derrida, op. cit., p. 58.
65. Ibid., p. 54.

The Failure of Postmodernity

1. The following are some of the basic texts of Africa's anti-imperialist discourse: Kwame Nkrumah, *Neo-Colonialism, the Last Stage of Imperialism*. Heinemann, London, 1964; Nkrumah, *Consciencism*. Heinemann, London, 1964; Cheik Anta Diop, *Nations nègres et culture*. Présence Africaine, Paris, 1955; Chinweizu, *The West and the Rest of Us*. Nok Publishers, Lagos, 1978; Chinweizu et al., *Towards a Decolonization of African Literature*. Fourth Dimension, Enugu, 1980.
2. See Walter Rodney's anti-imperialist book, *How Europe Underdeveloped Africa*. Bogle-L'Ouverture, London, 1972.
3. Chinweizu, op. cit., p. xxiii.
4. Frederik Nietzsche, *The Will to Power*, trans. Walter Kaufmann. Vintage, New York, 1967, p. 550.
5. Jürgen Habermas, *The Philosophical Discourse of Modernity: Twelve Lectures*. Polity Press, Cambridge, 1987, p. 253.
6. Michel Foucault, 'Nietzsche, genealogy and history', in *Language, Counter-Memory, Practice: Selected Essays and Interviews*. Basil Blackwell, London and New York, 1972, p. 154.
7. Chinweizu, op. cit., p. 23.

8. Marcien Towa, *L'Idée d'une philosophie négro-africaine*. Editions CLE, Yaoundé, 1979, p. 54.

9. Nietzsche, *On the Genealogy of Morals and Ecce Homo*, trans. Walter Kaufmann and R.J. Hollingdale. Vintage, New York, 1967, p 76.

10. Nietzsche, *Will to Power*, op. cit., p. 386.

11. Two historical novels, Chinua Achebe's *Things Fall Apart* (Heinemann, London, 1958) and Cheikh Hamidou Kane's *Ambiguous Adventure* (trans. from the French by Katherine Woods; Heinemann, London, 1972), contain useful details on the way the authentic natives interpreted colonial conquest. In the first, the 'unmoralized' reaction to the white man's intrusion is illustrated by Okonkwo's decision to fight it on the ground that it was an alien encroachment on the community's power and its gods. Obviously, the proud, slave-selling, tribe-conquering pagans could not have imagined that colonial conquest was a 'sin' or a crime against humanity. Similarly, in *Ambiguous Adventure*, the most influential character, called the Grande Royale, was quick to divine, behind the rapidity of the conqueror's victory, the morality-free force that drives world history. To her, the conqueror's easy and total victory amounted to 'l'art de vaincre sans avoir raison'. In other words, if the colonialists won, it was because they had power and not rightness on their side. Therefore, she sent her cousin to Europe to acquire this 'secret of winning without being right'. This was a clear intuition of world history as the arena for the implacable clash of powers.

12. Vincent Descombes, *Modern French Philosophy*. Cambridge University Press, Cambridge, 1980, p. 164.

13. Nietzsche, *Genealogy of Morals*, op. cit., p. 44.

14. Ibid., p. 45.

15. Ibid., p. 45.

16. Ibid.

17. Nietzsche, *Will to Power*, op. cit., p. 386.

18. Senghor's negritude politics of forgiveness and unconditional reconciliation with Europe is a good illustration of this impotence-induced moralism characteristic of many Afrocentric thinkers. Today, we often smile at his sublime self-deception that interpreted the powerlessness of a colonial subject as 'forgiveness of sins' and 'prayer for peace', even though the enemy had not said he committed a crime let alone that he needed forgiveness (see Senghor's '*Prière de paix*', *poésies*. Editions Seuil, Paris).

19. Nietzsche, *Genealogy of Morals*, op. cit., p. 83.

20. Ibid., p. 87.

21. Jean-François Lyotard, *La Condition post-moderne*. Minuit, Paris, 1980.

22. Nietzsche, *Will to Power*, op. cit., p. 402.

23. Schürmann, quoted in Habermas, op. cit., p. 402.

24. Nietzsche, *Will to Power*, op. cit., p. 395.

25. Lyotard, op. cit., p. 76.

The Marco Polo Syndrome

1. For instance, see J. Hunter, 'Inaugural disputation on the varieties of man' 1775, in T. Bendyshe (ed. and trans.), *The Anthropological Treatises of Johann Friedrich Blumenback*. London, 1865, pp. 357–94.

2. Geeta Kapur, 'Tradición y contemporaneidad en las bellas artes del tercer mundo', in Open Debate, 'Tradición y Contemporaneidad en la Plástica del Tercer Mundo', 3rd Bienal de La Habana, 1989, p. 12.

3. Gerardo Mosquera, *El diseño se definió en octubre*. La Habana, 1989, pp. 31–3.

4. Amílcar Cabral, 'O papel de cultura na luta pela independência', in *Obras escolhidas de Amílcar Cabral*, Vol. 1. Lisbon, 1978, pp. 234 and 235.

5. 'Despite all its noble aspirations and achievements, we should acknowledge that the culture of modernity . . . has also been always (but not exclusively) a culture of interior and exterior imperialism.' Andreas Huyssen, 'Cartografía de postmodernismo', in Josep Picó (ed.), *Modernidad y postmodernidad*. Alianza Editorial, Madrid, 1988, p. 239.

6. In literary theory the first warnings appear with the Russian Zhirmunski (1924), in the *Tesis* of the Linguistic Circle of Prague; in the Russian Konrad (1957); in the French Etiemble (1958); in the Polish Swarczynska (1965), Ingarden and Ossowski (1966). Desiderio Navarro, 'Un ejemplo de lucha contra el esquematismo eurocentrista en la ciencia literaria de la América Latina y Europa', *Casa de las Américas*, Vol. XXI, No. 122, La Habana, September-October 1980, pp. 83–5.

7. About the double condition of European borders as a western bastion and contact zone, see Leopoldo Zea, *América en la historia*. Mexico and Buenos Aires, 1957, pp. 118–54.

8. The processes of transculturation occurred above all in daily life and artistic-literary culture. Western discourse transformed very little within intellectual thought. It is connected with that cultural dichotomy, pointed out by Shuichi Kato, between a native ego and a western superego, according to Dufrenne. Mikel Dufrenne *et al.*, *Main Trends in Aesthetics and the Sciences of Art*. New York and London, 1979, pp. 37–8.

9. René Etiemble, *Essais de littérature (vraiment) général*. Gallimard, Paris, 1974, p. 9. The Marxists are in no better a position. For instance, the four volumes of Lukacs, under the all-encompassing title *Aesthetics*, do not take a single non-western work into account. And even worse, the Soviet manuals of literary theory ignored the Oriental literatures of their own country (Navarro, op. cit., pp. 88–90); and socialist realism in art and literature was imposed from western canons. All these are evidence of the Russocentric politics towards other nationalities which, together with other factors, provoked the dismemberment of the union.

10. See his testimony in *Made in Habana: Contemporary Art from Cuba*. Art Gallery of New South Wales, 1988, p. 20.

11. A critical interpretation of Botero from this perspective can be read in Luis Camnitzer, 'Boteros: falsos y auténticos', *Brecha*, Montevideo, 16 August 1991, p. 20.

12. Joseph Cornet, 'African art and authenticity', *African Arts*, Vol. 9, No. 1, Los Angeles, 1975, p. 55.

13. Néstor García Canclini, 'Modernismo sin modernización?', *Revista Mexicana de Sociología*, Vol. L1, No. 3, Mexico, July-September 1989, p. 170.

14. Mirko Lauer, 'Notas sobre plástica, identidad y pobreza en el tercer mundo', in *Tradición y Contemporaneidad*, op. cit., pp. 19–27.

15. Kapur, op. cit., p. 11.

16. Nelly Richard, 'Latinoamérica y la postmodernidad', *Revista de crítica cultural*, Santiago de Chile, Vol. 2, No. 3, April 1991, p. 15. What must be extended to include the whole South is the recognition of Latin America as a 'zone of experience (be it called marginalization, dependency, subalternity, decentredness) common to all

countries situated at the periphery of the Western dominated model of centred modernity'.

17. Jorge Luis Borges, 'La supersticiosa ética del lector', in his *Páginas escogidas*. La Habana, 1988, p. 105.

18. Boris Bernstein, 'Algunas consideraciones en relación con el problema "arte y etnos"', *Criterios*, Nos. 5–13, La Habana, January 1983–December 1984, pp. 266–7.

19. Rodrigo González changed his old Castillian aristocratic name into Rockdrigo, and became one of those who transformed rock into a vehicle of expression of marginal youth and the lower classes in Mexico City, by using international rhythms for local ends.

20. Rasheed Araeen, 'Our Bauhaus others' mudhouse', *Third Text*, No. 6, Spring 1989, pp. 3–4; James Clifford, 'Histories of the tribal and the modern', *Art in America*, April 1985, New York, pp. 164–77, included in *The Predicament of Culture*. Harvard University Press, Cambridge, MA, and London, 1988; Gerardo Mosquera, '"Primitivismo" y "contemporaneidad" en jóvenes artistas cubanos', *La revista del sur*, Malmö, Vol. 2, Nos. 3–4, 1985, pp. 52–5, and *Universidad de La Habana*, No. 227, January – June 1986, pp. 133–9.

21. Gerardo Mosquera, 'Speakeasy', *New Art Examiner*, Vol. 17, No. 3, Chicago, November 1989, pp. 13–14.

22. Robert Farris Thompson, 'Breakshadow art (Pasula Klini): towards an African reading of "Modernist Primitivism"', in *Rediscovered Masterpieces of African Art*. Paris, 1988, pp. 65–73.

Globalization

Scene and Obscene

1. Mike Gane (ed.), *Baudrillard Live*. Routledge, London, 1993, pp. 61–2.

2. Mark Poster (ed.), *Jean Baudrillard: Selected Writings*. Polity Press, Cambridge, 1988, p. 168.

3. Pierre Bourdieu, 'Le Champ intellectuel: un monde à part', in *Choses dites*. Les Éditions Minuit, Paris, 1987, p. 171.

4. Edward W. Said, 'La Trahison des intellectuels', in *Le Monde diplomatique*, August 1999, p. 7.

5. Thomas Mathiesen, *Prison on Trial: A Critical Assessment*. Sage, London, 1990, pp. 70–2.

6. Ibid.

The 'New Asian Museum' in the Age of Globalization

1. This paper is a revised version of my talk at the international symposium *The New Asian Museum: Twisting the Box*, organized by The Vancouver Center for Contemporary Asian Art, 5–6 May 2000.

2. To retrieve an earlier history of pan-Asianism in India, we need to recall Rabindranath Tagore's seminal contributions on the subject, enhanced by his close friendships with other advocates of 'one Asia', notably Okakura Tenshin (whose name is

synonymous with the Japanese collection of the Museum of Fine Arts, Boston). Unfortunately, this history has been marginalized in studies of early modernism in the Indian subcontinent. When Tagore's universal humanism is invoked in the discourse of the social sciences, it is generally inscribed in the context of anti-imperialism and *The Illegitimacy of Nationalism*, as Ashis Nandy (New Delhi, Oxford University Press, 1994) has conceptualized the poet's attitude without sufficiently acknowledging his embrace of modernity. In the process, Tagore's inter-Asian *cosmopolitanism* remains insufficiently inflected, if not undermined.

3. For a critical overview of this Foucauldian discourse, which shows no signs of disappearing, read the special issue on 'Asian ways: Asian values revisited', *Sojourn*, Vol. 14, No. 2, October 1999, specifically Clive Kessler's lead article on 'The abdication of intellectuals' (ironically subtitled, 'What everybody needed to know about "Asian Values" that social scientists failed to point out').

4. Addressing the Renaissance City Report on 9 September 2000, the Singapore Minister for Information and the Arts, Lee Yock Suan, clarified that the use of the term 'renaissance' was not meant to 'hark back to the post-medieval days of [the] European Renaissance'; rather, it was aimed primarily at establishing 'Singapore as a global city of the arts', while 'providing cultural ballast in our nation-building efforts'. 'Go international' is one of the key strategies of this cultural resurgence, which demands nothing less than 'an arts and cultural "renaissance" economy'. For an alternative view, see Anwar Ibrahim, *Asian Renaissance*. Times, Singapore, 1997.

5. For an elaboration of inter-Asian theatre practice in the context of global capitalism, see my monograph *Consumed in Singapore: The Intercultural Spectacle of 'Lear'*. Centre for Advanced Studies Research Paper Series, Singapore, CAS and Pagesetters, 2000.

6. The multicultural polemic on 'boxing the local' can be read in the animated and reflexive exchanges between the representatives of the Asian-Canadian artist community and the organizers of the symposium in Vancouver. See: www.centrea.org

7. Presented at a conference organized by the Rockefeller Foundation and the Smithsonian Institute, this essay is included in *Museums and Communities: The Politics of Public Culture*, eds Ivan Karp, Christine Mullen Kreamer and Steven D. Lavine. Smithsonian Institution Press, Washington and London, 1992.

8. Ibid., p. 51.

9. Ibid.

10. Ibid., p. 36.

11. Tapati Guha-Thakurta, 'The museumised relic: archaeology and the first museum of colonial India', *The Indian Economic and Social History Review*, Vol. 34, No. 1, 1997. All references to Guha-Thakurta in this paragraph are drawn from her essay, pp. 47–51.

12. Ibid., p. 51.

13. Tapati Guha-Thakurta, 'Instituting the nation in art', *Wages of Freedom*, ed. Partha Chatterjee. Oxford University Press, New Delhi, 1998, p. 122.

14. These 'blow-ups' and 'close-ups', interspersed with vivid tropical colour-plates, are central elements in the design of the brochure featuring *Street Dreams: Contemporary Indian Studio Photographs from the Satish Sharma Collection*, eds Val Williams and Anna Fox. Booth-Clibborn Editions and the Shoreditch Biennale, 1997. In a recent conversation (New Delhi, July 2000), Sharma has clarified that the brochure is clearly

an orientalist representation that sensationalizes the subaltern content of the photographs themselves. The question remains: How does one represent the reality of
Indian streets in the diasporic transmission of 'street dreams'?

15. Countering the implicit moral condemnation of cosmopolitanism as 'uncommitted
bourgeois detachment', Pheng Chea and Bruce Robbins have invented the 'cosmopolitical' to focus on 'the mutating global field of political, economic, and cultural
forces', in which the discourses of nationalism and cosmopolitanism intersect. See
their edition of *Cosmopolitics: Thinking and Feeling beyond the Nation*. University of
Minnesota Press, Minneapolis, 1998.

Cybersublime

1. *Zaningeha Med* was broadcast daily, for an hour, at 5 p.m. GMT. The only educational programme to be broadcast in Kurdish, it offered a unique insight to its
viewers while, at the same time, ensuring the survival and propagation of Kurdish
languages. *Zaningeha Med* was programmed by Dr Musa Kaval, who was kind
enough to facilitate this broadcast. As such, I personally owe him my regards and
kind wishes.

2. *Sterka Med*, issue two, October 1998, pp. 1–2.

3. Ibid.

4. Catherine David and Jean-François Chevenier (eds), *Politics–Poetics, Documenta X, the
Book*. Edition Cantz, London, 1997.

5. Catherine David (ed.), *Documenta X: Short Guide*, Edition Cantz, London, 1997, p. 7.

6. On the subject of the sublime, I am here referring principally to Lyotard's two
articles published in *Artforum*. These are 'Presenting the unpresentable: the sublime',
Artforum, Vol. XX No. 8, April 1982, pp. 64–70; and 'The sublime and the avant-
garde', *Artforum*, Vol. XXII No. 8, April 1984, pp. 36–43. There are also clear
references to both the 'avant-garde' and the 'sublime' in the appendix to *The
Postmodern Condition: A Report on Knowledge*, which I will refer to later in the article.

7. Versions of these two articles are also to be found in Jean-François Lyotard, *Political
Writings*. University of Minnesota Press, Minneapolis, 1993. In *Politics–Poetics*, they
can be found in the section titled 'Budapest' (which, ironically, is in the section next
to 'Algeria') on pp. 204–5 and 207–8 respectively.

8. This question is discussed at length by Heidegger in 'The origin of the work of art',
in *Poetry, Language, Thought*. Harper & Row, New York, 1971.

9. Attributed to 'the editors', *Politics–Poetics*, op. cit.

10. Nick Ryan, 'Television nation', *Wired*, March 1997, p. 92.

11. Hikmet Tabak, Director of Med TV, from an unpublished conference paper
delivered on 3 September 1998, at the Ninth International Symposium on
Electronic Arts, Liverpool Art School, Liverpool John Moores University, UK.

12. Ibid.

13. Quoted by Nick Cohen, 'Little Biggam man', *Guardian*, 19 May 1999.

14. Reproduced in Jean-François Lyotard, *The Postmodern Condition: A Report on Knowledge*,
trans. Geoff Bennington and Brian Massumi. Manchester University Press,
Manchester, 1991, pp. 71–82.

15. Ibid., p. 73.

16. Ibid., p. 74.

17. Ibid., p. 77.
18. Meaghan Morris, 'Postmodernity and Lyotard's sublime', in *The Pirate's Fiancée: Feminism, Reading, Postmodernism*. Verso, London, 1988, pp. 213–39.
19. Ibid., pp. 216–17.
20. Ibid., p. 235.
21. Ibid., p. 236.
22. Ibid., p. 218, citing Jean-François Lyotard, *The Differend: Phrases in Dispute*, trans. Georges van den Abbeele. Manchester University Press, Manchester, 1988.
23. From 'ITC revokes Med TV's licence', the ITC's website: http://www.itc.org.uk (23 April 1999).
24. Ian Black, 'Kurdish anger as TV station closed down for incitement', *Guardian*, 23 March 1999.
25. For example, see David Pallister ' "Hypocrisy" protest at BAe meeting', *Guardian*, 28 April 1999.
26. Reprinted as 'Messages in a bottle', in Slavoj Žižek, *Mapping Ideology*. Verso, London, 1994, pp. 34–45.
27. Ibid., p. 36.

Obscene from Any Angle

1. See James Watson (ed.), *Golden Arches East: McDonald's in East Asia*. Stanford University Press, Stanford, CA, 1997.
2. See George Ritzer, *The McDonaldization of Society*. Pine Forge Press, Thousand Oaks, CA, 1996.
3. See Martin Parker and David Jary, 'The McUniversity: organization, management and academic subjectivity', *Organization*, No. 2, 1995, pp. 1–20.
4. See Emiko Ohnuki-Tierney, 'McDonald's in Japan: changing manners and etiquette', in Watson, op. cit., pp. 161–82.
5. See Alan Bryman, 'The Disneyization of society', *Sociological Review*, No. 47, 1999, pp. 25–47.
6. See George Ritzer, *Expressing America: A Critique of the Global Credit Card Society*. Pine Forge Press, Thousand Oaks, CA, 1995.
7. See George Ritzer, *Enchanting a Disenchanted World: Revolutionizing the New Means of Consumption*. Pine Forge Press, Thousand Oaks, CA, 1999.
8. Paco Underhill, *Why We Buy: The Science of Shopping*. Simon & Schuster, New York, 1999.
9. Ibid., pp. 206–7.
10. Ibid., p. 207.
11. Ibid., p. 33.
12. Jean Baudrillard, *Fatal Strategies*. Semiotext(e), New York, 1983/90.
13. Paul Virilio, *The Art of the Motor*. University of Minnesota Press, Minneapolis, 1995, p. 65.
14. Zygmunt Bauman, *Intimations of Postmodernity*. Routledge, London, 1992.
15. Zygmunt Bauman, *Postmodernity and Its Discontents*. New York University Press, New York, 1997, p. 14.

Epilogue

A New Beginning

1. Zygmunt Bauman, *Modernity and Holocaust*. Polity Press, Cambridge, 1991.
2. In the Indian subcontinent, the debate about modernity vs. tradition started at the end of the nineteenth century when the westernized middle classes began to demand the implementation of the Enlightenment's ideas and a share in the colonial administration, which, among other things, led to the emergence of Indian modernism with incorporated indigenous elements.
3. On the struggle of Afro-Asian artists, see Rasheed Araeen, *The Other Story*. Hayward Gallery, London, 1989. See also the special issue of *Third Text*, Nos. 8/9, Autumn/Winter 1989; and Rasheed Araeen, 'The other immigrant: the experiences and achievements of AfroAsian artists in the metropolis', *Third Text*, No. 14, Summer 1991, pp. 17–28.
4. Rasheed Araeen, 'The art of benevolent racism', *Third Text*, No. 51, Summer 2000, pp. 57–64.
5. See Ziauddin Sardar, *Postmodernism and the Other*. Pluto Press, London, 1998.
6. See Marcos Becquer and José Gatti, 'Elements of vogue', *Third Text*, Nos. 16/17, Autumn/Winter 1991, pp. 65–81.
7. Slavoj Žižek, 'Multiculturalism, or the cultural logic of multinational capitalism', *New Left Review*, No. 225, London, 1997, pp. 28–51.
8. This development reflects the crisis of western culture I spoke about in the beginning, but this reflection is turned into a celebration. See Julian Stallabrass, *High Art Lite*. Verso, London, 2000; see also Rasheed Araeen, 'Hello Giuliani, we love you!', *Two Nine Two*, No. 1, Edinburgh College of Art, Edinburgh, Scotland, March 2000, pp. 86–95.

Contributors

Jorella Andrews, a member of *Third Text*'s editorial board, is a lecturer in art history and visual culture at Goldsmiths College, University of London.

Rasheed Araeen, the founding editor of *Third Text*, is an artist, curator and critic. He curated 'The Other Story' at the Hayward Gallery, London, in 1989 and is the author of *Making Myself Visible* (1989).

Roger Bartra, anthropologist, is a research fellow at the University of Mexico. He is the author of *Wild Men in the Looking Glass: The Mythic Origins of European Otherness* (1994), *The Artificial Savage: Modern Myths of the Wild Man* (1997) and *Blood, Ink and Culture: Miseries and Splendors of the Post-Mexican Condition* (2002).

Zygmunt Bauman is Professor of Sociology at the University of Leeds and the University of Warsaw. His most recent books include *Modernity and Ambivalence* (1991), *Life in Fragments: Essays in Postmodern Morality* (1995), *Globalization: The Human Consequences* (1998), *In Search of Politics* (1998), *Liquid Modernity* (2000) and *Society Under Siege* (2002).

Jonathan L. Beller is Visiting Professor of the History of Consciousness, University of California, Santa Cruz. His work has also appeared in *Postmodern Culture*, *boundary 2*, *Polygraph* and *Public Culture*.

Rustom Bharucha is an independent writer, director and dramaturge based in Calcutta. He is the author of *Theatre and the World* (1993), *In the Name of the Secular* (1998) and *The Politics of Cultural Practice: Thinking through Theatre in an Age of Globalization* (2000).

John Byrne is a Senior Lecturer in Contextual Studies at Liverpool Art School, John Moores University. He has written and published widely on the subjects of art, technology and aesthetics.

Zeynep Çelik is Professor of Architecture at the New Jersey Institute of Technology. She is the author of *Displaying the Orient* (1992) and *Urban Forms and Colonial Confrontations: Algiers under French Rule* (1997).

James Clifford is Professor of History of Consciousness, University of California, Santa Cruz. His books include *Writing Culture* (1986), *The Predicament of Culture* (1988), *Person and Myth* (1992) and *Routes: Travels and Translation in the Late Twentieth Century* (1997).

Annie E. Coombes, a member of *Third Text*'s editorial board, teaches in the School of History of Art, Film and Visual Media, Birkbeck College, University of London. She is the author of *Reinventing Africa: Museums, Material Culture and Popular Imagination* (1994) and co-editor of *Hybridity and Its Discontent: Culture, Politics and Science* (2000).

David Craven is Professor of Art History and Latin American Studies at the University of New Mexico. He is the author of *Diego Rivera* (1997), *Poetics and Politics in the Art of Rudolf Baranik* (1996), *Abstract Expressionism as Cultural Critique* (1999) and *Art and Revolution in Latin America* (2002).

Sean Cubitt is Professor of Screen and Media Studies, University of Waikato, New Zealand. He is the author of *Digital Aesthetics* (1998) and *Simulation and Social Theory* (2000), and co-editor of *Aliens R Us: The Other in Science Fiction Cinema* (2001).

Merryl Wyn Davies, a member of *Third Text*'s editorial board, is a writer, anthropologist and television producer. She is the author of *Knowing One Another: Shaping an Islamic Anthropology* (1988) and *Introducing Anthropology* (2001), and co-author of *Distorted Imagination: Lessons from the Rushdie Affair* (1990) and *Barbaric Others: A Manifesto on Western Racism* (1993).

Jimmie Durham is an artist, essayist, cultural activist and curator of contemporary Native American art. He currently lives and works in Germany.

Denis Ekpo teaches contemporary French thought and comparative literature at the Department of Foreign Languages at the University of Port Harcourt, Nigeria.

Ticio Escobar is a historian and art critic from Paraguay. His books include *Textos varios sobre cultura, transición y modernidad* (1992), *Sobre cultura y Mercosur* (1995) and *Maldición de Nemur* (1999).

Jean Fisher, a former editor of *Third Text*, is an artist and writer on issues of contemporary art. She teaches at Middlesex University, London, and the Royal College of Art, London. She is the editor of *Global Visions: Towards a New Internationalism in the Visual Arts* (1994) and *Reverberations: Tactics of Resistance, forms of Agency in Transcultural Practices* (2000).

Tony Fry is Founding Director, EcoDesign Foundation, Rozelle, New South Wales, Australia, and Adjunct Professor, Faculty of Design, Architecture and

Building, University of Technology, Sydney. He is the author of *Old World, New Visions* (1989) and *Remakings: Ecology, Design, Philosophy* (1994), and editor of *Rua TV: Heidegger and the Televisual* (1994).

Stuart Hall is Professor Emeritus of Sociology at the Open University, England. He was Director of the Centre for Contemporary Cultural Studies at the University of Birmingham during the 1970s. His most recent publications include *Cultural Identity and Diaspora* (1994) and *Stuart Hall: Critical Dialogues in Cultural Studies* (1996).

Ihab Hassan is the Emeritus Vilas Research Professor of English and Comparative Literature at the University of Wisconsin-Milwaukee. His books include *The Dismemberment of Orpheus: Toward a Postmodern Literature* (1982), *Slaves at Risk: Patterns of Quest in Contemporary American Letters* (1989), *Rumours of Change: Essays of Five Decades* (1995) and *Between the Eagle and the Sun: Traces of Japan* (1996).

Geeta Kapur is a critic and curator living in New Delhi. She is the author of *When was Modernism: Essays on Contemporary Cultural Practice in India* (2001). Her curatorial work includes 'Bombay/Mumbai 1992–2001' in the exhibition 'Century City: Art and Culture in the Modern Metropolis' at the Tate Modern, London, in 2001. She is a founder-editor of *Journal of Arts & Ideas* and has held research fellowships at the Nehru Memorial Museum and Library, New Delhi.

Johan Lagae teaches in the Department of Architecture and Urban Planning at the Ghent University, Belgium. He is author of a catalogue on architect Claude Laurens (2001).

Sebastián López is Guest Lecturer at the Art History Institute of Leiden University, and Director of the Gate Foundation. He is the editor of *Van het PostModernisme* (1985) and *Talking Back to the Media* (1985).

Kobena Mercer writes about and teaches visual studies in the black diaspora. He is a fellow of the Society for the Humanities at Cornell University. His books include *Welcome to the Jungle: New Positions in Black Cultural Studies* (1994) and *Mirage: Enigmas of Race, Difference and Desire* (1996).

Gerardo Mosquera is a freelance writer, critic and curator based in Havana. He is the editor of *Contemporary Art from Cuba* (1994) and *Beyond the Fantastic: Contemporary Art Criticism from Latin America* (1996).

Olu Oguibe is a Senior Fellow of the Vera List Center for Art and Politics at The New School, New York. He is the author of *Uzo Egonu: An African Artist in the West* (1995), *Reading the Contemporary: African Art from Theory to the Marketplace* (1999) and *Fresh Cream* (2001).

Nikos Papastergiadis is Senior Lecturer at the Australian Centre, University of Melbourne, Australia. He is the author of *Dialogues in the Diaspora* (1998) and *The Turbulence of Migration* (1999).

Benita Parry is Honorary Professor at the Department of English and Complementary Literature, University of Warwick, Coventry. She is the author of *Conrad and Imperialism* (1983), co-author of *Delusions and Discoveries: India in the British Imagination, 1880–1930* (1998) and co-editor of *Postcolonial Theory and Criticism* (2000).

George Ritzer is Professor of Sociology at the University of Maryland. His publications include *The McDonaldization of Society* (1993), *Expressing America: A Critique of the Global Credit Card Society* (1995), *The McDonaldization Thesis: Explorations and Extensions* (1998) and *Enchanting a Disenchanted World* (1999).

Edward Said is University Professor of English and Comparative Literature at Columbia University. His publications include *Orientalism* (1978), *Beginnings: Intention and Method* (1987), *The World, the Text and the Critic* (1984), *Culture and Imperialism* (1994) and *Out of Place: A Memoir* (2000).

Ziauddin Sardar, writer and cultural critic, is the editor of *Third Text*. His most recent books include *Introducing Cultural Studies* (1998), *Orientalism* (1999), *The Consumption of Kuala Lumpur* (2000) and *The A to Z of Postmodern Times* (2001). He is a Visiting Professor of Postcolonial Studies at the Department of Arts Policy and Management, City University, London.

Julian Stallabrass, a member of *Third Text*'s editorial board, is a lecturer in art history at the Courtauld Institute of Art. He is the author of *High Art Lite: British Art in the 1990s* (1999) and *Paris Pictured* (2002).

Michael Wayne lectures in Film and Television Studies at Brunel University, London. He is the author of *Political Film: The Dialectics of Third Cinema* (2001).

Anne-Marie Willis, photo-historian and cultural critic, is Director of Research, EcoDesign Foundation, Rozelle, New South Wales, Australia. She is the author of *Picturing Australia: A History of Photography* (1988) and *Illusions of Identity: The Art of Nation* (1993).

Slavoj Žižek is Senior Researcher at the Institute of Social Studies, Ljubljana, Slovenia. His books include *The Sublime Object of Ideology* (1989), *The Plague of Fantasies* (1997), *The Ticklish Subject* (1999) and *The Fragile Absolute* (2000).

List of Illustrations

INDEX